# Transforming Light

## The Living Heritage of World Religions

ALBERT VAIL

AND

EMILY MCCLELLAN VAIL

HARPER & ROW, PUBLISHERS

NEW YORK, EVANSTON, AND LONDON

*To those who believe there is a truth which will
    set men free from prejudice, from the greed
    that wrecks the social order, from degrading
    poverty, from crime, from fear, from war,
To those in all lands who labor for a united world,
To those who pray, Thy kingdom come on earth,
To those who seek the light that does not fail,
    the peace that passes understanding, the love
    that heals, the secret of divine civilization,
    the religion of the future,
This story of the rise and decline and ensuing resurrection
of Prophetic influence is dedicated.*

# Contents

# *Foreword*

THE TEMPLES of the world and their beauty; the sacred books of the great religions and their prestige; the believers in these religions and their service to their fellow men; the believers and their testimony that their religion sustained and transformed them—these are momentous facts of history.

In the following story of the great world religions the facts of each religion are presented as they have been lived and testified to by those who found their Prophet a potent influence in their lives. We cannot know our own religion until we believe it. We cannot understand another's religion until we translate ourselves sympathetically into the time when the Prophet gathered around him his first disciples and so filled their hearts with love for him and for his teachings that they gave their lives into his keeping and joyfully accepted his commission to carry his message to all mankind.

# Introduction

BY ERIC BUTTERWORTH

TODAY MANKIND IS FACING what may be his greatest test. Man has
split the atom and unlocked the tremendous forces of a subatomic
world. He has overcome his gravity chains and thus opened a new
horizon of extraterrestrial adventure. And yet he is still enmeshed
in the conflicts of "man's inhumanity to man" because he doesn't
really know who he is. He searches for the answer in scientific study,
in psychological confrontation and "sensitivity training," in psychic
research, and in a broad spectrum of contemporary philosophies and
religions.

In the universal law of both spiritual and historical cause and
effect, man is what he is because of what he has been. Educators
have known this and have attempted to bring wholeness to the student by giving him a sense of the history of his culture and of
mankind. This is a book that deals with mankind's living heritage
of world religions. We cannot really understand or rightly build
upon history without a knowledge of the religious life and consciousness of the people who have made it.

The great contribution of this book, *Transforming Light: The
Living Heritage of World Religions,* is that it compacts and com-
presses the long ages of religion into one setting, giving the reader
a unified impact which is subtle but extremely dynamic. One begins
to see his own religion in all religions and his own time in all times.
And he senses that in the broad sweep of man's quest for Truth,
the various religious movements with all their trappings and shrines

may well be the rough mangers in which the "wider experience can come forth."

And this is presented in a work that is scholarly without being pedantic, historical and yet reading like a novel, amazingly informative of the great religions without the usually complicated study of creeds and "outwardisms." The prophets and founders of the great religions are presented as *real* people and not as unidentifiable "holy men." It is more the rule than the exception that in any religious study one becomes so involved with the divine man that he tends to miss completely his revelation of divine Truth.

The Vails have attempted more than just an excellent outline of world religions. The work is not only a history but a forecast. Showing, as it does, the roots of the various religions and the amazing similarities of foundation and early concepts, it points to the need for the ultimate achievement of a universal synthesis.

I recall the shocking concept given by du Noüy in his book *Human Destiny*. He says that people always ask, if God is all-powerful, why did He not create a perfect being right away? Why the trials and gropings as revealed by history? He shows us an interesting answer through the relativity of time. Every natural event, as far as the observer is concerned, depends upon the speed at which it happens. A slow phenomenon would not exist in the eyes of an observer whose life was too short to cover its beginning, its evolution, and its end.

For instance, a phenomenon which extended over ten thousand years would not exist for an animal whose life spans only a few years. It exists for man simply because experiences are prolonged by traditions. But a phenomenon accelerated to the point where direct observation is impossible escapes an observer until the moment when recording methods more delicate and quicker than his sense organs enable him to see it. Compressed time photography shows growth of flowers. Accelerated cinematography slows down the penetration of a bullet through a metal piece, or the motion of a fly's wing. The phenomenon is "instantaneous" but the camera is able to decompose it into observable phenomena.

Thus when we examine the growth and unfoldment of man's quest for Truth through all history and in all the cultures of the world, what seems to be the slow progress of unfoldment is slow only as we observe it. To an imaginary being with a life span of ten thousand million years, religious evolution would seem very rapid. To God, whom we cannot even conceive in relation to time, it is "instantaneous."

With the excellent overview provided by *Transforming Light . . . Living Heritage of World Religions* we have the means of seeing the evolution of unique and individual concepts that will ultimately come together to form the strong moral and spiritual fiber of the "golden age" of man's life on planet Earth. Reading the dull and faded tomes of the many religions might make this religious evolution seem like dragging eternities. In this work it appears to be but a few scenes of a prologue to the main drama which is to come.

The Vails have clearly shown that all the great religions reveal a common pattern of evolution. All began in a moment of inspiration in one great life. A little celestial spark was fanned into a living flame in the life of Gotama or Jesus or Lao-Tzu or Mohammed. Then followed a period of teaching and healing. This was normally followed by a similar period of teaching and healing by disciples and students. And, after this there was usually an organization of a movement to perpetuate the ideas and memory of the founder. And finally the organization has become devoted almost exclusively to the worship of the founder.

Christianity is no exception, but is in fact a good case in point. After the age of the disciples and the widespread ministry of Paul there developed a strong machinelike organization that created creeds and doctrines by majority vote of bishops and cardinals, and, once created, they became inviolable, whether or not they had any similarity with Jesus' own teaching.

*Transforming Light . . .* reveals that there is a common ground on which the different religious traditions rest. The same elements appear in the experiences of the prophets of all the religions. People are, after all, people, regardless of the color of their skin or the age or geographical location where they have lived. All are seeking the same goal, through different schools of thought or under different banners. And when we cut through the formulas and the rigidities of regulations (as this book so effectively does), the same spiritual life is found.

Arnold Toynbee writes that he would "express his personal belief that the four higher religions that were alive in the age in which he was living were four variations on a single theme, and that, if all

the four components of this heavenly music of the spheres could
be audible on earth simultaneously, and with equal clarity, to one
pair of human ears, the happy hearer would find himself listening,
not to a discord, but to a harmony."*

The universality of fundamental ideas which historical studies
demonstrate is the hope of the future. All religions teach the mystical
nature of love. But though the dogma may differ, in the end when
one gives expression to live in his relationship, it has no sectarian
tag on it. The Buddhist, whose religion would describe love in one
way, might fall in love with a Christian, whose background would
lead him to define it in another way. Their love for each other may
be fulfilling and meaningful, for love is a universal energy and language, and certainly not the property or dialect of any religious
group.

Even as love is universal and is a force for unity, so is religion
as a whole. For there is a deep spiritual unity of all mankind. Religion has always come out of that intuitive awareness of unity. The
word itself, coming from *religio,* means "a binding together." The
tragedy of history is that what began as a universal or purely spiritual
movement has inevitably deteriorated into a sect. While true religion
is always unifying and all-inclusive, sectarian religion has invariably
been divisive and exclusive. From earliest times zealots have cried,
"Put away your gods and come and worship ours, or we will kill
you and your gods"—as one of the characters of Dostoevski's
*Brothers Karamazov* puts it. The Vails have clearly shown us that
the narrow, jealous, and parochial attitudes of the religious have
always arisen from overzealous followers of the founding prophet.
Here they bring into clear context the fact that the prophet himself
always calls for unity of all religions.

Today the world calls for unity. However, it may well be that
present attempts at Ecumenicity are directed toward the merging
of the machines and the uniting of the creeds which would lead
toward a unity of sameness or uniformity. So long as people differ
in temperament and background culture, they will prefer and choose
different forms of worship. So long as they differ in mind, in education, in everyday experiences, and in cultural influences, they will
approach life's meaning from a different level. Thus, it would be
a tragic loss to religion, to Truth, to life itself, if it should ever be

* *A Study of History,* Vol. II, 1954, p. 428.

possible to force all men to feel and think and act alike in matters of religion.

The ideal is a spiritual ecumenicity, a unity of objectives with a diversity of methods and means of achieving it. There is nothing so peculiarly one's own as his religion, because nothing proceeds so directly from his deepest divinest self. He may express it in different ways and use different symbols and means of devotion, but there is always something deeper than this, the spiritual consciousness that wells up in his being and ultimately expresses in love and faith and understanding and brotherhood—which are universal and nonexclusive characteristics.

I have said that this work is prophetic in nature, but it doesn't spell out the makeup of the religion of the future, its organization, its creeds, its form of worship and places of worship. It simply points in a futuristic direction and implies a unity of ideal even if in a diversity of expression.

Perhaps the purpose of the universal religious organization of the future will be—not to make people better Christians or Jews or Muslims or Taoists, but to make them better people. Perhaps the churches will eventually minimize groupism and sectarian labels and engage primarily in spiritual research and discovery. With a violinist or engineer, we are little concerned with where or how he was trained. What counts is how does he perform. The time is coming when people will not be identified as members of a religious group, but only by the quality of their lives.

This is a significant book that should be read with enthusiasm and great profit by Truth seekers everywhere. It should be a great catalyst in bringing about religious tolerance and a movement toward "universal synthesis." *Transforming Light* . . . articulates a great Truth that through all the many and diverse pathways of religious seeking, there is a light, "the same light that lighteth *every* man coming into the world." Cardinal Newman puts this in a context most relevant for this important work in our troubled times:

> Lead, kindly Light, amid the encircling gloom;
> Lead thou me on!
> The night is dark, and I am far from home;
> Lead thou me on!
> Keep thou my feet; I do not ask to see
> The distant scene; one step enough for me.

# Book I

## Buddhism

# 1

## *The Search: About 600 B.C.*

SUDDHODANA WAS RAJA of a little principality at the foot of the Himalays in northern India. His wide-spreading rice fields were watered by unfailing streams from the highlands to the north of his lands, and he was rich in cattle. But he had no heir. His wife, Maya, forty-four years old, was now to have a child. Blindly Suddhodana hoped that the baby would be a boy. "The love of a son," he said, "cuts into the skin; having cut into the skin it cuts into the flesh, the ligaments, the bones; having cut into the bones it reaches the marrow and dwells in the marrow."

Maya dreamed that this child was a glorious being, and when the day of his birth was near she asked that she might go to her mother. Elaborate preparations were made for the journey and, with many attendants, Maya started for her parents' home. Arriving at the Lumbini Grove, a group of beautiful sal trees, she halted her party that she might rest. It was springtime. The birds were singing in ecstasy. High into the blue sky north of the principality of the Sakyas, Suddhodana's clan, the shining snow-capped peaks of the mighty Himalays soared in eternal peace. All around Maya the trees were in full bloom. She walked into the grove and reached for a branch to pick the lovely blossoms; the time suddenly came, and the child was born, bright and perfect.

Many supernatural stories are told of this event—stories of the glorious light that filled the world, of the angels singing paeans of joy who descended from heaven and cared for the baby and his mother. To later generations this was no ordinary occurrence and in their longing to express the inexpressible and pay due homage to their Enlightened One the legends were more and more embell-

ished. To Suddhodana, the father, came just the good news that
a son, a beautiful and perfect child, was born.

Maya with her baby returned to her husband's palace. And, as
was the custom, seers were invited to visit the raja and foretell the
future of his son. When they saw the child they declared that he
would be either a mighty king or a universal teacher, a Buddha
who would "roll back the veil from the world." A saintly man,
Asita, soon after the baby's birth saw in vision many angels singing
songs of praise with joy and rapture, while waving their garments
in celestial rhythm. "Why," asked Asita, "is the company of angels
so exalted and happy? Why do they wave their robes and shout
and sing, making music?" The answer came, "The Boddhisatti, the
future Buddha, the excellent pearl, the incomparable is born for
the good and for a blessing in the world of men, in the town of the
Sakyas, in the country of Lumbini."

Straightway Asita hastened to Suddhodana's palace and asked,
"Where is the prince; I wish to see him." When the clansmen
showed him the child, Asita declared, "This prince will reach the
summit of perfect enlightenment; he will turn the wheel of the law,
he who sees what is most pure. This prince feels for the welfare
of the multitude, and his religion will be widely spread. My life
here will shortly be at an end. In the middle of his life there will
be death for me. I shall not hear the teachings of the Incomparable
One. And therefore I am sad, unfortunate and suffering."

Gotama grew up unaware of the prophecies made at his birth,
for his father wished him to become a maharaja, not a spiritual
redeemer. The prince was tenderly cared for and Suddhodana
gave him three mansions, one for the cold weather, one for the
summer, and one for the three or four months when it rained. In
the pools in his gardens blue, white, and red lotuses were trained
into lovely blossom for the joy of the boy. He dressed in choicest
Benares fabrics, and day and night a white umbrella was held over
his head lest he be uncomfortable from the heat, the dust, or the
dew. Unspoiled by his father's wealth, the youth lived the rugged,
athletic life of his caste. To walk fifteen miles or so a day was easy
for him.

Beyond Gotama's homes were the luxuriant rice fields of his

people, the Sakya Clan, and their herds of cattle grazed in the nearby meadows and forests. The ancestors of the Sakyas were the warlike Aryans. Centuries before Gotama was born they left their home in the highlands northwest of the Himalayas to invade northern India and take possession of its fertile valleys. Here they became the celebrated and valiant kshatriya, or warrior caste, proud of their fair complexions which bespoke their origin, strong and stalwart, possessed of abundant wealth. Gotama was of noble descent for seven generations; so Suddhodana dreamed of the day when his son would become an important figure in the political life of India, possibly a universal conqueror.

Every little village of the Sakya Clan was self-governing, under the King of Kosala; and "Gotama" was a Sakya surname. Once in a while the chief clansmen gathered in moot halls to discuss the affairs of their community. Decisions were made by unanimous acclamation, or by a committee if a compromise was necessary.

When Gotama was grown to manhood a strange uneasiness arose in his mind, and his idyllic existence in his earthly paradise had for him no charm. He reasoned to himself: The flowers are beautiful today; but they wither, and tomorrow will be gone. These pleasures, deemed important, are fleeting and transitory things.

He realized how inexorable is time: how a man, strong and comely in his youth, will grow old and become weak in body, of trembling hand and stumbling step, so that he may fall as he walks. Gotama perceived how impermanent is the vigor of life. And his pride in his own youth departed.

He considered how human beings become sick, and what pain they endure. He realized that he too might some day be ill, that even his strength was transitory. And his pride in his splendid health departed.

He faced the fact of death, the fact that the fairest body, the most beautiful loved one some day will die; that all living beings go through the stages of youth, maturity, decline, dissolution; it is an inevitable destiny. All his people, all India he saw enmeshed in this net, bound on the wheel of birth, youth, old age, sickness, death. No one could escape. The sorrows and suffering of life confronted him and he understood the futility of clinging to the impermanent. Could he not find something enduring?

He must solve the problem, and knowing this was impossible in his home, under the watchful eye of his father who was determined that he should become a mighty ruler, Gotama decided to escape into the forest. There in silence and peace, living the life of a recluse, he would, he hoped, find salvation for his people.

Many legends are woven around the night of Gotama's departure. The most popular tells how he decided to leave his home, his wife, and his son; how with firm resolve he rose from his bed at midnight and going to the window called softly, asking who was on guard in the palace grounds. Channa, his faithful charioteer, answered. Gotama bade him saddle his horse. Then he went into the room where his beloved wife was sleeping. She lay surrounded by flowers, one hand resting on the head of their little son. Gotama had hoped to take the child in his arms for a moment; but if he should touch him he would awaken the mother. With one last, loving look at his wife and his son he tore himself away, and with Channa rode through the palace gates into the night.

It was July and the moon was full. As their horses galloped along, Mara the Wicked One, the Tempter, appeared in the sky before Gotama and urged him to stay his flight. Mara promised that if Gotama would abandon his quest, in seven days' time he would give him sovereignty over all the world. And it is not surprising that such a temptation should have come into Gotama's mind, for all his life he had heard that he might be a great monarch, a maharaja. He quickly put the temptation from him; and the Devil departed, saying to himself, "Sooner or later some hurtful or malicious or angry thoughts will arise in his mind. In that moment I shall be his master."

With invincible purpose Gotama rode on. He left far behind him the Sakya lands and came to the Anoma River which flowed south into the Ganges. On the river's bank he dismounted, and with his sword cut off his long black hair. Then he took off his ornaments and princely robes and bade Channa take these with his horse to his parents and tell them that Gotama had retired from the world.

"Sire, I also will retire from the world," said Channa.

Gotama told him No. He must go to the king and queen and say that their son wished to be a recluse. How would they know what had become of him if Channa did not carry back this word?

This is the popular story of Gotama's flight, related in latter-day Buddhism. In the earliest Buddhist Scriptures, which give the Buddha's autobiographical story of his renunciation, he says very simply, "There came a time when I, being quite young, with a wealth of coal-black hair untouched by gray and in all the beauty of my early prime—despite the wishes of my parents, who wept and lamented—cut off my hair and beard, donned the yellow robes, and went forth from home to homelessness on pilgrimage."

Gotama put on the yellow robe of the ascetic, and entered the forest, following the immemorial custom of those who sought to open the eye of the spirit and behold while living in this world the city which is eternal. Life, he saw, was a conflict of discordant ideas, desires, and feelings. Everyone was unhappy. Gotama had now one purpose: to find the way to inner harmony. Gladly would he give up his luxuries, cheerfully would he undergo the discomforts of the homeless life, as it was called, if he might behold the radiant face of Truth, and discover for himself and his people "the path to the peace beyond compare."

Soon he decided that he must have a teacher. He journeyed to Rajagaha, capital of the kingdom of Magadha, south of the Ganges, and there found a celebrated brahmin, Alara Kalama, who lived in a cave outside Rajagaha and taught his students what he called, "the consciousness of naught"—that is, the realization of the impermanence of all physical things, and the significance of the life which is immortal.

Gotama quickly learned Alara Kalama's system of thought and knew his doctrine by heart. He told the master of this, and was invited to become his assistant. Gotama asked himself: Does Alara Kalama practice what he teaches, has he attained that exalted state which he describes? He perceived that Alara Kalama had not advanced very far. And he left this teacher to find one wiser and more spiritually developed.

He went to Uddaka, the son of Rama, who taught the way to a state of mind which was "neither perception nor non-perception." Gotama followed Uddaka's instructions and attained so perfectly this state of seeing but not seeing—seeing the pleasures and treasures of the world without desiring them—that Uddaka showered honors upon him and made him his assistant teacher. But Gotama found that Uddaka's philosophy gave no ultimate answer to the problem of life, and his form of meditation brought neither wisdom nor peace.

He left Uddaka, and wandered on until he came to the beautiful district of Uruvela. He had discarded two forms of meditation. He now decided that he could find no teacher to help him and must try the way of ascetic discipline by which, his contemporaries believed, men could rise higher than the gods. The spiritual life, said the philosophers of India, is the highest state of mind. To attain this mental state a person must train himself to think of spiritual things, must practice meditation for endless hours until he is absolute master of his thoughts and can do with his mind as he choses. The greatest hindrance to the spirit is the body. The desires of the body, its insistent demands hold the spirit chained so that it cannot soar to heavenly realms. The way to break the chains is to crucify the flesh, wear away the body. The less body, the more spirit. The body grows strong and aggressive when its demands are satisfied. Ignore its wants, heed not its suffering, and at last it will succumb and the spirit will be free.

One regrets to see Gotama enter upon this gruesome path with its austerities and starvings. He went deep into the jungle, in the district of Uruvela, and with unparalleled rigor commenced his ascetic practices. He lived for long periods of time in utter solitude, pledged to speak to no human being. If anyone approached he darted away like a deer lest he break his vow. He stayed in the heart of the forest, in "depths so awesome that it was said no one but the passionless could venture in without his hair standing on end." He tortured himself with incredible fidelity, staying in the open at night even though it was winter and the snow was falling, and in the dank jungle by day. In the summer's heat he wandered on under the baking sun, crawling into a breathless thicket at night. He slept on heaps of bones, with bones for a pillow, where he would be found in the morning and driven away by the cowherds who pelted him with dirt.

In all history there is no more tragic instance of a human soul searching for truth, willing to find it anywhere, through any prescribed method, yet refusing to accept man-made substitutes or traditional hypotheses. The only cup that could satisfy Gotama must be filled with the pure water from the Eternal Fountain, for that only was unpolluted by the imaginations of men.

Gotama tried by rigorous methods of concentration to win a direct apprehension of Reality, to gain release from the ever-present self and attain the peace beyond compare. He tried to force his thoughts into right channels, to master and crush all wrong thinking. He endeavored to enter into divine comtemplation by refusing to breathe. He reduced his food to a grain of rice a day, until his arms and legs were like dried canes and his skin was as empty and withered as a wild gourd baked by the hot son. He wore garments of bark or grass, or rags picked from the dust heaps. For months at a time he never lay down but always remained in a upright position. His control of his mind became almost perfect.

But he did not find in his asceticism a satisfying answer to his problem.

For nearly six years Gotama practiced these austerities which in India, the home of asceticism, were believed to be the best, perhaps the only, way to spiritual attainment. Five ascetics, watching him, marveled that any one could survive such torturing. Thinking that Gotama would surely soon find the way to immortality, and could teach them his method of concentration and take them with him, they attached themselves to him. Starved and weak, Gotama finally fell to the ground in a faint. A cowherd's daughter passing by gave him a little rice soup and offered him some solid food. He ate this and was revived. Whereupon his five disciples lost confidence in him and went off to Benares. How could they follow a teacher who was so spiritually weak as to need a square meal!

But now Gotama's austerities were at an end. He had proved that ascetic practices were not the path to the Imperishable. The years of heroic struggle had borne other fruit, for he had attained superb concentration of mind. Pure of heart was he and master of himself. He knew that his search was almost over and soon he would see the face of Truth.

He remembered a day in his youth when he sat in the cool shade of a rose-apple tree in his father's land and a wonderful spiritual happiness welled up in his heart. Thinking of this he said, "There is no harm in happiness and joy."

With mind at peace, a sublime anticipation singing in his heart, he approached a pipalos tree and sat down in its shade. Vibrant with quiet strength he waited. And night stole down upon the world. Silence fell all about as Gotama waited, his noble head erect and still against the darkness. Even the leaves of the trees and the wild beasts and the little birds seemed strangely hushed before the coming great event.

*King and high Conqueror, thine hour is come;*
*This is the night the ages waited for.*

Presently into Gotama's heart shone a light not of this world, and joy and gladness and the consciousness of freedom. He thought with amazing clearness, his perceptions were acute. His powers of decision, reflection, reasoning became luminous. A new unity of heart and mind lifted him, as upon the crest of waves from an eternal sea, toward the harbor of a shining serenity. This was the first state of contemplation: the first ecstasy, he called it. The wonder of it, however, did not alone possess his thought, to hold him at that level. With adamantine concentration he soared to another height of insight.

The tranquillity deepened, like a boundless ocean, there in the silence of the night. His brilliant powers of reasoning and observation he suppressed, that intuition, higher still, might arise. Joy and a sense of fathomless ease filled his body and mind. He was in the second ecstasy. Oh, the wonder of it! Yet, so perfect was his self-control it could not take possession of his thought and prevent his rising to a higher level.

The rapturous joy became a quiet peace. The eager elation was gone. Sublime patience enveloped him. His mind was vividly awake and conscious. Ever more amazed, he was lifted into the third ecstasy. But he did not let his wonder hold him there.

"Rejecting joy and sorrow, rejecting former gladness and sadness" he attained a still higher consciousness, the fourth contemplation. Here he rose far above all concern as to whether he was happy or unhappy, above the eager elation of spiritual joy, up to a pinnacle of bliss, a state of pure spirituality and poise. Insight, his heavenly eye, was opened, and cycles in the world's history were unfolded before him."

With mind "cleansed of dross, supple, ready for action, firm, incorruptible," he perceived how souls left the body. He saw them depart from this world, the "common and noble, beautiful and ugly, happy and sorrowful." If their deeds had been evil, their words not true, their thoughts not right, if they had reviled the good and admired what was dangerous, lo, after the dissolution of the body they went to one of the mental hells or purgatories. If their deeds and words and thoughts had been good and beautiful, if they had admired what was worthy and lived rightly, he saw them enter "the blissful way to the heavenly world."

In the last watch of the night Gotama perceived the cause of unhappiness and the path to its cessation—the knowledge which made him the immortal teacher of Asia.

A child, he observed, is born, and hardly has his life begun when accident or illness comes upon him. Surviving this, still is the child in trouble, for soon the turmoil of adolescence has arrived. In his manhood he makes a fortune; the next day perhaps, it is gone. Toil and accumulate as he may, however vast his wealth, this man cannot buy enduring happiness. No sooner does he acquire a thing than the joy in it has vanished. Fear and worry rack his pillow; and his family life is often full of grief. This is the first truth: the fact of suffering, of inner discord, of fear is so universal that it seems as though man is born for trouble only.

What causes man's suffering? What is it that with lashing whip drives him from sorrow to sorrow, from problem to perplexity? Pondering, searching, Gotama looked upon the Cosmic Law Sublime, which is the righteous order of the universe. Attachments, he saw, are the cause of unhappiness: the longing for physical pleasures, the love of self, the delusion that in self can one find permanent happiness. These states of mind are deadly floods. Sweeping over the soul they extinguish the higher impulses until the lights of the spirit, like vanishing stars, are gone. He who is enmeshed in selfishness can never be at peace. He who pursues the pleasures of the flesh cannot know rest. He who lives for selfish ambition plunges into ever-denser darkness. The cause of unhappiness: this is the second truth.

The third truth shone into Gotama's mind: break the fetters of fear, physical desires, love of self, and the soul is free.

How can these fetters be broken? How may a man extricate himself from his selfish cravings?

In celestial beauty the fourth truth was revealed to Gotama: it was the noble Eightfold Path of right beliefs, right ideals, right speech, right efforts, right actions, right means of earning a living, right thoughts, right meditation. Everyone who follows this path attains to freedom.

As Gotama meditated, the inexorable laws of causation were unfolded to him. So vividly did he see them, and the beauty of the perfect life, that a marvelous thing happened: his lower self with its cares, its fetters, its worries vanished and he entered into a radiance pure and holy. He was lifted above the call of the senses and the stream of thoughts that rise and flow and ebb, to rise again. There were for him no more becoming and passing away: he *was* the glorious ideal which he saw. The Immortal One had come to abide in the purified spirit of Gotama.

As morning broke, the Buddha sat, a transfigured being. Later centuries declared that for seven days he sat under the Bodhi-tree, the tree of Enlightenment, in the glory of emancipation. So beautiful was his spiritual radiance that the sun and the moon seemed dim beside him. For him the eternal morn had come, the morning of a day that had no ending. It was nirvana, heaven.

# 2

## The Buddha Calls His First Disciples

THE BUDDHA QUESTIONED, "Who shall be the first to hear my teaching, and who will understand it quickly?" Gotama remembered the five ascetics who had believed in him in the days of his austerities. "They served me well in my struggle to purge me of my self," he reflected. "Suppose I choose them for my first hearers." Considering where they might be, his intuitive knowledge told him he would find them at Benares in a public deer park.

He set out for Benares, his alms bowl hanging by a cord around his neck. In the cool of the evening Gotama entered the park where his former friends were staying. The five ascetics saw him from afar, and took counsel together.

"Here he comes," they said, "the recluse Gotama, the one who ate too much, who abandoned the struggle and reverted to gormandizing. We must not welcome him, nor rise to receive him, nor relieve him of bowl and robe—yet, let us put out a seat. He can sit on it if he wants to."

As the Buddha walked toward them an irresistible something touched the wary five. Awestruck they stepped forward, one to take his bowl and robe, one to offer him a seat, another to bring him water that he might wash his feet. And saluting him, they called him "Teacher."

"Harken to me, ascetics," said the Buddha. "The Immortal has been won; I teach it; I preach the true way. Live up to what I enjoin and soon you will come, of yourselves, here and now, to discern and realize, to enter on and abide in that supreme goal of the higher life, for the sake of which young men go forth from home to homelessness on pilgrimage."

The ascetics replied, "Brother Gotama, the life you led, the path you trod, and the austerities you practiced all failed to make you transcend ordinary human scope and rise to special heights of discernment of the truly Noble Knowledge. How shall you rise to those heights when you abandon the struggle?"

The Buddha repeated his advice.

The ascetics asked their question again: How could Gotama, failing in his ascetic practices, rise to exalted heights of spiritual attainment?

The Buddha admonished them as before.

Yet a third time, unable to accept the idea of attaining illumination while eating food and living in a normal way, the five ascetics asked their question.

For the third time, the Buddha in serene certainty answered as before. "Will you not agree," he asked, "that I have never heretofore spoken like this?" They admitted that he had not.

During the days that followed, Gotama taught the five ascetics his way of life. Two of their number would go with their bowls to beg for food and, returning to the deer park, would share it with the others. Again, the Buddha would teach the two while the other three went out for alms; and what food they brought back would suffice the six. For many days he taught them and as they gazed at his luminous face, and felt the power in his words, their hearts slowly responded.

Kondanna was the first of the five to see with "the pure and spotless eye of truth." Understanding came to him in a glorious moment, and with it the peace of nirvana.

"Of a truth, Kondanna has perceived it!" exclaimed the Buddha.

One by one, the other ascetics gained the same sublime understanding. Their minds were illumined, insight was born, and they attained the peace beyond compare. Now there were five disciples ready to help the Buddha. When this happened, the Buddhist Scriptures say, all the gods and angels shouted in joy, "The Blessed One has set going, at Benares in the deer park, called Isipatana, the wheel of the Law, which none can oppose, neither god nor devil, neither priest nor ascetic, nor any being." And an infinite light shone through the world.

In Benares lived a rich young man, Yasa. His parents loved him dearly and showered upon him every luxury their imagination could devise. He had a palace for each season, and was surrounded by a host of attendants whose task it was to guard him from boredom.

One night, while women musicians played for him, Yasa fell asleep. Hours later, as day was dawning, he woke and looked about him. An oil lamp flickered feebly, throwing its unwholesome light upon the women in the room, who slept at their posts, their musical instruments lying rakishly across arm or neck. Their hair was disheveled, their beauty was a travesty, and they muttered in their sleep. So different were they from the lovely creatures of the evening before that Yasa thought he must have fallen into a cemetery.

"Alas, what distress! Alas, what danger!" he cried as, utterly disillusioned, he perceived the emptiness of his pleasures. Picking up his gilded slippers he fled from the room. Away from his home he ran, and through the city gate, which by chance stood open. Hurrying along he knew not where he came to the deer park, and to the Buddha.

It happened that the Buddha had risen before dawn and was walking to and fro in the silent morning. He saw Yasa a long way off and sat down to wait for him. As Yasa ran, he whispered to himself, "Alas, what distress! Alas, what danger!"

"Come, Yasa," said the Buddha, "and sit down here, for here is no distress, here is no danger. Come, and I will tell you of the divine order of life."

These words filled Yasa's heart with joy. Taking off his slippers, he approached the holy Gotama, saluted him respectfully, and sat down beside him. The Buddha, knowing that Yasa was ready to receive his teaching, told him in glowing words of the happiness of a life of holiness and love, and the futility of vanity and selfishness.

In the meantime Yasa's home was in commotion. His mother, coming to see him in the early morning, was told that her beloved son was gone, no one knew where. Running to her husband, she cried, "Your son Yasa, householder, has disappeared; your son Yasa is gone!" Yasa's father, distracted at the news, sent searching parties on horseback to the four quarters of the horizon while he went in the direction of the deer park. The Buddha saw him coming and called to him quietly, "Sit here, householder, and perhaps you may see your son." Yasa's father, his excitement suddenly stilled, sat down beside the Buddha, and listened to him spellbound. Never, thought he, had man spoken as this radiant stranger spoke. Concealing for the moment Yasa's whereabouts the Buddha explained to the father the path to freedom. And to Yasa, listening also, came understanding. The candle of wisdom and insight was lighted in his mind, and turning away forever from his selfishness he approached the holy state of peace.

Yasa's father soon spied his son, and cried, "My son Yasa, your mother is mourning and grieving; give life to your mother." Yasa looked with questioning eyes at the Buddha, who said, "Do you think now, householder, that Yasa could enjoy worldly pleasures as he did before?" The father, perceiving that a new mind and heart had come to Yasa, answered, "It is supreme joy to Yasa that he has become free from attachment to the world."

After securing a promise that the Buddha and Yasa would take a meal with him the next day, the householder went home. On the following day, before this visit was over, Yasa's father, his mother, and his wife joined the new Buddhist brotherhood, as lay members. Repeating words, which were later the celebrated formula for the Buddhist convert, they said:

"Glorious, lord! Glorious, lord! Just as if one should set up, Lord, what had been overturned, or should reveal what had been hidden or should point out the way to one who had lost his way, or should bring a lamp into the darkness, in order that those who had eyes might see invisible things, thus has the Blessed One preached the law in many ways. I take refuge, lord, in the Blessed One, and in the Teachings, and in the Brotherhood. May the Blessed One receive me from this day forth, while my life lasts, as a lay disciple."

Fifty more rich and highborn companions of Yasa, when they heard the amazing story of his conversion, came to the Buddha, listened to his words, and declared that they wished to take refuge in the quiet harbor of the Blessed One. There were now sixty disciples.

With this brotherhood of sixty the Buddha made his plans for the spiritual emancipation of Asia. He said to his disciples, "I am delivered, friends, from all fetters. You, friends, are also delivered from all fetters. Go ye now, friends, and wander for the gain of the many, out of compassion for the world. Let not two of you go the same way. Preach, friends, the teaching which is lovely in the beginning, lovely in the middle, lovely at the end, in the spirit and in the letter. Proclaim a consummate, perfect, and pure life of holiness. There are beings whose mental eyes are covered by scarcely any dust, but if the teaching is not preached to them they cannot attain salvation. They will understand the teaching."

The friends taught far and wide, and spread their faith like a divine contagion. They brought disciples to the Buddha, some from distant provinces, to be ordained by him. Since the long journeys were very burdensome, the Buddha soon gave his disciples permission to ordain, themselves, the new teachers. The *Vinaya*, the book of rules for the Buddhist Brotherhood, tells the form of ordination. The one who wished to become a Buddhist monk cut off his hair and beard, put on a yellow robe, and bowed his head at the feet of the brethren. Sitting down, he raised his joined hands and said, "I take refuge in the Buddha. I take refuge in the *dhamma*, the teachings. I take refuge in the *sangha*, the brotherhood." This he repeated three times.

The Buddha taught from place to place and came in time to Uruvela, the scene of his austerities. Here in the forest beside a river lived the celebrated ascetic, the great Kassapa, with five hundred followers. The insignia of their society was matted hair. Farther down the river were two more groups, one of two hundred, the other of three hundred ascetics, presided over by the Great Kassapa's two brothers.

Gotama asked the Great Kassapa if he might spend the night with him; and while they sat in the evening's stillness he told of his illumination. As they talked Kassapa thought to himself, "Truly Gotama possesses great power and authority; but he is not holy like me."

At last Gotama said to Kassapa, "You are not holy, Kassapa, nor have you even entered the path of sainthood, nor do you so live that you will become holy or enter the path of sainthood."

The Great Kassapa, amazed, threw himself at the Buddha's feet and asked that he might be his disciple.

Gotama replied, "You, Kassapa, are leader of five hundred ascetics. Go first and inform them of your intention, and let them do as they think fit."

Kassapa assembled his followers and said to them, "I wish, sirs, to lead a religious life under the direction of the great Buddha. You may do, sirs, as you think fit."

The ascetics replied, "If you will lead, sir, a religious life under the great Buddha's direction, we will all lead a religious life under the great Buddha's direction."

Overjoyed to have for their master the holy Gotama, the five hundred ascetics cut off their matted hair and threw it into the river along with their implements for sacrificing to the gods. Kassapa's brother who lived farther down the river was astounded when the hair and other things came floating by, and he feared some clamity had happened to his brother.

The other brother, when all the debris floated past his part of the river, was also appalled and, sending a few messengers at top speed, he hurried after with his ascetics to find out what had happened. But he only beheld Kassapa's joyous face as he stood beside the Enlightened One. The two brothers with their five hundred followers at once became disciples of the Buddha.

After they had been in Uruvela for a time Gotama and his company of a thousand followers climbed an eminence overlooking a beautiful valley. Most of these men with their leader, the Great Kassapa, had been worshipers of Agni the fire god. As they sat on the hilltop watching a fire burning in the jungle the Buddha gave them a talk which became his celebrated "Fire Sermon."

"Everything," he said to them, "is burning, and how, O friends, is everything burning? It is burning with lust, with hatred, with ignorance, grief, lamentation, suffering, dejection and despair"; and he pictured in thrilling words the way of escape.

In his wanderings before his illumination Gotama came one day to the capital city of King Bimbisara, a mighty monarch of northern India. As Gotama went from door to door asking for food, the king standing on a terrace in his palace grounds watched him, in the street below.

Struck by Gotama's dignity, the king said to his companions, "Sirs, mark this man. He is handsome, great, and pure. Self-possessed is he; verily, of no mean birth. Let the king's messengers make haste and discover where the monk will go."

The messengers followed Gotama at a discreet distance and saw that he left the city when his bowl was filled with food, and went to a cave in a nearby hillside. They carried his word to the king, who ordered out his state chariot and hastened after Gotama. When he reached the hill, King Bimbisara alighted from his chariot and climbed on foot to Gotama's cave.

"Young thou art," exclaimed Bimbisara in astonishment when he stood face to face with Gotama. "Fine is thy color, like a highborn noble's. As the glory of the vanguard of the army, at the head of a band of heroes would I give thee wealth"; meaning to offer Gotama a high place in his kingdom.

Bimbisara never forgot this meeting. Now, nearly seven years later, word was brought him that Gotama of the Sakya Clan, with many followers, was stopping in a grove near his city. When the king was told of Gotama's spiritual attainment, he said, "Truly he is the blessed, holy Buddha, who understands all worlds, the highest one, who guides men that are teachable, the teacher of gods and men. He makes known the truth, which he has understood himself and seen face to face. It is good to obtain a sight of holy men like that."

Bimbisara made his second visit to Gotama. Reverently he approached the Blessed One and sat down beside him, letting his company of attendants draw near. These people were astonished when they saw Kassapa with the Buddha, and they thought, "How now is this? Does the Buddha teach Kassapa, or does Kassapa teach the Buddha?" That all might know that he, Kassapa, the celebrated ascetic of Uruvela was the Buddha's disciple, he rose from his seat and adjusting his upper robe to cover one shoulder, a sign of highest respect, prostrated himself before the Buddha, saying, "My teacher is the Blessed One. I am his pupil."

When King Bimbisara departed, he invited Gotama and his followers to a meal on the morrow. It was a great occasion—the Buddha and his thousand companions entertained at the king's palace. Bimbisara himself helped to serve them; and when the meal was over he presented the Buddha with a golden bowl, symbolic of another gift, a bamboo grove in a quiet place where Gotama and his disciples might live whenever they chose. Accepting his offering, the Buddha gave the king in return a wonderful talk.

The Buddha with his disciples journeyed toward the province of the Sakyas. Two brahmin merchants brought word to Gotama's wife that they had seen him and he was soon to visit his family. The stories of Gotama's return to his home are elaborate and conflicting, for they were not written out until centuries after the event. On the central facts, however, all accounts are agreed.

Suddhodana, Gotama's father, was certain that Siddartha (Gotama's first name) should be his heir and some day become lord of the Sakya lands. When he heard that Siddartha was traveling to Kapilavastu, the capital city of the Sakyas, Suddhodana sent noblemen to ask an early visit, and made sumptuous preparations to receive his son, thinking he might yet win him to a worldly life.

While the Sakyas made gayest preparations to receive their prince, he came, one morning, unannounced. Clad in the mendicant's yellow robe, and accompanied by two disciples, Gotama begged his meal from door to door, an awestruck crowd following him.

When this news was brought to Suddhodana and his brothers they were furious. They knew it was the custom for certain holy men to wear the plainest robes and live on meager fare. They were aware that such men went from door to door begging their daily meal; and the people willingly filled their bowls with rice, provided them with needed clothes, and now and then gave them shelter, for these holy men taught and served them.

But Siddartha, the prince, must not beg this way. Suddhodana mounted his war horse and rode madly to meet his son.

"Why, master, do you put us to shame? Why do you go begging for your food? Do you think it is not possible to provide food for so many mendicants?" cried Suddhodana.

"O Maharaja, this is the custom of all our race," Siddartha replied.

"But we are descended from an illustrious race of warriors, and not one of them has ever begged his bread," said the father.

Gotama answered, "You and your family may claim descent from kings; my descent is from the prophets [Buddhas] of old, and they, begging their food, have always lived on alms. But, my father, when a man has found a hidden treasure, it is his duty first to present his father with the most precious of the jewels." The Buddha told of his great discovery, the path to peace, and concluded with the ringing words:

> *Rise up! and loiter not!*
> *Practice a normal life and right.*
> *Who follows virtue rests in bliss,*
> *Both in this world and in the next.*
> *Follow after the normal life.*
> *Who follows virtue rests in bliss,*
> *Both in this world and in the next.*

The Raja told Siddartha that all these years his wife had eaten but one meal a day and had slept on a mat, striving to follow her husband. Gotama now paid a visit to his wife and his son, Rahula, to tell them of his discovery. And they became his disciples.

During Gotama's visit to Kapilavastu his cousins, Devadatta and Ananda, joined the new brotherhood; also the young nobleman, Anuruddha, who later became a brilliant Buddhist philosopher. Another new disciple was Upali the barber. In the lower caste, where he was held by custom, Upali had no chance. In the Buddhist brotherhood, where

> *Not by birth does one become low caste,*
> *Not by birth does one become a brahmin;*
> *By his actions alone one becomes low caste,*
> *By his actions alone one becomes a brahmin,*

Upali became in time an important intellectual leader.

# 3

## Spiritual Teachings

QUIETLY THE NEW teachings spread through northern India. The Buddha had two powerful friends: King Bimbisara who ruled Magadha, a large country south of the Ganges River; and King Pasenadi of Kosala, the most important kingdom in northern India. Kosala extended from the Ganges almost to the Himalayas and included the province of the Sakya Clan. For forty-five years Gotama traveled on foot to and fro in these two countries.

His days were much alike. He rose before dawn, put on the ascetic's yellow robe, a two-piece garment of skirt and coat, and spent the early hours of the morning in meditation. He then went to the nearby village or city to beg his meal of rice. Sometimes he was accompanied by the brethren, sometimes he went alone. When his bowl was filled by the kindly people, he returned to the grove which was his stopping place and ate his one meal of the day. When his stay at a place was finished he traveled with his disciples to the next grove, a distance of, perhaps, ten or fifteen miles. As soon as the people heard of his arrival they came to listen to his discourses and ask their questions.

A certain man found it very amusing to contradict everything that he heard, and cause an argument. He saw the Buddha one day as he slowly walked in meditation, and he thought, "What if I approach him, engage him in conversation, and whatever he says I will maintain the opposite." He went to Gotama and demanded curtly that he recite a philosophic verse. Gotama replied in verse that he could not teach one who was antagonistic, for "strife and discord of the mind" make it impossible for a man really to understand what is said to him. The gainsayer stared at Gotama who could thus read his motive, deep love and reverence welled up in his heart and he became the Buddha's disciple.

King Bimbisara tried to persuade his wife, Queen Khema to go to see the Buddha; but Khema was infatuated with her peerless beauty and, afraid that the Buddha would read her thoughts and know how vain she was, she would not go. The king told Khema's attendants to praise the bamboo grove where the Master was staying and make the queen want to see it. Khema, unable to resist her curiosity when she heard so much about the grove, thought she would take just one look at the place, going nowhere near that part where the Buddha was staying. The grove was so entrancing that Kema forgot her resolution and wandered farther and farther in until suddenly she found herself in the Buddha's presence. As she stood before him, a vision came to her, it is said. Beside the Master she saw a young woman beautiful as a goddess. "Alas, I am nothing compared to that wondrous being," sighed the queen. While Khema gazed at her, the beautiful girl became middle-aged; then all in a moment she was old, with broken teeth, wrinkled skin; so old and week that she fell to the ground. "I, too, will fade like that," thought lovely Khema. She returned to her palace; and with the king's consent she joined the Buddhist Sisterhood. She was one of the most influential of the women teachers of early Buddhism, famed for her wisdom and saintliness.

Often the Buddha's disciples brought him sick souls to be healed.

Kisagotami was married to the only son of a rich householder. She had everything to make her happy—a beautiful home, a lovely baby—until, just as he was learning to walk, her baby died.

In her despair Kisagotami took the dead child in her arms and went from house to house begging for medicine to bring him to life. A disciple of the Buddha approached her and said, "My good girl, I myself have no such medicine as you ask for, but I think I know of one who has."

"Oh, tell me who that is," said Kisagotami.

"The Buddha can give you medicine; go to him."

Kisagotami ran to the Buddha and bowing reverently said, "Lord and Master, do you know any medicine that will be good for my child?"

"Yes, I know the medicine, but first I want some mustard seed."

That is easy, thought Kisogotami, and she promised to bring it quickly.

"You must get it from some home where no son, or husband, or parent, or slave has died," the Buddha told her.

"Very well," Kisagotami answered, and started off to find the mustard seed.

She knocked at a door and asked for mustard seed. "Of course here is mustard seed; take it," said the people.

"In my friends' home has any son died, or a husband, or a parent, or slave?" asked Kisogatami, remembering the Buddha's requirement.

"Lady, what is this that you say; the living are few, but the dead are many," the people answered her.

Kisagotami went on, from house to house. In one a son had died; in another·the children's parents. At last she understood. Not a family was untouched by sorrow and death.

In the silent forest Kisagotami laid away the body of her little boy.

She returned to the Buddha.

"Have you the mustard seed?" he asked.

"My lord, I have not; the people tell me that the living are few but the dead are many."

The Buddha explained to her the impermanence of all things, and that those who are most near and dear must some time pass away. She comprehended, then, this law that underlies the world; and understanding opened to her the door to peace.

King Pasenadi of Kosala was interested in philosophic specula- tion and Gotama's intellectual approach to his teachings greatly pleased the king. But the Buddha's claim to supreme knowledge disturbed Pasenadi, for Gotama was just the king's age, too young for such attainment, it seemed to Pasenadi. One day he said to Gotama,

"There are many well-known teachers who have their following but make no claim to supreme enlightenment, and you who are so young, a mere novice, make this claim."

The Buddha replied, "There are four young creatures, sire, who are not to be disregarded because they are youthful. What are the four? A noble prince, a snake, a fire, a bhikku [religious mendicant]. Yes, sire, these four young creatures are not to be disregarded or despised because they are youthful."

Again King Pasenadi asked, "What experiences rise within a man for his harm, suffering, and discomfort?"

"Greed, hatred, dullness," said the Buddha.

One time Gotama gave some very practical help. King Pasenadi's kingdom was harassed by the notorious bandit, Angulimala. The accounts say "he showed no mercy to any living creature. From every human being whom he slew he took a finger to make him a necklace, and so got his name, Necklace of Fingers."

Early one morning Gotama went alone to meet Angulimala.

He enered the robber's district and Angulimala, watching, said to himself, "I will kill this recluse."

Carrying his sword and buckler, also his bow and quiver, he started for Gotama who was far ahead of him.

Angulimala could run like a deer; yet somehow, he could not catch up with Gotama. He became angry, and called to Gotama to stop.

"I have stopped, Angulimala. You stop, too," Gotama called back.

"What does this mean?" thought the robber. "This Sakya recluse, who supposedly tells the truth, says he has stopped when he is still walking; and bids me stop too. I had better ask him about it." He shouted to Gotama to explain himself.

Gotama answered that he had stopped violence; but Angulimala was still destroying life.

Amazed at Gotama's fearlessness, also at a new feeling of awe in his heart, Angulimala threw away his weapons and begged that he be admitted into the Buddha's Brotherhood.

While Gotama and Angulimala had their encounter, a crowd of people beseiged the inner gates of King Pasenadi's palace, demanding that he do away with the terrible Angulimala. The perplexed king called for his chariot and went to ask counsel of Gotama.

Gotama asked what the king would say if he should see Angulimala as a Buddhist brother, as one who neither killed, nor stole, nor lied, who ate but one meal a day, who led a goodly life.

Pasenadi replied that he would salute him, protect him, and give him all that such a brother needed. But could redeeming power touch a heart so depraved as Angulimala's!

During this conversation a monk in a yellow robe sat quietly beside the Buddha. Turning to him, Gotama said, "Here, sire, is Angulimala."

"It is wonderful, it is marvelous, what a tamer of the untamed is the lord!" said the king.

Angulimala did not backslide, the story says, but daily grew in grace until he could, with patience, take a beating from the angry people of the countryside. Little children, also, joined the Brotherhood. One little brother was Sopaka, whose mother, a pauper, gave birth to him in a cemetery and died. The watchman of the cemetery found the baby and adopted him. When he was seven years old the child saw the Buddha, and so loved him that he longed to become a brother. His foster father consented; and the Brotherhood received Sopaka. The Buddha told him to practice love to all beings. As Sopaka's heart became illumined he sang this little song:

> *E'en as she would be very good*
> *Toward her only child, her well-beloved son,*
> *So too ye should be very good*
> *Toward all creatures everywhere and everyone.*

In the India that the Buddha taught were three important religious groups: brahmins, recluses, and wanderers. The men who had their homes and carried on their profession or secular business were called "householders."

The brahmin caste, and the kshatriya, to which the Buddha belonged, were the highest castes of India. Brahmanism, the religious system of the brahmins, was built upon the Vedas, poems written a thousand years or so before the Buddha appeared. The earliest Vedas are such splendid poetry that the brahmins were sure they were written by angels. Although some of these poems proclaim a noble monotheism, most of them are songs to the parsonified powers of nature, the gods of the Brahman pantheon. To the Vedas were added charms supposed to have a magical effect for those who used them. Also were added, later, the Upanishads, written by philosophers and mystics of ancient India. In passages of surpassing beauty and insight the Upanishads describe the wonderous experience when man is conscious of God's presence in his soul, and knows that God sustains, animates, and inspires the universe. These portions of the Upanishads were the background and preparation for the Buddha's message of spiritual freedom, and many brahmins were looking for the teacher who could show them how to recapture the lost experience.

A set of laws given, tradition said, by Manu, one of the earliest sages, was a standard of conduct for the Brahman civilization. In these laws the weakness which the Buddha had come to heal was apparent. One could believe that the compliers of the Code of Manu were priests and princes, for the interests of both were well protected. Like most of the ancient codes, they made women inferior to men. They declared:

> *A faithful wife who wishes to attain*
> *The heaven of her lord, must serve him here*
> *As if he were a god, and ne'er do aught*
> *To pain him, whatsoever be his state,*
> *And even though devoid of every virtue.*

Also, "Day and night must women be made to feel their dependence on their husbands. Let not (a husband) eat with his wife. Women have no business to repeat the texts of the Veda, thus is the law established. As far as a wife obeys her husband so far is she exalted in heaven. A husband must continually be revered as a god by a virtuous wife."

The brahmins were well educated, and from their caste came the priests and teachers of Brahmanism. Many brahmins were householders, and some carried on the secular affairs of their society.

Recluses were brahmins, and others, who lived in the forests and spent their lives in meditation and ascetic discipline.

Wanderers traveled from village to village hoping to find some one with whom to carry on their interminable arguments about metaphysical matters and the central problems of the universe. They considered the creation of the world: how it began and would it ever end. They speculated as to the relation of mind and body. They pondered pre-existence and immortality: "Have I verily been in bygone times or have I not been? What have I been in those bygone times? How have I been in bygone times? What was I before I became what I was in the far distant past? Shall I verily be in far-off days to come or shall I not be? What shall I be in those far-off days to come? How shall I be in the far-off days to come? What shall I be before I become what I shall be in the far distant future? Am I now or am I not? And if I am, what am I and in what way? This present being—whence has it come and whither is it going?"

Some wanderers were called annihilationists. In seven ways they taught the annihilation of a being at death. Others were sophists. Others were called eel-wrigglers because they wriggled like eels out of every philosophic difficulty. Some speculated and refused to commit themselves; they lived up in the air on suspended judgments.

The Buddha was confronted by this welter of metaphysical thinking in which many of the ablest people of old-time India were entangled, each person insisting that his way to truth was the surest. Gotama's attack was that of simple reasonableness. He said: if a man is wounded by a poisoned arrow he does not insist that the arrow cannot be removed until he knows who shot it: whether the person was a brahmin, or a noble, or a peasant; whether he was tall or short, his complexion dark or fair; whether he shot from a long or a cross bow; whether his bow was strung with sinew or hemp. Before the wounded man obtained answers to all these questions he would die. If a man has been shot by an arrow, take out the arrow.

So Gotama refused to answer unprofitable questions. These

unanswered questions were called the indeterminates. For instance, Vaccha, a wanderer, came to see Gotama, in Jeta's Grove, and commenced his questions:

"Do you hold, Gotama, that the world is eternal?"

"No, Vaccha," answered Gotama.

"Do you hold, Gotama, that the world is not eternal?"

"No, Vaccha."

"Do you hold, Gotama that the world is finite?"

"No, Vaccha."

"Do you hold, Gotama, that the world is not finite?"

"No, Vaccha."

Vaccha asked about life and the body: Are they identical or distinct? Does the Buddha pass to another existence after death or does he not? To all his questions Gotama answered No. Vaccha was much disgruntled. Gotama then explained that such questions led, not to illumination and peace but to unprofitable distraction and pertubation. "The silence of Buddha" has sometimes been called his agnosticism. But he never said, "I do not know." He merely said, "No, Vaccha," to questions which would cause endless metaphysical arguments among a people whom he was trying to teach to be practical. Asked by a very argumentative wanderer for the essence of his message, Gotama replied: "Let past and future alone. I will preach the Doctrine to you: If *that* is, *this* comes about; the rise of *that* makes *this* arise; if *that* is not, *this* comes not about; the ceasing of *that* makes *this* cease."

Of the sacrifices and rituals, and the false philosophies of his day, the Buddha spoke with commanding definiteness. When King Pasenadi caused to be slaughtered, in a great sacrifice for his personal well-being, five hundred bulls, five hundred bullocks, and as many heifers, goats, and rams, while the slaves and menials and craftsmen, hectored by blows and by fear, made the preparations, weeping, the Buddha gave forceful talks on the folly of a man's thinking he could attain heaven by sacrificing some other creature's life. It was not the sacrifice of the innocent goat or bull, but of the living beast within himself that would bring salvation to a man.

At times Gotama was very severe. A young disciple wanted to show his superiority to a man much older than himself and planned to ask the older man, before all the people, questions he knew he could not answer. His purpose failed, for the Buddha chanced to come that way, and asked the young man a question which bewildered him, while the other man answered it without hesitation. Said the Buddha to the younger man, "If a man is a great preacher of the sacred text, but slothful and no doer of it, he is a hireling shepherd, who has no part in the flock."

Many brahmins and recluses believed that within them was a static, ready-made soul which was eternally and unchangeably perfect, like Brahma, the great World Spirit. If they could actually realize this omnipotent, infinite Self they could be "lord and master in all the worlds."

Some other philosophers taught that man had no soul at all.

The Buddha declared that both these ideas imperiled the spiritual life, that *becoming* was the purpose of existence. He told a brahmin visitor that no brahmin was made regenerate by Vedic lore and the repetition of verses. If "he stirs up effort, puts forth strength, advances with ever vigorous stride," he may though he be a "noble, brahmin, commoner or laboring man, or though he belongs to the pariah class, attain the purity supreme."

Building upon the noble teaching in the Upanishads of a spirit within man which could be trained into divine life, the Buddha instructed those who did not believe in such a spirit that they could develop a soul, just as a wayfarer might, if he chose, leave the bewildering bypaths which led nowhere, and walk the true road to his destiny.

Seeing what crowds visited the Buddha, a prominent brahmin became curious and presented himself before the Buddha. Straightway Gotama asked him what a true brahmin might be.

Looking around impressively at the large assemblage of people, the visiting teacher answered that a true brahmin must have five characteristics. First, noble birth on both sides of his family for seven generations. Second, mastery of the Vedas, all ritual and exegesis, knowing mystic verses by heart. Third, a beautiful complexion, fair color. Fourth, good character. Fifth, learning and wisdom.

"Which one of the five is it possible to leave out and still be a brahmin?" asked the Buddha.

"Color," the brahmin replied.

"What next?" asked the Buddha.

"The knowledge of the Vedas."

"What next?" asked the Buddha.

"Birth," answered the unhappy brahmin, for he must tell the truth, though an outcry had arisen from the listening brahmins.

Of the five essential characteristics there were left, under the Buddha's searching questions only two: good character, and learning and wisdom—each needing the other. The brahmin became the Buddha's disciple, but secretly, for fear of his colleagues.

The Buddha's followers could not break with the customs of their environment; hence the Brotherhoods and Sisterhoods among the early Buddhists, and the believers who lived in the forests where they could meditate according to their belief that salvation could best be attained in solitude.

To these devoted ones there were four degrees of attainment on the path to sainthood. The first degree was belief in the Buddha. By concentrating their thoughts upon the Buddha, his law of life, and the holy community of his saints, they experienced a quickening, a reinforcing of their inner life. This was conversion.

The second degree was release from attachment to the world. It was in order to make this liberation sudden, final, and complete that they left their homes, and the more drastic among them fled into the forests. To some, the emancipation came in the moment of having their hair cut off—their first real sacrifice of personal vanity. The Great Kassapa was a beacon light on this ascetic path. Of him the Buddha said, "If he has no robe he is not disturbed. If he possesses a robe he enjoys it without clinging to it. He never thinks that the people should give him more food than he receives. He never even wishes that they give him food."

Those who attained the third degree were free from malice. And joyous indeed was he who found in his heart no trace of ill will toward anyone.

The fourth stage of the path ascended to the heights of universal love, utter unselfishness and equanimity, which is sainthood. He who attained this goal, having few desires, was content, serene and "ne'er upset."

The Buddha raised women to a station unknown to ancient

India. Asked, "Who here below is the comrade supreme?" he
replied, "The wife is here below the comrade supreme." Many
women were among his important apostles. He did not wish them
to establish monastic Sisterhoods, for, he said, if they left their
homes and did not educate their children his good doctrine would
decline in five hundred years. If they served in their homes, his
teachings would not be corrupted for a thousand years. It was only
after persistent beseeching from Pajapati, his aunt and foster
mother, that he allowed the Sisterhoods to be formed. It is no
wonder that the women longed for the priceless boon, escape into
the Buddhist Order, for many women were practically prisoners
in their homes. One woman, after she became a Buddhist sister,
wrote a brief autobiography telling how, in her home, morning and
evening she had to bow and kneel at the feet of her husband's
parents, and how, like a slave, she must groom and dress her
husband.
She wrote:

> *I boiled the rice, I washed the pots and pans;*
> *And as a mother to her only child,*
> *So did I minister to my good man. . . .*
> *For me he nothing felt but sore dislike.*

Few were as fortunate as the woman of Rajagaha who, as she
prepared her husband's dinner, improvised a song of praise telling
her joy in the Buddha's teaching. Her husband, a brahmin, heard
her and shouted, "Now, wretch, will I give that teacher of thine
a piece of my mind," and strode off to find Gotama. In the Buddha's presence he became quieter, and asked peaceably what must
one do to be happy. Gotama answered:

> *Wrath must ye slay, if ye would happy live,*
> *Wrath must ye slay, if ye would weep no more.*
> *Of anger, brahmin, with its poisoned source*
> *And fevered climax, murderously sweet,*
> *That is the slaughter by the Aryans praised;*
> *That must ye slay in sooth, to weep no more.*

This brahmin became the Buddha's devoted disciple.

The emancipation women found in the carefully supervised Buddhist Sisterhoods, free from brahmin oppression, was wonderful. The songs of relief and happiness written by some of the women saints of the Order are among the most moving and beautiful poems in Buddhist literature.

Ajatasattu, son of King Bimbisara and successor to his throne, went one night to visit the Buddha and ask a question he was pondering. He found the Buddha sitting in the midst of a large company of the brethren, and climbing down from his elephant the king sat beside him.

Said Ajatasattu, there were many people who practiced, each, a particular calling and enjoyed from it definite and visible fruits. They provided for their families, they lived happily and in comfort, and gave gifts to recluses and brahmins. "But can you, sir, declare to me any such immediate fruit, visible in this world, of the life of the recluse?" Ajatasattu had asked this question of teachers and recluses but they all answered evasively.

The Buddha replied that a follower of his was honest, chaste, truthful, peaceful, courteous, had good judgment, was "satisfied with suficient robes to protect his body and sufficient food to keep his stomach going," had no perplexities concerning what was good and no uncertainty as to what he should do. "Ashamed of roughness and full of mercy he was compassionate and kind to all creatures who had life." Therefore "gladness springs up within him. He is filled with a sense of peace. And in that peace his heart is stayed."

After many years of this happiness in the Buddhist Brotherhood, Devadatta, a cousin of Gotama, decided he would like to be head of the Order. He proposed this to the Master. When he was refused, he asked that the Buddha make some very strict regulations for his followers, commanding that they must live in the forests under trees, that no one should ever live under a roof or ever accept an invitation to a meal. The Buddha replied that such requirements could not be made compulsory.

Devadatta then went about among the brethren, telling them the Master had given himself over to luxury. He aroused such discontent among the younger brothers that five hundred formed a hyper-ascetic party and went off by themselves.

The Buddha sent two disciples Sariputta and Moggallana, to win them back. Devadatta thought the two had come to join his party; and when they sat down quietly and listened while he talked to his group he was sure of them. Far in the night, when he was tired, Devadatta asked Sariputta to continue his address, and lay down. While he slept, Sariputta and Moggallana talked to the young monks so convincingly that they had repented and returned to the Buddha.

Forty-five years had passed since Gotama became the Enlightened One. King Bimbisara had died; some said his son murdered him to get the throne. Gotama and King Pasenadi were eighty years old. The great Teacher was adored by multitudes of the people. King Pasenadi was having trouble with his ministers, and his hold upon his throne was weakening.

Pasenadi had always liked the Buddha's philosophy. He came one day, on his last visit, to tell the Buddha he had proved to himself Gotama was the perfect teacher.

Everywhere, said Pasenadi, he met recluses and brahmins who had been ascetics from ten to forty years; yet they still indulged the weaknesses to which they were addicted. The Buddha's disciples lived the higher life.

There was always strife among kings, nobles, and princes; between householders; between mother and son, father and son, brother and brother, between friends. The disciples of the Buddha lived peaceably, loving each other. The king found no such harmony in any other group of people.

Gotama warned his disciples that he was soon to leave them, saying:

> My age is now full ripe, my life draws to a close;
> I leave you, I depart.
> Be earnest then, O brethren, holy, full of thought.
> Be steadfast in resolve. Keep watch o'er your own hearts.
> Who wearies not, but holds fast to this truth and law,
> Shall cross this sea of life, shall make an end of grief.

Kunda, a worker in metals, invited the Buddha and some of the brethren to a meal, and prepared for them sweet rice with cakes, also a quantity of dried boar's flesh. When they sat down to eat, the Buddha said to Kunda, "As to the dried boar's flesh you have made ready, serve me with it, Kunda; and as to the other food, the sweet rice and cakes, serve the brethren with it."

"Even so, lord," said Kunda; and no one but the Buddha ate the meat.

When the meal was over the Buddha said to Kunda, "Whatever dried boar's flesh, Kunda, is left over to thee, that bury in a hole."

Soon after he and his friends left Kunda's home, Gotama was taken with "a dire sickness, the disease of dysentery, and sharp pain came upon him, even unto death. But the Blessed One, mindful and self-possessed, bore it without complaint."

The little band walked on slowly. Near a village Gotama turned from the path and sat down at the foot of a tree, saying to Ananda, "Fold, I pray you, Ananda, the robe; and spread it out for me. I am weary, Ananda, and must rest awhile." The faithful Ananda, who for twenty years had taken care of the Buddha's personal needs, did as he was bid.

As Gotama lay there, very ill, a young man, Pukkusa, came by. He said to the Buddha, "How wonderful a thing it is, lord, and how marvelous, that those who have gone forth out of the world should pass their time in a state of mind so calm." Love for the Master filled Pukkusa's heart, and taking from the package he was carrying two robes of cloth of gold, he put one on the Buddha and one on Ananda.

When Pukkusa had gone, Ananda looked at the Buddha, and lo, he was transfigured, so that the robe of cloth of gold was pale beside his glory.

In wonder, Ananda exclaimed that the Buddha was shining and beautiful beyond description. The Buddha replied that this radiance had come to him twice: when he received full enlightenment, and now that he was about to enter into eternal nirvana.

He rose and they journeyed to a grove belonging to the nobles of the district. He lay down again, under a tree, and the brethren gathered around him.

Ananda, seeing that the end was very near, went aside and

began to weep. "Alas," he thought, "the Master is about to pass away from me—he who is so kind."

"Now the Blessed One called the brethren, and said, "Where, then, brethren, is Ananda? Go and say, Brother Ananda, the Master calls for thee.' "

When Ananda came, the Buddha told the disciples how devoted and trustworthy he had always been.

Ananda, knowing not what to say, asked Gotama why he must pass away "in this little wattle and daub town, in this town in the midst of the jungle, in this branch township." Why could he not pass away in a large city, like Rajagaha or Savatthi or Benares?

The Buddha bade Anada go to Kusavati, the nearby village, and tell the nobles that he was about to leave the world.

When they heard this, the nobles, who were all his friends, were filled with grief and came with their young men and maidens, their wives and children and retinues to the Blessed One, staying with him until the second watch of the night.

In the third watch of the night came Subhadda the mendicant. He had heard that Gotama was to leave the world that night, and, knowing that very seldom did a Buddha appear on earth, he thought perhaps Gotama could clear away his doubts and give him peace of mind.

He asked that he be permitted to see the Buddha, but Ananda answered, "Enough, friend Subhadda. Trouble not the Master. The Blessed One is weary."

The mendicant made his request three times, and each time Ananda urged him not to trouble the Master.

Gotama overheard them, and said to Ananda, "Do not keep out Subhadda. Whatever Subhadda may ask of me, he will ask from a desire for knowledge, and not annoy me. And whatever I may say in answer to his questions, that he will quickly understand."

"Then the venerable Ananda said to Subhadda the mendicant, 'Enter in, friend Subhadda; for the Blessed One gives you leave.' "

Subhadda asked the Buddha whether the teachers whom he, Subhadda, knew, understood things aright.

The Buddha replied that only those became saints who walked the noble eightfold path, and added:

*But twenty-nine was I when I renounced*
*The world, Subhadda, seeking after good.*
*For fifty years and one year more, Subhadda,*
*Since I sent out, a pilgrim have I been*
*Through the wide realms of virtue and of truth,*
*And outside these no really "Saint" can be.*

After a few words to the disciples near him, "the Blessed One addressed the brethren, and said, 'Behold now, brethren, I exhort you, saying, decay is inherent in all component things. Work out your salvation with diligence.' This was the last word of the Master." As the Buddha departed, the Buddhist Scriptures say, an earthquake shook the world.

One night, six of the Buddha's devoted disciples met under the beautiful sal trees in the Gosinga Wood. The trees were in full bloom and the air was sweet with perfume, while in the clear sky the moon shone radiantly.

As they sat together Sariputta asked the question: "What type of disciple would illumine the Gosinga Wood?" meaning, What method of teaching would best spread the Buddha's light through the world?

Ananda answered first, saying that the disciple who treasured the Master's words, who learned them by heart and knew them in letter and in spirit, who explained them so fluently, exactly and comprehensively that he destroyed the selfish desires of the brethren and the sisters and the faithful laity whom he taught—he would illumine the Wood.

Revata, trained in meditation, thought that he who lived in quiet places and tranquilized his heart, who practiced contemplation and attained to insight—he would illumine the Wood.

Anuruddha, the Buddha's cousin, believed that the disciple who attained the eye celestial would be like one who surveyed a thousand worlds from an exalted pinnacle. He would illumine the Wood.

The Great Kassapa spoke. He was sure that the disciple who lived the ascetic life in the forest and commended the forest life to others, who was content and temperate, who shunned lay society would attain to spiritual freedom and would commend to others what he had attained. He would illumine the Wood.

Moggallana believed that the disciple who could answer questions on abstruse subjects and give enlightenment to others would illumine the Wood.

Sariputta spoke last, saying that he who in the morning chose the type of thought he wished to think that morning and held it during the morning, who chose the kind of thoughts he would think at midday and thought those thoughts, who determined the kind of thoughts he would think at eventide and thought those thoughts—he would illumine the Wood.

# 4

## King Asoka Spreads the
## Buddha's Teachings

SOON AFTER the Buddha's passing the Brotherhood met in a general Council. The Buddha's nearest disciples had heard his public addresses so often that they were fixed in their memory; Ananda repeated some of these addresses to the Council, and they made plans for a widespread campaign of spiritual and moral education. For the Buddha had said to one of them, "Go, Punna; saved thyself, save others. Comforted thyself, comfort others. Thou with thy great gift of patience mayest indeed essay this task."

Knowing that his disciples would some day teach not only in the valley of the Ganges where the people were tolerant, but among the fierce tribes of other regions, Gotama adminished them, "If villainous bandits were to carve you limb from limb with a two-handled saw, even then the man that should give way to anger would not be obeying my teaching. Preserve your hearts unmoved, abide in compassion and good will, enfolding in radiant thoughts of love the bandit (who tortures you)."

It is not certain what Gotama's first students were reborn into the heroism of saintly living as instantaneously as the collection of the Buddhist Scriptures called the Pali Canon relates. The narrators may have foreshortened into one glorious moment the educative process of months or years. That in early Buddhism were hundreds of true saints, like Queen Khema, Sariputta, and Ananda who became the second patriarch, there is no doubt. Spiritually radiant men and women made heroic efforts to serve their world and their Buddha; and through the centuries many thought courageously and with astonishing effectiveness.

A hundred years after the meeting of the first Council the brethren came together again, from all northern India where they were studying, meditating, and teaching. Some teachers were changing Gotama's words, forgetting his high standards, relaxing the monastic discipline of the brotherhood. The Council insisted on the rules for living as given by Gotama; and the brothers went forth to teach until the power of the arrogant priests was curbed, the barriers of caste were broken down, and a better social order established.

Chandragupta's father was King of Magadha, his mother was a woman of the people. The young man showed such energy and initiative that the king became uneasy for his throne, and exiled him from Magadha. Chandragupta became an outlaw, and when Alexander the Great in 326 B.C. marched his army into the Punjab, Chandragupta hung about the Greeks' camp, until he got into trouble and fled for his life.

He now set about in earnest to advance himself. He got together enough bandits and adventurers to attack Magadha; he conquered the country and made himself king. From that vantage point he conquered the Greek settlements that Alexander had left in the Punjab and became king of all northern India.

He governed well, and added to his empire until it comprised immense territory. He had a large standing army controlled by an elaborate war-offce system. A most important asset of the army was the elephants and every provision was made for their care and training. Departments and subdepartments managed artisans and workmen of every class, took care of commerce, irrigation, the building and upkeep of roads, the collection of taxes, conservation of the country's natural resources, public health, census-taking.

The Greek ambassador Megasthenes wrote of the delightful character of the Indian people: their courage, their scrupulous honesty. Skillful in their work, industrious and peace-loving, they lived in harmony with their chieftains. The women were chaste. There were few slaves. The courage of the men was unsurpassed in Asia. No Indian was ever known to be untruthful. Thieving was so rare that the street doors were not locked. The people were good farmers and careful workmen. Few quarrels were taken into the courts. Chandragupta could not have trained such characters among his subjects as Megasthenes described. Here was undoubtedly apparent the result of two hundred years of Buddhist teaching.

Chandragupta died in 298 B.C. after twenty-four years of power, and his son became king. He was succeeded about 273 by his son, Asoka. The empire now included most of Afghanistan and Baluchistan, and all of India except the extreme south. There was also Kalinga, a small kingdom on the eastern coast, which was independent. Asoka determined to have it, and let his army into Kalinga. One hundred and fifty thousand of the people were taken captive, a hundred thousand were slain on the battlefield, and many more thousands perished from the effects of the invasion or were rendered homeless.

As Asoka, followed by the despairing captives, rode home through the desolation, his campaign suddenly seemed horrible to him and he resolved never again to fight a war of aggression. Soon after, a remarkable thing happened: through the teaching of Upagupta, the foremost Buddhist of the time, King Asoka became a Buddhist.

For two and a half years Asoka quietly studied the Buddha's teachings. Under Buddhist influence Asoka became a new kind of ruler. The kings of India spent much time and money in hunting and traveling for their pleasure. King Asoka gave up hunting, he forbade the killing of animals in sacrificial ceremonies, he resolved to travel only in the people's service. Making his own life ever more rigorous, he used the money usually spent on wars and the king's pleasures in a tremendous campaign of education and in public improvements.

For forty years he reigned and carried out his great purposes. He built thousands of monasteries, in which the monks could live and conduct the schools of the empire. He supported two universities, one at Taxila, one at Nalanda. He built rest houses beside the excellent highways, and had trees planted along the roadsides and wells dug at frequent intervals "for the enjoyment of man and beast." He laid out new roads and gardens and planted groves of mango trees for public use. He founded hospitals for men and women and for animals, and imported and cultivated valuable medicinal herbs.

On beautiful slender pillars of stone which were polished until they looked like metal his artists carved in flawless writing his plans for the best possible government. Written on one lovely pillar is the King's account of his war on Kalinga, and his remorse. The war drums shall beat no more, he says. They have been replaced by the dhamma, the Buddha's law. To the remote parts of his empire he sent his linguistic artists to carve his messages on the rocks and boulders. In caves cut in the rocky side of the Barabar hills Asoka's instructions are still to be found.

These carved edicts were Asoka's method of education. Some of his pillars and rocks are still standing, others have been unearthed by archaeologists. The edicts relate the wonderful story of the king's mighty works. He took the people into his confidence and told them how he expected his officials to treat them. He told the people what was his attitude toward them. He advised them how they should live if they wished to help themselves. His Pillar Edicts, as they are known, bore the news that all his subjects were his children, he reigned to serve them, and considered himself their father.

Carved on one pillar are his words, "Whether I am dining, . . . in my bedroom, . . . in the palace gardens, the official reporters should keep me constantly informed of the people's business, which business of the people I am ready to dispose of at any place, at any hour." This used not to be his practice, he wrote; but he had changed his attitude toward his people and toward the government: "For work I must, for the welfare of all the people; and of that the root is energy and dispatch of business; for nothing is more essential than the welfare of all the people. And whatsoever effort I make is made that I may be free from my debt to all creatures; so that while in this world I make some persons happy, and they may win heaven in the world beyond."

He ruled with a strong hand. He had regulations and laws, prisons and strict officials. He knew that he was obeyed throughout his vast dominions. Slaves and servants must be treated kindly; the well-being of everyone must be guarded. To this end the king appointed ministers, called Censors, to watch over the people and help them to follow the Buddha's dhamma.

To those officials who did not live up to his requirements he wrote on a pillar, "Fulfilment of these orders bears great fruit, non-fulfilment brings great calamity. By officers who fail to give such guidance neither the favor of heaven nor the favor of the King is to be hoped for. My special insistence on this duty is profitable in two ways, for by following this line of conduct you will both win heaven and discharge your debt to me." He rewarded, the edict stated, those who are mild, efficient, patient, kind. Those who were not, must be disciplined.

His edicts informed the people of his purpose that good practices "may grow, including self-control and the distribution of alms." "But no gift, no aid, is so good as giving to others the gift of the divine Law, as aiding others to gain this Law" for "both this world and the next are difficult to secure save by intense love of the divine Law, intense self-examination, intense obedience, intense dread, intense effort." "Man sees but his good deeds, saying: 'This good act have I done.' Man sees not at all his evil deeds, saying 'That bad act have I done, that act is corruption.' Self-examination is hard. Yet must a man watch over himself saying: 'Such and such acts lead to corruption—such as brutality, cruelty, anger, and pride. I will zealously see to it that I slander not out of envy. That will be to my advantage in this world, to my advantage, verily, in the world to come."

The king appointed a minister of justice to safeguard the Buddha's teachings. This minister must also watch over the subject races and the aborigines and see that they were kindly and justly treated. To the border tribes who could not come to him, Asoka sent a Rock Edict telling them "that they should not be afraid of me, that they should trust me and should receive from me happiness, not sorrow," for he would deal patiently with them.

Asoka sent Buddhist teachers throughout his world. Traveling in parties of a leader and four assistants they made their way into the Himalayas, journeyed west to the Greek kingdoms of Syria and Egypt, and east toward Burma. It is said that the king supported sixty-four thousand priests and teachers.

After thirty-five years and more had passed, King Asoka reviewed, on seven carved pillars, the results of his educational campaign. He found that the sacrifice of animals had decreased; the superstitions of the people, the foolish ceremonies to bring good luck, the worship of false gods had decidedly abated. The many teachers whom he sent into far-off countries had achieved good results in those lands. The king had made clear to the people that the laws of his dominions were the cosmic laws, the universal order of cause and effect as taught by the Buddha. Of all the words of the Buddha, Asoka liked the most, "The good Law will long endure."

"From the unreal lead me to the real, from darkness into light, from death to immortality," the brahmins had intoned for centuries. This prayer was answered in the beautiful, peaceful civilization which arose at the foot of Asoka's throne, in the light of the Buddha's teachings.

Responding to their teachers, laymen expressed in art and handicrafts their contentment, their aspirations and joy, until a new dimension of sweetness and happiness entered into India's art. King Asoka's palaces were so beautiful that Hsuan Tsang, the Chinese pilgrim of the seventh century A.D. wrote they must have been built by angels.

All over his realm, at every place where had occurred some conspicuous incident in Gotama's life, the king built a shrine; and shrines to hold the priceless relics of Buddhism. On these shrines Buddhist symbols were carved in bas-relief. In Astoka's time no one made an image of the glorious Buddha; his presence was but suggested by an empty seat. A tree meant his illumination. A young elephant symbolized his coming into the world. Seven trees side by side were seven Buddhas who had come before him. A wheel was Gotama's teachings. A riderless horse his departure from this world.

Asoka built a chapel beside the Bodhi-tree under which Gotama became the Buddha. At Sanchi, in central India, stands a gate which archaeologists believe dates from Asoka's reign. On this gate the story of the king's visit to the famous tree is carved in bas-relief: In the middle of the lower bas-relief is the tree, with Asoka's chapel beside it, half as high as the tree, a procession of musicians attending. A royal personage, believed to be King

Asoka, is dismounting from a horse. Peacocks in the carving symbolize Asoka's House, the Maurya or Peacock.

Tissa, King of Ceylon, was Asoka's friend. The kings had already exchanged ambassadors when Asoka sent his younger brother, Mahinda, and a band of monks to Ceylon with the good tidings of his religion. King Tissa soon became almost as devoted to the Buddha as was Asoka. Tissa built a beautiful temple in Anuradhapura, his capital city, and also two monasteries; and gradually Buddhist monasteries and schools rose all over Ceylon.

The Buddhist monks from India taught India's culture and her fine art of stone-carving, also Asoka's practical methods of irrigation and government, as well as their religion. In the rocky side of a hill eight miles from Anuradhapura, Prince Mahinda hewed a cave, and there he lived and directed the Buddhist teachers in their beneficent work. Professor T. W. Rhys Davids, English scholar and translator of Buddhist literature, writes of his visit to Mahinda's retreat:

On the precipitous western side of the hill, under a large mass of granite rock, at a spot which, completely shut out from the world, affords a magnificent view of the plains below, he had his study hollowed out, and steps cut in the rock over which alone it could be reached. There also the stone couch which was carved out of the solid rock still exists, with holes either for curtain rods, or for a protecting balustrade beside it. The great rock effectually protects the cave from the heat of the sun, in whose warm light the broad valley below lies basking. Not a sound reaches it from the plain, now one far-reaching forest, then full of busy homesteads; there is only heard that hum of the insects which never ceases, and the rustling of the leaves of the trees which cling to the side of the precipice. I shall not easily forget the day when I first entered that lonely, cool, and quiet chamber, so simple and yet so beautiful, where more than two thousand years ago the great teacher of Ceylon had sat, and thought, and worked through the long years of his peaceful and useful life. On that hill he afterwards died, and his ashes still rest under the Dagaba [shrine] which is the principal object of the reverence and care of the few monks who still reside in the Mahintale Wihare.

While the new temple in Anuradhapura was building, some of the women of King Tissa's family decided to become Buddhist nuns. Mahinda sent to India for his sister, Sanghamitta, to come and teach them. She brought with her a company of women teachers, and through the years she gave to the women of Ceylon the same service that her brother gave the men.

Sanghamitta brought a present from King Asoka: a branch cut from the Bodhi-tree. The branch was planted in Anuradhapura and grew into a tree. It stands today, the oldest historical tree in the world. A constant succession of monks has cared for it. When it became weak with age they built terraces around it into which the tree grew new roots from its lowest branches. A careful and accurate record was kept of the tree's history, and it is an assured fact that the present tree was grown from the branch sent by King Asoka and planted in Ceylon in 245 B.C.

After King Tissa's death, in 230 B.C., the island was overrun by the Tamils, energetic people of southern India, who stole the northern provinces. About sixty years later they were driven out by King Tissa's grandnephew.

He was a devoted Buddhist, and under him the good Law advanced. In Anuradhapura he built a huge monastery, called the Great Brazen Palace because its roof was of metal. The sixteen hundred granite pillars of this monastery stand near the Bodhi-tree.

After this Buddhist king died, part of Ceylon was again conquered by the Tamils. About 88 B.C. they were driven out by a nephew of the king who erected the Great Brazen palace. The new king built a large Buddhist temple two hundred and fifty feet high. During his reign the collection of the Buddhist Scriptures called the Pali Canon was written down, in Ceylon.

True Buddhism, as practiced and taught by King Asoka, prompted good government, integrity of character, the spirit of service; and therefore prosperity. Under its inspiration and guidance Ceylon's civilization came into being. Widespread irrigation works were carried out, hospitals for human beings and for animals were founded, and homes for the convalescent. Art and literature, and useful cities, appeared. Every village had its school where peasant and prince received the same education and worshiped together at the temple shrine. Buddhist scholarship advanced and students from all the Buddhist world came to Ceylon to study.

Women were educated, and thousands of women became teachers.

In the most beautiful spot in every community the Buddhist temple and monastery were placed, and near each monastery was a lovely pond of lotuses. Every full moon the people, dressed in spotless white, gathered at the village monastery and in the peaceful evening light the monks told them incidents in the Buddha's life and explained his teachings. From Ceylon the good religion was carried to Burma and Siam.

# 5

## The Buddhist Bible

BUDDHISM REACHED its first zenith in the reign of King Asoka. Love, action, service, that all mankind might enjoy the good life on earth and in heaven beyond was Asoka's interpretation of the Buddha's life and teaching. With this vision of social service and with the faith that moves mountains Buddhist teachers traveled to the four corners of the world to educate and unify the nations.

Gotama was a man of action who taught an almost pragmatic philosophy and refused to consider anything not of practical social value. His viewpoint was that of the prophet of science. He would not discuss ultimate or far-off things but dealt with immediate causes. He saw everywhere cycles of dissolution and renovation, composition and decomposition, death and life, winter storms and spring, seedtime and harvest, autumn and decay, night and then a new morning. Like the true scientific investigator he perceived the orderliness within nature. He invited men and women to observe and experiment as he had done; to see for themselves the reign of law in the mind of man. The joy of his emancipation vibrated through India. His love shone into the hearts of his disciples; they transmitted it from person to person. The Buddhist Scriptures proclaim as an eternal law: "All the means that can be used as bases for doing right are not worth the sixteenth part of the emancipation of heart through love. That takes all those up into itself, outshining them in radiance and glory. Just as whatsoever stars there be, their radiance avails not the sixteenth part of the radiance of the moon. That takes all those up into itself, outshining them in radiance and glory—just as in the last month of the rains, at harvest time, the sun, mounting up on high into the clear and cloudless sky, overwhelms all darkness in the realms of space, and shines forth in radiance and glory—just so all the means that can be used as helps toward doing right avail not the sixteenth part of the emancipation of heart through love."

The Buddha told his followers that he preached the dhamma, and they must live according to the dhamma. He said to a brahmin:

> *I lay no wood, brahmin, for fires or altars,*
> *Only within burneth the fire I kindle.*
> *Ever my fire burns, ever tense and ardent,*
> *I work out the life that's holy.*

Dhamma meant to him the purpose of the universe, which could never be corrupted by man's wrong thinking. It was the moral law of nature. It was the electric, vivid, vital life or Spirit which kept the universe moving forward; the creative energy which urged all things toward perfection. It was the vitality by which men lived and worked and progressed. It was man's conscience, which caused him to prefer moral and spiritual living to degrading thoughts and deeds. It was the ultimate moral and spiritual values; the standard of perfection.

The loving-hearted Buddha saw that people were in all stages of development. "As in a pond of lotuses, blue or red or white, some lotuses of each kind are born and grow in the water, never rising above the surface but flourishing underneath; while others, born and growing in the water, either rise level with the surface or stand right out of the water and are not wetted by it"—so some people were immersed in the material world, others were rising above it, and others had risen quite out of the muddy water, had clear vision, and would understand. He declared:

> *Nirvana's doors stand open wide to all*
> *with ears to hear.*
> *The weary task ahead made me forbear*
> *to preach to men my Doctrine's virtues rare.*

The Buddha's radiant experience was like Isaiah's vision when he saw, mentally, the Lord of Hosts in the temple. To each prophet was given the message: action, service. At intervals through the years Brahma, this spiritual Presence, pointed out the path to the Buddha. When he pondered how best to present his message to mankind, Brahma spoke to him in the silence of his mind and told him that the Buddhas of the past and the Buddhas of the future honor only the dhamma, Truth, and live under Truth. When Gotama sat alone on a mountainside, grieving over Devadatta's treachery, the same glorious Being came to him "when the night was far spent, shedding radiance with his effulgent beauty over the whole of Vulture's Peak Hill," and comforted him.

The Tevigga Sutta, a great book of the Buddhist Scriptures, tells of two young brahmins who, having found in the Buddha the teacher who could show them the way to union with God, came to him with their questions which, they said, had been answered thus-and-so by various brahmins. The Buddha told the young brahmins that a person to be united with Brahma, God, must be like him. Brahma was free from anger and malice, his mind was pure, he was self-controlled, he was love, compassion, perfect peace. If the brahmins would be united with Brahma they must possess Brahmalike, Godlike qualities.

"Arise, thou leader of the caravan, tour the world, and teach the Law divine," Brahma bade Gotama. Many of the Buddha's influential followers, however, were meditative, metaphysically minded ascetics to whom the tendency to ascetic seclusion was eventually as strong as the will to action. This group was first led by the Great Kassapa, patriarch of the Buddhists. Kassapa never deviated a hair's breadth from his asceticism; even the Buddha's suggestion that he have a new garment was refused and Kassapa clung to his "coarse rag robes which were past wearing."

As the years piled up into centuries, Buddhism slowly succumbed to the ascetics, and to a peril greater than asceticism: a decadent form of Brahmanism and a powerful polytheism.

The poems, Vedas, upon which Brahmanism was founded cover a wide range in their conception of human needs. Some of these poems approach the thought of the divine. One such Veda says:

*Him let us praise, the golden child that rose*
*In the beginning, who was born the lord—*
*The one sole lord of all that is—who made*
*The earth, and formed the sky, who giveth life,*
*Who giveth strength, whose bidding gods revere,*
*Whose hiding-place is immortality. . . .*
*Whose mighty glance looks round the vast expanse*
*Of watery vapour—source of energy,*
*Cause of the sacrifice—the only God*
*Above the gods. May he not injure us!*
*He the Creator of the earth—righteous*
*Creator of the sky, Creator too*
*Of oceans bright, and far-extending water.*

Other Vedas express the ideas of a primitive people singing at the dawn of their history and praying to the forces of nature which they have personified.

Only the priests of Brahmanism knew the Vedas, and could properly intone the rituals, only they could teach the Brahman theologies. In their religious services they chanted prayers to the sun; to the gods of the sky and rain; to the goddess of the dawn; to Soma, god of the sacred juice, to whom were offered sacrifices innumerable. They worshiped the god of fire, they invoked the gods of storms and thunder, The supreme rain and storm god, Indra, was very popular in the Buddha's day. Indra was the god who helped the Aryan invaders in their conquest of India. One time he routed fifty thousand of the black race and shattered their citadels. He was a gigantic being of gross passions who ate enormously and freely. When he had drunk too much he did not know his left hand from his right. In elaborate ceremonies which often took days to consummate, the priests conducted the sacrifice of animals to these gods; and for this service they must be paid.

The Buddha declared the animal sacrifices, the priestly ceremonies and magical charms to be superstitions and he roused some priests to storms of pride and anger and invective. Yet in time a multitude of gifted brahmins joined the recluses and wanderers who became the Buddha's followers. Into the new religion many of these disciples brought their excessive stress on asceticism and motionless meditation, their beliefs concerning immortality, and their polytheistic ideas, also their skepticism and agnosticism.

As the centuries went by and, after Asoka, no energetic dynamic king appeared to safeguard the Buddha's teachings, the ascetics adopted a high-sounding but cold idealism. In the boundless leisure of the monasteries the monks sat and thought, without troubling themselves with any scientific study of facts. The wise Buddha warned his countrymen of the danger of excessive theorizing and refused to answer purely metaphysical questions. His followers, like those of the other great Prophets of history, forgot their Teacher's instructions when they went contrary to their particular predilections, and speculated as recklessly as ever. Eventually otherworldly philosophies dominated the Brotherhood until, by the first century B.C. all Buddhism was in decline.

Seeking to please their brahmin associates, Buddhist teachers purged and purified many of the Brahman gods, gave them an infusion of Buddhist kindness, and accepted them as subordinate deities. The wild Indra thus became the Buddhist god Sakka, a much better-behaved deity. These gods were thought of by the Buddhist philosophers as imperfect beings, less developed than the Buddhist saints and not yet having attained nirvana.

More and more, nirvana was defined by the Buddhist philosophers in negative terms, until it almost negated personal existence after death. To the Buddha, nirvana was peace of mind, a radiant life of universal love, Dynamic service to mankind. It was always necessary to avoid an argument which speculative minds might continue interminably; therfore when Gotama was asked whether or not the man who entered nirvana at the death of his body would be extinguished as an individual and not be seen again; or, whether or not the saint at death lives eternally, a distinct person, in nirvana, he refused to answer, saying in substance that these were not important or practical matters at that time. If he had said that the saint remained a distinct individual after death, those brought up on Brahman philosophy would have considered his teaching lower than Brahmanism, for, through the centuries, many brahmins believed the ultimate sacrifice to be that of individuality; therefore the saint at death was merged in the Ocean of God's being. Of course, then the drop entered the Ocean it added nothing to the

Ocean; the saint just went out of existence.

Through Buddhist literature is reflected the predilection for fine-spun theorizing. The Buddha taught that heaven and hell are states of mind, and man's life is determined by his thoughts: if a man harbors thoughts of selfishness or anger or passion he is caught in a trap. If he thinks the right thoughts he enters into joy, freedom, eternal life. Out of suffering and sorrow, if one thinks aright, faith rises. Faith causes joy, and a spiritual happiness which leads to serenity. Serenity is the prerequisite for concentration on spiritual subjects. He who has this concentration can see realities. In many vivid figures of speech Gotama describes the different mental states, explaining that his word pictures were symbols. The later theologians, liking the current flamboyant mythology, made his symbols into actual facts and a basis upon which they evolved and placed in space, endless tiers of heavens and vast abysses in a series of hells.

Considering the Buddha's denial of any omnipotent Self, some Buddhist philosophers came to the conclusion there was no self at all, that man's inner life was just a stream of fleeting states of consciousness which were bound together by a chain of causation. When their speculation eliminated the soul and nothing was left to pass from one existence to another they were in difficulty. Thinkers who saw that this conclusion would make memory impossible, and that there must be something to carry the burden of consciousness, came to their help with the good news that the self was a principle of continuity in the stream of consciousness.

With this much saved, the philosophers elaborated the principle of causation. The deeds done in this life, they said, brought into existence another life, upon this earth or in the unseen world, just as a fire sweeps from tree to tree in the forest, leaps the river and sets another forest on fire. The trees do not pass over the river; it is the flame on this side which causes the conflagration on the farther side.

This idea was bound up with the belief in karma. Karma is the character that a person builds up, the habits of mind that are established, the results, good or evil, which come to a person through his mental habits. Karma is the future results of one's character, determined by natural law. In other words, as a man soweth so shall he also reap. In one doctrine of Karma, "rebirth" is return to this world for reward or punishment for the deeds of the previous life. Hence transmigration and reincarnation.

Reincarnation is the return of the soul in a human body. Transmigration is the return of the soul in a human being, an animal or plant, a bush, a tree. If a man or woman was cruel and selfish that person in the next life here might be born in a beast's body. If a person was mentally and spiritually indolent he might return as a vegetable. Though a woman was beautiful, if she has bad tempered, after her death she would be born again into the world very ugly. If she was self-controlled and kind in this life she would be reborn on earth beautiful and of graceful figure. If a person in this world was niggardly in giving to brahmins and recluses, in the next life here he would be poor; if he was generous he would be reborn into a family of wealth and high social position. Karma executes itself automatically.

In the Buddhist Scriptures is the story of Queen Mallika who came to the Buddha and asked why she was not beautiful. The Scriptures make the Buddha tell her. "Mallika, when a woman has been irascible and violent, and at every little thing said against her has felt spiteful, angry, enraged, and sulky ... then, when she leaves that existence and comes to this one, wherever she may be born, she is ugly, of a bad figure, and horrible to look at, and indigent, poor, needy, and low in the social scale."

The poor queen caught the idea, and cried, "From this day forth I will not be irascible, nor violent and, though much be said against me, I will not feel spiteful, angry, enraged, or sulky, nor manifest anger, hatred and heart-burning."

Belief in reincarnation and transmigration may have commenced in an effective figure of speech, to show that people who let their animal qualities determine their conduct eventually become beasts. Speculative minds endlessly amplified this belief in reincarnation and transmigration.

The Buddhists defined the Buddha not as a unique and isolated phenomenon but as one of a type of prophetic teachers who appear on earth in each cycle. A thousand years or so before Gotama, in the childhood of the Aryan race, tradition tells, a Prophet or Buddha lived, named Brahman. The Book of Patanjali, an ancient Brahman document, says: "God is knowing, speaking from eternity. It was he who spoke to Brahman, and to others of the first beings in different ways. On the one he bestowed a book; for the other he opened a door, a means of communicating with him; a third one he inspired so that he obtained by thought what God bestowed upon him." The Buddhist Scriptures made it clear that these great teachers, Buddhas, all reflected one light, proclaimed one truth. Later tradition said they all attained illumination under the same tree; that before his illumination each Buddha ate from a golden bowl; all threw their bowls into the same place in the river; and the golden bowl of Gotama, when it sank, struck the golden bowls of the Buddhas who had preceded him in past cycles and ages.

After the Buddha's passing, those of his followers who accepted the ancient Brahman theory decided that Gotama having attained perfect insight was merged into the ocean of nirvana, and gods and men would never see him again. This, they said, was his teaching. Others declared he was living in eternal glory. Others explained the Buddha as the victory of many previous lives of discipline and struggle. These lives are described in the section of the Pali Scriptures called Jataka, a charming collection of stories which to the Buddhists seemed shot through with heaven's own light.

As the Buddha became the center of their life, his followers in their enthusiastic appreciation of what he had done for them magnified his station. Sariputta, trying to express his ever-growing adoration, said to him. "Lord, such faith have I in the Exalted One that methinks there never has been nor will be, nor is there now any other, who is greater and wiser than the Exalted One."

The Buddha replied that to make such a statement Sariputta must know all the Buddhas of the past and all the Buddhas of the future, their minds, teaching, wisdom, lives.

One day when Buddha was addressing a large company of people in a mango grove near the city of Nalanda, the young man Kevaddha was present. Seeing so many people listening with such remarkable interest Kevaddha thought how fine it would be to

speed up their conversion with an astounding miracle. He asked
the Buddha to command a disciple to perform a miracle of surpassing power. The Buddha replied that his own miracle was that of
education.

During this period of speculation and decline the Buddhists
divided into two groups: the Mahayana or northern, and the
Hinayana or southern, Buddhists. The Mahayana Buddhists were
those of northern India, and later of Tibet, Korea, China, and
Japan. The Hinayana Buddhists lived in Ceylon and, later, in
Burma, Cambodia, and Siam.

Each group compiled Scriptures. The Mahayana Buddhists,
while they told of the Buddha's sublime love for humanity and
preserved his original thought of God, embroidered their record
of his life with many miracles. The Hinayana Buddhists, weak in
their conception of God, gave clear, detailed stories of the Buddha's life and teaching.

The tendencies and changes through the centuries were reflected in both groups through each purported to preserve the
Buddha's pure teachings. Sects or schools arose and eventually the
divergencies were very pronounced. Members of the different
schools lived peaceably together in the same monastery; and for
two thousand years not a drop of blood was shot in the name of
the Buddha. The Buddhists were not always strict and scholarly
in preserving the integrity of their original documents. But where
is another such record of tolerance and peace?

The Buddhist Scriptures, memorized by the brethren of each
generation, were divided into three groups, called Pitakas or Baskets. One Basket contains the Buddha's talks on various subjects,
collections of sayings, and lovely psalms of exquisite feeling written by the brothers and sisters of the Order. Another Basket, the
Vinaya, gives the rules which regulated the Brotherhood, and
many anecdotes of the deeds of the Buddha and the early Buddhist
heroes. The third Basket, the Abhidhamma, contains interminably
long analyses of spiritual stations, also many subtle psychological
and philosophical discourses.

The southern Buddhists wrote down the Three Baskets, or
Tripitaka, in the Pali language and closed their canon. These Scrip-

tures the Malayana Buddhists called the Hinayana, the Little Vehicle. The northern Buddhists wrote the Tripitaka and other Scriptures in Sanskrit, calling them the Mahayana, the Great Vehicle.

Reading these records is like excavating an ancient city. The student finds layer after layer of life and thought and story deposited one upon the other, century after century. For instance, the scholar reads in the Samyutta Book of the Pali Scriptures the story of Nakula's father. The old man came to see the Buddha, and said, "Master, I am a broken-down old man, aged, far-gone in years, I have reached life's end, I am sick and always ailing. Moreover, Master, I am one to whom rarely comes the sight of the Exalted One and the worshipful brethren. Let the Exalted One cheer and comfort me, so that it be a profit and a blessing unto me for many a long day."

The Buddha told him with loving sympathy it was true his body was sick and cumbersome. He must then say to himself, "Though my body is sick, my mind shall not be sick. Thus, householder, must you train yourself."

The melancholy old man was so transformed that Sariputta, meeting him, asked why he looked so bright and happy. Nakula's father related his conversation with the Master.

Such was evidently the original incident. To it material was added. Into the mouth of the disciple Sariputta was put an elaborate metaphysical talk about the wheel of causation, explaining the Master's words. That dissertation was probably produced by some Buddhist philosopher a hundred years or more after Sariputta, of simple speech, had passed away. This record shows the way in which the artificial and ponderous portions of the Pali Scriptures were brought into being.

The monks in the monasteries, weary at last of abstractions, and perpetual meditation on Truth, focused their thoughts on the evil ways of the people who lived in the world. Believing less and less in action service, they sank into spiritual apathy. A Sanskrit Buddhist Scripture tells of the tragic surrender:

*Afterwards, the evil world multiplied.*

*Goodness diminished,*
*Conceit abounded,*
*Love of money was supreme.*
*And men drifted far from God.*

At the same time over the world the light went out.

From the sixth to the third centuries B.C., while the Buddhists taught India the cosmic law sublime, a wave of rationalism ran high in other countries. The Hebrew prophets thundered out God's ethical requirements. Socrates presented high ideals with persuasive reasonableness. Confucius and Lao Tzu proclaimed in the Far East the need of a scientific treatment of intellectual and social problems. Zoroaster and his strong followers, King Cyrus and Darius the Great, raised Persia to unprecedented heights.

By 100 B.C. the sun was set. These teachers' voices were stilled. And in the worldwide silence, apathy, agnosticism, and unthinking imitation of useless customs smothered progress.

# 6

*The Buddhist and Brahman*

*Renaissance*

IN THE FIRST century A.D. as Jesus in Palestine laid the foundation for a new era, Rome again advanced in intellectual and worldly splendor, Greek reformers recalled the brilliance of the early Greek philosophers and their ethical teachings, and Buddhist and Brahman India awoke to triumphant progress. A century later, Persia under the Sassanians rose as from the dead.

For five hundred years Buddhists and brahmins had lived side by side and the brahmin thinkers had witnessed the transforming power of the personality and teachings of the Buddha. Reacting to this influence they put the Code of Manu into its present form, inserting many Buddhist teachings. The book now contains noble requirements for judges; rules for self-discipline; humility and hard study for brahmins; and instructions in righteousness, forgiveness, and good deeds for all the people. The Code of Manu says to kings: "Determination not to retreat in battle, protection of the people, and obedience to brahmins is the highest duty of kings, and secures their felicity in heaven." The brahmins purified their interpretation of the Vedas, and added to their literature two great epics, the Ramayana and the Mahabharata, which contains a heaven-sent poem, the Bhagavad-Grita.

The Ramayana and the Mahabharata are tales of mighty heroes who lived long before Gotama was born. Their thrilling deeds personified the struggle between good and evil; and told from generation to generation were a means for the moral education of the youth of India. These epics, raised to higher ethical standards under Buddhist influence, were written in their new form early in this Brahman renaissance.

The Ramayana is the story of Rama, a young prince, whose father reigned over a happy city where

Peaceful lived the righteous people, rich in wealth, in merit high,
Envy dwelt not in their bosoms and their accents shaped no lie, . . .
Men to plighted vows were faithful, faithful was each loving wife,
Impure thought and wandering fancy stained not holy wedded life, . . .
Twice-born men were free from passion, lust of gold and impure greed,
Faithful to their Rites and Scriptures, truthful in their word and deed,
Altar blazed in every mansion, from each home was bounty given,
Stooped no man to fulsome falsehood, questioned none the will of Heaven.

The Mahabharata, the epic of another group of godlike heroes, is the jewel casket which now contains one of the world's sublime poems, the Ghagavad-Gita, written by an unknown author during the first or second century B.C. The Bhagavad-Gita is in the form of a conversation between Arjuna, a prince of India, and Krishna, his charioteer. The poem embodies the thought which spread during the first two centuries of the Christian era that, when the world is in dire need God sends his greatest ambassador, his Holy Spirit, to earth in the form of a man to teach anew the right way of life. The Gita says that Krishna was God himself in human form. The poem opens on the battlefield of a civil war. Arjuna and Krishna stand in their chariot ready to drive forward to fight. As they await their summons Arjuna sees in the enemy's army some of his kinsmen. He does not want victory, distinction, wealth at the cost of their lives. He asks Krishna why he must slay them.

The great argument begins, and continues through the Gita. When the war was impending Krishna went before the king's Council and pled for peace; but the Council decided against him. Since this war must be fought, and since for Arjuna's country it is a lawful war, the Prince must do his duty valiantly, unafraid, knowing that if he fights "in devotion to pure devotion" he will fulfill the highest law. There is, says Krishna, a "sad righteousness which calculates" reward on earth and in heaven. In this spirit some people repeat the Vedas and do good works, hoping for wealth and power. Arjuna is not these. He must

> *Find full reward*
> *Of doing right in right. Let right deeds be*
> *Thy motive, not the fruit which comes from them,*
> *And live in action.*

The Gita discusses profound problems of life: man's relation to God; the nature of God, about which it says:

> *Only by fullest service, perfect faith,*
> *And uttermost surrender am I known*
> *And seen, and entered into, Indian Prince. . . .*
> *Four sorts of mortals know me: he who weeps,*
> *Arjuna, and the man who yearns to know;*
> *And he who toils to help; and he who sits*
> *Certain of me, enlightened. . . .*
> *By me the whole vast universe of things*
> *Is spread abroad;—by me, the Unmanifest.*
> *In me are all existences contained;*
> *Not I in them. . . . My Being*
> *Creating all, sustaining all—still dwells*
> *Outside of all.*
> *See! as the shoreless airs,*
> *Move in the measureless space, but are not space,*
> *(And space were space without the moving airs);*
> *So all things are in me, but are not I. . . .*
> *The splendor of the splendid, and the greatness of the great,*
> *Victory I am, and action, and the goodness of the good. . . .*
> *I come, and go, and come. When righteousness*
> *Declines, O Bharata! when wickedness*
> *Is strong, I rise, from age to age, and take*
> *Visible shape, and move a man with men,*
> *Succoring the good, thrusting the evil back,*
> *And setting Virtue on her seat again.*

So exalted are the ethics and spiritual insight of the Gita that the poem has often been compared to the New Testament; some saying its author learned from the Christians, others that the authors of the New Testament borrowed from the Gita.

Brahmanism steadily incorporated the best Buddhist teachings into its sacred writings. In this changed form it is present-day Hinduism. The Bhagavad-Gita is the Hindus' New Testament, the most beloved book in their literature.

The new Buddhism, started in northern India, was called Mahayana. Many of the reforms and most of the writings of its inspired teachers were included in the Mahayana collection of the Buddhist Scriptures.

The Mahayana Buddhists believed that progressive revelation came not only through the Buddha but through chosen saintly persons, and that Gotama had thus taught. "The Illumined appear on earth, but are not quickly recognized." Therefore new teachings must be carefully studied and tested lest one miss God's most recent revelation. If the new communication bears striking fruits of righteousness; if under its influence covetousness and ill will decrease and spiritual experience deepens. Truth must be present in it, and it is worthy to be included in the sacred Scriptures.

The Brahmin priest, Asvaghosa, was a philosopher of exceptional ability; he was also a poet and a musician; and he lived as do the saints. After long acquaintance with the Vedas he studied the Buddhist Scriptures. He became a Buddhist; and was soon chosen to be patriarch of the Buddhist world. Asvaghosa led the Buddhist renaissance.

In his book, *The Awakening of Faith*, Asvaghosa explains God as the Eternal Soul of the universe, the True Eternal Form, the Divine Essence within the invisible and visible worlds. His book says that materialists, "who are dependent upon the senses alone," are blinded and bewildered by "unruly thoughts more numerous than the sands of the Ganges." Those who are trained by a Buddha, the True Exemplar, are enlightened with "the Eternal Mind." Seeing beyond the transitory life of nature, they know that the universe is only the garment of God. This book, rationalistic, sober, and free from miracles, clarified many of the complex ideas of the Buddhist thinkers who, in their effort to eliminate Brahma so bedimmed the thought of God that almost no scholar can find him in the Pali Scriptures. Asvaghosa wrote a stately poem, *The Buddha Charita*, the life of Buddha, as well as dramas and short spiritual poems that were set to music and sung in every part of India.

During Gotama's last days on earth, says one of the Mahayana books, he described to Sariputta the four Buddha-countries; one in the east (Confucianism), one in the north (Zoroastrianism), one in the south (Buddhism) and, far in the west, a country called the Pure Land, or Western Paradise. This Western Paradise is like the New Jerusalem of the Book of Revelation. It is a city with trees of gold and silver, and when the wind blows through the trees lovely music is heard. In the city are rivers, and those who bathe in them are made new. The city is of vast dimensions. To enter it one must die and be born again. In the center of the city is Amitabha who manifests God's Infinite Light. He is boundless mercy and lovingkindness, and he fills the world with life eternal and glory and unspeakable joy.

Amitabha is the name of the second great Buddha who would come after Gotama. To the Mahayana Buddhists it was one of the sublimest names they knew for God's Manifestation; and as the centuries passed a large portion of the human race cried, "Amitabha! O Amitabha!" The devout Buddhists of the north could have said, with Keats,

> *The very music of the name has gone*
> *Into my being.*

The Western Paradise became to the Mahayana, or northern, Buddhists the vision of heaven, and for many millions it took the place of nirvana. Innumerable pictures in Buddhist temples portray the coming of Amitabha and his angels over the hills and mountains to receive, at death, the souls of those who have served and loved God.

Another book, *The Lotus of the Pure Law*, which was the bread of life to the Buddhists in their renaissance, was believed by the Mahayana Buddhists to contain discourses and teachings of Gotama not to be found elsewhere. Like many Buddhist documents, material was imposed upon it through the years until the original words were almost lost under fanciful and incomprehensible exaggeration. In this form the book even contains sectarian disparagement of the great Sariputta. The Chinese Buddhists separated the life-giving original section from the spurious parts; and this essence was translated from the Chinese into English in 1910 by Dr. Timothy Richard, a Presbyterian Missionary in the Far East. Dr. Richard writes of the book, "Its chief teaching of Life, Light, and Love is in the main the same as that found in the Gospel of St. John, the consolation of all the devout of Christendom." *The Lotus of the Pure Law* likens the Buddha to a Gate:

> *The Gate of Infinite Law*
> *Explains all things,*
> *Opens the Way to the Immortal,*
> *Delivers from the bondage of custom,*
> *Removes the worries of existence,*
> *And gives great rest to the soul. . . .*
> *All the Buddhas—the Illumined Ones—*
> *Teach the same secret,*
> *From age to age,*
> *That their goal is God.*

Says *The Lotus of the Pure Law*, the Infinite may live in a Buddha, in all true disciples, and in a book until through its pages the sincere may behold, "clearly, distinctly" God's presence.

The art of Buddhist India for the first five centuries A.D. shows a gentle, cultivated people who devotedly loved their Prophet. In his honor and that of his holy apostles they painted pictures, wrote poems, and erected thousands of temples. Carvings of the first century A.D. still represent the Buddha by an empty chair under the tree of Enlightenment. When Greek influence was introduced into India the sculptors of Ghandara in the southwest carved many statues of the Buddha. For a time these statues were much like the Greek Apollo. When the Indian sculptors had mastered the new technique, they breathed into their work the genius of Buddhist India for portraying the life of the spirit. They made statues of the Buddha with eyes closed and on his face a divine smile, for he gazed with the eye of the mind into the glory of God's presence.

In a wild and lovely valley in central India they cut out of the solid rock of a mountain side the cave temples and colleges of Ajanta; above them were the eternal music of high waterfalls, and below a rushing stream. In these temples are statues of the Buddha and his disciples, also lovely columns, and on the walls are some of the earliest paintings known to India. The artists did not try to make photographic reproductions of people or scenes but to give the thought, the purpose, the living quality of the people they painted. To this end they used strong lines, not rounded forms, and color contrasted rather than light and shadow. Though the paintings are now faded, one can see in the gentle faces of the men and women the refinement, idealization of women, and the adoration of holiness in this Buddhist civilization. Of these paintings the most wonderful is "The Beautiful Bodhisattva." He represents the supreme ideal—the saint who travels through the world educating and serving the people. On this pensive face is a deep, far-away look as he grieves for a suffering world which he prepares to serve.

For five hundred years and more after the birth of Christ, the Buddhists carried forward one of the great educational campaigns of history. This campaign was so closely identical in its aims and results with that of Christ's apostles, and the Buddhist Scriptures proclaimed so nearly the exalted ethical and spiritual teachings of the Gospels, that many Christians have thought Mahayana's ardent teachers borrowed directly from the New Testament. It is clear that the Buddhists of the early years of the first century knew there was a great Prophet in the world, for certain Chinese records tell that Asvaghosa said a Buddha was living on earth for the year A.D. 1 onward. That these Buddhists knew any details about the Christ there is no evidence other than phrases in the Mahayana Scriptures which are very similar to those in the New Testament. Both Buddhists and Christians were evidently receiving light from the same celestial source; therefore the Buddhists of this age, reborn from on high, went forth to teach their part of the world.

In those days books, because they were inscribed by hand, were so costly that only a few could own or read them. So the Buddhist teachers carried with them the art of India as well as the Buddhist Bible and the Higher Law; and they trained artists to use painting and sculpture in their spiritual teaching. As the conception of the

Buddha's greatness grew, the statues of Gotama became larger. In Burma is a statue so high that a man standing on its mighty arm looks like a speck. This statue has four faces, which means to the people that the Buddha, the real ruler of that world, can see in all directions simultaneously. When size seemed insufficient to convey their idea the kings had statues cut out of the eternal rock, or made of bronze. When Buddhism was at its zenith in Afghanistan the artists carved in the cliff overlooking the highway of the nations at Bamian, the Great Buddha, a statue taller than Niagara Falls. For fifteen hundred years this statue has been to Buddhist travelers a symbol of the grandeur of the Law of God.

With spiritual awakening came intellectual quickening and improved government. The great King Kanishka ruled northwestern India about A.D. 100. Like Asoka he became a Buddhist after he succeeded to his father's throne; and he gave every assistance to the spread of his religion. Asvaghosa's book, *The Buddha Charita* led many princes of India to the Buddha's dharma, and the Buddhist teaching concerning good government reminded them that their true wealth lay not in the number of their chariots and soldiers and the abundance of their costly apparel but in the prosperity and happiness of their people.

In this renaissance Buddhists and Hindus strove for and attained an ideal of perfection which lifted their philosophy, literature, art, the handicrafts, and all their social life to a pinnacle approaching the days of King Asoka. Delightful poetry was contributed, and some of the world's best short stories.

Ceylon was led into the new life by men like Dhammapala and Buddhaghosa. Dhammapala wrote entrancing biographies of the early Buddhist saints. Buddhaghosa, born in northern India at a place not far from the Bodhi-tree lived most of his life in Ceylon and translated into Pali many commentaries on the Buddhist Scriptures. He was an indefatigable worker and wrote some twenty books, in addition to his translations.

Fa-hien, the young son of a Chinese Buddhist, as sent by his father to a Buddhist monastery, in China, to be trained by the brothers. The child so loved the peaceful life and the atmosphere of study in the monastery that, with his father's consent, he became a monk. When he was twenty-five he resolved to travel to India. He longed to read the Buddhist Scriptures in the original Sanskrit and many of these documents were to be found only in India. He was gone from China for fifteen years. His diary account of his journey gives a priceless picture of Buddhism in the fifth century A.D.

With four Buddhist monks for companions, in the year 399 Fa-hien started for India, on foot, by the long northern route. Fa-hien and his companions pressed on to east Turkistan and found Buddhist monks, also kings and their subjects, practicing, with different degrees of ardor, the Buddha's law. Arriving in Khotan, a pleasant an prosperous city in a Turkistan kingdom where lived thousands of monks who followed the Mahayana teachings, Fa-hien and his companions attended a festival for the Buddha.

On the great day an enormous four-wheeled car, like the hall of a monastery moving along the road, approached the city. In the car was a huge statue of the Buddha, on either side of it was the statue of a bodhisattva, a saint, and suspended above the three were angels carved in gold and silver. When the car was almost at the city's gate, the king came down from his tent and took off his crown and royal robes. Barefooted, and dressed in simple garments, with his hands full of flowers, he awaited the car while the queen and her ladies in the tent above made ready a shower of blossoms. The festival lasted ten days, each monastery having its day and car.

Fa-hien and the others traveled on, and in western Turkistan found Tartars who were loyal Buddhists. Farther on they visited a country where every five years, at the call of the king, a convocation was held to which Buddhist monks came "in clouds from every direction." In Hidda, a city of southern Afghanistan, Fa-hien visited a monastery "adorned all over with gold leaf and the seven sacred substances." In this monastery, which was so well built that "though heaven should shake and earth be rent, this place would not move," a bone was kept which the people believed was a piece of the skull of Gotama Buddha. Eight men from the noblest families of the kingdom guarded the treasure.

The travelers came to the Indus River at a place where its banks were walls of rock ten thousand cubits from base to top and not a crevice to put one's foot into. They crossed this gorge, arrived in the Punjab, and were received with joy. How wonderful, said the Buddhist brethren, that brothers of the Order in far-away China should come to visit the Buddhists in India!

There were four centers of pilgrimage in India: the place where the Buddha was born, the Bodhi-tree under which he attained supreme Enlightenment, the deer park at Benares where he taught the five ascetics, and the place where he departed from this world. Fa-hien visited all these shrines, and many monasteries, in the holy land of Buddhism. Everywhere he was greeted with loving-kindness. The hospitable monks would take his baggage and alms bowl and bring him water to wash his feet, for generous entertainment of visiting monks was an international service of the Order.

In a Mahayana monastery were copies of the Scriptures for which Fa-hien had traveled so far. He spent three years in India learning Sanskrit that he might translate these documents. Then he went south to Ceylon.

In Ceylon there were sixty thousand monks teaching in the schools and temples. These teachers were cared for from a common fund, and were so loved that the people gave their monasteries priceless jewels and treasures.

Fa-hien attended a Buddhist festival which lasted for ninety days, also many other festivals, and was given copies of some Scriptures which he had not found in India.

With his precious manuscripts and many a recollection, he sailed for China, on a ship with two hundred men.

When Fa-hien landed on China's shore the prefect of the city came to meet him. The famous traveler made his way to the capital, to show the scholars of China the treasures he had brought from India—the manuscripts given him, and the drawings he had made of the wonders he saw.

It took Fa-hien six years to get to India; he spent six years in India; and three years passed on his homeward journey. He traveled through almost thirty countries.

He reported that from the sandy desert, westward to India, "the beauty of the dignified demeanor of the monkhood and of the transforming influence of the Buddha's law was beyond the power of language fully to describe." To his diary account of his fifteen years of travel a friend later added a postscript saying that, with all his achievemnts, Fa-hien was always modest and humble.

# 7

## Lao Tzu and Confucius

ACCORDING TO the oldest Chinese records, semihistorical perhaps, Yao the sage was King of China about 2300 B.C. His home was a simple little house. He dressed in cotton in the summer and deer skins in the winter, and he drove white horses to his red chariot. His chief food was soup. His joy was the welfare of his people and his favorite music their happy singing. He obeyed Heaven's decrees; therefore peace reigned in China and the people were contented. He traveled about to learn how his rule was succeeding. When he heard the people singing,

> *Great is Heaven's son the mighty Yao,*
> *On whom we rest*
> *As creatures sleep*
> *Upon the breast*
> *Of Tuh,*
> *Secure, contented, peaceful, blest;*
> *While stars with noiseless measure sweep*
> *In view.*
> *We nothing know nor understand*
> *But how to keep the King's command,*

he knew that he was a successful king, and he said, "Lo, I have not distressed myself, and yet the people are well governed. I have remained in obscurity, and behold, the people shine!"

There was, in the days, a citizen of Chung-Kuo (China) named Shun, who by his kindness and courtesy drew the people to him like a magnet. King Yao needed just such a helper, and offered him a place in the government. Shun served with such exceptional efficiency that Yao, when his life was drawing to its close, sent for him and said, "Come, Shun, I have studied your actions and taken account of your words. Your actions are great and your words are small. Do you therefore ascend the throne, for I find no virtue in my son Tan-Chu." Shun protested that he was not worthy; but finally he accepted the King's appointment.

These two kings and sages, Yao and Shun, were for forty centuries the exemplars of ideal government in China.

Yu, a government official under King Shun, was a remarkable administrator and engineer. He surveyed the provinces and divided the land, he drained the marshes, built bridges, enlarged the canals, and stayed the devastating floods with dikes and channel outlets to the sea. For eight years he traveled over China on this service, not going home in all that time. When King Shun was old he gave his kingdom to Yu, saying, "Take care of my people."

King Yu ruled well, for Heaven gave him the Great Plan—a simple, logical outline of cause and effect in human society. According to the Great Plan, the first requirement for good government is a ruler of exemplary character whom the people can trust to guard their happiness. The fundamentals for their happiness are long life, financial security, health of body and mind, virtuous living in accordance with the will of God. The people must have food, and sufficient income to purchase the current commodities. They must have a competent and faithful Minister of Public Works, a Minister of Education, a trusty Minister of Crime to safeguard property. The government must provide for hospitality and kindness to strangers, and for the maintenance of the army. The people must have time from their labors for their religious observances; otherwise they can have no real peace of mind. In later centuries the Great Plan was much amplified.

At the request of the people, Yu appointed his son Ch'i to be his successor. Thus the Hsia dynasty began. For four hundred years this dynasty continued, through eighteen generations. Chieh, the last Hsia king, reigned from 1818 to 1766 B.C. He "gave himself up to luxury and wantonness, piling up fresh and dried meats, and forming a pool of wine, whereon a boat could float, and of which, at the roll of a drum, three thousand men drank like oxen until they were inflamed with it." He had a concubine, a young woman named Mei-hi. He preferred Mei-hi's advice to that of his ministers of state. He built for her a room of coral, opening into ivory passages; and from her couch of fine chrysoprase she looked out upon terraces sparkling with precious stones. He got the money for all this by such exhorbitant taxes that the country was almost ruined.

The people cried so loudly for a deliverer that Prince T'ang, advised by the wise sage I-Yin, led the nobles in a rebellion and drove King Chieh from the palace. In 1766 B.C. Prince T'ang became king and made I-Yin his prime minister. Prince T'ang put an end to oppression. And his subjects loved and trusted him.

The Shang dynasty which Prince T'ang founded lasted until 1122 B.C. Most of the Shang kings reigned long and well and under them the people prospered and were happy. Chou-Hsin, the last Shang king, was corrupt and cruel and everyone was afraid of him, for he was so strong he could kill a wild beast with his hands.

His Highness Wên, the heroic Duke of Chou, was the hope of the people during these terrible years. The old poem says, "God set right measure to his thoughts"; therefore fearlessly and in plain terms he reproved the king. After the third rebuke the king sent Wên to prison. During the two years that he was in prison he compliled, it is believed, the classic *Book of Changes*.

As Wên was dying, he charged his son, Lord Fa, to save the country from the tyrant king. Lord Fa led an army against Chou-Hsin and defeated him in a fierce battle.

The immense quantities of grain and treasures that King Chou-Hsin had stored up for his own use, King Wu divided among the people. He sent the soldiers home, he equipped the farmers with horses and oxen to work their fields, he built schools, and homes for the old and helpless. His devoted assistant in this reconstruction was his younger brother, the Duke of Chou, who is a glorious hero of China. In a beautiful prayer, the brother offers his life in exchange for that of King Wu, seriously ill.

The Chou dynasty, which began with King Wu, lasted until 255 B.C. During this dynasty, and the Shang which preceded it, Chinese civilization evidently advanced in refinement and artistic ability, for the bronzes, vases and sacrificial caldrons of the time, vital and graceful in design, show a well-developed technique and mature feeling for distinguished art.

After two centuries, the kings of Chou became self-indulgent and weak; and by 600 B.C. their kingdom, a country lying mainly because the Yellow and Yangtze rivers, was in chaos. The feudal lords of China now did about as they pleased, and cared only for pleasure and revenues for themselves. The kings of Chou kept their throne only because the jealous overlords would permit no one among themselves to take it. Famine killed multitudes of the people, and many were murdered by the savages who continually swarmed in from the desolate steppes of the north and west to ravage the country, which looked to them so prosperous.

In the confusion, two teachers raised their voices—Lao Tzu the mystic; and a generation later, Confucius the prophet of political science.

Lao Tzu was a spiritual philosopher. He is pictured as a saintly, distinguished looking very old man; and he was living when Confucius was a youth. Lao Tzu was keeper of the archives and librarian for the king; and that is about all that is known of him personally. His name is made immortal by the little book, *Tao Tê Ching*. Not all the sentences in this book are his; some are interpolations of his followers. His own words show his goodness and sagacity, words like these: "Requite injury with kindness. To the not-good I will be good in order to make them good." He told his followers to observe nature and learn from it. It is not the spasmodic storms and violent winds; it is the silent shining of the sun, the gentle breeze, the quiet rain, that cause the crops to grow and help mankind. The wise man, then, will cultivate inner repose; for he who lives in excitement and hurry wastes his energy.

Lao Tzu taught that war is a tragedy, and men should make war only when absolutely necessary, never because they wish to be the masters of others. "Wherever a host [army] is stationed briars and thorns spring up," he said. "He who has killed multitudes of men should weep for them with the bitterest grief." "He who overcomes others is strong; he who overcomes himself is mighty."

*Tao* was Lao Tzu's name for God, who was to him the Way of Life, the Unknowable Essence from which all life comes, the Order of Nature, Eternal Reason. The name *Tao* includes these attributes. Lao Tzu taught that "all things depend upon It [*Tao*] for life and It rejects them not. Its task accomplished. It takes no credit. It loves and nourishes all things, but does not act as master." Heaven which "takes its law from *Tao*" and the earth which "takes its law from heaven" will long endure. "And why can heaven and earth endure and be lasting? Because they do not live for themselves. On that account they can endure."

Said Lao Tzu, "I have three precious things, which I hold fast and prize. The first is gentleness; the second is frugality; the third is humility, which keeps me from putting myself before others. Be gentle, and you can be bold; be frugal, and you can be liberal; avoid putting yourself before others, and you can become a leader among men. The Sage puts his own person last and yet is found in the foremost place." He does great things because he does not make himself great. "He is free from self-display, and therefore he shines; from self-assertion, and therefore he is distinguished; from self-boasting, and therefore his merit is acknowledged; from self-complacency, and therefore he acquires superiority."

Lao Tzu tried to guide his countrymen back to their ancient Sages, and forward to an age of reason, nonviolence and kindness. But a greater than he was needed for the task.

As Confucius grew to manhood he realized that China must have a good central government; and this became his primary interest. He was especially fitted to understand his nation, for although he belonged to the nobility he lived among the common people. According to the traditional accounts, his father, the soldier-governor of a small city and an exceptionally courageous man, died in 548 B.C. when his son was not quite three years old. Confucius' mother believed that education was essential, and though she was very poor, for her husband left little property, she managed to send Confucius to school.

For centuries the Chinese had considered education of utmost importance and in every community the learned man held the place of honor. Therefore, when Confucius at twenty-two began to teach, around him quickly gathered a group of serious-minded young men, who became the nucleus for his reforms.

To Confucius, political science began with knowledge of human nature: as it was, as it might be changed for the better. The only way to a better State was through better people. The only way to make people better was to educate them. To educate them one must know their needs and interests, their prevailing motives, their secret thoughts and longings. Confucius was a careful observer. With scientific accuracy he studied his people: their life at court, the life of the masses.

To train his students in his methods he used a very original textbook. With amazing candor ancient China expressed in verse the most unconventional feelings. Men, and especially women who were free to study and to write, told their inmost thoughts in poems, which were sung throughout the land. Three hundred and five of these poems were collected into a book. This anthology, the *Book of Poetry,* Confucius told his students to study that they might become intimately acquainted with their nation.

In the book are stately poems of the court which picture the elegant gentlemen of old-time China—the graceful ease with which they leaned from their chariots, their humor, their courtesy, their skill in archery and warfare. There are war songs of triumph. There are drinking songs, and songs of feasting:

> *Amuse yourselves, but no wildness!*
> *Good men are always on their guard.*

Poems by farmers, workmen, and soldiers, by housewives and brides, describe their work and their hunting, their feasts with joyous music and dancing, their love affairs. Through these poems is what Walter Pater calls "the dynamic fact of poetry." Many verses are the poignant cry of the oppressed. The servant tells of the harshness of his master, the seamstress of the stinginess of her mistress. The forgotten soldier writes of the march over the snow, of fatigue and hunger—will they ever end? Sometimes a soldier writes a song of victory, but more often it is of the hardships of camp life, and his loneliness away from his home and his wife. Different is the householder's poem, which tells—and it must have been in a time of peace—of his new home:

> *Here shall we live, here rest,*
> *Here laugh, here talk.*

Some poems are cries for pity for the toiler, for the lonely man of the road, for the overworked farmer. A farmer tells how rats overran his farm and ate his crops. He fought the rats for three years, then moved to another district, leaving all his little property behind him. Other poems describe the peril of famine and floods. Some reveal the superstitions, the religion, the home life of the people, and their deep affection for good kings and princes.

The women who wrote were ever the equal of the men in their gift of expression, and their telling sincerity. A bride is pictured, beautiful in person and character:

> *How comes it that she is like a heavenly one,*
> *How comes it that she is like a god? . . .*
> *Truly such a lady*
> *Is a beauty matchless in the land.*

Another poem is the plaint of the girl whose lover is unfaithful to her:

> *He swore that truly he was my comrade,*
> *And till death would love no other.*
> *Oh, mother, ah, Heaven,*
> *That a man could be so false!*

Vivid, unpremeditated, unsophisticated, these charming poems had gone throbbing through the centuries. Study them, said Confucius, they stimulate the mind, they teach one carefully to observe social life and individual behavior.

It was the custom in ancient China to pay homage to ancestors and near relatives in the unseen world. The custom was based on the belief that these relatives although they could not be seen by their family were present among them and could be helped and comforted. So the Chinese affectionately placed small offerings of flowers and food before little shrines in their homes, assuring their ancestors of their untiring love and allegiance.

And there was the primitive worship of nature spirits. Into the mind of man came in time a vague apprehension of powerful presences who could help him in his struggle for food and the other things that kept life in his body. Groping to find these presences he raised his thoughts to the sun, which caused the crops to grow, which drove away the angry clouds and forced the rivers back into their channels, which gave man warmth and comfort and cheered his whole environment. Reverently and trustingly he told the sun his needs and offered it presents of food and flowers, in gratitude for blessings in the past and with the hope of protection in the future. As the sun became the object behind which a mighty person hid, surrounding nature assumed a similar life until the mountains, rivers, harvest-time, all the earth and sky were alive with unseen spirits who watched over, or tried to destroy, men. Intellectual men called these beliefs superstitions; but to the less informed they were very real.

As thought advanced, China's best teachers saw in the universe a divine mind and a moral order. In early Chinese literature this divine mind, or cosmic order, is called Heaven, and this became the name for God, the Omniscient, the Beneficent. He is also called Shang Ti or the Supreme Lord. In Confucius' time the emperor held imposing services twice a year when he offered his gratitude and allegiance to Heaven, God. But the masses of the people still prayed to and tried to appease the nature spirits.

As a rule, to wean the people from their customs, Confucius used his own example. A disciple asked if he, Confucius' student, should pray to the spirits? Confucius replied that *he* had not so prayed for a long time.

Leaving alone for the most part the many customs and foibles of the time Confucius concentrated upon his master subject: good government.

To him government was one of the most important activities in which intelligent and noble men can engage. There are three things, he taught, which are essential to good government: sufficient food, sufficient military equipment, and confidence on the part of the people in their ruler. Of the three, the most important is that the people have confidence in their ruler.

A reigning duke asked Confucius, "Is there a single sentence which can ruin a country?"

Confucius answered, "Such an effect as that cannot be expected from one sentence. There is, however, the saying which people have—'I have no pleasure in being a prince, only in that no one offers any opposition to what I say.'"

Government, Confucius taught, should exist only for the economic, physical, moral, and spiritual welfare of the governed. The principal function of government should be rectification: correcting evil. Confucius fearlessly attacked the political procedures, mistakes, and feuds of his people, saying, "At first, my way with men was to hear their words, and give them credit for their conduct. Now my way is to hear their words, and look at their conduct."

The strongest influence for good government, said Confucius, is the example of the ruler. "The virtue of the prince is like unto wind; that of the people, like unto grass. For it is the nature of grass to bend when the wind blows upon it." The rulers of the people should be superior men. Superior men must be well educated. It was Confucius' mission to train such men. "Scholar" and "Confucianist" are the same word in Chinese.

Said Confucius, "The superior man composes himself before he tries to move others; makes his mind restful and easy before he speaks. The superior man thinks of virtue; the small man thinks of comfort. The superior man thinks of the sanctions of law; the small man thinks of favors which he may receive. The mind of the superior man is conversant with righteousness; the mind of the mean man is conversant with gain."

The Sages of the past, who were all superior men, lived by the *li. Li*, the Chinese scholars says, is untranslatable. It means propriety, the laws of courtesy, the code of social behavior, "the right thing to do." It means the essence of religion, the science of social relations, good government. Its application is dependent upon man's conscience. Laws regulate the outer deeds of men; *li* regulates the inner life. *Li* teaches that goodness in mankind can become spontaneous, although "there is no end of things by which man is affected; and when his likes and dislikes are not subject to regulation from within he is changed into the nature of things that come before him." Said Confucius, "If in government you depend upon laws, and maintain order by enforcing those laws by punishments, you will see that the people will try to avoid the punishment and that they will gradually lose the sense of shame. If, on the other hand, in government, you lead the people with virtue and regulate their actions with *li,* you will see that they will have a sense of shame for wrong-doing, and that they will emulate what is good." According to *li* the sovereign did not have absolute power, God being above him. A sovereign should have the allegiance of his subjects only so long as he obeyed God; who is right principles. The people should rise against a king who was unchangeably corrupt and drive him from the throne. "Do not think yourself so large as to deem others small," said a prime minister of old to his king. *Li* allows nations and religions to be different from each other; it teaches tolerance and sympathy for these differences.

Duke Ting of Lu, ruler of the province where Confucius lived and taught, was for a time interested in Confucius' ideas for good government. When the Duke understood, however, that Confucius' plan required the ruler to dismiss corrupt officials, and reform *himself,* he talked with Confucius no more. Sadly Confucius left the Duke's capital city, and for the next thirteen years, accompanied by a few devoted disciples, he wandered from one province to another, hoping to find a prince or a governor who would be willing to try his plan.

Confucius said of himself that he was "simply a man who, in his eager pursuit of knowledge, neglects his food; and in the joy of its attainment forgets his sorrows; and who thus absorbed does not perceive that old age is coming on." He died in 478 B.C. seventy-three years old and apparently a failure.

Duke Gae of Lu, hoping to remind the people of Confucius' unique mission, soon built a temple to him as to a Sage and, as always happens when so great a teacher leaves the world, Confucius' disciples placed upon their own shoulders his mantle of self-sacrificing service.

Mencius, Confucius' greatest disciple, lived from 372 to 289 B.C. He belonged to the Mangs, one of three powerful clans in Lu. The

Duke of Lu was afraid of these families and finally drove them from the state. The Mangs settled in a small province near Lu, and there Mencius grew up. His mother, left a widow when he was about three years old, wishing to give her son the best possible education, moved from place to place until she found, near some scholars, the right environment. Through the centuries she has been celebrated in China as the ideal mother.

When Mencius was in his forties China's feudal system was still causing woe to the common people, compelled to fight the wars of the overlords who made no effort to improve the central government lest any one among them become the master of others.

Quietly Mencius studied the situation, and decided that the best way to help the country was to show the results of just government. Although China was supposed to be one nation it was in fact divided into seven states, the seven kings treacherously watching each other. Mencius would find a king who would let him manage his state for a while. The people in a few years would throng into this well-governed kingdom, and would unite to make its king the chief ruler of China.

The learned man still held the highest social position; and Mencius was the most celebrated scholar of the time. Confident that he would be well received at the several courts, Mencius set out, with some eminent disciples, to visit the kings of China. He was courteously received everywhere and treated with marked respect, although he paid no compliments and often spoke with disconcerting frankness.

He asked a king why he went to war. The king answered, "My object is to seek for what I greatly desire." Mencius asked, "May I hear from you what it is that your Majesty greatly desires?" The king, embarrassed, was silent. Mencius pressed him for an answer. Did he want more "rich and sweet food," or more "light and warm" clothing, or more "beautifully colored objects," or attendants and favorites? No, answered the king. Did the king wish to enlarge his boundaries, or to be more widely known, or "to rule the Middle States and to attract to [himself] the barbarous tribes that surround them?" To do these things would be like climbing a tree to catch a fish. Is it as bad as that? asked the king. It is far worse, replied Mencius, for it one climbs a tree to catch a fish he will find no fish, that will be all. But what calamities follow these wars of conquest!

Asked by another king to describe the great man in office, Mencius answered, "To dwell in kindness, the wide house of the world; to abide in *li*, the correct seat of the world; and to walk in righteousness, the great path of the world; when he obtains his desire for office, to practice his principles for the good of the people, and when that desire is disappointed, to practice them alone; to be above the power of riches and honors to make dissipated, of poverty and mean condition to make swerve from righteousness, and of power and force to make bend—these characteristics constitute the great man." The wise king, said Mencius, will so manage the country that the people will have plenty, and in years of adversity will not suffer and perish. With financial security the people can be serene of heart and happy, and crime will diminish.

For twenty years Mencius visited the various courts. The kings and ministers listened to him civilly, but refused his request that he be permitted to demonstrate the amazing prosperity that wise government would achieve. They offered him subordinate positions and a salary, and twice he accepted the office of minister to the Prince of Ch'i. But each time he resigned, for he would not compromise his high standards.

Finally he ceased to make the rounds, and spent the last twenty years of his life teaching his disciples, and writing. Confucius was his ideal; he followed Confucius' principles and hoped to apply his teachings.

This distinguished scholar gave a tremendous impetus to the study of the Confucian Classics, three of which books existed before Confucius and to which his own writings were later added. By the middle of the third century B.C. Confucian scholars were teaching throughout China, using Mencius' writings and the Classics as their textbooks. Kings and ministers now sought out trained scholars to fill government offices, and the whole country moved slowly forward toward the time when it could be united under Confucius' plan for cooperation between a devoted, energetic king and honorable conscientious subjects.

As Confucius' teachings spread, the nation lived more and more by the Classics. The *Book of History* includes Old documents which Confucius had gathered into one book. It tells in terse and vivid sentences of hero kings of long ago: the success of the ideally righteous, and how those failed who did not follow the dynamic laws of true political science.

Confucius had also gathered up the historical records of the State of Lu, covering the years from 722 to 481 B.C., and used them as subject matter for lectures to his students. The records showed that Lu had fought four hundred wars in two hundred and forty years. The Master considered the legality of each war and the character of the reigning duke, showing the merit or corrupt motives in every case. The collection of brief, statistical records which he used in this case-system was called *Spring and Autumn*, meaning the swinging of the year from spring to autumn, and autumn to spring. Three of his followers in time wrote books worthy to supplement this Classic; Confucius' interest in history caused later Chinese scholars to specialize in this subject, until they rank with the most careful and interesting historians of the world.

Another Classic, the *Book of Changes* is a set of documents, partly compiled, partly written, by King Wên when he was in prison, with later additions by his son, the beloved Duke of Chou.

In the twelfth century B.C. when King Wên and the Duke of Chou lived, the Chinese were zealous fortune-tellers. By very complicated manipulation of divining stalks, little sticks which the people believed were "spirit things," a person would build up a hexagram, a figure of six broken or unbroken lines, one above the other; perhaps this one:

Sixty-four hexagrams are to be found in the *Book of Changes;* and these sixty-four are all that can be made with the six lines.

A person wishing to know the future would build up, at random, a figure of six lines. Then he would take the *Book of Changes* and hunt out from among its sixty-four combinations the one he had made. Under his hexagram he would read his fortune—written for him by the two Sages, who did not try to wean their countrymen away from their love of the game of chance, but used it to good account.

A king who was planning a military campaign and wanted to know in advance how it would come out would send for a diviner, who would juggle his little sticks into a hexagram, would look in the *Book of Changes* for their duplicate, and might read that the king would have the best of luck if he was sure to choose able commanders. If the king tried fortune-telling to learn how to govern his country he might be told that his projects would succeed if he would gather around him "men of brilliant ability." One hexagram tells a person about to travel to a distant country that, if he is "firm and correct as he ought to be there will be good fortune." A man is afraid his business is going to ruin. He investigates his future through a combination of the fortune-telling stalks, and reads in the *Book of Changes* that the crash may come, but if he keeps "smiling and talking cheerfully" all will be well. Under one arrangement the seeker reads that "it will be advantageous to see the great man," the wise teacher and adviser, for superior men have a particular influence and brightness. The book begins with a description of the superior man: what he will do when he has full command, how he will act if he is a subordinate official. Wise advice is given to him, and he is told that his safety lies in humility; for even he may fall if he becomes proud and lords it over others.

So the clever device goes on, through sixty-four readings. Whenever the people took up their *Book of Changes*, said by some historians to be the most popular book in China's history, they were told the science of right living. Confucius' followers did not delay to study this book and write commentaries upon its meanings.

The *Great Learning*, another Classic, was written by a follower of Confucius. It outlines the education necessary for princes and government officials, and says that the efficient ruler must with infinite care train himself, for even when alone the superior man controls his thoughts.

One of the greatest of the Classics, the *Chung Yung* or Golden Mean, is attributed to K'ung Chi, Confucius' grandson and a famous scholar. The book contains high requirements for self-control and good government. It says, "When the ruler pays attention to putting in order his personal conduct, there will be respect for the moral law. When the ruler honors worthy men, he will not be deceived. . . . When the ruler shows respect to the high ministers of state, he will not make mistakes. When the ruler identifies himself with the interests and welfare of the body of public officers, there will be a strong spirit of loyalty among the gentlemen of the country. When the ruler becomes a father to the common people, the mass of the people will exert themselves for the good of the state. When the ruler encourages the introduction of all useful arts, there will be sufficiency of wealth and revenue in the country."

Within a century after Confucius' passing, his followers made a compilation of his sayings, and the stories of his life and wonderful influence, calling their book the *Analects*, or Sayings, of Confucius. This little Classic contains about all that is known of Confucius himself.

Because the Master praised the *Book of Poetry* it was added to the Classics.

In time these books became the revered Scriptures of the Chinese people.

# 8

## Buddhism Enters China

BY THE END of the second-century B.C. the Confucian teachers had lost the vision which the Master gave them. They omitted from their books his teaching of God and immortality, and, concentrating upon ethics and political science, drifted into agnosticism. Ssu-ma Ch'ien wrote that in his day "educated people mostly deny the existence of a spiritual world." The teachers gave disproportionate attention to forms and ceremonies, emphasizing additions to the *Analects* which purported to tell just what the Master did: how he got into and out of a carriage, how he ate and what he ate. They taught their students that they must do all things as the Master did them.

The people at large, finding cold comfort in agnosticism and stony literalism, turned to Taoism. Here also was confusion for, about two hundred years after Lao Tzu, his follower Chuang Tzu began to write. Brilliant, dilettante, irresponsible, Chuang Tzu played with ideas and wove marvelous romances. Preferring paradox to seriousness, in irreproachable literary style he told many a fanciful tale and reduced Lao Tzu's exalted teaching of power through quiet self-control, in large part to a doctrine of inaction. He wrote, "By following nothing, by pursuing nothing Tao may be attained." "Fools think they are awake now, and flatter themselves they know if they are really princes or peasants. Confucius and you are both dreams and I who say you are dreams—I am but a dream myself."

He wrote autobiographically, "Once upon a time, I, Chuang

Tzu, dreamt I was a butterfly, fluttering hither and thither, to all intents and purposes a butterfly. I was conscious only of following my fancies as a butterfly, and was unconscious of my individuality as a man. Suddenly, I awaked, and there I lay, myself again. Now I do not know whether I was then a man dreaming I was a butterfly, or whether I am now a butterfly dreaming I am a man."

Butterfly Chuang, as he was called after he had this dream, knew that the universe must be one. But how could opposites become one? He solved the problem by deciding there were no opposites: that right and wrong, high and low, good and evil, virtue and vice were all the same. Therefore in the world there was only unity. With easygoing pantheism he opened the door to any superstition which the vagrant minds of men might introduce.

Following Chuang Tzu's lead, others expounded the doctrine of unity and inaction. Their words were written into the *Tao Tê Ching*, the little book of Lao Tzu's teachings, and in time passed for Lao Tzu's own. These additions advise: "Practice inaction, occupy youself with doing nothing. Learn not to learn, and you will revert to a condition which mankind in general has lost. Leave all things to take their natural course, and do not interfere. Practice inaction, and there is nothing which cannot be done. The Empire has ever been won by letting things take their course. He who must always be doing is unfit to obtain the Empire."

One of the most popular and extravagant of the Taoist vagaries declared that somewhere in the world was a water which gave immortal life to him who drank it. It was believed that the philosopher Huai-nan actually discovered the elixir, drank some of it, and floated heavenward, in the daytime. As he sailed over his courtyard, in unphilosophic excitement he dropped the elixir, the bottle broke, and the water was spilled. His dogs and chickens drank the water and immediately rose into the air. A number of Taoist emperors experimented with concoctions which charlatans gave them, each claiming to have found the real elixir. Several emperors died of the dose.

By the first century B.C. Taoism was almost strangled by miracles and superstitions, and had materialized its thought of immortality until Taoists were hunting everywhere for the elixir of life; some believing it was a draught, a swallow, just enough for a

person; others sure it was an inexhaustible fountain forever flowing.

In this moment, the Chinese Emperor Ming Ti had a dream, in
the year 61. The record says he saw, in this dream, a dazzling light
high in the sky over the imperial palace. As his eyes became
accustomed to the light he beheld in it the shining figure of a man,
who carried in his hand two arrows, holding them so that they
made the word sign *Fu*, the Chinese for Buddha.

The astonished emperor inquired of his retinue for an interpretation of the dream, and one of his ministers told him that he had
seen the mighty Prophet of India, the Buddha. Something was
already known of India's religion or this minister could not so
readily have explained the dream, but the accounts were largely
legendary. A celebrated traveler of the first century B.C. had
brought news of a golden statue of the Buddha. And later traders
told confused stories of a Holy One adored in countries outside
China. Emperor Ming Ti called eighteen scholars to him, and sent
them to India for firsthand information.

The scholars took the long route over the Himalayas and had
a hazardous journey. When they arrived in Magadha in the valley
of the Ganges they found Buddhism in the beautiful renaissance
of the first century A.D.

The friendly Buddhists gave them copies of the Mahayana
Scriptures written in Sanskrit, works of art, and some of their
relics. The Chinese pilgrims loaded these treasures on a white
horse, and accompanied by two Indian scholars started China-
ward. Six years after Emperor Ming Ti had his dream the envoys
he sent to India presented themselves at his palace to tell him its
meaning.

The Indian scholars at once commenced to translate the Sanskrit manuscripts; but one of the two soon died. The other scholar
worked indefatigably until he died, at sixty, and he made invaluable translations of the Scriptures. Emperor Ming Ti built in
Loyang, his capital, China's first Buddhist temple, naming it White
Horse Temple in honor of the horse that brought the Buddhist
treasures to him. This name was later given to many Buddhist
temples in China.

Now that the way was open, teachers came from India and

central Asia, until for more than six hundred years a steady stream of Buddhist monks poured into China. In the second century A.D. a Parthian, a prince of Persia, gave up his throne that he might become a Buddhist teacher. He lived in China for many years, and became a famous translator of the Buddhist Scriptures. These early missionaries taught with heroic courage, and many a monk spent his long life in a tiny cell laboriously translating the Buddhist literature. With the assistance of Chinese scholars, by the end of the later Han era they had translated three hundred and fifty Buddhist books into dignified and polished Chinese.

The Confucianists and Taoists at first welcomed the Buddhist teachers as co-workers for universal law. The Confucian Classics lost none of their popularity because of the new religion, for the Buddha became another in the succession of China's Sages. While under Buddhist influence, the Taoists' desire for immortality took on a form more attainable than physical longevity, and the Taoists discovered, in their books, references to the Immortals of the West whom the Buddhist saints easily resembled.

Through Asvaghosa's book, *The Buddha Charita* the Buddha now spoke to a vast new audience, saying: "From pure behavior comes self-power, which frees a man from dangers. Pure conduct, like a ladder, enables us to climb to heaven. As age and disease waste youthful beauty, so pride of self destroys all virtue. As I am conqueror amid conquerors, so he who conquers self is one with me."

The people in far-away China could be one with the Buddha as the people in India were one with him. He had changed the life of India. He would change the life of China and give freedom to untold millions.

The teachers from India brought their mathematics, astronomy and literature, their sculpture, architecture, painting, and all the sciences they knew; and they introduced China to the outside world. Chinese architects borrowed from the Indians the pagoda form of building which so pleased the people that almost every city in China built a Buddhist pagoda symbolizing humanity, endowed with limitless possibilities, climbing to the pinnacle of life's eternal values.

In the later Han period, the dynasty again became famous for literature and the arts, for lovely pottery and embroidery, for carving in jade and work in bronze. In A.D. 105 paper was invented, and soon bamboo books and even books written on silk were but strange reminders of old limitations.

Eminent poets, novelists, and historians wrote during the later Han era, among them women who almost outranked the men. Lady Pan-Ch'ao is one of the most celebrated of these Chinese writers. Her father commenced a history of China where Ssu-ma Ch'ien left off, about 100 B.C. When her father died Lady Pan Ch'ao assisted her brother, who continued the work. He was accused of changing the records and was sent to prison. The Emperor gave the history to Lady Pan Ch'ao and she finished it with scholarly care. In addition to this monumental task she wrote sixteen volumes of poems, essays, commentaries, and elegies. She was an advocate of education for women and in her book *Precepts for Women* gave her countrywomen excellent advice, from the Confucian standpoint. When Lady Pan Ch'ao died, the emperor proclaimed a national time of mourning.

During the later Han period other master stylists dipped their pens in the new light and wrote commentaries on the Confucian Classics. Illustrious scholars revised the *Li Chi* into its final form; and the Confucian Canon was closed. The Classics were so highly prized that Emperor Ling Ti had them engraved on stone. In the year A.D. 175 by his order the poet Ts'ai Yung wrote them in red ink on stone tablets, and stonecutters chiseled out his idiographs or characters.

After more than a hundred years of prosperity, political troubles returned, and under them the later Han dynasty sank to an ignominious end in 220. Soon after, the empire was divided into three kingdoms: Wei in the north and center, Shu in the west, Wu in the south. The several kings fought each other ceaselessly, until Wei conquered the other two.

The victorious family, the Tsin dynasty, ruled most unworthily for a hundred and fifty-five years, until 420. The second king of this dynasty lost his capital, Loyang, and much additional territory to the Tartars; the Tsins continued to exist only because the Tartar chiefs fought violently among themselves.

In 397 an enterprising Tartar chieftain, the first king of the House of Toba, conquered Wei; which left the Tsin king almost no provinces north of the Yangtze River. China was divided until 589, when the empire was once more united under a Chinese ruler.

Strangely enough, during this time, while the soldiers fought innumerable battles and the Tartars fiercely murdered the helpless people, while the kings and princes schemed and quarreled and exploited their subjects, literature, art, refinement of feeling, intellectual excellence steadily advanced. Buddhism gave the people the hope and courage they so needed and the religion spread until by 381 nine tenths of the people of northwestern China were Buddhists.

The first ruler of the Tartar House of Toba in the north persecuted the Buddhists and ordered that every monk and nun who could be found be killed, also that all Buddhist literature be destroyed. His successor, who reigned from 466 to 470, became a Buddhist, and assisted the Buddhists in every way. Other kings of the Toba dynasty encouraged the Buddhists to build monasteries in northern China. In the sixth century there were thirty thousand temples and more than two hundred thousand monks and nuns protected by the Toba kings.

Under the quiet influence of Buddhist teaching, the wild Tartars who settled in China slowly assimilated the culture and learning of the people until they were absorbed by and became a part of the people they had conquered.

Early in the fifth century a king of the Tsin dynasty sent an army to conquer Chinese Turkistan, instructing the commanding general not to return to China without the famous Indian scholar Kumarajiva. The scholar was therefore captured and brought to the Chinese king—who freed him and set him to work translating the Buddhist Scriptures.

In the true Buddhist spirit of service, Kumarajiva did his best work and made translations which have never been improved upon. The Buddhist Diamond Sutra, or Discourse, translated by him won more of the highly educated Chinese to Buddhism than all the other Scriptures.

The Diamond Sutra is a philosophic analysis of the spiritual and intellectual reality of a Buddha. The Buddha, says the Sutra, is not merely a physical body walking and speaking on earth for a few years. Those who think of him in this way do not understsand him. The Buddha is above time and space, and to know him one must think of the truth which he teaches. His body, his appearance, his cast of speech, his name, these are not the Buddha, for the Buddha is nothing that will pass away. In other words, one may look with joy at a beautiful flower. The flower in a few days will fade. The beauty which it embodies is eternal and will return in another flower.

Says the Diamond Sutra: as the world is of no ultimate value to the Buddha, it may be without final value to human beings for they also partake of the eternal. Physical life may seem in youth to be enduring. As the years pass and the body wears away, those with discerning eyes see the mirage which is at the center of physical things. Look upon the physical life, says the Sutra, as "a lamp, a phantom, dew, a bubble, a dream, a flash of lightning and a cloud." If the saint thinks, I have attained, he depends only upon himself, and breaks the link which joins him to the reality which makes achievement immortal.

The Confucianists of the fifth century A.D. who were trained in high principles of good government and self-discipline found, in this analysis of a reality above politics, a philosophy of life by which they could be independent of worldly prizes. The man who was driven from his position in society, by the whim of his superior, could take humiliation with equanimity when he was taught by the Diamond Sutra.

To the Confucian moral code was added the loving heart of the Buddha and his promise of life's fulfillment in the immortal realm where he lived and served humanity. Confucianism, become mechanical and stereotyped, was quickened into new life by Buddhist contact. One emperor likened the two great teachings to the wings of a bird, each complementing the other. A sixth-century emperor, seeing a queerly dressed scholar, inquired of him, "Are you a Buddhist?" In reply the man pointed to the Taoist cap which he was wearing. "Are you then a Taoist?" asked the emperor. The scholar put his hand on his Buddhist scarf. On the wall of a Buddhist temple of those days was a picture of the Buddha surrounded by a halo; on one side of him stood Confucius, on the other, Lao Tzu. In another picture a wise man held in his hand a scroll, symbolic of the three religions which were three flames blended into one.

During China's dark centuries the Buddhist monastereies were havens for many despairing people.. Many monasteries were built high in the mountains in quiet, lovely places and here the monks were so gentle that the wild animals came to them for food and shelter as fearlessly as did the travelers. The mountain monasteries became the refuge of poets, artists and scholars, who learned from the tranquil monks to love and be satisfied with nature. Chan Fang-sheng, a poet of the fourth century, wrote his soul into these beautiful lines:

> *Cliffs that rise a thousand feet*
> *Without a break,*
> *Lake that stretches a hundred miles*
> *Without a wave,*
> *Sands that are white through all the year,*
> *Without a stain,*
> *Pine-tree woods, winter and summer*
> *Ever green,*
> *Streams that for ever flow and flow*
> *Without a pause,*
> *Trees that for twenty thousand years*
> *Your vows have kept,*
> *You have suddenly healed the pain of a traveler's heart,*
> *And moved his brush to write a new song.*

After the translation of the Diamond Sutra, Buddhism spread so rapidly at the southern Court and among the educated people that several kings of India, also the King of Ceylon, sent ambassadors to King Sung Wen Ti, who reigned in the south from 424 to 454, to congratulate him and express their wish to be friends with their Buddhist brothers. Liang Wu Ti, the founder of the Liang dynasty which lasted from 502 to 557, was so devoted to Buddhism that three times he gave up his throne and retired to a monastery; but each time at the insistence of his court he returned to rule the kingdom. King Asoka was his ideal and, distinguished in appearance, character and deeds, he was an eminent pupil of his elder

Indian brother. He built thousands of temples, he had the Scriptures copied, and encouraged new monks to teach the people. Buddhism so flourished during this dynasty, the fourth of the five dynasties in the south, that the Indian patriarch Bodhidharma came in 520 to live in China.

Confucius taught the Chinese to appreciate and benefit by their Sages; and became himself one of the Sages. Buddhism lengthened their vision into an immortal period beyond death and gave them assurance of the eventual fulfillment of their aspirations. Trained and sustained by these two great systems of education, the Chinese were able to endure the perpetual menace of the wild barbarians of the north. When the peril which they feared became reality and the barbarian deluge poured over their country they were not overwhelmed, but taught their conquerors all that they knew, until Tartars, Mongols, and Manchus became a constructive part of their civilization. The central government of China, at its best, allowed the maximum of freedom to provincial and local units and to each individual. And the Chinese, at their best, from the humblest worker to the emperor, were worthy of such independence and did not impose upon it. For the nation as a whole revered the Law of Heaven as taught by the Confucian Classics and the Buddhist Scriptures—a system of education which, until it became corrupted through many centuries of interpretation and misinterpretation was a Way of Life for truly superior men.

# 9

# Japan

LIKE OTHER PEOPLES the Japanese did not wait for help from science, but decided for themselves how creation began. In heaven, high up in the sky, they said, lived gods and goddesses. By them the god Izanagi and the goddess Izanami were commanded to consolidate a certain coagulated substance then floating in water, and make it into earth. Izanagi and Izanami stirred the substance well with a jeweled spear. When they drew out the spear some drops fell from it, thickened, and became the island of Awaji which lies across the eastern entrance to the Inland Sea. Izanagi and Izanami went to live upon this earth which they had created. With this beginning, more islands of Japan appeared, were peopled by gods and goddesses, and were supplied with the food and other things needed.

The beautiful daughter of Izanagi and Izanami climbed into heaven by the pillar which connected heaven and earth, and became the Sun Goddess. As time went on and the gods good and evil living on the earth increased in number there was such confusion among them that the Sun Goddess sent her grandson, Ninigi to bring order, giving him, when he left heaven, a mirror (symbol of her spirit), a sword taken from a dragon's tail, and a jewel. These three gifts were later placed in the shrine of the Sun Goddess at Isé, and were carefully guarded through the centuries. Ninigi conquered the earth gods and forced them to submit to orderly government. Meanwhile heaven rose so high above the earth that they were separated, and communication between the two was practically at an end.

Ninigi's two sons quarreled, and the older brother refused to make peace. As the disconsolate younger brother walked beside the sea wondering what to do, an old man appeared and invited him into his basket boat. Younger Brother stepped into the boat, and was carried down to the bottom of the sea. He got out of the boat and wandered on until he came to the palace of the Sea-god. He married Rich Jewel, the Sea-god's daughter, and lived in the palace with her for three years.

The Sea-god then gave him two jewels with which he could control the tides, and sent him back to earth. With one of the jewels he called the incoming tide and almost drowned the island where his quarrelsome brother lived, making his brother submit to him.

Younger Brother built a hut beside the sea. His wife, Rich Jewel, there gave birth to his son, and immediately returned to her father's palace, leaving the newborn baby in the hut.

When the boy grew up he married his mother's younger sister. They had a son, Jimmu Tenno, who became a mighty warrior. Equipped with a sword of supernatural power given him by the heavenly gods, Jimmu Tenno conquered all his enemies. He built a palace in the province of Yamato; he married the Princess Ahira and lived to be a hundred and twenty-seven years old. He was the first emperor of Japan. Through him the long line of Japan's emperors is descended from the Sun Goddess, a line unbroken to this day, the oldest dynasty in the world.

This Shinto myth was taught for centuries in Japan, as part of the nation's history. The educated people knew it for what it was. The uneducated believed it meant that Japan was unique among all nations, ruled by a god.

In a New Year's Rescript of December 31, 1945, Emperor Hirohito pronounced the story of the Sun Goddess pure myth, and officially repudiated the idea of the emperor's descent from the gods.

Japan's earliest history, full of supernatural tales, is told in the nation's two oldest books. The first, the *Kojiki* or Records of Ancient Matters, was written A.D. 712. It carries Japan's history to the year 697.

During these centuries Japan's religion was Shinto. It taught devotion to the emperor, obedience to the government, and the worship of a multitude of gods and godlike heroes about whom were told miraculous stories. Shinto had priests, but no regular ritualistic services. Scattered through the country were primitive little shrines before which the people laid their offerings of grain and flowers, and besought the good deities to protect them from the anger of the wicked gods who sent upon helpless mortals drought and disease and many other calamities. When the supplicant came to a shrine to pray he did not go into the building, but pulled a rope hanging outside which sounded a gong and attracted the god's attention. He then made his prayer silently, for the gods could hear thoughts.

In A.D. 552 the King of Paikché, the second kingdom of Korea to accept Buddhism, sent some Buddhist priest to the Japanese emperor with portions of the Buddhist Scriptures, and a gold and copper statue of the Buddha. The priests were told by the king to say from him to the Japanese emperor, "This law is the most excellent of all teachings; it brings endless and immeasurable blessing to all believers. It has come to Korea from far-off India, and the peoples of the countries lying between are now zealous followers of it."

The Japanese have a prayer:

> There are beings without limit,
> Let us take the vow to convey them all across ... [to safety].
> There are truths without end,
> Let us take the vow to comprehend them all.

The emperor's court was interested in investigating every new idea and would probably have encouraged the Korean king's messengers. But the Shintoists raised such an uproar that the emperor to get rid of his presents gave them to Soga, his prime minister. Soga moved the statue to his house, and commenced to study the manuscripts. A pestilence spread through the country, and the Shintoists at the court cried that the gods were angry because of the new religion. To appease the gods the Shintoists burned the prime minister's house and threw the statue of the Buddha into the canal.

More teachers came from Korea. But again the Shintoists drove them away.

The triumph of the Shintoists lasted only until the year 593, when Princess Suiko became empress. She was an ardent Buddhist; and her nephew, Prince Shotoku, one of earth's superior men, was Buddhism's champion.

Prince Shotoku, the heir apparent and virtual regent during twenty-eight years of Empress Suiko's reign, studied Confucius, Mencius, and the Buddhist Scriptures with scholarly precision, and decided that the Buddhist teachings held unusual possibilities. He explained Buddhism to his subjects as a blending of Confucian science, Buddhist idealism, and Chinese culture; and he convinced many people. A monologue written, it is said, by him gives an emperor reasons for accepting the Buddhist gospel. Shinto, says this document, served the early period of Japan's life. Confucianism is a code of morals for the nation's steady growth. Buddhism is a religion for intellectual maturity.

The Prince sent to China and Korea for Confucian and Buddhist scholars and teachers, artists and craftsmen and with their aid launched a new campaign of education for Japan. He also sent young Japanese of ability to China to study art, science, industry, political science and medicine. Some of these students were in China's capital when the great T'ai Tsung of the T'ang dynasty was emperor. They returned to Japan with the tidings of many reforms, and were largely responsible for the organization of a strong central government to supersede the feudal system. In the eighth century, as a result of these reforms the army was made a profession. The samurai, the military group, became in time a foremost power of the nation. With the nobility they were the intellecutal and cultured class.

It was Prince Shotoku's ideal that every family should be a Buddhist sanctuary, and every province a cathedral. He received enthusiastic support from the court, for Buddhism meant art, learning, science, all the intellectual and cultural equipment of the Chinese and the Indians from whom it came. It had an international outlook; it taught immortality; it upheld allegiance to the government and the emperor. In those early days of saintly teachers of pure motives it seemed about perfection. Prince Shotoku proclaimed Buddhism the state religion. Under its influence the Japanese nation grew up.

Thinking that every Buddhist monarch considered himself a member of the international brotherhood, Prince Shotoku wished to correspond with the Chinese emperor and wrote him a letter, beginning with the salutation, "The Ruler of the Land of the Sunrise sends his message to the Ruler of the Land of the Sunset." The emperor addressed was Yang Ti of the Sui dynasty. Lacking his father's strength of character, and generosity, Emperor Yang Ti replied arrogantly, "The Emperor speaks to the Prince of Yamato." Prince Shotoku forthwith sent Yang Ti another letter, commencing, "The Heavenly Ruler of the East speaks to the Emperor of the West," and the bearer of the letter explained to Yang Ti that the Japanese Regent had supposed all Buddhists to be in one brotherhood and therefore equal. When T'ai Tsung became Emperor of China, Prince Shotoku's dream of an ideal monarch was realized.

Empress Suiko and Prince Shotoku were the first of a long line of Buddhist sovereigns, five of them women. The illustrious Emperor Jomei who succeeded Empress Suiko was followed by Empress Kogyoku. After three years on the throne she resigned in favor of Prince Karu, who became Emperor Kotoku and reigned from 645 to 655.

The *Nihongi* tells how Emperor Kotoku ruled. He ordered that a box and a bell be placed in his palace court; and he sent out a decree that anyone who had a complaint to make might put it in the box. If he did not receive attention quickly, he could ring the bell. An engineer commenced the construction of a canal which was harmful to the farmers of a certain district. An appeal from the farmers was found in the box; and Kotoku stopped work on the canal. Complaints that forced labor was practiced in Nara were dropped into the box; and this abuse was stopped.

Kotoku reminded the people that China's Sages and best kings gave the government's offices to the wise men of the kingdom. Following this example Kotoku commended his officials who ruled justly. He broadcast the names of those who practiced graft, and made them pay back to the people twice the amount they had extorted. Rapacious landlords had seized the large and fertile valleys, leaving the peasants with farms "too small to stick a needle into." Emperor Kotoku broke up these huge estates, recompensing the owners; and he sent out the decree, "Let no man without due authority make himself a landlord, engrossing to himself that which belongs to the helpless." The *Nihongi* comments, "The people were greatly rejoiced." He distributed the land among the peasants and arranged for a redistribution every six years; he reduced the taxes. Said Kotoku, "He who would be a ruler, whether Lord or Minister, should first correct himself, and then correct others," and he gave a large part of his own estates to the people.

Emperor Shomu who reigned from 724 to 749 built roads and bridges, almshouses and hospitals. After a life of good works, he left his palace to become a Buddhist monk. His example was followed by the Empress, by his daughter, and later by many emperors and court nobles.

In 782 Kwammu, one of Japan's greatest emperors, began to reign. Through his many government reforms, and under the honest and efficient men whom he placed over the provinces, the nation prospered. Emperor Kwammu was the Confucian ideal of the practical scholar, who founded schools, and at the same time helped the farmers with canals and the commercial life of the nation with roads and bridges. Under the kindly teaching of the Buddhist priests the Japanese became within a hundred years a great nation.

At first the Japanese copied Chinese civilization. When they discovered that a vital religion is a mighty force for originality they trusted their own inspiration. Encouraged by their emperors, the artists and architects of the new era built in many places lovely temples; also monasteries and convents which became the schools, hospitals, and orphan asylums of the nation. They decorated the temple walls with frescoes picturing the deeds of early Buddhist saints and heroes and the wonderful paradise to which they had gone. Among the monks were master artists, the Fra Angelicos of the East, who worked by an inner light. They filled their monasteries with treasures of sculpture and scrolls, showing the charm and possible perfection of human life.

The Buddhist monks in Japan gave every form of service known to them, and many monks and nuns dedicated their priceless lives to the total life of the nation. The monks dug canals for irrigation, and drained the death-breeding swamps, built roads and aqueducts, planted fruit trees, and trees where shade was needed. They explored the mountain fastnesses and discovered possible passes. They were physicians, scholars, dieticians who made known new and valuable foods. For the benefit of their age they made researches in astronomy, mathematics, and the sciences. They were marvelous woodcarvers, and later were master workers in lacquer, pottery, and other exquisite handicraft. With patience and beauty of workmanship they made thousands of handwritten copies of the Buddhist Scriptures. On scrolls they painted the saints in paradise, and the wicked in awful hells. For hundreds of years these realistic scrolls hung upon monastery walls and were used by the priests to illustrate the moral Law.

While the emperor's court and the intellectuals of the nation accepted the Buddhist and Confucian teachings, the common people clung to their Shinto gods. Their problem was finally solved by the monk Kobo Daishi. He studied for two years in China, and in 807, when he was thirty-three, returned to Japan and spent the rest of his saintly life, until his death in 835, teaching his form of Buddhism, called Shingon.

Kobo Daishi was a master of Pali, Sanskrit, and Chinese. He complied for the Japanese a simplified alphabet. His theology also was simple. The Buddha, he taught, had three aspects: the physical body in which he appeared in India; the radiant reality which was his perfect mind and spirit; the eternal reality which was one with God. This eternal reality, being God, was omnipresent. It lived in flowers, and rushing waters, it stirred in stones, it blazed in the sun and stars. It was the Great Illuminator of all the worlds. He who knew the immortal reality of a thing found God's light. Kobo Daishi expressed his teaching in this poem:

> The bird has a voice for singing,
> A man has a mind for thinking,
> The voice and the mind,
> The clouds and the stream,
> Express the Buddha-wisdom.

He simplified the elaborate Buddhist Scriptures, as he simplified the complicated Japanese alphabet. The God-reality was in man's mind. Know this, said he, and you may attain, on this earth, the boundless life of nirvana. A modern Shingon teacher puts it this way: "Nothing is so wonderful as the mind. If the direction of the mind is changed, it can make a man good or bad."

When the common people heard from the Shingon teachers that God's reality and mind were in everything the problem of deserting their Shinto gods was solved; for God and the Buddha were, then, in all their gods.

In the eighth century smallpox broke out in the south, and spread until it reached Nara. Emperor Shomu promised to build a colossal statue of the Buddha if the plague stopped. The common people cried to their nature gods for help. To appease the people, Emperor Shomu sent a Buddhist priest to the temple of the Sun Goddess at Isé to inquire what she thought of the Buddha. He received a favorable answer; and the next night the Emperor dreamed that the Sun Goddess appeared to him and told him the Buddha was an incarnation of herself.

From this experience the soil for Kobo Daishi's version of Buddhism was preparing for nearly a century. Buddhism, it seemed, was Shinto with moral and ethical teachings and the hope of immortal life added. The Buddhist saints were Shinto gods in a new dress. Rejoicing that they need not give up the gods of their ancestors, the common people joined the Buddhists until the old Shinto almost disappeared from Japan. In time thousands upon thousands of people became monks and nuns. Many were sincere; others simply wished to have a comfortable home, to escape from hard work, or to have a safe retreat when the country was torn with civil war.

About 1200 the form of Buddhism called Zen was brought to Japan by a Japanese monk who learned it in China where it had been popular since the ninth century.

In every world religion has arisen at times the mystic idea: God's spirit is in me. This was the essence of Zen. God's life was in a man and to live by that life was the thing most worthwhile. Zen taught that he who so lived would release inner resources which would make him invincible. The keynote was meditation upon the eternal values of courage, honor, beauty, trustworthiness, upon the never-failing Buddha-light in one's heart. Zen was a wonderfully inspiring and refining influence.

It was a religion of democracy. It taught brotherhood and the rights of the common people. It told the rulers that the greatest virtue of the strong was sympathy for the weak.

Its ideal was poise under all circumstances. It taught the samurai that in their archery practice the chief objective was not to hit the target but to attain poise, harmony of motion. It told the soldiers they must never become excited, for war was base and brutal when men lost their composure. It was accepted by the samurai, for it taught a philosophy which made soldiers indifferent to the hardships of army life and enabled them to go to battle courageously.

Zen was the religion of the best Hojo regents. Tokiyori, the fifth Hojo, who ruled from 1246 to 1261 was its follower. Preparing for the day when he would govern Japan, he traveled in disguise through the country, searching for the best men that he might give them important positions. A judge whom he later appointed was so uncanny in recognizing dishonest officials that it was almost believed he used sorcery.

To test Tokiyori's self-control his Zen teacher one day struck him with his fist three times when he hesitated in answering a question. The ruler of Japan remarked calmly that the blows gave him pleasure only.

This soldier, poet, and man of letters in the latter part of his life became a Buddhist monk, and he died with the restraint with which he lived. Sitting upright, in the meditative position, and writing a poem, which contained the line, "Now opens smooth the Great Road," he passed away.

Zen Buddhism was the inspiration for many artists. One of the greatest was the Zen priest and teacher, Sesshu, born in 1420. China in the flower of the Ming dynasty was the center of artistic inspiration. Sesshu wished to study under the Chinese masters and went to China, but found no one who could teach him. His pre-eminent genius was quickly recognized, and the Emperor of China invited him to paint landscapes on his palace walls. Sesshu stayed in China for several years, for what the Chinese masters could not tell him he learned from the mountains and the rivers.

He painted almost entirely in black and white, with broad rugged lines. Whether his subject is a splendid landscape or a little bird on the branch of a tree, the effect is tremendous. His portrait of Daruma, a founder of Zen in China, gives a glimpse of the soul of the spiritual teacher.

Sesshu had disciples, Buddhist priests and teachers second only to himself. Their studios were in Buddhist temples, their paintings were their prayers, their pictures were beauty and grandeur made visible.

In 1603 the Tokugawa period began with Shogun Ieyasu and with it came two hundred and fifty years of peace. Shogun Ieyasu and his first successors were Buddhists and followers of Confucius. Ieyasu ordered that the Buddhist priests teach every child to read and write. In 1614 the decree went out that every person should become a member of the Buddhist group in his neighborhood and his name be recorded in the temple register.

Buddhism became again a vital force for peace and compassion. The Buddhist monastery schools carried on the education of the nation and taught the Buddhist and Confucian ideals of loyalty, and sacrifice for the common good. Many schools were supported by the feudal chieftains, who paid every expense of the students.

Through Buddhist instruction love of nature was a part of the people's religion. Even the arrangement of flowers in a vase became an art which lovers of flowers studied carefully for as many as fourteen years. A flower design was symbolic of man's life. The highest branch of the design was the heights of heaven; the lowest branch was the earth, a lesser place; between the two was the middle branch, the human being who in his soul united heaven and earth.

Buddhist poets like Basho were a vital influence for moral and spiritual living. Basho's home was a little hut surrounded by banana plants. Here he taught his students, the school of poets who rose under him, that the aim of life was to love nature, to be serene and happy and keep a sense of humor; that the secret of writing great poetry was to live unbewildered, undisturbed by the vicissitudes of loss or gain; that graceful writing was accomplished through spiritual discipline.

The common people, who had no access to the masterpieces, clamored for them. In the eighteenth century, to meet this demand color prints by famous artists appeared; but they were disparaged by the nobility, for they portrayed the ordinary life of ordinary men and women in the country, in their homes, at work. Hokusai, a great landscape artist of the nineteenth century, made many such paintings for prints. Hiroshige, who lived nine years longer than Hokusai, painted "every aspect of his own country in every weather." Hiroshige painted his picture "The Bridge at Ohasai" more than a hundred years ago, yet in this picture the wind still blows so strongly one wonders if the people caught on the bridge in the pelting rain can hold up their umbrellas against the storm.

A village policeman once diverted street traffic so that an artist who had placed himself in the middle of the street might paint his picture undisturbed.

When the doors that had been closed for more than two centuries were opened and Western travelers were at liberty to visit Japan, they found even as late as the nineteenth century a land still uncrowded. In the peace of many years, when the people did not have to give their all to support the devastating wars, there was enough for their needs. They lived in an atmosphere of beauty and furnished their homes with good taste. Color prints were so inexpensive everyone could buy them. The poorest coolie could have a spray of blossoms or some little work of art to enjoy.

Lafcadio Hearn, skeptical, critical and caustic, a journalist and, later, university professor, went to Japan in 1891 and lived there for fourteen years, marrying a Japanese girl. He wrote many books relating his expeiences in Japan. He tells that in the Japan he found, everything "is delicate, exquisite, ... The bank bills, the commonest copper coins are things of beauty. ... The bright, pretty streets ... the bay and the mountains begirding it ... the luminous atmosphere. Fujiyama's white witchery overhanging it in the speckless sky." The artistic sense of the people was almost automatic and instinctive. They were devoted to learning, and many rich noblemen, manufacturers, and merchants educated groups of students giving them board, room, books, tuition, and often their clothes. Poorly paid teachers saved out of their scanty salaries enough to educate several students. One professor lived on sweet potatoes and saved enough to educate, clothe, and board a number of students. For a student to fail in his courses through his own fault was a disgrace, almost a criminal act.

The Tokugawa rule had numberless minute laws that regulated every phase of the people's life: the size, cost, form of a man's house, his occupation, his marriage, his right to hold or sell property. Religious custom determined how the people should "dress, walk, sit, speak, work, eat, drink." Everyone accepted these laws and customs as the best possible way of life. "Everybody greets everybody with happy looks and pleasant words; faces are always smiling. . . . Before the Buddhas and the gods folks smile as they pray."

Of the problem of crime, Lafcadio Hearn wrote: "I have lived in districts where no case of theft had occurred for hundreds of years—where the newly-built prisons of Meiji remained empty and useless—where the people left their doors unfastened by night as well as by day."

It was Buddhism, said Lafcadio Hearn, that brought to Japan the "new gospel of tenderness. . . . In the highest meaning of the term, it was a civilizing power. . . . Architecture, painting, sculpture, engraving, printing, gardening—in short, every art and industry that helped to make life beautiful—developed first in Japan under Buddhist teaching. . . . As teacher, it educated the race, from the highest to the humblest, both in ethics and in esthetics. All that can be classed under the name of art in Japan was either introduced or developed by Buddhism; and the same may be said regarding nearly all Japanese literature possessing real literary quality—excepting some Shinto rituals, and some fragments of archaic poetry. Buddhism introduced drama, the higher forms of poetical composition, and fiction, and history, and philosophy. All the refinements of Japanese life were of Buddhist introduction, and at least a majority of its diversions and pleasures. There is even today scarcely one interesting or beautiful thing, produced in the country, for which the nation is not in some sort indebted to Buddhism."

# Book II

## Christianity

# 10

## God's Guidance in Israel

LIGHT IS ESSENTIAL to life. In the organic world it causes growth; in the human world progress. Light is man's due, for by it he achieves the purpose of his existence. Christianity was founded on the belief that the Light which lights everyone in the world appeared in Christ.

According to the Bible, Christ was not the first Prophet of Messianic station. The New Testament states that his likeness to Melchizedek, a previous Prophet, was proof that Jesus was the Messiah. The 110th Psalm says, "Thou art a priest for ever, after the order of Melchizedek." Jesus in one of his arguments with the Pharisees quoted this psalm as referring to the Messiah who was to come, and who had come in him. The author of the Epistle to the Hebrews devotes a chapter to proofs that Jesus was like Melchizedek, who, "King of Salem, which is, King of peace; without father, without mother, without genealogy, having neither beginning of days nor end of life, but made like unto the Son of God, abideth a priest continually." That is, transcending earthly origin, his station abides forever.

Who was Melchizedek? The Book of Genesis tells that Abraham after his conquest of "the four kings" went to him for a blessing. This is the first time Melchizedek is mentioned. He was King of Salem, or Jerusalem. He was also "the high priest of the most high God." It seems remarkable that the Hebrews in their Bible gave to a "foreign" priest-king the station which became the standard for the Messiah. The Book of Genesis says that Abraham in obedience to a command from God left Ur in Mesopotamia and went to live in Canaan. Was it the divine purpose that he find not only the Promised Land, but the Messiah, Melchizedek?

Of Abraham's immediate descendants his great-grandson Joseph was the noblest and ablest. When, after many vicissitudes, Joseph became prime minister of Egypt his brothers and their families followed him to that country and settled there. Each of the twelve brothers became the patriarch of a tribe, all clinging to each other and to the religion of Abraham until their descendants formed the small Hebrew nation, a separate unit among alien people. Pharaohs mighty and terrible made them slaves, to work at forced labor on Egypt's monumental buildings, and under this exploitation they became a weak, degraded, broken-hearted people.

In ancient Egypt, a Sage deliverd the Hebrews from their enslavement. Moses, the Israelite, was adopted by the Pharaoh's daughter and brought up in the palace as her son. Although in his youth he was trained in the wisdom of the Egyptians he remained at heart a Hebrew, and when he was grown to manhood, he killed an Egyptian taskmaster who was beating a Hebrew. This drew the Pharaoh's attention upon him and reminded the ruler that Moses belonged among his slaves. Moses fled for his life, away from Egypt to the land of Midian and became a shepherd for the priest Jethro.

While Moses served Jethro in Midian, the Pharaoh of Egypt died. "And the children of Israel sighed by reason of the bondage, and they cried, and their cry came up unto God by reason of the bondage. And God heard their groaning, and God remembered his covenant with Abraham, with Isaac, and with Jacob. And God saw the children of Israel, and God took knowledge of them." He spoke to Moses as he stood alone one day near a bush beside Mount Horeb and told him to take the Hebrews away from Egypt. God gave Moses a spiritual sign to prove to him who spoke. He opened Moses' mental eyes so that he saw in the bush near him a light bright as fire.

Like most ancient Scriptures, the Bible of the Hebrews is full of miracle stories: only after many supernatural occurrences, according to the Book of Exodus, did Moses escaped from Egypt with his throng of terrified, half-willing people. During the years of desert life that followed, when the Israelites wandered through unoccupied country, the goal was always the Promised Land. They believed Canaan to be theirs by right as heirs of Abraham and they seem never to have considered any other land. The right or wrong of the conquest of Canaan has been a much-disputed question among modern teachers of ethics; but with the Israelites the only problem was how to get possession.

For many years the Hebrews wandered up and down the Sinai desert. During that time Moses held them together, guided them, restrained them. Because of their love for him and their confidence in him, his authority was supreme. One time he went up on the mountain and stayed there alone, working out the people's problems. The story says that there he met God face to face. God gave him the Ten Commandments, the code for right behavior for the Jewish nation, and Moses wrote them on tablets of stone. He saw so clearly these fundamental laws his people must follow, and the illustrious nation they could become by means of these laws, that he was transfigured with a joy almost supernatural. When he went back among the people and they saw the light in his face, they said their leader had been talking with God himself.

Like every Sage, Moses worked by faith to lay the foundation for his people's progress. Although he lived to be a very old man he did not see the Hebrews established in Canaan; and probably most of those who followed him out of Egypt ended their life in the desert with him. The young man Joshua, whom Moses appointed to carry on his work, was worthy to succeed him; and the Israelites under Joshua's generalship conquered enough country in Canaan to give them a home. They were surrounded by enemies and for centuries fought almost continually to save themselves from their neighbors, and to gain territory. The valiant conqueror David about 1000 B.C. drove out the last of their enemies and won for them undisputed possession of Canaan.

David and his son Solomon were the most illustrious kings who ever ruled Israel. David was so beloved, and so many romantic stories were told about thim, that it seemed, to later generations, the Messiah, who, their prophets promised them, would be like King David.

Under Solomon the Hebrews attained prosperity and contentment and approached righteous living. Solomon's kingdom extended from the Euphrates River on the north to Egypt on the south. His ships sailed the seas as far as India, perhaps. Arts and crafts flourished in his day. He was an enlightened, powerful monarch.

Solomon's son Rehoboam who ruled after him also kept Moses' covenant. But Jeroboam, one of Solomon's officers, made war on Rehoboam and took from him the northern portion of Palestine, setting up a separate kingdom. For more than two centuries the Hebrews were divided thus into two kingdoms: ten tribes in the north, two tribes in the south of Palestine.

The northern kingdom under Jeroboam turned to the worship of the idols and nature deities of the nations around them, to visible gods that they could talk to and take in their hands. Gradually the vision of the people of Judea, the southern kingdom, became clouded and they also inclined to the gods of the neighboring tribes, gods that made no ethical requirements. It was easy to follow what Milton calls

> *gay religions full of pomp and gold,*
> *And devils to adore for deities. . . .*
> *For those the race of Israel oft forsook*
> *Their Living Strength, and unfrequented left*
> *His righteous altar, bowing lowly down*
> *To bestial gods; for which their heads, as low*
> *Bowed down in battle, sunk before the spear*
> *Of despicable foes.*

They gave their courage and national vigor as the price of disobedience; and as their morals weakened the nation sank into living death.

In the ninth century B.C. the intrepid Elijah tried to reform his countrymen. From his cave on Mount Carmel he descended, at intervals, upon the people to scourge them and their king with his fiery anathemas. The moral collapse of the Hebrews was by this time so complete that Elijah despaired of them all. But he finally gathered together a little band of disciples, a nucleus to preserve the laws and religion of Moses. Elijah's personality was so vital that he became the symbol of the one who would herald a better day in Israel, even the coming of the Messiah. By this criterion, said each successive generation, would they recognize the Messiah: immediately before him would come one like Elijah.

After Elijah, other teachers, "the later prophets," accused Israel of faithlessness, and warned the people that they lost God's protection when they broke their covenant with him. These prophets all proclaimed the same message: There is only one God; away with your irrational and impotent idols; live according to God's laws. Amos, the eighth-century shepherd, left his flocks and journeyed to Bethel where the people had set up idols and were singing and dancing and sacrificing animals before them. He told the Israelites they would pay for their disobedience by captivity beyond Damascus. The priests who led the idol worship found Amos so obnoxious that one of them sent word to the King, "Amos hath conspired against thee in the midst of the house of Israel: the land is not able to bear all his words. For thus Amos saith, Jeroboam shall die by the sword, and Israel shall surely be led away captive out of his land." The priest asked Amos to go to Judea in the south, and make his unpleasant prophecies there. The prophet Hosea tried gentleness; he told the people of the northern kingdom that God loved them and would receive them back no matter how disobedient they were. But Hosea warned them that their continued faithlessness would result in captivity in a foreign land. After Hosea, the prophet Micah cried to Israel, "What doth the Lord require of thee, but to do justly, and to love mercy, and to walk humbly with thy God."

Even Isaiah, majestic and distinguished, could not change the hearts of the people and save them from their impending fate. Like Amos and Hosea he pled with the Hebrews to cease worshiping nature deities and idols, and to return to their ethical religion. The northern kingdom refused to listen to these inspired friends, and the terrible thing happened which the headstrong people had laughed to scorn as impossible. In 721 B.C. the Assyrians overwhelmed them, carrying off a large part of the northern tribes—and they were never heard of again. The Assyrians left most of the peasants on the land, trusting to the Arabs and others who settled in the north to kill any national spirit that remained. This part of

Palestine became a province of Assyria. Judea, about forty miles wide and sixty miles long, was all that was left to the Hebrews.

After the north was lost, Judea managed somehow to escape the enemy, and continued to be an independent kingdom. The authors of the Books of Kings say God protected the Hebrews. Perhaps the tact and discretion of some of Judea's kings, and the barren, unproductive, hilly land had something to do with it. But the best people of Judea believed only God could save them from the grasping Assyrians.

In 720 B.C. the mighty Assyrian army swept down the coast and encircled Jerusalem. Hezekiah, King of Judea, sent three men from his palace—his steward, a secretary, and a historian—to the Assyrians' camp to inquire of King Sennecharib's commander his purposes. The arrogant Assyrian general told them Jerusalem had better surrender, for the city was already his. It would be of no use for the Hebrews to trust to the Holy One of Israel to save them. Many a Syrian City that had trusted to its gods was now helplessly in Assyria's power.

When King Hezekiah received this ultimatum he sent a special deputation in sackcloth and ashes to ask the prophet Isaiah if God would save Jerusalem. Isaiah told Hezekiah not to surrender but to hold firm, for God would deliver his people. In the night an awful epidemic spread through the Assyrians' camp and so many thousands died that King Sennecharib and the survivors of that night of horror fought no more in Palestine but returned to Nineveh.

Isaiah told the people of Judea that the Assyrians were sent by God to chastise them for their idol worship and their unrighteousness. The Lord speaks thus, said Isaiah: "The ox knows its owner, and the ass its master's crib, but Israel does not know, my people doth not consider." There could be no prosperity for them until they sincerely turned to God.

Manasseh, King Hezekiah's son, was an idol worshiper, and for the fifty-five years that he reigned he encouraged Judea's idolatry. Manasseh's son and successor, Josiah, was a devoted follower of Moses' God. King Josiah prohibited the worship of pagan gods, and tried to rid his kingdom of idols. To keep their religion pure the Hebrews now centered their worship in the temple in Jerusalem. But many shrines to the nature gods in the country districts, on hilltops—"high places" the people called them—escaped Jerusalem's vigilance.

When Josiah died his sons "did what was evil in the sight of the Lord." The prophet Jeremiah wrote a book detailing the Hebrews' unrighteous deeds and how they had oppressed the poor and helpless. And when Nebuchadnezzar, King of Babylonia, threatened to invade the little kingdom of Judea, Jeremiah warned King Jehoiakim, son of King Josiah, that submission to the Babylonians was the only way to save his people from annihilation. King Jehoiakim would not listen to Jeremiah. He had the prophet arrested, and burned his book; and he tried to make an alliance with Egypt against King Nebuchadnezzar. But Jeremiah was right, for in 597 B.C. the Babylonians conquered Judea and carried princes, nobles, and many other Hebrews to captivity in Babylonia.

Zedekiah, another son of Josiah, was made King of Judea, under King Nebuchadnezzar. Zedekiah, like his brother, schemed to persuade Egypt to fight with him against the Babylonians. Jeremiah warned King Zedekiah that he would ruin Judea and pled with him to submit to the army Nebuchadnezzar sent to suppress his rebellion. To silence Jeremiah lest he weaken the people's fighting spirit, the King had the troublesome prophet put into a dungeon pit where he sank deep in the mud and was left to starve.

Jerusalem was surrounded by the Babylonians and became desperate for food. King Zedekiah was much in need of a favorable prophesy, and hoping Jeremiah's days in the pit had changed his mind ordered that he be brought out. The King's servants put strong bands of cloth under Jeremiah's arms and thirty men pulled him out of the mud. He was taken to the King, and gave the same counsel as before: surrender. But again Zedekiah would not listen.

In 586 B.C. the Babylonians captured Jerusalem. They razed the walls, burned the beautiful temple of Solomon, and laid the city waste. King Zedekiah's sons were killed in his presence, Zedekiah's eyes were then put out, and he was taken to Mesopotamia with seventy thousand captives. After the city fell, Jeremiah and a large party fled to Egypt and there Jeremiah died.

In the Book of Psalms is the cry of the broken-hearted Jewish captives:

*By the rivers of Babylon,*
*There we sat down, yea, we wept,*
*When we remembered Zion.*
*Upon the willows in the midst thereof,*
*We hanged up our harps.*
*For there they that led us captive required of us songs;*
*And they that wasted us required to us mirth, saying,*
*Sing us one of the songs of Zion.*
*How shall we sing the Lord's song*
*In a strange land?*

The priest Ezekiel was taken to Babylonia in 597 B.C. with the first party of captives; and he and the young man Daniel tried to comfort the despairing Hebrews who arrived in 586. Evidently they were in no state of mind at first to listen, for Ezekiel tells in his book that God warned him the children of Israel might be like briars and thorns and scorpions, but he must not be afraid of their words, nor dismayed by their looks. So he gave them God's message that the real Jerusalem would never be destroyed; it would rise again and in it would be built a new temple from which would flow a water of life to quicken into fruit and flower the waste places of Palestine and the withered hearts of the people.

In 538 B.C. Cyrus the Great conquered Babylonia. He issued an edict that the Hebrews should go back to Palestine and should rebuild their temple. In 516 B.C., after seventy years of captivity, they returned to Judea as Jeremiah had prophesied they would.

Cyrus' successors, Darius the Great and Artaxerxes, assisted the Hebrews in many ways to recover their temple and national life. Never had conquerors been so kind to a captive people as were these Persian emperors. A second Isaiah, living at this time, saw visions of a glorious future, and he cried, "Comfort ye, comfort ye my people, saith your God. The grass withereth, the flower fadeth: but the word of our God shall stand for ever. They that wait upon the Lord shall renew their strength; they shall mount up with wings as eagles; they shall run and not be weary; and they shall walk, and not faint."

In this new day for the Hebrews the wise governor Nehemiah administered the affairs of their restored community. And Ezra the priest gathered up the laws of Moses, as best he could, and taught them to the people.

The Hebrews now wrote out and signed a promise that they would obey God's laws as revealed by Moses. Noble priests and rabbis who came after Ezra educated the people in the way of Moses and the prophets. Precept upon precept, line upon line; here a little, there a little, they taught their nation love of God, holy living, social righteousness. The Scriptures became the people's daily bread from heaven. They read them in the morning, and in the evening, and in the middle of the night. They committed them to memory and taught them to their children. They bound Moses' words upon their foreheads and adored them, as they adored God. The center of their social and spiritual existence was the synagogue; and the law of the Lord was their life. Prophets like Zechariah and Nahum, Malachi and Joel continued their education, and for some two hundred years Israel enjoyed the rewards of sincere obedience to God. Says the psalmist, "Sorrow may endure for a night, but joy cometh in the morning." Never again did the Hebrews return to idol worship.

When Alexander the Great conquered Palestine in 332 B.C. Judea became a Greek province. Alexander's empire was divided after his death into four parts. As a result, in 170 B.C. Antiochus Epiphanes became ruler of Palestine.

Antiochus Epiphanes was an admirer of Hellenic culture, and he determined that the Hebrews should give up Moses. In the persecution he authorized, many men and women died rather than break the least of Moses' laws, which were to them the words of God.

A noble Jewish family, the Maccabees, led a revolt, and in 166 B.C. threw off Greek domination. For a hundred and three years the Hebrews were again an independent nation—until in 63 B.C. they were conquered by the Romans.

In the second and first centuries before Christ no prophets appeared in Judea. Those Hebrews who were faithful to their religion faced skepticism, hopelessness, unbearable social injustice—and no one to help them. They knew that by the prophets Israel had advanced. In desperation, some writers invented what they so needed—prophetic counsel. They chose a hero of long before—Enoch, Noah, Moses, Solomon, Elijah perhaps—and put into his mouth a prophetic story of Hebrew history from the prophet's time onward. The procedure went along smoothly enough to the period of the actual author, say the first century B.C. The author now wrote, or found in an unknown document and used, a striking prophecy describing the coming of the Messiah, the triumph of the Hebrew nation, the time when God's guidance would reach its sublime culmination. The Book of Enoch, the Assumption of Moses, the Apocalypse of Elijah are a few of these books, and may contain true prophecies.

Apocalypses of this order became increasingly popular. Believing all their golden sentences to be the utterances of the true prophets, the Hebrews found reason for hope during the tragic years of their declining religion, and their humiliation under Greek and Roman despotism.

# 11
Through Criticism to the True Bible

THE SURVIVAL of the Hebrews is one of the striking facts of history. In Egypt the Hebrews lived a separate people. They left Egypt and entered Palestine and remained a distinct nation. The ten northern tribes, taken captive by Assyria, were lost and forgotten; they were the ones who most persistently worshiped the nature deities and the idols of Canaan. The two remaining tribes, called Jews because of their residence in Judea, survived captivity in Babylonia, conquest and persecution by the Greeks, conquest and persecution by the Romans, persecution by the Christians. After the destruction of Jerusalem by the Romans in A.D. 70 the Jews were scattered to the uttermost parts of the known world, yet they remained one people. Their physical strength and family life overcame all tribulations. They advanced intellectually until their contributions to scholarship, science, literature and the arts, to finance and medicine are today outstanding. They have survived persecution, dispersion, misfortune for a longer time than any people in history.

The great prophets declare that by moral and spiritual behavior does humanity endure. Who survive, in the long run? It is the people who practice self-control, chastity, sound hygienic habits, who love their children and sacrifice for them, who obey the laws of community life and serve each other, who adapt themselves to an environment physical, social, divine.

It was their devotion to Moses and their prophets which sustained and united the Hebrews. Where there is no vision a persecuted people perish. The Hebrews looked backward to their origin, upward to their God, and forward to their destiny.

This vision was made immortal in their Bible. The foundation of the Bible is the Torah, or Pentateuch, those first five books of the Old Testament in which the Law thunders from Mount Sinai. The Hebrews were a Torah-educated, Torah-centered, Torah-illumined people. Hillel, the beloved rabbi of two thousand years ago, said to them, "Be disciples of Aaron, love peace, pursue peace, love all men too, and bring them nigh unto the Law." The power of the law lay not in its penalties, but in its origin, "Thus saith the Lord." The Hebrews were united by a law upon which they could all agree because they were sure it came from God. They were united by a divine promise of a glorious future which would be theirs if they followed this law. They were sure of this future because it was revealed to them by their prophets, who said to them always, "Thus saith the Lord."

Science today questions everything. Scholars make a systematic study of ancient documents. In the balance of critical investigation they weigh the dialogues of Plato, the orations of Cicero, the poems of Homer, the dialogues of the Buddha, the Old and New Testaments, and many other classics. They criticize the text to be sure they have the most authentic manuscripts; this they call textual criticism. They carefully study authorship and genuineness, search for the dates when the documents were actually written, and try to separate additions from the original manuscripts; this is higher criticism. They make inquiries as to the accuracy of the historical statements the documents contained, study the relation of these ancient documents to other ancient writings and try to build a connected history of actual events; this is historical criticism.

"Higher critics" analyzing, in this way, the first five books of the Bible have found that they are largely compilations of documents, some much older and more primitive than others. The earliest compilation they named "J," or the Judean document, because its author lived in Judea. This document gives the most childlike account of God, and contains some of the Bible's most beautiful narratives. The author probably used earlier collections of laws, poems, and ballads. He calls God "Yahweh."

Another authority whose work was incorporated in the Torah has been called, by the higher critics, "E" because he calls God "Elohim," and probably lived in Ephrahim, the northern kingdom of Palestine. He is not so vivid a narrator as the Judean source, but he gives a more spiritual account of Moses and his relation to God, and records important events.

Another biblical record is the Book of the Law. In 621 B.C. Hilkiah the high priest found it in Solomon's temple, and carried it to King Josiah. The description of this manuscript in the twenty-second chapter of Second Kings has led many higher critics to conclude it is the Book of Deuteronomy, or the nucleus thereof. Deuteronomy is a clarion call such as Jeremiah might have raised to remind Israel of the Law and the One God. "Hear, O Israel," it cries, "the Lord our God is one Lord; and thou shalt love the Lord thy God with all thine heart, and with all thy soul, and with all thy might."

During the Babylonian captivity or shortly after, a fourth compilation was made. This record was written by priests, to exalt priestly law and ritual and give them the sanction of immemorial custom. It appears in the story of creation in the Book of Genesis, is to be found here and there through Genesis and Exodus, and comprises the whole of Leviticus. The higher cities call this document "P."

In the time of Ezra the scholar, or later, these four records were combined into the five books of the Torah. To them was added the Book of Joshua, put together from old sources. The six books are sometimes spoken of as the Hexateuch. To them were added compilations relating Hebrew history in the time of the Judges, Samuel, David, and the Kings. They tell how debased, how cruel and barbaric the people became when they forsook the laws of Moses; and what a transformation took place in their life through obedience to those laws.

To the Torah and the history books were added the writings of Isaiah, the Second Isaiah, Jeremiah, Ezekiel, and twelve minor prophets; also the Psalms, beautiful poems which were sung by Israel. Proverbs, Job, Ecclesiastes which make up the books of wisdom; Chronicles, Ezra, and Nehemiah which are later history books; Lamentations, the Song of Songs, and the two little books Ruth and Esther, were also added to the Law and the Prophets.

The Hebrew Bible was completed a hundred years before Christ. The Christians added to it their New Testament, and this compilation became the social and spiritual guide book of the Western world.

For centuries the brilliant, educated, thoughtful people of the West accepted the inspiration, the fundamental truth in the Bible. Men of genius like Milton, Dante, and Augustine lived on the Bible; it shaped their thinking. Men of science like Blaise Pascal, Sir Isaac Newton, Clerk Maxwell, and Lord Francis Bacon believed in it and counted it essentially inspired.

But the scientific victories of the nineteenth century were so amazing that young critics, sighing for worlds to conquer, looked askance at the subject matter in the Bible. Searching the pages of the Old Testament these critics uncovered contradictions and inconsistencies in the historical narratives, and found many impossible miracles. They read that the world was created in six days; that Joshua made the sun stand still for a day; that during the forty years the Hebrews wandered in the desert God sent them every day except the Sabbath a shower of food sufficient for the day's needs. They found a very anthropomorphic God, fickle, easily angered, who dwelt most of the time in heaven, high above the sky. Now and then he sent an angel to earth to inquire what was going on. Sometimes he regretted he had ever created those human beings, they were so disobedient and wild and he seemed so unable to manage them. He decided to wipe them out with a flood. Then he held off, for the time being. He showed favoritism to certain people; and ignored all his other children. He was very narrow-minded.

Finding in Genesis and the history books, even in the stories of King David, an astonishing absence of ethics the 19th century critics asked the pertinent questions: How could they be expected to accept such a book? The Christian philosophers of Alexandria and Athens had asked the same question seventeen hundred years earlier. Origen, the great Christian philosopher of the third century, wrote of the first chapters of Genesis: "Who that has understanding will suppose that the first, and second, and third day, [of creation] and the evening and the morning, existed without a sun, and moon, and stars? and that the first day was, as it were, also without a sky? And who is so foolish as to suppose that God, after the manner of a husbandman, planted a paradise in Eden, towards the east, and placed in it a tree of life, visible and palpable, so that one tasting of the fruit by the bodily teeth obtained life? and again, that one was a partaker of good and evil by masticating what was taken from the tree? And if God is said to walk in the paradise in the evening, and Adam to hide himself under a tree, I do not suppose that any one doubts that these things figuratively indicate certain mysteries, the history having taken place in appearance, and not literally."

With the torch of modern science as they called it in their hands young German and French theologians of the nineteenth century launched a campaign of debunking the Bible. In their recast of the Old Testament the new critics decided that authentic Hebrew history began in the time of Moses who, they said, was just a sort of tribal chieftain with no particular spiritual gifts. Much of the teaching of the Torah, especially its monotheism, they decided was surely beyond the mental capacity of a Hebrew living in Moses' time; so it must have been a later development. The laws attributed to Moses must have been put in his name to give them authority and dignity. King David, they said, was not much of a character or much of a poet; therefore he could not have written the psalms attributed to him. Moreover, the psalms were too advanced in thought for his age; they must have been written after the return of the Israelites from Babylonia, five hundred years after David lived. Nor could the idea of individual salvation have appeared in a time as mentally undeveloped as that of David; it must have arisen in the sixth century B.C. after Jeremiah. Nor was Solomon competent to write the proverbs ascribed to him.

The critics decided that a prophecy, or inspiration from God as described in the Bible, was impossible. They, at the pinnacle of nineteenth-century progress, had never foretold the future. They had never heard God speak. No thinker in the past was greater than the scientific man of their day. Therefore all these accounts of revelations from God which filled the pages of Scripture were mistakes. Men *thought* God spoke to them; that was all. These higher critics tore the books of Isaiah, Jeremiah, Zechariah, and Daniel into fragments. If in these books they found a prophecy they dated it, if possible, after the prophesied event happened. And what did they not do to the New Testament! In their hands the foundations of real Christianity became a mass of ruins. One record which mussed up their thinking was the Gospel of John. To get rid of it they dated it as having been written well into the second century. Auguste Comte bowed God out of the universe with thanks for his provisional services. By the end of the nineteenth century radical critics did the same for Moses and Christ. In their places they put a tribal chieftain and a liberal theologian. They called their creations Moses and Christ; but the new figures bore little resemblance to the Moses and Christ adored through the centuries by millions of true Jews and Christians.

To their conclusions the critics felt impelled perhaps by the nineteenth-century theory of evolution; the idea that mankind gets better and better as the centuries fly by. The Renaissance was better than the Middle Ages; the nineteenth century was better than the eighteenth. Look how evolution burst into mechanical, industrial, scientific creativeness in the nineteenth century. The monotheistic and ethical teachings of Amos and Hosea and Isaiah in the eighth century B.C. should be higher than those in the time of Moses, which was at least five hundred years earlier.

The critics forgot the central fact of historic religion: that the prophets of God were spiritual geniuses who towered far above their age. It was because of his genius that a great prophet could found a world religion. Furthermore, the critics and the prophets lived in different worlds. The critics thought of man's descent from his physical forebears. The prophets taught his descent from heaven also and how the word of God could reshape human destiny. The prophets considered why men were living, where they were going, how they might reach their destination. Only a revelation from God, they said, could answer these questions. Many critics, looking always for flaws and mistakes, through their life-destroying doubts made an alliance with death, and the living water of divine revelation was for them nonexistent. The lesser critics, remembering what the higher critics had said, lost their power of appreciation and for them the Hebrew and Christian religion became devitalized. This school of thought is often called "enlightenment."

The swinging of the pendulum to the left was of service, however, in pruning off the excrescences of literal-mindedness. While they were destroying old foundations these skeptics were forcing us to a much sounder faith, for through bold thinking that is not afraid to face the truth we have laid aside our superstitions, our foolish outworn dogmas, our unquestioning faith in miracles, our idea that we must believe the Bible inspired from cover to cover.

The influence of the Bible rested in the past upon the sublime certainty, "Thus saith the Lord." Can this certainty be maintained by the modern man who selects what he likes in Scriptures and believes and obeys their statutes as he pleases, making himself the judge and the jury in the court of the Eternal? What kind of a Bible can he have?

Parts only of the Bible claim to be inspired. The prestige and splendor of these portions carry along the rest of the book. The essence of these passages is awareness of the One God who through his Spirit spoke to and guided the Hebrew nation. The man who could draw upon this radiant Energy was quickened into exceptional ability as thinker, administrator, prophet, workman, artist, artificer of beautiful things, according to his particular gift. Joshua was filled with wisdom by God's Energy, which passed to him from Moses. From Moses and Joshua it entered the hearts of the Hebrew soldiers and inspired them with courage and confidence to undertake the conquest of Canaan. This same Spirit, present in their memory of Moses, brought to birth in his followers heroic strength, and the gift of prophecy.

An ordinary book has but one meaning. A divine revelation may have many hidden significances. So let us be sure we understand the Bible, its poetry, parables, symbols, its account of the way in which through the centuries wise teachers educated their nation. When the prophet says the mountains dance for joy, and the trees clap their hands, he is using figures of speech. When he says it shall come to pass in the golden day of God on earth "that the mountains shall drop down sweet wine, and the hills shall flow with milk, and all the brooks of Judah shall flow with waters; and a fountain shall come forth of the house of the Lord, and shall water the valley of acacias," he is using metaphors. When he speaks of the "sun of righteousness" which shall rise in the latter days "with healing in his wings," he has employed a figure of speech.

Furthermore the truth of the Bible is always relative to the minds for whom it was written. As Paul said, one does not give meat to babies. Moses had to win the people from their idols, from their golden calf. He told them that Jehovah was a jealous God, jealous of obedience to himself. This was plain, understandable language. The "jealous" Old Testament God was a device by which to get over to the Hebrews God's counsel that it would be much better for them if they would love goodness and truth above all things.

In the desert Moses was the only lawgiver and there were no prisons or penitentiaries. To keep the people in check, in that primitive life, punishment must be swift and visible. In what measure ye mete so shall it be meted to you. Therefore, the law of an eye for an eye and a tooth for a tooth; also, the law that a thief should have his hand cut off; and the death penalty. The "wrath" of God was a means of getting Israel to recognize the inexorable sternness of the moral law. If Moses had told the Hebrews of the operations of natural causation, that as a man soweth so shall he also reap, they would not have understood him, for the people whom he led out of Egypt were not philosophically minded. Today wrath often means a lack of self-control or selfish, unjust anger. To the Hebrews with whom Moses dealt God's wrath was perfect justice, and the fear of it was for them the beginning of wisdom.

The covenant is an eternal symbol based on the contracts and agreements men make with each other. Moses told his followers that Jehovah was a covenant God, who had chosen the people of Israel for his own. God gave his promise to send Israel a shining succession of prophets. Israel accepted his promise; and agreed to recognize, love, and obey the prophets when they came. By this covenant, God guaranteed the Hebrews divine and temporal prosperity. If they broke the covenant, disaster and spiritual death would be the result, for, as a later prophet told them, the soul that sinneth shall die. If they followed Moses' God they would become a strong and united people.

The so-called books of Moses were put into their present form after the Babylonian captivity, and they undoubtedly contain ancient ballads, songs, legends, and material of different dates. The style of the Hebrew historians who wrote the Old Testament may have been faulty. These historians may have so loved miracle stories that they could not resist incorporating some of them into their narratives. But mixed up with childlike fancies and questionable stories is a superb social science that runs through the Old Testament like a shining thread. On this thread are strung the most exalted ethics. Through the undesirable material the jewels of Moses' teachings are scattered, and in it is to be found the simple philosophy of the Bible.

Says the Old Testament, God is the creator, life of all that is. He is apparent in nature to a degree, for he rides on the wings of the wind, and the heavens declare his glory. If man flees to the uttermost parts of the earth, God the omnipresent, the eternal is there. Yet nature alone cannot reveal him. Until he speaks in definite personalities men cannot know his will or his reality, or unite to perform his laws. For each person, interpreting God for himself, will be inclined to make God's will accord with his own interests, prejudices, predilections, and justify his particular wishes and behavior.

Judaism and Christianity believe that God spoke to men through his true prophets, and the Bible contains a record of his messages. To some prophets he spoke in moments of inspiration; to others he was an indwelling presence and divinely potent light more or less continual.

Strip away the myths and legends of the Old Testament. Cull out the evidences of human weakness. What remains? A revelation of God's method of educating Israel through the prophets—one of the most thrilling and inspiring stories ever written. Moses did bring spiritual water to the poor Hebrews in the Sinai desert to lift them out of their stony griefs. Spiritual bread surely came down from heaven upon starving Israel; it was very potent there in the wilderness and adapted to a half-barbaric people. Nourished by this bread Israel grew stronger and wiser. Truly God's presence, as Israel's eyes were opened, became like a sheltering cloud by day, a guiding fire by night, their consolation in the midst of the desert's perils. And of one thing the Hebrew historians were certain: Moses was the savior and the lawgiver of their nation. To them there was no prophet like Moses. He alone, they said, knew God face to face. It is a fact that under his training the Hebrews advanced until they became one of the immortal nations of the earth. If Moses had not led them out of Egypt they would have remained in captivity and weakness, and as a nation would have perished.

When the prophets of Israel—Amos, Hosea, Micah, Isaiah, and the others—commenced an announcement with God's signature, "Thus saith the Lord," or "It shall come to pass in the latter days," and the priestly rulers of Israel were convinced that these passages had the ring of the very word of God, the scribes preserved them with a fidelity known only to those who really love God. Later copyists may inadvertently have modified the text when they tried to interpret a symbolic or prophetic passage. They may have added sentences, believing they belonged to the original. But they tried with rare fidelity to preserve the words of the prophets, and in the main they succeeded.

The most destructive critics see no living flowers on religious altars. To them the religion of Israel and the Christ are but pressed flowers in a herbarium which through custom they call the Old and New Testaments. They spend their time in criticizing what they cannot understand in the Bible, or its mistakes, and quite forget something which made it despite its mistakes the inspiration of the inner life of Western civilization. The real meaning of the Bible is like the coming of morning light. Its inspiration is alive and life-imparting. Deep speaks to deep. When we recognize and understand for ourselves the truth in the Bible we need not go to the critic for guidance, for, after many years of linguistic and historical study, his brain may not be able to record spiritual impressions.

If we have never looked through a telescope are we qualified to decide there is no such thing as the heavens its lens reveals? If we have not climbed to the top of a high mountain can we rightfully deny the sublime panorama there to be seen? If we have never known assistance from God in a time of trouble shall we forbid another the comfort of the Everlasting Arms? "Cast thy burden upon the Lord, and He shall sustain thee," cried the Hebrew poet, speaking from experience. Wrote the author of the 91st Psalm, "He that dwelleth in the secret place of the Most High shall abide under the shadow of the Almighty." Because, and when man has made the Most High his habitation in thought he rises serene and victorious above his troubles; the 91st Psalm is a record of such attainment. "Be still, and know that I am God," says the 46th Psalm; that is, be free from the selfishness and doubts that keep one's heart in turmoil. "Cast me not away from thy presence," cries the author of the 51st Psalm, and his is the prayer of one who has been aware of God and his glory. "Wash me and I shall be whiter than snow," is the supplication of one who has felt the cleansing inrush of the Holy Spirit which purifies the heart of its temptations. He who has known only the humdrum drabness and struggle of everyday life may not understand what the psalmist meant when he cried, "The Lord is the strength of my life; of whom shall I be afraid?" "In thy presence is fulness of joy."

It requires colossal power to launch a new religion in the face of conservatism; a religion which asks the sacrifice of man's apparent interests, which invites men to work for far-off rather than immediate rewards, which requires them to forsake the fleshpots of Egypt and travel through the wilderness in pursuit of a remote and seemingly impossible ideal called the Promised Land. What scholar who disparages Moses and his methods could take a company of thousands of helpless, disorganized people into the wilderness, care for them, and train them into an orderly, united nation? What scholar even of genius could remain for three thousand years a potent living influence in their education?

By the end of the nineteenth century a group of scientific historians led by Professor Adolf von Harnack of Berlin, while accepting the essential findings of higher criticism, realized that the essence of the Bible, its moral, ethical, spiritual teaching, is eternally true. Bishop Lightfoot with Professors Westcott and Hort were a generation ahead of them in doing this service for England; the English scholars never let the pendulum swing so fast or so far as did some scholars on the Continent. Also archaeology with its astonishing discoveries has steadily reinforced early historical records of the Bible, making the monotheistic teaching of Moses and the accomplishments of David and Solomon quite possible.

Today there are at least four kinds of Bible critics. The beliefs of some critics approach zero. Others see somewhat of the glory of the Law and the Prophets. Other critics declare that one must follow the assured findings of higher criticism, but reach the conclusion that God really speaks in certain portions of the Bible. To some, religion is a universal experience and the world prophets are God's teachers.

## 12

# Christ Walked among Men

FOR NEARLY a hundred years the Hebrews had been ground under the heel of their Roman conquerors. Even joy in the law of the Lord was gone, for a minute legalism called the religion of the scribes and Pharisees, with its petty laws attributed to Moses, was forced upon the people by their religious leaders.

As the Roman despotism became every day more unbearable the Hebrews lived upon the prophecies of the Messiah who would save them. Moses foretold a Prophet; Isaiah, Micah, Daniel, Zechariah, Ezekiel proclaimed the Messiah. In the apocalypse the Book of Enoch, they read beautiful parables describing the spiritual glory of the Messiah:

> For he is mighty in all the secrets of righteousness,
> And unrighteousness shall disappear as a shadow,
> And have no continuance;
> Because the Elect One standeth before the Lord of Spirits,
> And his glory is for ever and ever,
> And his might unto all generations.
> He shall be a staff to the righteous whereon to stay
>     themselves and not fall,
> And he shall be the light of the Gentiles,
> And the hope of those who are troubled of heart.

Isaiah saw the Messiah as a suffering servant of God, and the people who followed him as a suffering servant. The revered Rabbi

Hillel, who was an old man when Jesus was born, was sure the Messiah would be a spiritual teacher.

But the Hebrews needed someone to deliver them from the Romans. Surely the Messiah would be a great warrior? Moses promised, "The Lord thy God will raise up unto thee a prophet from the midst of thee, of thy brethren, like unto me; unto him ye shall hearken. . . . And the Lord saith unto me, . . . I will put my words in his mouth, and he shall speak unto them all that I shall command him." Moses was the Hebrews' teacher and ruler; he believed they should fight for their freedom. The prophet Micah wrote in the eighth century B.C. "But thou, Bethlehem, Ephrathah, which art little to be among the thousands of Judah, out of thee shall one come forth unto me that is to be ruler in Israel; whose goings forth are from of old, from everlasting." Other prophets wrote of one like David. David was a spiritual singer; he was also an unconquerable warrior who fought battles for his people. An apocalyptic psalm written about 50 B.C. and put into Solomon's mouth told that the Messiah would purge Jerusalem "from nations that trample her down to destruction. With rod of iron he shall break in pieces their substance. He shall destroy the godless nations with the word of his mouth. He shall reprove sinners for the thoughts of their hearts." He shall "gather together a holy people. Heathen nations [will] serve him under his yoke." This was the Messiah the religious leaders wanted; those leaders of Israel who self-righteously fasted and prayed and gave alms in puplic to impress the world with their good deeds, while in their hearts they longed for worldly power.

As though drawn by the tense expectation, an ascetic of the desert, John the Baptist, suddenly appeared among the people and announced, in words which rang through Palestine, that the day of judgment was at hand. "And this is the judgment," the Fourth Gospel explains, "that the light is come into the world, and men loved the darkness rather than the light; for their works were evil. For every one that doeth ill hateth the light, and cometh not to the light, lest his works should be reproved."

John the Baptist was stern and uncompromising and lonely, like Elijah. John called the people to social righteousness, for, he said, one was at hand who would winnow out the wheat of Jewish civilization. "In the midst of you standeth one whom ye know not, even he that cometh after me, the lachet of whose shoe I am not worthy to unloose," said John. He did not embarrass this one whom he announced by frankly calling him the Messiah. But he quoted verses from Isaiah which everyone knew foretold the Messiah. I baptize with water, said John, but this glorious one will baptize with fire and the Holy Spirit.

The people, trembling with excitement, said a prophet, as of old, had come. In their eagerness to recognize him they crowded around John daily, for the blessing of his baptism. Among them one day was John's younger kinsman, Jesus. When John saw Jesus, the veil was lifted from John's eyes, and he said in wonder to those near him, "Behold the Lamb of God which taketh away the sin of the world." As Jesus rose from the Jordan's waters after receiving John's baptism the sign came and God spoke to him in the silence of his soul. His forty days in the wilderness were but his final hours of dedication.

Jesus' quick popularity when he began to teach disturbed John's disciples, and they went to John with the news that everyone was turning to Jesus. John assured them, "Ye yourselves bear me witness, that I said, I am not the Christ, but that I am sent before him. He that hath the bride is the bridegroom; but the friend of the bridegroom, which standeth and heareth him, rejoiceth greatly because of the bridegroom's voice; this my joy therefore is fulfilled."

Jesus told the people that laws which sanctioned an eye for an eye, a tooth for a tooth, love your friend and hate your enemy, were necessary in Moses' time. But a new age had dawned, and now the law of forgiveness was infinitely higher than the law of retaliation. "I say unto you, resist not him that is evil," he said to his disciples. "If a man strikes you on one cheek turn to him the other also. . . . Forgive, seventy times seven, even . . ." Anger at a personal affront puts one in danger of the spiritual judgment. And hatred, which is anger become habitual, excludes one from the presence of God.

It was Jesus' mission to tell mankind of the blessings which would be theirs if they attained that social and individual life which he termed the kingdom of God. His first commandment was the sublime requirement stated in Deuteronomy: Love God with all they mind and soul and strength. His second commandment: Love thy neighbor as thyself, he took from the Mosaic law in Leviticus. He gave a new and universal meaning to "neighbor." One's neighbor, he proclaimed by word and deed, was the foreigner from Tyre or Sidon, the Roman tax gatherer, the poor who had no helper; every human being, even an enemy. God sends his rain impartially on the just and the undeserving, even on those who break his law, defy his will, deny his existence.

"I am the way, and the truth, and the life: no one cometh unto the Father but by me," said Jesus, telling his disciples, and through them the people, that the priests and the Pharisees could not lead them to God, for Jesus alone among the teachers of his day lived and proclaimed the life required by God.

To him the spiritual life is the highest human experience. It is destined to begin on this earth and become eternal. Life without it is as dark as the existence of the child in the matrix. As the life of the child when born into the physical world is incredibly enhanced, so is man's life glorified when he lives according to the will of God. Therefore Jesus called this spiritual awakening "the second birth." This life within life must be made real and attractive. Jesus could convey to mankind the splendid reality. But men must believe that he transmitted the priceless energy. Therefore he made strong statements about himself. "I and the Father are one," he proclaimed. "I am the living bread which came down from heaven." He saw himself as the mirror which reflected the attributes of God. When he said, "Before Abraham was, I am;" or when he called himself the Son of God, he meant that he was the Spirit, the Mouthpiece of God. He was certain that God was with him to an unlimited degree, for he lived always according to God's will.

He called himself both the Son of man and the Son of God. He said to one who addressed him as Good Master, "Why callest thou me good? None is good save one, that is God," trying to make his hearers understand that they must see the Spirit which shone through his personality. His perfections were God's gift to him and to humanity. He was a mirror in which God's mind was shining. He was the vine; and mankind might, if they chose, be the branches to whom he gave his life. Those who believed his words and followed them would find him a veritable fountain of spiritual energy by which to attain to God's gifts of life abounding, truth, immortality. He could show mankind what the Father was like. No one else could do this for no one else then in the world really knew him. Jesus therefore was the Light of the world.

All holy men are sons of God and everyone may have the Father's life in proportion to the amount of self that he conquers. As there was only one Socrates in Greece, one Shakespeare in England, as supreme genius is rare in philosophy and art and science, so is divine genius unique in a Messiah. In a peculiar sense, Jesus was the Son of God. He was not divine because of virgin birth, he was divine because as in Melchizedek, God's Spirit in him was not alloyed by human personality. That Jesus was conscious of the mighty Spirit which was himself was natural.

"Come unto me all ye that labor and are heavy laden and I will give you rest," called Jesus to the people. And his words were as water from heaven to those who were despondent and afraid, and wanted God. They hung upon his sentences with rapture; and he made them see the life within the universe and hear the call of God in his voice. Though they had been lame in their spiritual life they were able by his radiance to walk once more. Even the Roman soldiers said that this man spoke as never man had spoken.

A scribe, stirred by the sweetness and power of Jesus' appeal, thought how wonderful it might be always to be near such a person, and he cried impulsively, "I will follow thee whithersoever thou goest." When Jesus told him that foxes had their holes, wild birds had their nests but he had nowhere to lay his head, the scribe said no more.

A rich young man seeing the love of God shining in Jesus' face asked, "Master, what good thing shall I do, that I may have eternal life?" Jesus—knowing that although the young man had followed, literally, the commandments of Moses, he had not yet attained to their essence, which was to love God above everything—answered him, "If thou wouldst be perfect, go, sell that thou hast, and give to the poor, and thou shalt have treasure in heaven." The young man wanted to keep what he had, adding to it the kingdom of heaven; and he turned away.

Realizing that they had no ordinary person to deal with, Israel's scholars tried by public argument and ridicule to silence Jesus. Routed and baffled in this, they drew about Jesus a net of jealousy and covert persecution, until those even who saw somewhat of his grandeur dared not befriend him. To be with him when he healed a sick man on the Sabbath might ruin the reputation of a very respectable person.

One day Jesus rose in the synagogue in Nazareth and read Isaiah's description of the Messiah: "The Spirit of the Lord is upon me, wherefore he anointed me to preach good tidings to the poor; he hath sent me to proclaim release to the captives, and recovering of sight to the blind, to set at liberty them that are bruised, to proclaim the acceptable year of the Lord." Jesus said this prophecy was fulfilled in him.

The priests of Israel looked for a Messiah who would be a sort of supernatural warrior. From an unknown place, some said, he would come, bringing with him an army of angels. He would sit upon a throne of glory, and with his rod, and the words of his mouth he would destroy the wicked—his enemies and Israel's. He would set up a new government. He would exalt his nation's leaders.

Did Jesus fit any of these expectations? No. All Israel knew where he came from: it was the despised little town of Nazareth. No angels were attending him; no throne was made ready for him. His followers were just a few illiterate fishermen, and he had not even a mat of his own. How did he treat Israel's leaders? He called them blind leaders of the blind. He told the people that unless their righteousness exceeded that of the scribes and Pharisees they would not enter the kingdom of God. Furthermore, these rigid followers of Moses were informed that Jesus did not observe all Moses' laws: he broke the Sabbath; he said he intended to change Moses' law of divorce; he did not require his disciples to keep the legal fasts.

John the Baptist was troubled when he heard what Jesus was saying. Like many lesser prophets, John believed in violent denunciation. He called the religious leaders of his day a generation of vipers, and wanted to bring down fire and vengeance upon them. Jesus said compassion was greater than vengeance. Unable to go to Jesus, for John was in prison condemned by King Herod to die, he sent two disciples to ask Jesus, "Art thou he that should come or look we for another?"

Tell John, answered Jesus, that the blind are receiving their sight, the lame walk, those who were as unclean as lepers are purified, the deaf are beginning to hear the music of God, the dead are raised into life, and to the poor and the disinherited has come the glad tidings of God's love for them.

Even Jesus' poor fishermen-disciples could not give up the idea of a worldly Messiah, and argued among themselves as to who would have precedence in Jesus' kingdom.

Blessed is any member of the old order, said Jesus, who finds in me no cause of stumbling.

One afternoon a little band of fishermen with other poor folk from Galilee trod the road to Jerusalem. In their center was the young workingman Jesus, riding a donkey borrowed for the occasion. A crowd of the people of Judea trailed after them.

As the party neared Jerusalem an unsuppressible enthusiasm swept those beside Jesus and they cut palm branches, and pulled off their garments, to throw them on the ground before him.

"Hosanna! Blessed is he that cometh in the name of the Lord: Blessed is the kingdom that cometh, the kingdom of our father David: Hosanna in the highest!" shouted the little group in ecstasy.

Jesus had announced that he was the looked-for Messiah. After being with him for the better part of three years his disciples believed anything was possible. The beloved Master had talked continually of the kingdom of God and how it contained every good thing. Now the time was come for him to ascend a throne of glory. His splendor would fill the world and the nations would be his subjects. Every enemy would be under his feet. Rome the magnificent would be as nothing before him. The righteous would flourish, sorrow and sighing would cease. The dream of the ages was come true.

The kingdom would belong to the poor, and Jesus' disciples would be rewarded for their faith in him. They would be his chief ministers and two among them, whom he would select, would sit one on either side of his throne. The king's name would endure everlastingly. His spirit would descend like rain upon the mown grass. There would be peace until the sun and moon were no more.

Think what this meant to the downtrodden, persecuted people of Israel! They soon would rule the world.

As the disciples climbed the long road to the heights of Zion joy gave wings to their feet. Blessed is the king that cometh in the name of the Lord! Peace in heaven and glory in the highest! they cried.

When the party entered Jerusalem, multitudes of the people said, "The prophet from Nazareth has come!" and a great excitement shook the city.

Jesus and his disciples spent the night in nearby Bethany, and the next morning went again to Jerusalem. Jesus now went straight to the temple; and with a little whip of cords drove out the tradesmen whom the priests allowed to have their stalls in the temple's court. The priests were personally interested in this business, for they conducted services in which they sacrificed the animals and birds the tradesmen sold to worshipers. The people's enthusiasm for Jesus knew no bounds. Have you heard, they said, how he makes the blind to see and the lame to walk? Is not he the Messiah? Soon he will overthrow Caesar and set us free!

When even the children cried, "Hosanna, hosanna to the Son of David!" the chief priests and the scribes came to Jesus.

"Hearest thou what these are saying?" they asked him angrily.

"Yea, did ye never read, Out of the mouth of babes and sucklings thou hast perfected praise?" replied Jesus.

The more the people acclaimed Jesus, the more the priests hated him and wished to be rid of him. But he was so popular with the multitudes they dared not arrest him.

Jesus came to the temple the second morning, and the people crowded around him. Another delegation of the chief priests with scribes and elders approached, to argue with him.

"Tell us," said they, hoping he would say something for which they could arrest him, "by what authority doest thou these things? and who gave thee this authority to do these things?"

Jesus replied, "I will also ask you one question, and answer me, and I will tell you by what authority I do these things. The baptism of John, was it from heaven or from men? Answer me."

They turned to each other, perplexed. What shall we answer? they thought. If we say, from heaven, he will ask us, Why did you not believe him? If we say, from men, the people might stone us, for they think John is a prophet.

Playing safe, they answered, "We do not know."

Jesus said to them, "Neither tell I you by what authority I do these things."

Jesus decided to take issue with these priests. For three years he had offered them his supernal tidings of love and life and they had refused to listen. In a parable he compared their form of religion to a fig tree with luxuriant foliage; full of pomp and cere- mony, with no spiritual fruitage. Jesus came to this tree on his visits to Jerusalem, and searched it for results, but there were none. Now he denounced the tree, saying, "Cut it down, for it is of no value in the life of the people."

The kingdom of God he described as a wedding feast which a king gives for his son. God, the King, invites the priests and Pharisees to his feast, the teachings of his Son. If they do not want this food from heaven and do not accept his invitation he will send his servants into the highways for other guests. If with these others anyone comes who has no wedding clothes, that is, whose motive is to turn the spiritual food of the King to worldly profit, such a person will eventually be put out of the kingdom.

Jesus likened the religion of Israel to a vineyard which God planted, sending his servants the prophets one after another to watch over the vineyard and lead Israel forward that her civiliza- tion might become a blessing to all nations. What did this chosen people do? They beat one prophet, they stoned another, they killed another. The Father then said, I will send them my beloved son. Surely they will reverence my son. When they saw the son they said, This is the heir. Let us kill him and take his inheritance: let us continue to usurp his spiritual office as revealer of God to the people. So they threw the son out of the vineyard of Israel, and killed him.

Said Jesus to the Pharisees, "Did ye never read in the scriptures, 'The stone which the builders rejected, the same was made the head of the corner'?"

The priests said to one another: "Does he think he is the Son of God! For this he shall die." But they feared the multitudes, for many believed Jesus a prophet, and some thought him the Messiah.

On the eve of Jesus' crucifixion he made a solemn ceremony of his last meal with his disciples, to prepare them if possible for the impending tragedy. His words to them, that night, recorded in the Gospel of John, are tender and compassionate beyond human capacity. He told of his martyrdom; that he would rise from it into immortal life; and in due time would come to the world again. He said he would return. Again, he said the Paraclete, the Spirit of Truth would come. The Spirit of Truth would guide them into all truth: "for he shall not speak from himself; but what things soever he shall hear, these shall he speak." Jesus wanted his disciples so to love one another that they would give their life for each other, as he was giving his life for them. The glory which God had given him he would bestow upon them, that the world might know God had sent him. If they remained one, as he and the Father were one, they could give his message and Spirit to the world. If his followers did not remain united his light would be dimmed, and the purpose of his mission obscured.

When their meal was over they went out into the tragic night, to an orchard called Gethsemane, near the city. Then something happened which has mystified the centuries. Jesus, who with transcendent courage had withstood the fury of the Pharisees, became troubled and in an agony of prayer besought the Father not to require him to drink the imminent cup of grief. Surely it was not for himself that he sorrowed, but for his disciples, who were so soon to be put to a test under which they would break. He pled with them to pray with him and receive strength from the Father. When he saw that he could not rouse them he became reconciled even to their desertion.

On that evil night in Jerusalem the chief priests and elders consulted in the court of the high priest Caiphas how to arrest Jesus. They must not take him during the feast of the Passover, they decided, for the people might rise against them. Then came Judas and offered to show them the lonely place where Jesus was to spend the night. The priests were so pleased to have their problem thus easily solved that they paid Judas thirty pieces of silver for his services.

A company of men and soldiers with Judas' assistance easily arrested Jesus, and carried him to the priests in Jerusalem. When morning came, the ruling ecclesiastical court and leaders of Israel, the Sanhedrin, composed of seventy-one members, assembled to question Jesus. He was brought before them; and they carried through a trial as dark as their souls.

The government was in the hands of the Romans, and the Sanhedrin did not have authority to put a man to death. They were obliged to take Jesus to Pilate, the Roman governor, for the death sentence. The priests did not enter into the Romans' pretorium (according to their religious beliefs that place would defile them), but sent a request to Pilate to come out to them. Pilate, humoring them, went out on his balcony and asked, "What accusation bring you against this man?"

"We found this man perverting our nation and forbidding to give tribute to Caesar, and saying that he himself is Christ a king," the priests told Pilate.

Pilate went back to Jesus. "Art thou the king of the Jews?" he asked.

"My kingdom is not of this world," said Jesus. "Everyone that is of the truth heareth my voice."

"What is truth?" questioned Pilate.

It was three o'clock in the afternoon when Jesus died. Joseph of Arimathea obtained permission from Pilate to take the body down from the cross and bury it. The Jewish Sabbath began at sunset of that day and according to priestly law no work could be done with the hands until after sunset of the following day. Because sunset was almost upon them Joseph of Arimathea, accompanied by Nicodemus, put the body temporarily in a new tomb near the place of crucifixion, the Gospel of John relates. The following evening they came again, many believe, and carried Jesus' body to its final place of burial. Joseph and Nicodemus were not in communication with the disciples, and did not tell them what they had done.

In Isaiah is a prophecy which says, "All we like sheep have gone astray; we have turned every one to his own way; and the Lord hath laid on him the iniquity of us all."

Jesus indeed suffered for the iniquity of the priests and the Pharisees of Israel. It was not he but they who stood on trial before the Highest Tribunal.

# 13

## Apostles of the Light

LIKE THE COMMAND given to Moses from the flaming bush, the sublime confirmation that descended upon Jesus after his baptism had consequences far more crucial than the victories of empire makers, or the crowning of the strongest king. On the third morning after Jesus' crucifixion came another of these magnificent spiritual events.

For two days after Jesus' martyrdom his few disciples, agitated and desolate, hid from the Jews. On the third morning Mary Magdalene, broken-hearted and faithful, went to the sepulcher where Jesus' body should be—and the sepulcher was empty. In consternation she hurried to tell Peter; and he, with John, ran to the tomb to see for himself. Finding it empty, as Mary had said, the two turned away, thinking nothing could be done in the face of the priests' fury.

To Mary it was a comfort just to stay for a while where Jesus' body had been. As she stood, weeping hopelessly, she heard a voice say, "Woman, why weepest thou?"

Mary looked up and to her amazement saw, not the gardener of the place as she expected, but Jesus. She made a movement to throw herself on the ground and clasp his feet, the vision was so real, but Jesus said, "Touch me not."

The same day two disciples were walking along the country road to the town of Emmaus. As they walked they discussed the incredible ending, as they thought, of Jesus' years of teaching and what they had believed of him. A young man joined them and, entering into their conversation, gave explanations of Jesus which had not occurred to them. When he left as suddenly as he came, they realized that they had been talking with the Christ. They went on to Jerusalem, to tell the apostles; and learned that Jesus had appeared to Peter. They were all in a room, pondering these occurrences when suddenly the Christ stood in their midst, and said to them, "Peace be with you." He appeared to the little group several times. The last time, he rose into the sky and they watched him until he vanished into space.

Many people questioned Jesus' physical appearances. The body that dies, they say, cannot be revived. Matthew tells that Jesus came, after his death, to the disciples when they were on a mountain in Galilee but some doubted if it was he. If his appearance after his crucifixion was physical, why were they unsure that they saw him?

Many other Christians have believed that these appearances of Jesus were physical, and that his ascension was in a physical body, to a physical heaven above the skies.

Paul states positively that flesh and blood cannot enter the kingdom of God. He tells us that as we have a physical body suited to this earth, so we will after death have a spiritual body, indestructible and suited to the immortal world in which we will now live eternally.

For two days after the stunning blow of Jesus' arrest and crucifixion his disciples only knew that Jesus, whom they believed to be the Messiah, had been crucified as a common criminal when they thought he was already mounted on a king's throne. When their spiritual eyes were permanently opened, his glorious spirit lifted them to a new dimension and established within them a new set of values. The lure of aggression and military conquest, of pomp and riches, now paled for them before the radiance of unselfish love and self-sacrifice. They were transformed from panic-striken men afraid for their lives into dynamos of faith and joy, indifferent to personal danger. They were raised out of an agony of doubt, which to them was living death, into love for their Master and faith in his immortality, which made them willing to go to martyrdom for their belief. It was the consciousness of Jesus' spiritual presence, within their minds, that did this for them.

The reward of the pure in heart, said Jesus, is that they may see the spiritual world, God. The apostles won that priceless consciousness.

One day, when they were praying together during the feast of Pentecost, there came, like the rushing of a mighty wind, a wondrous spiritual baptism. To some it seemed that flames of fire descended upon them. They were so translated by an ecstasy of faith and longing to serve their Master that the universal language of love came to them, and people from Rome, Mesopotamia, Egypt, Asia Minor, Crete, and Arabia recognized their glorified spirit of kindness as though it were expressed for each in the tongue of his own country. To the hard of heart, however, they seemed a group of men strangely elated, and these exclaimed in derision, "They are filled with new wine." It *was* a new and intoxicating wine, their love for their Messiah. As they stood together after this holy experience, a little group distinct among th Jews, Peter spoke to the Crowds who gathered around them. Jesus, he told them, who was crucified, was now sitting in heavenly splendor at the right hand of God, and would conquer the world: "Let all the house of Israel therefore know assuredly, that God hath made him both Lord and Christ."

Jesus promised his disciples that they would have power when the Holy Spirit was come upon them. The strange new force which a great Prophet brings into the world, love for himself and his teachings, which draws his disciples to him like a magnet, Jesus' apostles now transmitted to others in an ever-widening circle like a mighty contagion, until the Christ's love shone in many hearts recreating and ennobling their lives. So radiant were the apostles as they proclaimed Jesus the Messiah that three thousand persons joined them in one day "and continued steadfastly in the apostles' teaching and fellowship." And every day others were added to their number. To help one another the new believers made a common fund of their possessions; Barnabas, an ardent new disciple, sold his farm and added the purchase money to the fund.

Peter and John the son of Zebedee were continually together during this time, speaking in the temple's courts. One day as they were about to enter the temple through the Beautiful Gate a lame beggar asked for alms. Peter, gazing intently at him, said, "Look at us." The beggar did this, expecting alms. Peter took his hand

and commanded him in the name of Jesus Christ of Nazareth to stand and walk. The astonished man rose to his feet and shouting and jumping with joy followed the apostles into the temple. Peter told the people that Jesus had given him the power to cure the cripple; Jesus, the Prophet foretold by Moses.

As he was proclaiming Jesus to be the Messiah, along came some priests and Sadducees, and ordered Peter and John to prison. The next morning the two were brought before the Sanhedrin; and in that group were Annas and Caiaphas, Jesus' bitter enemies. "By what power, or in what name have ye" healed this cripple? asked the priests. Peter, living now in a world far above any fear of these men, answered, "By the name of Jesus Christ of Nazareth, whom ye crucified, whom God raised from the dead, even by him doth this man stand here before you whole. He is the stone which was set at nought of you the builders, which is become the head of the corner."

The priests knew that Peter and John were uneducated men; yet listened to their knowledge of the Scriptures and their eloquence! With them stood the one whom they had healed, a man over forty years old. There was no gainsaying the fact of the healing. To ask Peter and John how they did it would give them opportunity to proclaim their Jesus. In a quandary, since they dared not do injury to the apostles because of the people, the priests ordered them to keep silent about Jesus; and let them go. Peter and John replied, "We cannot but speak the things which we saw and heard." When they were released they went to the other apostles and told what had happened. And they all praised God, and prayed for more boldness and power to proclaim the Christ.

In these days of danger and persecution Peter was so spiritually glorious that the people laid the sick in the streets, on beds and pallets, that perchance as he passed his shadow might fall on the afflicted ones and they would be healed.

Again the high priests and the Sadducees had Peter and John taken to prison. In the middle of the night, the story says, an angel of the Lord brought them out and told them, "Go ye, and stand and speak in the temple to the people all the words of this Life." It may be that a means of escape was shown them by a prison guard who was secretly a follower of Christ.

When the Sanhedrin assembled in the morning to try Peter and John they were teaching in the temple's court. Soldiers were sent for them, they were brought before the Sanhedrin and commanded to stop teaching. Peter replied that God gives the Holy Spirit "to them that obey him." He and John declared they must obey God rather than men, and accused the Sanhedrin of crucifying their Messiah. The priests became so angry they wanted to kill the prisoners at once. Then Gamaliel, a learned and revered doctor of the Law, rose and asked that the men be taken from the room. When they were gone, he said to the Council, "Ye men of Israel, take heed to yourselves as touching these men, what ye are about to do. For before these days rose up Theudas, giving himself out to be somebody; to whom a number of men, about four hundred, joined themselves: who was slain; and all, as many as obeyed him, were dispersed, and came to nought. After this man rose up Judas of Galilee in the days of the enrolment, and drew away some of the people after him: he also perished; and all, as many as obeyed him, were scattered abroad. And now I say unto you, 'Refrain from these men, and let them alone: for if this counsel or this work be of men, it will be overthrown: but if it is of God, ye will not be able to overthrow them; lest haply ye be found even to be fighting against God.'

"And to him they agreed: and when they had called the apostles unto them, they beat them and charged them not to speak in the name of Jesus, and let them go."

The young man Stephen was a fearless teacher for the new Messiah during these days. Jews from Alexandria, Asia Minor, and Cilicia disputed with him in the streets, but were unable to cope with his inspired wisdom. Exasperated by their repeated defeat in argument, they instigated men to accuse Stephen of blaspheming Moses and God, until some of the elders and scribes carried Stephen before the Sanhedrin with these false charges.

The high priest asked him, "Are these things so?"

In reply Stephen reviewed the history of Israel, to show how the Hebrews had abused and repudiated their prophets. As he spoke, his face shone like an angel's.

The listening priests went wild with rage. They gnashed their teeth, they shouted, they stopped up their ears that they might not hear Stephen. Rushing upon him they drove him outside the city's gates and stoned him to death. Stephen knelt in prayer and received their blows. As he prayed, "Lord, lay not this sin to their charge," he died.

Those who killed Stephen took off their long robes which interfered with their running and the throwing of stones, and laid them for safe-keeping at the feet of Saul who stood and watched, approving the deed of the priests.

Saul was a young Pharisee of Tarsus, a student of Gamaliel; and in the observance of the Mosaic law he was considered blameless. After Stephen's death, Saul led a persecution of Jesus' followers. Hunting them out in their homes he dragged men and women to prison in an effort to stamp out the new movement. Many disciples fled from Jerusalem and spread their belief in Jesus through Judea and Samaria.

Saul determined to carry his persecution to Damascus, and secured letters from the high priest authorizing him to hunt out heretics and bring them, bound, to Jerusalem. As he was hurrying along the road to Damascus, Jesus appeared to him—in his mind, he later explained. The vision was so real that Saul cried out, and asked what Jesus wanted of him. Saul was so overpowered and dazed by the awful majesty of the vision that for three days afterward he was as one gone blind.

Ananias, a follower of the Christ, who lived in Damascus also had a vision and in the vision Jesus told him to go to a house in the street called Straight, for there Saul awaited him. Ananias found Saul and called this dreaded persecutor "Brother." Saul had been unable to understand his experience. When Ananias explained it, light came to dispel his bewilderment and his spiritual eyes were opened.

Saul went off to Arabia, undoubtedly to think over what had happened to him. He had seen and talked with Jesus, not in the physical world but in his mind, where undreamed-of possibilities were uncovered, and spiritual sight, beyond his ken, was suddenly added to his other faculties. He who had determined to stamp out any allegiance to Jesus as heresy was asked to prove Jesus to be the expected Messiah. Saul believed his experience to be from

God and he testified in later years that he was not disobedient to the heavenly vision. But he had many problems to solve. He had received his education in Jerusalem from the best Jewish theologians; he was a thoroughly trained and brilliant scholar. He knew with utmost exactness the laws attributed to Moses, and was versed in the intricacies of Jewish doctrine. He must think out the relation of the new Messiah to Pharisaic theology. He must reconcile the teachings concerning observance of the Mosaic law with faith in a present-day Prophet.

The disciples proclaimed the Christ throughout Judea and Samaria, and in other parts of Palestine, going north through Phoenicia to Cyprus and Antioch. In Palestine and Syria they taught only Jews. In Antioch they gave their message to Gentiles and many became believers.

When the believers in Jeusalem heard of the eager new group in Antioch they sent the kindly Barnabas to help them. Barnabas soon found he must have assistance in the wonderful campaign and went to Tarsus for Saul, now called Paul. For a year the two were guests of the new community, the first group to be called Christians.

Paul and Barnabas traveled westward. When they reached a city they went first to the synagogue. If they were invited to speak to the Jewish congregation they gave their tidings that the Messiah had come. They would stay with the Jews until driven from the synagogue, then would go to the Gentiles.

Thus they journeyed from city to city. Some Jews believed their message; others opposed them bitterly and forced them to leave their town. After many trials and triumphs they made their way back to Antioch and told "all that God had done with them, and how he had opened the door of faith unto the Gentiles" and that little groups of believers had formed in many cities, with elders to guide them.

By this time believers from Judea were making trouble for the Gentile Christians in Antioch, insisting that they be circumcised, and observe the Mosaic laws. Paul and Barnabas remonstrated with the Judeans but were unable to silence them.

The two teachers decided to lay the matter before the apostles and traveled to Jerusalem that Paul might explain the issue to a

Council of the apostles and elders. Paul argued from his own experience: he had been a meticulous follower of the Mosaic law. He read Moses' commandment, Thou shalt not covet, and knew intellectually that he ought not to covet. He did not wish to covet; but what he did not wish to do he continued to do. He found no power to help him; and cried to himself, "Wretched man that I am! who shall deliver me out of the body of this death." Christ revealed himself to Paul's inmost consciousness; and Paul found that his old temptations were gone and Christ's Spirit had transformed his character until he was a new being. According to the so-called Mosaic law, Christ was accursed because he hanged upon a tree. The law was mistaken or its time of service was ended, reasoned Paul. Many of the Mosaic laws were outgrown, and it was foolish for those who spread the gospel for the new age to insist that these be retained.

Radiant with the Spirit of the Christ, Paul visited again the churches he had founded in Galatia and Asia Minor. In Lystra he was stoned by the enemies of the new Light and left for dead. In other places he was imprisoned and beaten. Singing in his soul, "I can do all things through Christ who strengtheneth me," he pressed on. He told in his letters that he taught not the opinions of men but "the teachings of God," and did not depend upon worldly and superficial eloquence. One of his disciples wrote of him, "Sometimes he seemed like a man, and sometimes he had the countenance of an angel." He loved those whom he taught, they were his "pride and delight," and he caused them to live in the presence of the Christ as the bird flies in the sustaining air, as the flower drinks in the sunlight. In return, his disciples welcomed him as a messenger from heaven, and gave him the devotion of all their life.

One night, about the year A.D. 50 Paul had a vision in which a man in Macedonia called to him, "Cross over and help us." Paul's reason told him to stay in Asia, where it was comparatively easy to teach. His spiritual guidance called him to Macedonia.

With Timothy and Silas for traveling companions Paul took ship, and two days later landed at Philippi in Macedonia.

# 14

## Athens — Rome

TRAVELING WESTWARD by sea routes or along the well-built Roman roads, Christian teachers soon came face to face with religions around which had grown a whole civilization, artistic, literary, architectural.

Could sophisticated philosophic Greece believe that a young Jewish workingman was the Messiah not only of the Jews, but of the Greeks? The Greeks lived in a historic environment shaped by Homer, Hesiod, Pindar, the Olympic gods, the Olympic games, the philosophers of Athens and Alexandria, the Stoics, and the rulers of Rome. The Jewish Christians lived with Moses and Jesus; and their language with its references to the symbols, allegories, and heroes of the Hebrew Bible was quite different from that of Greece and Rome. The center of the Christian message was an uneducated Jew. The center of the Greek religion was Homer, the Greek poets and philosophers, and the Delphic Oracle. At Apollo's shrine in Delphi was a priestess whose utterances were so momentous that kings of many nations sent envoys to inquire of her concerning the management of their states. Her purported messages from the Unseen were considered oracular, and she was believed to have the gift of prophecy.

The Delphic priestess served a system of nature deities in which Jupiter, or Zeus, was the sky god. Subject to him were Apollo god of the sun, Diana goddess of the moon, Aphrodite the goddess of love, and many others. Walter Pater describes them as "a series of wondrous personalities, of which the Greek imagination became the dwelling place; beautiful, perfectly understood human outlines, embodying a strange, delightful, lingering sense of clouds and water and sun." Possessed of supernatural powers beyond the grasp of mortals, they used these to further their own desires and ambitions, to injure their enemies and vanquish their opponents. Wherefore Psyche wandered forlorn from shrine to shrine begging assistance from gods and goddesses, no one daring befriend her because of vindictive Venus.

The poets of Greece created these gods; and the gods so made often lived a wild life, acting just as unrestrained mortals would if magic powers were given them. The old Greek philosopher Xenophanes said that if bulls or lions made God they would make him in the form of a bull or a lion. As the poets developed, the gods improved. Zeus even acquired ethics and reduced the number of his evenings out. When righteous poets began to write, Zeus became the noble god of Aeschylus. But the prevailing gods of Greek literature were made in the image of very imperfect men.

The noblest philosophers of Greece tried to reform this popular religion and attain something approaching true monotheism. Philosophers and scientists, they carried their world forward. The philosopher Pythagoras was a pioneer in mathematics and geometry, in the theory of evolution, and the science of sound. He was a scientific investigator who thought through the physical into the eternal order. The famous biographer of Greek philosophers, Diogenes Laertius, wrote that Pythagoras was "so eager for knowledge he left his own country and had himself initiated into all the mysteries and rites ... of foreign countries." He traveled even "among Chaldeans and Magi." Some Eastern historians say he visited the Hebrew prophets in Palestine and received from them his noble ideas.

Pythagoras' followers had no prejudices of race or class. They taught that religion should stimulate scientific research, for science is knowledge of how God works in nature. They believed that philosophy, since it endeavors to discover ultimate realities, should quicken all the human faculties. These bold thinkers declared the earth was spherical, and suggested that it revolved around the sun, as a stone would swing from the end of a string. The religious communities Pythagoras founded endured for centuries.

The Greek philosopher Thales of Miletus, like Pythagoras, appreciated the knowledge of other countries and traveled widely. He studied the astronomy of the Babylonians and the sciences, geometry, and practical achievements of the Egyptians; and he returned to Greece and, developing his knowledge, became a pioneer in Greek wisdom. For hundreds of years the astronomers of Babylonia had kept records of the motions and eclipses of the sun and moon. From the periodicity of eclipses recorded by these scientists, Thales predicted an eclipse of the sun to occur in the year 585. The eclipse came on schedule during Thales' life, as a battle raged between the Medes and the Lydians. Day was turned into night, and the armies were obliged to stop fighting. As a consequence, Thales the philosopher-astronomer became immensely famous.

Hippocrates, the Greek philosopher and physician of the fifth century B.C., developed clinical medicine with scientific precision. He was aided in his work by the Chaldeans and Egyptians—the exalted ethics in the Hippocratic Oath, which physicians of the West have taken for centuries, came in part from the Egyptians. Hippocrates' students and successors, inspired by the achievements and high character of their master, used in their researches an experimental, inductive method, and became founders of scientific medicine. The writings of these brilliant Greek scientists, with those of Hippocrates, form the famous Hippocratic Collection.

Developing into a new dimension the process of scientific thinking which they learned from Egypt and Chaldea, Greek philosophers laid aside the belief that planets moved, eclipses occurred, and diseases came upon human beings by the caprice of the gods or the malevolence of demons. Seeking natural causes, the Greeks discovered a natural order. Some saw in this physical order of nature a moral order and one God, "the mind of the universe."

The best Greek philosophers now taught one supreme God and the reign of law. They were aided by great artists: Phidias who created his glorious statue of Zeus; Sophocles whose dramas taught the cosmic moral law; Aeschylus whose classic verse proclaimed that righteousness exalts a nation and injustice is national ruin.

Leading the Western world in science, philosophy, and aesthetics, Greece advanced with pomp and splendor. With a genius for simplicity of form and aesthetic values, her art gave to the world some of the most brilliant literature ever written, and some of the most vital, perfectly proportioned statues ever created. Yet, Greek civilization was built upon a multitude of slaves, and the culture of the free citizens barely hid the yawning abysses of vices and primitive emotions current among them. The young men were insatiable for power and fame and more gold. The lesser dramatists portrayed so vividly their heroes' passions and prejudices, hatreds and lust for revenge that they awakened these destructive emotions in the populace who crowded the theaters. Even Athenian democracy was always on the verge of collapse.

What a strange figure must the independent, unselfish, shabbily dressed Socrates have seemed in this city as he walked among the cultivated upper classes who were not aware of the rudiments even of disinterested conduct. He was a hardy soldier who could tramp barefoot over the snow, and he was intrepid in battle. He lived with rigid simplicity. Often times when he looked at the wares displayed for sale in the bazaars he would say, "How many things I can do without."

This rugged ascetic, with all the virtues that strong men admire, believed God had appointed him a teacher for Athens. His convictions, based upon logic and upon intuition, made him the greatest moral educator of Greece. He taught pure reason; and declared that he was guided by an oracle in his mind. Every day he went to the marketplace of Athens and took his seat, and soon the young men of the city gathered around him. They admired his mighty intellect and nobility of character, even when he upbraided them for their vices.

On one occasion a brilliant discussion took place between Socrates and Protagoras, while the young nobles of Athens listened. Socrates came to the conclusion that knowledge and virtue are one: he who has knowledge has goodness; he who sees what is right will do what is right. For Socrates this was undoubtedly true. He was a saint and a prince of philosophers, independent and fearless. When he was called to trial by the High Court of Athens and accused of corrupting the young men, of neglecting the gods of Greece and teaching "new divinities," Socrates was tranquil.

His words to the Court who sentenced him to death have rung through the centuries: "Wherefore, O judges, be of good cheer about death, and know this of a truth—that no evil can happen to a good man, either in life or after death."

Socrates tried to reform men's characters, that they might become fruitful.

Socrates' disciple, Plato, gave to the world in his magnificent writings the processes of two almost superhuman intellects—Socrates' and his own. Plato's great student, Aristotle, made stupendous findings in philosophy, ethics, politics, biology, and other sciences. He is one of the world's great pioneers in aesthetics, logic, and the development of the scientific method.

Plato, Aristotle, and Socrates formed a triumvirate who won for a time in the battle with the materialists and Sophists. A momentous opportunity lay in their hands, for the Greeks became the intellectual leaders of western Asia and Egypt. Rome even acquired art, science, and philosophy largely from the Greeks. The Greeks founded the beautiful city Alexandria and equipped it with a library of five hundred thousand books; also schools and theaters to impress truth upon the minds of the people. Here the Ptolemies established and supported their museum or university. In this noble center for learning, men of science studied mathematics, medicine, and astronomy. Erastosthenes measured the diameter of the earth, correctly within fifty miles. The eminent astronomer Hipparchus developed trigonometry and discovered the precession of the equinoxes.

Intellectual understanding, however, is not the whole of life. Another element is necessary: a dynamic which strengthens man's will to do what is right.

Socrates and Plato could not reach the masses. They had devoted friends; yet no one undertook for their sake hazardous journeys to educate the barbarians. Evidently they could not satisfy even the elite. For despite philosophy, wealth, and culture a sense of despair and frustration spread, like a deadly intellectual paralysis, from city to city of that Hellenic world. By 200 B.C. the independent science developed by Aristotle and Archimedes and Aristarchus had practically disappeared.

Unable to prevent the collapse of Athens' city-state, or the break-up of Alexander the Great's colossal empire, or the gradual disintegration of Hellenic culture, the best thinkers of Greece decided their philosophy was too up-in-the-air, too theoretical. It was concerned with every abstruse problem, and ignored the vital one: how to live heroically in a decadent world.

Stoicism came to the front, with a program for practical living. Its founders were Zeno of Athens, a Semite from the East; Chrysippus the Boxer; and Cleanthes, a Hercules of physical strength who wrote many of the Stoic hymns. The Stoics believed in one Supreme God, the Eternal Order and Administrator of the universe. They also believed in a certain number of secondary gods.

By means of philosophic thinking the best Stoics found profound reasons for self-control and temperate living. They taught that man has at the center of his mind a will which by its own choice can change evil into beneficence. It is, they said, always within the power of the will to transcend the world. Epictetus declares that men are slaves when they do what they do not want to do, or live where or as they do not want to live. This is true of emperors and bondsmen. Let all things over which man has no control, things like wealth, fame, exile, humiliation, be matters of indifference to him. Let that over which he has control, his will, be supremely important. Physically man is only a speck on the earth. Mentally he can encompass the universe, can be one with the gods. Why then should man devote so much attention to his body, and neglect the significant, divine, eternal? There is no permanent evil in the universe, for God does not miss the mark. What seems evil is due to a narrow perspective of the seen and the unseen. Cooperation is the law of life. The world is one city of men below and the gods on high. Human beings are ordained to live for each other as parts of one body. Never speak or act in anger. Serve mankind.

This philosophy strengthened those who already wanted to do what was right. On this principle, Socrates willingly accepted his imprisonment; and therefore he was free.

Stoicism became the prevailing religion among the educated classes. For long periods of time the government of the Roman world was in the hands of Stoics.

What an impressive group of men they were: Cicero, the delightful man of letters and workers for peace; the Elder Pliny with his encyclopedic intellect and his just and noble character; Pliny the Younger, nephew and adopted son of the Elder Pliny; Marcus Aurelius, ruler of his world.

"You advise me," wrote Cicero to a friend, "to give myself up to books. What else do you imagine I do? Could I live at all, were it not for my books?" When someone gave him a statue of the god of war, he wrote, "And what, again, shall I, a promoter of peace, do with a statue of Mars?"

Another great Stoic was Seneca, tutor of Emperor Nero and for a time virtual ruler of the Roman empire. Seneca's teachings were so close to the Gospels that the early Christians thought he must have been a disciple of Paul.

Epictetus the slave lived heroically his Stoic philosophy. His profligate and cruel master, a freedman of Nero, one day put him on the rack. As the wheel was turned tighter and tighter Epictetus remarked calmly to his torturers, "You will certainly break my leg." The wheel was turned again, and Epictetus said, "Did I not tell you that you would break it?" He was freed from slavery, and became a famous teacher. For "what else can I, that am old and lame do but sing to God," he said. "Were I a nightingale, I should act after the manner of a nightingale. Were I a swan, I should act after the manner of a swan. But now since I am a reasonable being, I must sing to God: that is my work: I do it; nor will I desert this my post, as long as it is granted me to hold it, and upon you too I call to join in this selfsame hymn."

As Rome conquered the world and plundered the nations, the plunderers quarreled with each other as to who should have the spoils. Julius Caesar created with his genius an apparently invincible military machine. But after his assassination came an orgy of civil strife. Horace, the Roman poet of the first century B.C., describes the collapse of justice, the crumbling of morals, the spread of dishonesty, the destruction of family life, the disintegration of his world. Laws are vain, he writes despairingly, when morals err. Now he advises the people to hasten to the imaginary islands of the West where is peace. Again, he pleads for the restoration of the old Roman religion and urges the people to

*Care for each neglected shrine,*
*And cleanse from smoke the forms divine,*

for the only remedy is that something happen to divine power. To what god shall they return? Which one has power to save them? A new god, Horace declares, is needed; a god incarnate on earth. Perhaps Mercury, or Mars, or Apollo.

Irresponsible thinkers revived the worship of Bacchus, god of the vine, and called intoxication through wine divine inspiration. The orgies in Rome in Bacchus' name were so terrible that his worship was forbidden. Other secret societies offered the lure of sacred mysteries and elaborate ceremonies of initiation. The Eleusinian Mystery of Greece was world famous. Its secrets were so well guarded through the centuries that not one of them was given away. Aesculapius, the god of healing, was popular for centuries and a huge temple was built to him in Epidaurus in Greece. He was a physician who healed so many people that, the legend says, Jupiter, fearing all mankind would be immortal, killed Aesculapius with a thunderbolt. For hundreds of years people made pilgrimages to Aesculapius' temples, which were often built in the high mountains, or near healing springs. Some testified that, while sleeping in his temple, the god healed them. In the time of the apostles one of the most popular of these shrines, on an island in the Tiber River, was visited by multitudes of Romans afflicted with various ailments.

From the Orient came mystery religions with all the glamour of novelty. The religion of Isis and Osiris, deities of Egypt, was one of the most popular. Osiris was the god of the spring and the harvest, and Isis was his wife. Osiris, prehistoric king of Egypt, founded that nation's amazing civilization. For centuries he was Egypt's god of immortality. Like the spring he came again, in perpetual resurrection. The goddess Isis, a gentle, serene deity, was worshiped in services composed of stately ritual and solemn processional.

The poet Virgil in the first century B.C. wrote, "The great line of the centuries begins anew. Now the Virgin [Justice] returns, the reign of Saturn returns; now a new generation descends from heaven on high." He described a wondrous child with life divine in whose day heroes and gods would be mingled. The iron man shall pass away, wrote Virgil, and "a golden race spring up throughout the world," a new race and a new civilization.

The hope grew among the Greeks and the Romans that a divine being would come to them, a supernormal man with knowledge and power to save them. Pliny the Elder, in his *Natural History* says that "To assist man is to be a god; this is the path to eternal glory."

# 15

## A New Humanity Arises

INTO THIS VITIATED, demoralized world came the teachers of the youthful Christ with the joyous tidings, "Behold, we have the Savior who makes all things new."

Peter, his wife sometimes with him, traveled and taught in Asia Minor, Italy, and Greece. Andrew, the brother of Peter, traveled, tradition says, in Asia Minor, up the Black Sea as far as the Volga River, and was crucified in Greece. Philip, after wonderful teaching in Palestine, settled with his two daughters in Hierapolis. From John Mark's teaching came the church in Alexandria. Other Christians with capacity to teach sold their property and went forth to spread far and wide "the saving seeds of the kingdom of heaven." Foreseeing the healing of their world, their hope became for them almost an ecstasy. Slowly they established Christian groups in Greece, Italy, and Gaul. An unknown teacher carried the Good News to Carthage whence it spread like a vivid contagion.

Peter and Paul helped to found the church in Rome. As the new group on the Seven Hills grew in numbers they were assisted by a succession of apostolic teachers. Titus and Timothy probably visited this group many times; and perhaps they were rejoiced by the presence of John the Divine who, it is said, lived until the reign of Emperor Trajan. It was a time of easy travel, and many Christians made it their mission to go to the Imperial City; also, Jewish Christians from the assemblies in Asia Minor went to live in Rome. Paul wrote to the group in Rome, "Your faith is spoken of throughout the whole world."

For nearly thirty years Paul traveled, and he established groups in Crete, Galatia, Philippi, Thessolonica, Corinth, Athens, Ephesus, and other cities.

In Athens, like Socrates Paul spoke in the marketplace, to any who paused to hear him. Among these one day were some Stoic and Epicurean philosophers. Remarking superciliously to each other, "What would this babbler say? He seemeth to be a setter forth of strange gods," they invited Paul to go along with them, and when they came to the Areopagus (known as Mars Hill) they directed him to explain to them his new religion. Paul addressed them, "Men of Athens . . . as I passed by, and beheld your devotions, I found an alter with this inscription, To An Unknown God. Whom therefore ye ignorantly worship, him declare I unto you . . . for in him we live, and move, and have our being; as certain also of your own poets have said, for we are also his offspring." The philosophers listened until Paul talked about a resurrection, when they laughed mockingly and the meeting evidently came to an abrupt end. A few, and among them was Dionysius the Areopagite, believed Paul.

After this, Paul spoke in Corinth with "fear and trembling," until in the night Christ came to him in a vision and told him, "Be not afraid, but speak, and hold not thy peace; for I am with thee, and no man shall set on thee to hurt thee: for I have much people in this city."

Paul's inner life was a laboratory of vital significance. His letters to the assemblies he founded and to the Christian community at Rome give his findings, upon which he built a philosophy that became a framework for Christian thinking.

For years Paul experienced a mental conflict; therefore he taught that man has two natures. When he became a follower of the new Messiah, and concentrated his thoughts upon the Christ, into his mind came a spiritual radiance so invincible and triumphant that in awe and wonder he cried, "It is no longer I that live but Christ that lives in me." In the presence of this life his inner conflict ended. The Christ who came to him was like God, for in him was no lower nature. In Christ therefore he could see God; and through Christ he could partake of God's life, a life which Paul called the Spirit. This attainment he testified brought him love, joy, peace, patience, kindness, generosity, gentleness, self-control. Prayer, which to Paul was conversation with God, through Christ, became unbelievably easy and the joy of his life. In his meditations he was caught up into heaven, as it were, like the prophets of old and, like them, saw God's glory. Because of his experience he told his disciples, "Devote yourselves to prayer, give your whole mind to it."

Paul wrote often to his disciples of the dynamic and glory of God in Christ's spirit. He recognized God in whoever might reveal him—Abraham, Moses, Isaiah; and God's truth when expressed by Greek poets and philosophers. All creation, said Paul, groans and travails to develop sons of God. Each person reflects only an aspect of God. The perfect mirror is the Christ.

From his experience Paul learned that to attain the spiritual life he must concentrate his thoughts upon the perfections of the Christ, not upon the world's evil. Jesus was homeless and persecuted, he often spent the night on a mountainside, perhaps in wind and rain storms, and his days as an itinerant teacher. He said that God is love. After years of a living martyrdom Paul could say, "All things work together for good to them that love God. Our light affliction which is but for a moment worketh for us a far more exceeding and eternal weight of glory." Paul experienced so deeply the nature, the permanence, the glory of the immortal Christ that on Christ's authority he was sure, whatever happened, that God is love.

In his classic, *The Republic* Plato pictures a society, a brotherhood, built upon justice and divided into classes which he likens to iron, copper, silver, and gold. In this utopia the philosophers, the golden stratum, will be the rulers. The silver men will be the soldiers. The artisans and farmers will be told they are made of copper and iron; this will keep them in their places and make them content to be ruled by the philosophers and the soldiers.

Now a greater than Plato had come, a workingman, from whose teaching and philosophy a new humanity was rising. In this social body, whose maker and sustainer was Christ, all were equal in that all could serve. Some would serve as do the hands and feet. Others, the eyes, would see with the insight of the inspired. Some, the ears, would listen to divine guidance. Some were destined by their administrative gifts to govern the whole body, as does the brain. The bloodstream feeds all. The digestive organs and the lungs feed the bloodstream. The principle of life is this: each for all. To all, food and strength according to their need. When each lives for the others and draws life from the spirit of God each may perform his function. Those who are socially least, said Jesus, may prove to be the greatest among you. Therefore the Christians considered society a living, growing organism.

The majority of the converts in the first century were working-men and slaves, people whom the philosophers and Stoics never thought of teaching, nor considered worth saving from their manifold afflictions. By the end of the century, however, some noble families of Rome had joined the new faith.

These early Christians were in every degree of mental and spiritual development. Some were wise. Others exulted in what they believed to be ecstatic visions. Some were matter-of-fact Romans. Some were foolish dreamers, docetists who said that Christ was not a human being at all and only appeared to live and die in a body. Some, the Gnostics, tried to reduce the practical gospel of Christ to profitless and impossible metaphysical speculation. Many continually slipped back and down into the world of nature and seethed with animal impulses just like the rest of us.

How could these diverse people be united? The Christians' answer was: put over them wise and pure-hearted executives who would bind them together in the love of God. Everything depended upon the teachers, deacons, and bishops. They must be "meek and not avaricious." No one must make "gain out of Christ." All must beware of false teachers. If two Christians quarreled they were told that until they were reconciled they could not come to the meeting of the believers on the Lord's Day, for their ill-will would break the unity and spoil the spirit of the meeting. All were advised to "seek out daily the faces of the saints that thou mayest be encouraged by their words." The early Christian groups flourished in the degree that they chose as presbyters and bishops men of blameless character, wise and loving. "How great and wonderful a thing is love," wrote Clement, Bishop of Rome late in the first century.

The believers obeyed their leaders because they loved them.

The letters written by Christian leaders of the first century show in what measure they returned the love given them. The devotion of the early Christians to Christ, to their teachers, and to each other is one of the beautiful facts of history. The joy and the timeless beauty of their unity and insight were a completely new dimension. At their meetings they often placed a chair for the Christ and gathered around it, imagining that he was with them. They enjoyed strangely simple pleasures. For recreation they listened to the epistles of Paul, or the story in the Gospels, or sang the psalms of Israel. They took a singular delight in prayer, and as they prayed their faces shone; some said they looked through gates ajar into life eternal. They would eat a meal together every few days, and they loved to say that as the bread they ate was once separate grains of wheat scattered over the fields and hills so they, although they came from the ends of the earth, were now one. Franks and Assyrians, Jews, Gentiles, Greeks, Romans, through the mighty power of their love for the Christ were slowly welded into the first real brotherhood in the Western world.

Never is the light so lovely or the air so sweet and still as at dawn. Never is nature so beautiful as in the springtime when the trees come to life, the fields begin to smile, the birds to sing. Yet never are the shadows so deep as in the early morning light. And into the most joyous days of spring storms may break, ominous and cruel, and hurricanes may tear asunder the most beautiful structure. For in the spring the more direct shining of the sun upsets the atmosphere and causes the harsher elements in nature to stir.

The first official persecution of the Christians came, apparently without any warning, in the reign of Nero. Suetonius was sure it was by the emperor's order that the fire was started which decimated Rome. The rumor that accused him of the ghastly deed must, however, be suppressed. Nero decided to clear himself by proclaiming the Christians in Rome the perpetrators of the crime and he ordered that they be "punished with the most exquisite tortures." The famous historian Tacitus wrote that in obedience to this command "a vast multitude were convicted. . . . And in their deaths they were also made the subjects of sport, for they were covered with the hides of wild beasts, and worried to death by dogs, or nailed to crosses, or set fire to, and when the day declined, burnt to serve for nocturnal lights. Nero offered his own gardens for that spectacle."

Tradition says that Paul was beheaded in Nero's reign. His martyrdom occurred, it is thought, not later than A.D. 67. Peter, after traveling and teaching for years, was martyred during Nero's persecution. When the Roman soldiers were about to nail him to a cross Peter begged that he be crucified with his head down for he did not think himself worthy to die in the same position as his Master. James, the brother of Jesus, was stoned by the Jews at Jerusalem.

All the apostles had died or been martyred by the end of the first century.

In Palestine in the first Christian century the Jews were obsessed with one idea—to throw off the yoke of Rome and again be a free, self-governing people. This revolution they still expected their Messiah to accomplish for them. Prophecies of his coming said he would have a sword, a throne, soldiers. Goaded by the tyranny and cruelty of Roman governors, and the promises of false prophets— adventurers who hoped to advance themselves by the people's wishful thinking—the Jews, contrary to the advice of the wise ones among them, in A.D. 66 rose against the Roman empire. Poorly armed, in a chaos of civil strife, with robbers everywhere, they were utterly unprepared. "They were to fight more by their rage than by sober counsel," wrote Josephus, Jewish historian of the first century and one-time governor of Galilee. The Roman soldiers were disciplined and obedient. They marched and fought in perfect order. They were well armed, and through hard exercise were prepared for the rigors of war.

After nearly four years of fighting the rebel Jews, in the year 69 Emperor Vespasian with his Roman legions advanced against them in northern Palestine. Many Jews then fled to Jerusalem and added their spirit of strife and sedition to the general turmoil of contending Jewish factions in the Holy City.

In A.D. 70 the Roman army under Titus, son of Vespasian, surrounded Jerusalem in a seige which lasted from spring until

September. The population of the city was enormously increased by pilgrims who had come to celebrate the Passover. The food supply was soon exhausted, and starvation faced those in Jerusalem.

Jerusalem was strongly built and was defended by three walls with soaring towers. Crowbars were of no avail; so the Roman besiegers brought up their battering-rams, and broke through two walls. They set fire to the gates of an inner wall and for a day and a night a terrifying conflagration raged. Then the Romans broke into the city. In the fury of fighting that followed, a Jew threw a burning torch and set fire to the temple. Titus wished to save the building for it was a ornament to the empire and he rushed into the court to try to extinguish the fire; but he could not. The Roman soldiers wanted to plunder the temple of its gold and when Titus left the court a soldier threw another firebrand and completed the destruction of the glorious building.

The Roman soldiers plundered and murdered women, children, and priests without mercy. The entire city seemed to be in flames, and everywhere were the war cries of the soldiers and the shrieks of the stricken people. The Romans set other buildings on fire, until all the temple hill was burning. In the madness, false prophets tried to check desertions from the Jewish army, telling the people to keep on fighting until God delivered them.

Jerusalem was ruined. Youths under seventeen years of age were sold into slavery. Other captives were sent to hard labor in Egypt, or to the Roman theaters to be killed by the sword or by wild beasts.

The Christians living in Jerusalem, when they saw that the city was determined upon rebellion, left in a body and took up their residence across the Jordan River twenty miles south of the Sea of Galilee. Here, they and their descendants after them lived and held to a form of Christianity of their own making, associating with neither Jew nor Gentile.

After a few years the Jews crept back to Jerusalem and tried to rebuild the city, even considering a new temple. They were again beguiled by a false messiah, Bar Kochba, who swore he was a star, come from heaven to set his people free. Vouched for by Rabbi Akiba, one of the most eminent rabbis of his century, Bar Kochba led a furious rebellion. In 135 Emperor Hadrian's powerful army wiped out the rebels. This time the Romans razed every building in Jerusalem, plowed up the ground, and forbade the Jews upon penalty of death to enter the place. The Jews now wandered to Babylonia, Arabia, Egypt, and the four corners of the world. Christinity now became a religion for Gentiles.

For many years the government had required, by law, the worship of the emperor as a god. This served a double purpose: it safeguarded the emperor's dignity and throne; it gave the populace a tangible god. Its observance consisted mostly of throwing incense on the altar of the god, the emperor. Every individual was ordered to perform this rite.

Jesus did not interfere with governments, or mention their functions. He said, "Render unto Caesar the things that are Caesar's; and unto God the things that are God's." But he explicitly taught one God and the worship of him only. Therefore, when the Christians were commanded by the Roman government to throw incense on the altar of the emperor, they could not. To them this meant not only a declaration that the emperor was a god, on a par with the God of Christ, but the acceptance of all the deities of the official religion.

The Jews also believed in monotheism and refused to sacrifice to the Roman and Greek gods and to the emperor. The Roman rulers struggled desperately with this determined people but finally acquiesced and allowed the Jews to live as a race apart. All over the empire were little Jewish communities. They were not increasing in numbers and the authorities decided they were not especially dangerous.

The community of Christians was different. It was growing rapidly and as it grew it threatened not only the religion of the empire but a very important commercial activity. About forty years after the martyrdom of Paul, Pliny the Younger was governor of a province in northern Asia Minor and he wrote a letter to Emperor Trajan. This letter is one of the earliest authentic documents written by a pagan about the Christians. He was persuaded, wrote Pliny, whatever "their opinions might be," that the Christians, because of "a contumacious and inflexible obstinacy certainly deserved correction." They seemed to be possessed by an "absurd and extravagant superstition" which was spreading rapidly through all ranks and classes, among both sexes. "In fact, this contagious superstition is not confined to the cities only, but has spread its infection among the neighboring villages and country." The Christians' chief error was that "they met on a stated day before it was light, and addressed a form of prayer to Christ, as to a divinity, binding themselves by a solemn oath, not for the purpose of any wicked design, but never to commit any fraud, theft, or adultery, never to falsify their word, nor to deny a trust when they should be called upon to deliver it up; after which it was their custom to separate, and then reassemble to eat in common a harmless meal."

Trajan replied to Pliny, "Do not go out of your way to look for them. If indeed they should be brought before you, and the crime is proved, they must be punished; with the restriction, however, that where the party denies he is a Christian, and shall make it evident that he is not, by invoking our gods, let him (notwithstanding any former suspicion) be pardoned upon his repentance."

In the middle of the second century, in the reign of Antoninus Pius a persecution of the Christians was launched in Smyrna. Eyewitnesses recorded that the martyrs were stretched upon shells, whipped almost to death and thrown to the wild beasts in the arena. The crowds in the amphitheater, craving more excitement, demanded Polycarp, "the father of the Christians." For fifty years he had been bishop of the church in Smyrna. He knew John the Divine, and others who had seen the Christ. He remembered their exact words and quoted them with much effort against the heretics who threatened to corrupt the gospel with fine-spun theories. His strength lay not in argument, for he was not intellectual but in his positive statement that so-and-so was not the teaching of the apostles.

When the Romans commenced to search for Polycarp he was hid in one Christian home after another and would have escaped had not a slave girl betrayed him. When the soldiers found and arrested him he was not disturbed, for in a vision he had seen himself lying on a blazing pillow. He asked the Christians with whom he was found to give the soldiers their evening meal; and when that was over he went with them cheerfully, to the arena. The proconsul commanded him to worship Caesar as a god, and revile the Christ. Polycarp replied, "For eighty and six years I have been his [Christ's] servant, and he has done me no wrong, and how can I blaspheme my King who saved me." The crowd quickly built a pyre. When they made ready to nail Polycarp down to prevent his escape he told them it was unnecessary for the power by which he would endure the fire would enable him to remain in the flames. He was placed unsecured on the pyre; and died rejoicing that he was drinking the cup Christ had drunk.

There were all sorts of religions in the Roman empire during these centuries of persecution, and all were tolerated by the government except Christianity. These other religions, most of them, offered prosperity and worldly advancement, tangible prizes. Those who accepted Christianity faced the possibility of stoning, imprisonment, torture, and martyrdom. Yet Christian communities arose in Lyons and Vienne, in Germany and Spain, and according to Pliny and Lucian, Asia Minor was full of them. The Lawyer, Tertullian of Carthage, wrote in the year 175, of Carthage and the surrounding districts: the Christians are everywhere.

For two hundred and fifty years Imperial Rome fought the Christians. The martyrs died so gloriously that many thoughtful Roman onlookers realized here was something never before seen. Tertullian testified it was the sight of the martyrs dying for their Christ that turned the scales for him and made him a Christian. The Romans were famous patriots and knew how to die for their country; but usually they went to war because they were compelled to go, and obeyed through fear or because they hoped for quick reward. Of the early Christians an unknown author in the second century wrote to his friend Diognetus, "They obey the prescribed laws, and at the same time surpass the laws by their lives. They love all men, and are persecuted by all. They are unknown and condemned, they are put to death and restored to life. They are poor, yet make many rich; they are in lack of all things, and yet abound in all; they are dishonored, and yet in their very dishonor are glorified. When punished, they rejoice as if quickened into life; they are assailed by the Jews as foreigners, and are persecuted by the Greeks; yet those who hate them are unable to assign any reason for their hatred."

The Roman officials were sure if they killed the Christians they conquered them. These seemingly helpless people turned death into victory, and even as they died spread their cause.

No explanation of the strength and endurance of the primitive Christians is to be found but this: they were sustained by divine power. All the forces of their world were against them. Their leaders were martyred one by one. The rest of them, simple people mostly, were hunted down by the Roman government and killed like wild animals.

Divine power it was, reinforcing something in human beings, at their best, which makes them follow what is right at any cost when once they see that it is right.

# 16

*Christianity and the Philosophers*

DURING THESE CENTURIES, while the Christians increased in numbers and were martyred, the Romans continued to build themselves mansions of illusion, and to experiment with mythical religions and with philosophy.

From Persia, the land of heroes, came the religion of Mithras the sun god. Mithras, according to the fable, was born from a rock, and the first object he saw was the god of evil. Without hesitation he attacked this god, and a mighty fight commenced.

When Mithras traveled west, like the he-goat in the Book of Daniel he moved so fast that he hardly touched the ground. Generals, officials, and people of high position welcomed with acclaim this militant mystery religion which taught men to be courageous soldiers, to fight the forces of evil. At the height of its popularity this superstition suddenly collapsed.

Mithras was popular with the administrators of the empire. Others looked to philosophy to accomplish their moral and social regeneration, as today many rely on science and social reform. If the dying Roman society was not healed, its philosophy was at fault and must be improved. The spiritually minded among the intellectual leaders realized that the Stoics were too cold, too rationalistic. The mystery religions, on the other hand, were fantastic. Only really balanced thought could be effective: truth, as Socrates and Plato taught it. So Neo-Platonism, or the new Platonism, was born.

Early in the third century, Ammonius Saccus, of a Christian family, opened in Alexandria a Neo-Platonic school, which soon became famous. In or near Alexandria lived the young genius Plotinus. Searching for truth, Plotinus went from one idle, superficial philosopher to another. When he finally came to Ammonius Saccus, he cried in joy, "This is the man I have been seeking."

After eleven years in Ammonius Saccus' classroom Plotinus enlisted in Emperor Gordian's army which was marching against Persia, for Plotinus hoped if he could somehow get to Persia he might have the wonderful privilege of studying with the sages of Persia and India. The Persians were invincible in those days, and Emperor Gordian's army was defeated. Plotinus fled for his life to Antioch, and journeyed on to Rome.

He was almost forty years old, and had written no books. In Rome, with Porphyry his student to help him, book after book came from his pen. Like a Plato become gentle, humbler, and seeing a light of which Plato was but dimly aware, Plotinus brought Plato up to date and almost made him into a Christian mystic.

Plotinus was brilliant, charming, friendly; and the leaders of Rome, an emperor and his wife among them, became his students. Parents sent their sons to him; some parents wrote in their wills that Plotinus should train their children and manage their estates. The hero of this adulation, one of the greatest philosophers of the world, lived simply and was kind and unassuming.

Plotinus meditated upon the constant procession of fashions in thought, in philosophy, and in speculation. There must be, he decided, an unchanging Mover behind this change. Without a primal, living, all-embracing Principle, distinct from and above the universe, the whole material world would drift aimlessly. Only this First Mind, whom he called the Nous, could give form to the material elements and guide them into and through the process of growth. The search for truth and beauty presupposes a changeless beauty, truth, justice. Plato called this eternal reality "the Good." Plotinus was convinced that beyond even the Good is the One. This One Eternal Essence was to him impersonal, self-subsisting, divine, beyond the knowledge and understanding of men. "The One," he writes, "is not absent from anything, and yet is separated from all things; so that it is present, and yet not present with them." "Whoever fancies that beings are governed by fortune and chance, and are held together by corporeal causes, is very remote from God, and the conception of the One." Plotinus believed the One to be the source of all order, life, goodness, beauty—all the ineffable splendor to which the soul aspires. An ocean of Light, it pours forth from itself the First Mind; this concept corresponds very closely to the Logos in the Gospel of John.

Like the Buddha, Plotinus saw that all physical substances finally disintegrate. He argued that man's soul must be distinct from his body: for, if the soul were a physical substance it could not preserve memory, could not receive diverse and successive impressions, and keep simultaneously in the mind yet distinct each from the other all the different forms which it perceives.

Transcending time and space, Plotinus perceived, the soul manifests perfections which are everlasting, can be akin to God and partaker of God's mind. If the soul could be free from the body it could return to its origin in the Perfect One, he reasoned. This return of the soul to God, he saw, was unattainable through the discursive thinking and conflicting theories of philosophers. If one could by rigid ascetic practices subdue the body, and through intense contemplation transcend discursive thinking, the wonder of wonders, God's Light, might appear. Porphyry testified that he was witness four times when Plotinus became conscious in meditation of this Light.

Plotinus reasoned that the immortality of the soul is proved by the universal respect shown the dead, as though they were still living; by the flashes of communion which come from those in the heavenly world; and, finally, by the testimony of oracles and prophets. He turned an expectant eye to the bright morning of a revelation from on High, which alone could baptize man with sufficient spiritual energy to enable him to escape in this life the bondage of the body.

Neo-Platonism, sponsored by Plutarch and Ammonius Saccus and arrayed in the logic of Plotinus, became one of the most alluring philosophies the intellect has ever framed. Explained in superb literary classics it was a religion of refinement and culture, a movement which had as its teachers Socrates, Plato, Plutarch, Plotinus. And back of it for momentum Homer, Pindar, Sophocles, Aeschylus, Euripides. Developed by Porphyry and Proclus and Hypatia it was Christianity's most formidable rival. Neo-Platonism had two paramount advantages for scholarly Greeks: it did not teach that the world was created in six days; it did not teach a physical resurrection.

Despite its rationalism, however, it condoned the polytheism of the Greek and Roman religion and gave fanciful and far-fetched interpretations of the unethical deeds of the many gods and godesses. It left the masses at liberty to follow the depraved life of their deities; and the people became ever more sensual and immoral. Courage and good citizenship steadily declined. The amount of silver in the currency dwindled. Agriculture languished and wide stretches of land lay waste while the people crowded to the cities where were excitement, gladiatorial shows, and debauchery. Matthew Arnold describes it:

> On that hard pagan world disgust
> And secret loathing fell.
> Deep weariness and sated lust
> Made human life a hell.

All the while the wild, white barbarians from beyond the Alps and the Danube thundered at the gates of the northern cities. Moral and spiritual death within. Destruction from without. Who could save the Roman empire?

And the Christians? They were increasing by the thousands among the simple people. To the Greek intelligentsia they were just another mystery cult from the East; ethically and intellectually inferior to Socrates and the Stoics. Prejudice against the Jews was almost universal among educated Greeks and Romans. The Cristians were looked down upon as a Jewish sect which practiced an impossible democracy, receiving into their groups thieves, outcasts, and slaves and claiming to reform these undesirables. The haughty intellectuals laughed at the Christians' claims as not worth investigating. Relying upon their philosophy, almost no one of intellectual or political prominence during the first two centuries of the Christian era believed that the Christians could make any contribution to Roman civilization.

True religion is a philosophy of life plus an inner experience of God. There are requirements which must be met before communion with God is possible. A few persons, with a strong bias toward a holy life, like Socrates and Marcus Aurelius, discovered some of the requirements and heroically obeyed them. Socrates from childhood had for companion a soundless voice, which he called a signal from God. It advised him what to do and helped him with philosophic problems the intellect alone could not solve. To Marcus Aurelius came visions in the night and rational conclusions during the day; and he lived by them. Epictetus said that whenever he might wander his spiritual dreams and divine signs would come to him.

But these strong men were unable to impart to others any clear knowledge of the means by which their experience was attained. To the Stoics generally, God was an intellectual abstraction, cold and unreal. To the Neo-Platonists he was pure mind, from whom they might receive an occasional illumination. The Stoics tried to attain higher knowledge by suppressing all emotion. They thought they could become perfect by means of their reason and will. This philosophy they carried too far, for they suppressed not only the baleful emotions of anger and fear, but sympathy, love, and joy. Epictetus may sing with his lips, yet one hears in his song a deep sadness as though in his heart he is weeping.

The Neo-Platonist believed in a divine life, and held it most desirable. The epitaph on Plato's tombstone read, "Earth in her bosom here hides Plato's body, but his soul hath its immortal station with the blest; Ariston's son, whom every good man, even if he dwell afar off, honors because he discerned the divine life." Plato wrote understandingly of the value of truth and love; he presented in stately sentences the laws of reward and retribution. Celsus the philosopher asserted that Jesus was rough and crude in style compared to Plato. Plato wrote, "Of all things which man has, next to the Gods, his soul is the most divine and most truly his own." Sometimes "he undervalues his wonderful possession; ... he sells her glory and honor for a small piece of gold; but all the gold which is under or upon the earth is not to be given in exchange for virtue."

Plato proved the existence of perfection to be the necessary basis of comparisons and value-thinking: a man says, "This is a better chair than that one," and thus leads from better to better, up at last to the best. He applies this method of reasoning when considering chairs, ideals, or the characters of men. Criticism and comparisons presupposed real objective standards and lead logically to perfection and God. This idea of the perfect, the true, the most beautiful is like a sublime presence in all exact thinking.

The Greeks made statues of their ideal of perfection: physically perfect gods and goddesses; and beautiful they were, with their rigid outlines.

The Hebrews seeing perfection in One God, who was free from any physical form, made not physical but word pictures of him: he was a pillar of light, the sun of righteousness, the light of loving-kindness, the glory which spoke through Abraham and Melchizedek, which shone in Moses' face.

As religion advanced from the anthropomorphic to the impersonal to the superpersonal, the thought of God, to the Greek philosophers, became so exalted as to be somewhat remote, and the need of an intermediary was apparent. The Stoics and the first-century philosophers said God's creative reason was the intermediary between himself and the world.

Philo of Alexandria, one of the most spiritually minded of Jewish philosophers, likened God, infinite beyond all comprehension, to the sun. The rays which the sun sends forth are its intermediary: they are the same as the sun, yet not the sun itself.

These rays the opening chapter of the Gospel of John calls the Word (in Greek, the Logos.) In the beginning was this Light and the Light was with God and the Light was God. This Light is the life of men, as the sun's rays are the life of the world. This Light shone visibly, into the world, in Jesus the Messiah. Of all the teachers, he alone could explain, in words universally understandable, the way of approach to a living God, so that anyone who followed his method could feel God's presence and guidance in his soul. The Christians, gazing steadfastly at the perfect life of Christ, filled their minds with the thought of his attributes until the lower emotions from lack of attention were conquered.

In the second century lived Justin the philosopher. He studied Plato assiduously, who told him that he could attain a state of mind so pure he could see God. But the vision never came. Justin went to the Stoics and the Peripatetic philosophers, the followers of Aristotle. Some he found sincere, some were too much interested in the fee. None of them knew God. How then could they reveal God to him? Justin witnessed some Christian martyrdoms. Of this he wrote that, while delighting in Plato's teachings, he heard the Christians abused, but he "saw them fearless of death and of all other things which are counted fearful."

Pondering these matters as he walked by the sea one day, he was aware that an old man followed him at a short distance. He let the meek old man join him, and soon the philosopher was telling of his quest through the long years, and how he hoped some day to see God. His hearer, a Christian, led him on until Justin proved to himself that his soul was a gift from God, and that the only way to know god was through the prophets, who heard his voice and lived in his presence. After the Christian left him, the happiness which Justin sought came singing into his heart, and in his soul burned a divine flame, "a love of the prophets, and of those men who are friends of Christ."

This first Greek scholar of whose conversion there is authentic and detailed record spent the rest of his life teaching Christianity as a philosophy. He wrote books, addressing them to the emperors Antoninus Pius and Marcus Aurelius; he traveled from city to city trying to win the educated people; in Rome, wearing the philosopher's robe, he taught Christianity in a hall he rented. His approach to his subject was simple: the Greek poets and philosophers had somewhat of the Logos; the Hebrew prophets had more; Christ had the whole.

After many years of devoted teaching, Justin with six other Christians was brought before the prefect of Rome, during a persecution in Marcus Aurelius' reign. The seven were commanded to worship the gods. They said they could not do this, for, by the grace and by the will of God, they were Christians. The prefect ordered his soldiers to scourge them, and then to take them away and behead them.

Other Greek philosophers, of sincere and inquiring mind, perceived there must be some powerful source from which came ideas so convincing that men and women cheerfully died for them.

Slowly and carefully they investigated this new statement of the life force in the universe, and read, in Greek and in Hebrew, the Old and New Testaments.

Athenagoras of Athens, sagacious and clear-headed, was one of the most accomplished writers among the early Christian philosophers and an admirer of Plato. He addressed to Emperor Marcus Aurelius a conclusive defensive of the Christians, describing their noble lives, their exalted conception of God. Some philosophers, wrote Athenagoras, worshiped nature. This was like worshiping the emperor's palace and forgetting the emperor. "But the world was not created because God needed it; for God is himself everything to himself—light unapprochable, a perfect world, spirit, power, reason. If, therefore, the world is an instrument in tune, and moving in well-measured time, I adore the Being who gave its harmony, and strikes its notes, and sings the accordant strain, and not the instrument."

Clement of Alexandria, educated in Italy and Athens, traveled through the Greek world in quest of an ultimate truth and finally became a Christian. In the Christians' theological school in Alexandria he taught his philosophic approach to the Christ. Among his students was the young man Origen, who became in his maturity the greatest scholar of third-century Christianity.

Origen was seventeen when his distinguished father was martyred with many other Christians. The ardent son encouraged his father to withstand his persecutors, and wished to die with him, but his mother by a ruse saved him from the premature sacrifice.

His father's property was confiscated, and the family faced destitution. Origen organized classes in Greek science and literature and supported his mother and his six younger brothers and sisters. He ws soon asked to reopen the catechetical school, closed during the persecutions; and before he was twenty was made head of this Christian college.

Pagans and Christians filled his classroom; and he had in time five secretaries and a staff of helpers, who took down and made copies of his lectures. Great numbers of students came to him. He was the most popular teacher of his day.

When he had taught in this way for twenty-five years, the bishop of his district called a meeting of other bishops and presbyters; and they voted to banish Origen from Alexandria. The real reason for this action was, undoubtedly, the bishop's jealousy of Origen's amazing popularity and his success as a teacher.

Origen seems to have made no protest. He just went to live in Caesarea in Palestine. He was joyfully received by the two Christian bishops of the district, and befriended in every way.

Again his classroom was filled with eager students, among them incipient bishops and notable scholars. His student Gregory, who became Bishop of Neo-Caesarea, tells of Origen's curriculum; how he trained his students to think clearly, speak exactly, and rid themselves of wrong ideas and habits. With geometry as a basis they investigated the physical universe. Knowledge of the sciences was preliminary to a course in Christian ethics. After Christian ethics came exhaustive reading of the Greek poets and philosophers. In a delightful letter to Gregory, Origen gives his reasons for such study: When the Hebrews fled from Egypt they carried with them Egyptian silver and gold; and out of these made vessels for the worship of the true God. "The ark with its lid, and the cherubim and the mercy-seat, were probably made from the best Egyptian gold." Origen advised his students to study the poets, philosophers, and sciences of the Greeks and use all the gold in Greek philosophy and learning for the new house of God. The climax of his curriculum was an intensive study of Christian philosophy based on the Old and New Testaments.

Origen was the founder of scientific criticism of the Scriptures. He compared the various texts of the Old Testament to find the most authentic readings; and published in six parallel columns the texts he had studied. He saw clearly that a literal interpretation of some incidents and passages in the Bible was impossible. He was sure that God speaks in the Bible, in parables and figures of speech. In his book *De Principiis* he gives proofs that the teachings of Christ were filled with divine energy. Many a philosopher and lawgiver, he reasons, wished to see all people obedient to his laws and practicing his philosophy; yet no philosopher spread his precepts throughout a nation. This astonishing Christ spread his laws and his gospel among Greeks and barbarians, not only through one country but through the world. He enlisted a multitude to espouse and practice his laws, and this when his followers were threatened at every moment with imprisonment and death.

The pagan philosopher Celsus argued that gods appeared "with all distinctness, and without illusion" to worshipers at the Greek and Roman oracles; while the "appearance of Christ to his disciples after his resurrection was like that of a spectre flitting before their eyes." Origen, who did not believe in the physical resurrection, replied that Christ's appearance after his resurrection was not a mere appearance or vision in "one place, like these so-called gods in human form"; it was a "divine power, felt through the whole world," drawing together "all who are found disposed to lead a good and noble life."

After long and glorious service Origen was thrown into prison by the Roman persecutors. The torture to which he was subjected ended, in the year 254, in his death. He was one of the most influential philosophers and theologians of early Christianity.

Justin and Origen, with other Greek scholars, taught the Christians how to present their message to philosophic Greece and Rome. When the Christians' appeal was no longer limited to the uneducated, all classes of society came into the Brotherhood. The Stoic Galen, famous medical authority of the ancient world and physician to Emperor Marcus Aurelius, wrote of the Christians, "They sometimes act exactly as true philosophers would. And some, in ruling and controlling themselves, and in their keen passion for virtue, have gone so far that real philosophers could not excel them."

By the year 300, from India to western Africa, from Armenia to Greece and Italy, through Spain and Gaul up to Britain a chain of Christian communities was established. A Christian traveling through these lands would find along the way groups who would receive him as a trusted friend, would care for him if he was ill, and if he wanted work would secure it for him if it was possible.

In 313, a year after he became ruler of the western half of the Roman empire, Emperor Constantine issued the Edict of Milan. This gave all the people of the empire freedom to worship as they chose. Moreover, Constantine joined the Christian Brotherhood while its members were still social outcasts. When he went to the meetings of the Christian bishops at Nicaea, although he was emperor he did not take his seat until invited. He became a Christian, he said, because he had observed that the character of the Christians was altogether superior to that of the pagans. In the beautiful church which he built in Constantinople in honor of the twelve apostles was a column with the inscription, "The city [Constantinople] and the Roman empire are dedicated to Christ."

Before Constantine became emperor, the Christians were still comparatively few in numbers. The historian Gibbon believed that not one twentieth of the population of the Roman empire was Christian. Today, many historians are inclined to make the figure one tenth. Aided by Emperor Constantine, who founded schools for the poor and built hospitals and churches, the Christians, for so many years reviled and persecuted, entered the summer season of their religion. Statesmen, philosophers, artists, the rich and the poor joined them. Hard Roman laws were replaced by humane regulations, brutal manners softened, and Roman society was revolutionized toward the kingdom of God.

# 17

### Anthony and Augustine

IN A VILLAGE in Egypt lived a well-to-do Christian couple of noble descent. About 250—the exact date is not known—their son was born and they named him Anthony.

The child was always serious and thoughtful far beyond his years, and he never played like other children. When Anthony entered a church one day as someone was reading aloud Jesus' words to the rich young man, "Go, sell that thou hast, and give to the poor."

Anthony decided that Jesus' words were meant for him. He straightway gave his "three hundred plough-lands fertile and very fair" to the people of his village; he sold all his movable property and devoted the proceeds to charity; he put his sister in the care of some "known and faithful virgins," giving her a sufficient sum to pay for her education. And he went to live in a house on the edge of the village, to support himself by manual labor.

He ate only bread and salt, and drank only water, taking his meager food after sunset, once a day. Often he ate but once in two or four days. When he was beset by tempting remembrances of his wealth and the pleasures of luxury, or "the harshness of virtue, and its great toil; and the weakness of his body, and the length of time," he turned "his thoughts on Christ, and on his own nobility through Christ, and on the rational faculties of his soul," trying "earnestly to make himself day by day fit to appear before God, pure in heart, and ready to obey his will, and no other."

He determined to make his life more rigorous; and left the house for a tomb in the cemetery near his village. Arranging with a friend to bring him bread once in a while, he went into the tomb and closed the door.

In this tomb he lived until he was about thirty-five. Then he left the place for one still more solitary and drear. On a mountain in the desert, on the east side of the Nile, was an old ruined fort. In these ruins he made a cell, with a door and a roof. For twenty years he lived here and battled with his thoughts, which became to him like incarnate demons. Two or three times a year friends brought him bread. Sometimes he talked with them; usually in silence they dropped the bread to him through a hole in the cell's roof'

As the news of his exceeding rigors spread, other men who wanted to become hermits found cells near him. Many persons came to him to be taught, some of them men of distinction. Almost always he refused them, saying he did not know enough to teach.

At last a multitude assembled at the door of his cell and demanded that he talk with them. Many were curious to see how he had endured his rigors, some hoped to learn from him. When they were about to take off the door and force their way into his cell he came out and stood before him. "And when they saw him they wondered; for his body had kept the same habit, and had neither grown fat, nor lean from fasting. . . . For he was just such as they had known him before his retirement. . . . They wondered again at the purity of his soul, . . . for he was neither troubled at beholding the crowd, nor over-joyful at being saluted by too many; but was altogether equal, as being governed by reason, and standing on that which is according to nature. Many suffers in body who were present did the Lord heal by him; and others he purged from daemons. And he gave to Anthony grace in speaking, so that he comforted many who grieved, and reconciled others who were at variance, exhorting all to prefer nothing in the world to the love of Christ. He persuaded many to choose the solitary life; and so thenceforth cells sprang up in the mountains, and the desert was colonized by monks, who went forth from their own, and registered themselves in the city which is in heaven."

In this way commenced Christianity's monastic tendency, which had a cataclysmic effect upon Europe's history. Anthony's friend and sometimes sharer of his desert life, Athanasius, bishop of the church in Alexandria, is alleged to have written the account of his life. From this fourth century-document these quotations are taken.

The first monastic settlement was made up of men whose purpose was so to live the Sermon on the Mount that all might see its practical usefulness. "So the cells in the mountains were like tents filled with divine choirs, singing, discoursing, fasting, praying, rejoicing over the hope of the future, working that they might give alms thereof, and having love and concord with each other. And there was really to be seen, as it were, a land by itself, of piety and justice; for there was none there who did wrong, or suffered wrong; no blame from any talebearer: but a multitude of men training themselves, and in all of them a mind set on virtue."

A few years later Anthony found a more solitary spot three days' journey deeper in the desert, on a high mountain with water and a plain nearby. Some of the brethren, wishing to help him, followed him with loaves of bread. Anthony asked them to bring him a hoe and a hatchet and a little corn, for he did not want to be a burden to anyone, and with the two implements and corn seed he could raise his own food. He lived in this place for many years.

The fame of his holy life spread until a constant stream of people made the long journey into the desert, just to look at him. According to Athanasius, "He was unto Egypt like a good physician who had been given unto the people thereof from God. For who ever came unto him being afflicted that did not go away rejoicing? Or who ever came unto him in sorrow because of the suffering which had come upon him that did not come back wholly encouraged? And who ever came unto him full of rage and wrath that was not enriched with graciousness and long-suffering? ... And what youth who was afraid of the war which had come upon him ever came unto him, and seeing his triumphant old age did not henceforward contend in the forefront of the battle? And what man ever came unto him troubled in mind who did not go away with it composed and in a state of reason? And many people used to come to him from outside Egypt, and unto all the questions he would return suitable answers; and he was so great, and was so much beloved by every man, that after he had departed from this world, and had left all men orphans, the memory of him never died among the people, and every man gave himself courage by the repetition of his triumphs and of his words. For although these men of God live in secret places and do not desire to be seen and known, yet our Lord [maketh them] to shine like lamps upon all men." Emperor Constantine and his sons sent letters to Anthony asking him to pray for them and write to them.

Anthony lived to be more than a hundred years old. To the end of his life "he possessed strength which was out of all proportion to his aged body." On the mountainside where he lived so long his devoted friends built a monastery. He was a hero to all Christians in whose hearts burned the longing for spiritual perfection.

As the educated people filled the Christian churches, during the fourth and fifth centuries, many families were divided in their faith. This was the case in the home of the young man, Augustine. His mother was born into Christianity and was brought up by an old servant of her family; his father was a thoroughgoing and violent-tempered pagan. Well educated himself, the father recognized his son's intellectual gifts and spared no effort or expense to give him an education.

With other students, Augustine read Virgil, Homer, and the poets, learned to admire the gods and, by citing Zeus, to justify their immorality. He did not marry, for his father thought that would interfere with his career. His father was unfaithful to his wife, and Augustine's companions lived by pagan standards. Augustine was somewhat more upright than the others, for when a child was born to him out of wedlock he loved the boy and was faithful for a time to the mother.

Inordinately ambitious and wayward, the youth's ideals were eloquence of speech and perfection of literary style. His Christian mother wept for him, but dared not protest. In fact she was fortunate above the women of her day, for her husband never beat her —due to no self-control on his part but because she was remarkably tactful and discreet and never by word or deed opposed him.

Augustine was seventeen when his father died in 371. He became a Christian shortly before his death; not through persuasion, for his wife dared not argue with him, but because of her unvaryingly beautiful life.

Augustine continued his studies, and when he was eighteen read

Cicero's *Hortensius*. In this book was an intriguing new idea: that somewhere, in some system of thought, was Truth.

He determined to find Truth wherever it might be. He studied Plato, and read *The Ten Categories of Aristotle*. In his *Confessions* he mentions "the nimbleness" of his intelligence at this time.

The Manichean doctrines were popular, and he studied them exhaustively. Manicheism taught philosophic dualism, that in the world were two permanent powers, good and evil, which ceaselessly fought for the possession of man. Augustine liked this idea of dualism; it explained his mental restlessness, and for nine years he was satisfied with the Manichean philosophy.

Then he decided it was unscientific and fallacious: its teaching concerning astrology did not accord with facts. It declared that a man's destiny was determined by the month, the day, and the hour of his birth. Augustine observed that in the same minute one child might be born to a slave mother and another to a free woman. Did anyone think their destinies would be alike? According to the Book of Genesis, the twins Esau and Jacob were born in the same hour; yet how different were their lives.

During these years Augustine taught in Tagast, the city where he was born, and later in the large college in Carthage. When he was twenty-nine he was a professor of rhetoric in Rome, and soon was appointed to a professorship in the great college in Milan. He was an intellectual genius and his career was assured.

He continued to search for Truth, and read Plato, Plotinus, and the Neo-Platonists. Their theory of one supreme God and a divine spirit in man's soul greatly pleased him. He had thought of God as a vast physical system. The Neo-Platonists told him God was much more than his creation. He was like an ocean, and the world was like a sponge, floating in the ocean and permeated by the waters of God's sea of being. God was perfection and could not create evil. Man possessed the power to act contrary to God's will. It was man, then, reasoned Augustine, who willed and created the evil in the world.

Following the instructions of the Neo-Platonists, he concentrated his thoughts one day upon God. And he saw, he testified, "the Light that never changes, above the eye of my soul, above my intelligence. It was not the common light which all flesh can see, nor was it greater yet of the same kind, as if the light of day were to grow brighter and brighter and flood all space. It was not like this, but something altogether different from any earthly illumination. He who knows the truth knows that Light, and he who knows that Light knows Eternity." A voice, as from on high, said to him, "I am the Food of the fullgrown; become a man, and thou shalt feed on Me. Nor shalt thou change Me into thine own substance, as thou changest the food of thy flesh, but thou shalt be changed into Mine." Augustine "heard as the heart heareth, and there was left no room for doubt."

He marveled that God was not a phantasm as he had believed, and wished to make his glimpse of God a habitual consciousness. But his habits of thought, his worldly desires closed the door. He writes, "I was swept up to Thee by Thy beauty, and again torn away from Thee by my own weight."

He cast about for help, and turned to the Neo-Platonists. Porphyry taught there was no universal way to freedom. Other Neo-Platonists. Porphyry taught there was no universal way to freedom. Other Neo-Platonists believed no one could in this life attain to perfect wisdom.

Augustine had rejected his mother's Christian books, for he considered their style unpolished. Plato's sentences were much better phrased than were the Gospels. Also, the eminent Neo-Platonist Porphyry declared that Jesus should have lived in a more "elevated substance" than flesh; he should not have been born of a woman; nor punished as a criminal.

By this time, however, Augustine had wrung from Neo-Platonism all it could give him. The Neo-Platonist seemed to him like a man standing on a wooden height whence he could see in the distance "the land of peace." Knowing not the way thereto he must struggle "vainly towards it through pathless wilds."

Worldly advancement and fame did not entice Augustine now. They seemed to him like striving for a crown of straw or for applause in the theater. His supreme interest was the nature of God and how to attain a permanent consciousness of God's presence. He must find comfort for his heart. The scholar's keen, scientific mind must also be satisfied.

In Milan was a Christian bishop, famous for his saintly character. He was well trained in law and, when a layman, was governor of the district, and gave capable service to his church. This aristocratic layman, Ambrose, was thirty-four years old when the time came for the election of the metropolitan bishop. A crowd packed the church for the momentous election. Ambrose presided and, in his effort to quiet the rising commotion among the sectarian groups, he addressed the people, beseeching them to be peaceable. When he ceased to speak an amazing thing happened: as though a single voice was crying, the shout arose, "Ambrose is bishop."

Ambrose did not want to be bishop and quickly said harsh and unjust things, hoping to show that he was not worthy to have the office. When this was of no vail, he ran from the church. The people followed him and brought him back, for they believed an angel's voice had somehow called for his election. Th emperor approved Ambrose and ordered that he serve. Selected, then, by the emperor and the people, and elected by the bishops, Ambrose became Bishop of Milan.

Tormented by his conflicting thoughts and groping for relief, Augustine wandered into Ambrose's church. At first he listened cynically to Ambrose's sermons. Then the professor of rhetoric was charmed by the eloquence of the able bishop. Contemptuous of his Christian ideas, Augustine gave attention not so much to what Ambrose said as to how he said it. Augustine wrote in his *Confessions* that after a while he discovered "with the phrases which I loved, the facts which I neglected began to trickle into my mind, because I could not keep them apart." He listened with respect to Ambrose the scholar, who proved to him the limitations of human reason, and made him acknowledge the futility of the "vehement quibbling" contained in the writings of "so many mutually destructive philosophers."

Augustine now read he Bible; and was astonished at some of its stories. He wrote later, "While I read those Scriptures in the letter, I was slain in the spirit." Ambrose in his sermons interpreted these stories as allegories, and removed stumbling blocks which had made the Bible impossible.

Augustine was irresistibly drawn to Ambrose, and watching Ambrose's blamelsss life resolved that he must know God as Ambrose knew him. Cautiously Augustine acknowledged how reasonable and beautiful were the teachings of Christ. They could not be so helpful if they were not true, he decided. Learned men had said a divine revelation was necessary only for the weak and childlike. But was he not, morally, a child? It was evident that the Christ, the "high road built by the care of the heavenly Emperor" was the only one by whom he could approach God. He was convinced that Christ was God's will and character made visible. If God's Manifestation could humble himself, until he accepted the ignominy of the cross even, should a man with but fragmentary learning and righteousness be proud, Augustine argued. He now understood that a Neo-Platonist like Porphyry turned away from the Christ because of "pride and vain knowledge," and that he himself had begun to "wish men to think" him wise. Christ could say, "Come unto me all ye that labor and I will give you rest, for I am meek and lowly." Such power and humility were unknown in Platonism. Christ's consciousness of God was continuous. The Neo-Platonist caught an occasional and momentary glimpse of Reality.

It was difficult to obtain an interview with Ambrose, for he was always surrounded by people or, if he had a few moments to himself, he rested his voice by reading. So Augustine, who saw the path but was "reluctant to pass through the straight gate," went to Simplicianus, who was Ambrose's teacher and from his youth had been entirely devoted to God. Augustine saw the grace of God shining in Simplicianus' face; and he told the old man his problems, and how he had studied the Neo-Platonists. Simplicianus replied that in their writings "God and his word were implied at every turn." Tactfully he told Augustine of the conversion of Victorinus, a celebrated professor of rhetoric in Rome.

Victorinus was translator of the Platonists. He was the tutor of illustrious senators. He was so famous that his statue was in the Roman Forum. He was a pagan and worshiped all the gods and goddesses. When he was old, he made a careful study of the Christians' literature, and told Simplicianus that he was a Christian. Many times he told Simplicianus this. Each time Simplicianus said he would believe Victorinus when he declared himself publicly. The famous professor hesitated. What would his friends say if they knew he was a Christian, he asked Simplicianus. Simplicianus replied that if he did not acknowledge Christ before his friends, Christ would not acknowledge him before the holy angels. Victorinus read and reflected, and suddenly announced his new belief at a vast public gathering, "to the great wonder of Rome and the great joy of the Church." His pagan friends were furious; the Christians rejoiced. Julian the Apostate, then emperor, had forbidden that a Christian be allowed to teach literature or rhetoric. Victorinus was dismissed from his professorship.

Augustine longed to follow Victorinus. But habit had stiffened his heart into resistance. He knew the time for his declaration had come; but like a drowsy man he delayed. "Presently, prsently," he said to himself. "But presently, presently had no present." Meanwhile belief in the Christ grew in his mind.

He was living in Milan with his life-long friend Alypius, who had a beautiful home and garden, when the crisis came. One day a high official of the emperor's court called on them. As he talked, the visitor noticed that a single book lay on a table near him. Curious to know that Augustine, the distinguished professor, might be reading he picked up the book, expecting to find it a classic or a treatise on rhetoric. To his amazement he held in his hand the writings of Paul. He asked Augustine and Alypius if they were Christians. When he learned they were interested he told them of people he knew who had become Christians. He told them of Anthony. And of his two friends, officials in the government, who had resolved to become Christians on the impulse of a chance reading of the biography of Anthony. They came to a cottage, entered it, and saw on a table a book, Athanasius' biography of Anthony. One of the two opened the book and read until his soul was ablaze. "What are we living for," he cried. "What is the goal of our toil? Is it the friendship of the emperor? How fickle is his love, and what dangers are on the path, before we can win that prize! But if I choose, I can be the friend of God from this moment. I have broken with ambition, and determined to serve God. I am going to begin this moment and here," he declared to his friend.

Augustine thought why could not he do this? He told himself how miserable his life had been. He had wasted twelve years, and for ten years had carried on his back a pack of vanity which was now so heavy he could not go forward. These two officials had, in a moment, cast off their load.

When the caller left, Augustine went into the garden. Alypius followed and they sat under a tree. Augustine was determined to win. But so great was his struggle with himself that he began to weep uncontrollably. He walked to another part of the garden and threw himself on the ground under a fig tree. Suddenly he heard a voice saying clearly, in a sort of chant, "Take and read. Take and read." What is this, he asked himself, and he wondered if children in a nearby garden were playing a game. He knew of no game with the words he had heard. He remembered what he had just been told of Anthony, how he chanced to enter a church as some one was reading Jesus' words to the rich young man. Augustine returned to Alypius, and picked up the book of Paul's letters. Opening it eagerly he read, "Not in rioting and drunkenness, not in chambering and wantonness, not in strife and envying: but put ye on the Lord Jesus Christ, and make not provision for the flesh to fulfil the lusts of thereof." He read no further, for peace filled his heart, "sweeter than any pleasure, though not to flesh and blood; brighter than any light, though hidden behind the inmost veil; exalted above all honour, though not to them that are exalted in their own eyes." He told his experience to Alypius and he, fired by the glory of it, joined him. It was easy for Alypius, wrote Augustine, for his heart was pure and humble, and he was accustomed to self-discipline.

When the summer vacation came, Augustine went to Alypius' country home and studied the Christians' Bible. Ambrose advised him to read Isaiah, probably because of the prophecies of the Messiah's coming. Augustine could not understand Isaiah and decided to wait until he "had more practice in the divine style." It was Paul and the Psalms that he loved, and as he read them the rough places of his life became smooth, the crooked ones straight, and he had no more apprehensions for his past. He was thirty-three when, with his son and his friend Alypius, he was baptized a Christian.

When Augustine's mother heard that her son was listening to

Ambrose, she sped to Milan, wrote Augustine, "over land and sea
... there to hang upon the lips of Ambrose, as a fountain of water
springing up to eternal life. She loved that great man as an angel
of God, because she had learned that by his instrumentality I had
been brought for a while to a state of wavering." She died soon
after Augustine joined the Christians. He describes in his *Confessions* one of his last conversations with her. Looking out of a
window upon the garden below, they realized that joy in "the
brightest conceivable earthly sunshine was not to be compared,
no, nor even named with the happiness of" the spiritual life. As
they talked and their hearts reflected to each other the light of the
Spirit they rose in their perception, until they were directly conscious of the life which is God. They "reached out and with one
flash of thought touched the Eternal Wisdom that abides above all.
Suppose this endured, and all other far inferior modes of vision
were taken away, and this alone were to ravish the beholder, and
absorb him, and plunge him in mystic joy, might not eternal life
be like this moment of comprehension for which we sighed? Is not
this the meaning of 'Enter thou into the joy of thy Lord'?"

Augustine attained the consciousness of God for which Plato
and Plotinus searched. Wishing that others might benefit from his
long researches and his investigation of Jesus as the true authority
on the way to God, Augustine wrote his book *Confessions* explaining how he arrived at his conclusions.

The Christians made him Bishop of Hippo, in Tunisia. Through
his office, and in many books and hundreds of letters, he used his
mighty intellect to proclaim the Christ by whose strength he lived.
He is one of the greatest philosophers of the Western world. His
theology, built upon the Bible, the Platonists, the Church Fathers,
and his own experience, shaped Christian thinking for more than
twelve hundred years.

In his *Confessions* he tells how he learned to love God and what
his love for God meant to him. It released him from pride, from
the inordinate drive of physical instincts, from love of himself, and
with this release came peace of mind and a power to love and help
others so marvelous he could hardly describe it.

His *Confessions* is his song of gratitude and praise to God. It is
a continual prayer telling God his love for him. He concentrates

his mind in adoration upon God's attributes: his omnipotent power and truth, unfathomable, inexhaustible; his mercy, his infinitely tender love. He sees God's Light, beautiful beyond the imagination of men. He can find no adequate words to describe it, and falls back upon the simple declaration that it exists and can be seen by the soul that is purified.

# 18

## From Mission to Monasticism

IN THE FOURTH century Christianity spread rapidly in southern Gaul. Shortly afterward, Martin of Tours went into northern Gaul where Christianity had not penetrated. Martin's pagan parents migrated from Hungry to Pavia, a town in northern Italy not far from Milan. When the boy was nine he ran away from home to a Christian community, and for the next five years wandered from monastery to monastery. His father, a soldier in the Roman army, finally put a stop to his nomadic life and compelled him to join the army. Three years later, when Martin was seventeen, his regiment was stationed at Amiens in Gaul. One bitterly cold day a detachment of soldiers, Martin among them, was approached by a man who stood naked at the city's gate and begged for alms. No one heeded him but Martin, who had already emptied his purse for starving beggars. Martin had on his white military cloak, and this he quickly took off and cut in two with his sword, giving half to the shivering beggar. Some of his companions laughed when they saw Martin in only half a cloak. And some were ashamed, remembering how much more they had to give than had he. That night the Christ came to him in a dream. He was wearing the half cloak Martin had given the beggar, and he said to the host of angels with him, "Martin, as yet only a catechumen has clothed Me with this garment." Martin soon left the army, and the rest of his long life he spent in the service of the Christ. With Hilary, an aristocratic and cultivated gentleman who was Bishop of Poitiers, he heroically spread Christianity through Gaul, founding monasteries and many churches in the north.

The conversion of the Germanic tribes north of the Black Sea and the Danube River was due to the Christians captured in the many raids of those tribes and to the traveling merchants. Ulfilas, a heroic missionary to the Goths, was the grandson of Christian captives taken in a raid in 264. For forty years Ulfilas taught in the region north of the Danube. He was finally driven away by a pagan chieftain, but sent many others to take his place. He translated the Bible into the Goths' language, omitting the Books of Samuel and Kings, as the Goths were warlike enough without the encouragement of such tales. Those fierce people judged a religion worth while in proportion to the success of its adherents' armies. When they saw the power of the Roman empire, then Christian, they decided that Christ must be stronger than any other god and worthy of their acceptance.

At the end of the fourth century the Huns pressed upon the Goths and the other Germanic tribes of the east and drove them westward. Among the Goths who migrated west arose the Christian chieftain Alaric. Seeking power and plunder, Alaric and his warriors raided northern Italy, and about 410, to the horror of the Western world, descended upon Rome and sacked that city which no enemy nation had entered for almost a thousand years. Alaric remembered his Christianity to the extent that he did not harm the Christian churches or bishops or teachers or nuns. After three days in Rome he departed with all the plunder he and his horde could carry. Compared with the way in which the pagans sacked a city his operations were mild.

The Vandals, Christians from northern Europe, pushed south through Gaul and Spain and established themselves in northern Africa. Augustine died during their seige of his city, Hippo, in 430. In 455 they crossed over to Italy and ruthlessly sacked Rome. These invaders were men of vigor and sometimes of budding genius. But they took their Christianity about as seriously as did a certain lawless boy who wanted to join the church and be baptized, and when he was told he was not spiritually fit, replied that he'd be damned if he were not a Christian.

Soon the barbarians were in possession of Rome's western empire. One of their most aggressive chieftains was Clovis the Frank. His wife was a Christian, but he would have none of her religion.

She must, however, have made an impression on him, for when he was about to lose a very important battle he vowed that if the God of the Christians would make him victorious he would become his follower. Clovis won, and kept his promise. The Bishop, Remigius, tried to train him in the way of Christ. Clovis declared, when he heard of the crucifixion of Jesus, "Had I and my faithful Franks been there, they had not dared to do it." The bishop baptized him into the church with the injunction that Clovis adored the cross which he had burned, and burned the idols which he had adored. Three thousand Franks were baptized with him. And soon the rest of his subjects became, nominally, Christians.

Britain under Roman government had a civilization which compared favorably with Rome itself. There were evidently Christian communities in this early Britain, for mention was made in the time of Constantine of the Bishop of Londinium and two bishops under him, who went to a Christian gathering in Gaul. Tertullian, Hilary, and Paula wrote of the Christians of Britain.

In the fifth century Rome concentrated all her energies upon defending herself against the northern barbarians and left Britain unprotected. The Angles, Jutes, and Saxons then swarmed across the North Sea and plundered and killed the people of Britain until by the sixth century the Islands were reduced to semibarbarism.

Ignorance, brutality, cold despair, and a paganism often expressed in tales of supernatural and savage cruelty now made up the people's life. Several monks were sent to Britain by the Church at Rome, but they had little success in their teaching. About 597, Pope Gregory sent a party of monks under a young man named Augustine. The historian Bede wrote of the expedition, "They having, in obedience to the pope's commands, undertaken that work, were, on their journey, seized with a sudden fear, and began to think of returning home, rather than proceed to a barbarous, fierce, and unbelieving nation, to whose very language they were strangers; and this they unanimously agreed was the safest course." Gregory the Great wrote them a letter, setting forth their missionary opportunities, and they continued the journey.

When Augustine arrived in Britain he sent a messenger to King Ethelbert with word that he had come from Rome with tidings which "assured to all that took advantage of it everlasting joys in heaven, and a kingdom that would never end, with the living and true God." Ethelbert had already heard of Christianity, for his wife was of the royal family of the Franks, and a Christian. Her parents had exacted a promise from Ethelbert that she should be allowed to worship in her own way, and when she left Gaul to marry the King they sent along a Christian bishop to help her preserve her faith among foreign people.

King Ethelbert gave Augustine and his monks an audience, receiving them in the open air where they could not get the better of him by any practice of magic. He listened to Augustine's reasons for coming, and gave the monks permission to live in Canterbury, also freedom to teach and gain as many believers as they could. And he promised to supply them with the necessary support. Many people soon forsook their paganism for the new religion. King Ethelbert, "among the rest, induced by the unspotted life of these holy men, and their delightful promises, which, by many miracles, they proved to be most certain, believed and was baptized." What the miracles were which made Augustine so successful is not known. Pope Gregory admonished him that he must not become proud of the amazing powers entrusted to him by the Christ. The real miracle, and perhaps it was the only one, was the transformation that gradually took place in the character and spirit of the people under the influence of the monasteries which became the schools and cultural centers of the country.

The hero of the conversion of Ireland was Saint Patrick. He entered the island in the fifth century, a nightingale singing in the dark night. He was so successful in conquering the pagan hosts that wonderful tales were told about him. This much seems sure: he was a native of western Britain, the son of a Christian. He was taken captive in a raid by the Irish and carried off to Ireland where he spent his youth in slavery, tending flocks, while the spiritual life grew in his soul. He fled to Gaul and years later returned to Ireland and taught many people the Christ's glad tidings.

Columba, a member of Ireland's royalty, was another important messenger of the Christ. With twelve assistants he taught in northern Britain and in Scotland, and he established a famous monastery on the Island of Iona west of Scotland. By his holy life he

spread Christianity and won the friendship and assistance of many
leading families. These Christians from Ireland consummated the
conversion of Britain. Boniface and other missionaries from Britain traveled into Germany and worked for the conversion of the
Germanic peoples.

While this renaissance was growing in the British Isles, the
Christian Church developed the organization which enabled it to
withstand the catastrophes and conflicts that befell the Western
world.

The apostles appointed the leaders of the first Christian groups.
Later, the bishops, as they were called, were sometimes appointed
by one in authority, sometimes elected by the groups. When there
were numerous assemblies the bishop of a large city presided over
the bishops of nearby regions. Antioch, Rome, Alexandria, and
Constantinople were the most important of the large cities and
among them the Church at Rome, founded by Peter and Paul,
became pre-eminent. Peter was the disciple who said to Jesus,
"Thou art the Christ, the Son of the Living God." Jesus answered:
"And I tell you, you are Peter, and on this rock I will build my
church, and the powers of death shall not prevail against it." Many
Christians believed that with these words Jesus appointed Peter to
be the center—his name meant rock—from which the Christian
unity should radiate.

The sovereignty of the Christians of Rome was founded, like all
true dominion, on love and wisdom. That luminous group by their
deeds of kindness knit together the Christian world. They sent
food and supplies to relieve poverty-stricken communities and
helped the brethren in the mines. The early Roman bishops as a
rule practiced love. They saw conflicts, usually, in high perspective, and decided disputes among the Christians with moderation
and justice. Their gentleness and wisdom shone through the centuries.

For five centuries Christianity went forward. Then over Christendom crept the pall of a strange disaster, and Europe sank gradually into the Dark Ages.

The reason often given for this tragedy is the barbarian inva-
sions. But why should Christian civilization have been strangled

by the barbarians, savage though they were? The Christian leaders really had help at hand, for the conquerors were nominally Christians; at least they were predisposed to Christianity. When the northern tribes, bloodthirsty and terrible, bore down upon China in successive waves of horror they threw that country into chaos for a time. The religion and civilization of the Chinese triumphed and in a century or so, sometimes in a generation, the descendants of the wildest barbarians become patrons of learning and culture. It is religion's function to transform the world; it should not surrender when it is most needed.

Pure and vital religion is the soul of civilization. Learning and literature, arts and crafts, science and education are its body. After the fall of Rome the monks of the West tried to eliminate the body from their civilization and have in their world only religion, the disembodied soul. This at first took the form of opposition to Greek and Roman learning and an insistence that only the Bible and the Church Fathers should be studied. The Christians gradually ceased to collect books or learn the Latin language into which their Bible was translated. The few who read the Bible were permitted no independent thinking about its contents. Origen was declared a heretic because he taught that much of the Bible was allegorical, and because he believed in a spiritual resurrection only. Jerome, a Latin father of the Church, was denounced because he studied Hebrew with Jewish rabbis.

The human mind is developed by contact with superior minds. Art and literature advance by the study of great art and masterpieces of good form. Beauty begets beauty. Scholars like Clement, Origen, and Augustine fully appreciated the importance of education and took every advantage of the scientific and cultural achievements of Greece and Rome. Augustine fashioned his terse and brilliant style on the Italian classics. Early Christian scholars used the large libraries of Caesarea and Alexandria accumulated under Greek and Roman influence. Augustine had an excellent library of his own at Hippo. Sidonius in one of his letters describes the library of a Christian friend in southern Gaul: it contained the writings of Plato and Augustine, Origen and Cicero—the classics of Greece and Christendom. The scholarly Jerome made free use of the classics.

In 529 Justinian, the Christian emperor of the Eastern empire, closed the Greek schools and colleges of Athens. The Christian leaders thereafter set their faces against science and its enlightening, critical spirit, which are the purifier of theology and the balance wheel of the soul. Gregory the Great, one of the best of the popes, opposed science and learning. Cathedral schools languished, public schools are gradually discontinued. Ignorance became the fashion; and with minds at rest the monks quoted Jerome as saying it was better to weep than to teach. Clement and Origen taught that the earth was round. The monks now decided it was flat. With the distribution of ignorance came a decline in morals, manners, and art.

In the early Byzantine art are rare mosaics in which the solemn splendor of God is shining: and paintings of the Christ whose face is strong and sweet and through whose eyes the love of the Eternal seems to pour ineffable beauty.

In later centuries came a change. The mosaic pictures of Christ and his disciples looked pinched and worn, with faces sorrowful even unto death; their faith seemed defeated, hope was gone, and with it spiritual light. For monastic Christendom now laid stress upon negations, upon extinction of the normal interests of life, upon contemplation of the cross to the exclusion of the glory of a resurrected world. Forgetting what God is like, they lost the way to him and went into decline along a path of their own making, which they called creedal, monastic, ecclesiastical salvation through Christ.

As the centuries passed and the glory of the spiritual life faded, many Christians, hoping to recover the lost radiance, turned to asceticism and made intense warfare on the flesh. During the centuries of persecution by the Roman government their life was so beset with danger there was no question as to sufficient tests whereby to prove and strengthen their faith and courage. When Christianity became popular some Christians felt they must manufacture, through asceticism, such tests as were ever present in persecution and poverty. Others reasoned that they were not spiritually strong enough to live in a corrupt world and remain unspotted; they must retire to a place where they would be safe from temptation.

The Christians should have continued this missionary work among all nations and peoples. They would then have met worthwhile hazards of physical hardships and social persecution. They would have been compelled to pray without ceasing a prayer of sincerity and importunity. As they traveled, educating the world, every day they would have received fresh strength from the King of their hearts and souls who takes especial care of his soldiers on the firing line and the outposts of his kingdom. True it is that many Christians did teach in this way. Suppose thousands of spiritually and mentally strong teachers had continued the work and had persistently taught true Christianity, the best Greek science and philosophy, arts and crafts, the Dark Ages might never have come upon the Western world and civilization might now be advanced to a point beyond imagining.

The teachers who might have been went into monastic cells. They substituted contemplation for service. They invented all manner of self-torture to take the place of the rugged and natural asceticism of the soldier at the front. While they gazed into the skies searching for God, the barbarians stormed through Europe. It was now the hour for Islam.

# Book III

## Islam

# 19

## Muhammad's Call

BY THE SEVENTH century A.D. the once thriving civilization of Arabia was barely a memory. The splendid cities of Petra and Palmyra in the north were in ruins. Yemen in the south was weak and despairing. The Sabeans of Yemen had been happy and industrious, and their embroidery was a symbol of beauty even in far countries; but Rome took away their trade in Chinese silks and Indian spices, and diverted into its own hands the stream of pearls and other treasures which poured from Persia and the East. The breaking of the marvel of ancient engineering, the mountain dam of Marid, and the dispersion of the life-giving water it held in reserve were a part of the economic and political confusion and the final collapse of the Sabean civilization.

In central Arabia the district of al-Hijaz boasted Medina and Ta'if as important cities, also Mecca where lived prosperous merchants who watched over sacred shrines. The Arabs were hospitable as of old, and poetry and eloquent speech were still admired. The poets, though they sometimes described the untamed beauty of nature, preferred to sing of war and women, wine, horses and camels, for al-Hijaz with its vast deserts was now recklessly barbaric and the prevailing purpose of the men was to fight, drink, and love without restraint. The northern tribes of Ghassan which were feudatory to Rome, and the kingdom of al-Hîra subject to Persia, as well as Yemen had been visited by Christian teachers and for a century or so had supposedly been christian. Their paganized form of Christianity, however, warmed no heart. Here and there in al-Hijaz were to be found Jewish and very small Christian communities who reminded the people of the One God; and there were the Hanifs, a group of devout ascetics who announced sporadically that the day of judgment was drawing near. Also once in a while some voice cried that a great Prophet was soon to come. But in the main, a barbarism cruel and sinister enveloped all central Arabia in its abysmal degradation. Human sacrifices were common, the unwanted girl babies were buried alive, and through the deserts roamed the wild Bedouin, making incessant war.

In a turmoil of hatred and bloody feuds, plundering of neighbors and stealing of slaves and women the orphan boy Muhammad grew up in the home of his uncle, Abu Talib. Nobility is a relative matter; his family possessed as much as there was at that time, his grandfather being the virtual ruler of Mecca. The young man Muhammad was very handsome, with fair complexion, black hair, and dignified bearing. He "was more modest than a virgin behind her curtain," most careful of his personal appearance, highly sensitive to pain. He was by trade a shepherd, and was so poor that often his only food was the wild berries of the desert. In savage surroundings, he lived austerely, and he was called by his neighbors, *El-Ameen*, the Honest, the Reliable. Because of his good character, a well-to-do widow, Khadeeja employed him to carry on her business. Before he had ever come to her home, it is said, she saw him in a vision, riding to her on a horse, surrounded by light; and when he entered her house for the first time, with him came such a radiance that she, thinking the sun was too bright, bade her maid close the shutters.

Across the desert, to Syria and Palestine, Muhammed traveled with Khadeeja's caravans. When he was twenty-five years old and she was forty Khadeeja asked him to marry her. For the twenty-five years of their marriage life she was a perfect friend and companion to him. Of their children the most celebrated is their youngest daughter, Fatima. Perhaps Muhammad was thinking of Khadeeja when he said, "Heaven lieth at the feet of mothers."

Muhammad's associates worshiped the sun, moon, stars, and innumerable idols. He set his face against this polytheism and went often into the silent desert near Mecca, where he stayed alone for days at a time praying to God to show him the way to relieve the miseries of the slaves and the very poor of his community.

When he was about forty, as he prayed thus in the desert, again and again his mind was flooded with light from an unseen Presence. Night after night, as he slept on the mountainside in a cave of red granite, he had wonderful dreams. And as he walked over the brown rocks in the silence of the day a voice called, "O Muhammad! O Muhammad.! Peace unto thee, O Messenger of God"; but when he looked about he saw only the bare stones and the blazing sun and the shrubs of the lonely mountain. In his perplexity, he feared he was becoming a sorcerer, a soothsayer—to him abhorrent.

One night he heard a voice say, "Cry! Cry! Cry!"

"What shall I cry?" asked Muhammad.

"Cry in the name of thy Lord, who taught man that which he did not know," answered the voice.

Muhammad, astonished, left his cave and started down the mountain. When he was halfway down, the voice called to him, "O Muhammad, thou art the Prophet of God, and I am Gabriel."

Muhammad looked, and beheld a dazzling Presence. Later, in his Quran, he described one who, endowed with wisdom and "terrible in power," from the highest horizon approached nearer and nearer to him.

Again the voice said, "O Muhammad, thou art the Prophet of God, and I am Gabriel." And the sky was filled with light.

For the third time the voice called, "O Muhammad, thou art the Prophet of God, and I am Gabriel."

Muhammad left the desert and went home to Khadeeja. "O Khadeeja," he said, "I have either become a soothsayer or a madman."

"You never told a lie nor ever returned evil for evil; you always kept your word and led a virtuous life. You can never be either a soothsayer or a madman," she answered.

Khadeeja told a Christian, her cousin, of the voice that had been spoken to Muhammad. The Christian said to her, "O Khadeeja, there hath come unto him the greatest Námús who came to Moses aforetime, and lo, he is the prophet of this people."

The mystic would explain that the ocean of God's being entered Muhammad's mind. The psychologist might suggest that Muhammad's subconscious mind touch a More than he, which brought to birth in his consciousness a new center of energy. His followers have simply said that God spoke to Muhammad, through the intermediary of his Holy Spirit, Gabriel.

The voice soon commanded Muhammad to proclaim to the people of Arabia the highest standard of honesty, philanthropy, and lovingkindness, and told him to denounce licentiousness. Muhammad's consciousness of direct communion with God was so compelling that he was immediately obedient.

His first convert was Khadeeja. Ali, his nephew, a gentle boy of ten, was the second. His third disciple was Zaid, a slave whom he had freed and adopted as his son. Other slaves became believers, as did a wealthy merchant, Abu Bakr, revered by his townsmen for his intelligence, efficiency, and integrity. Of Abu Bakr, Muhammad said in after years, "I never invited any to the faith who displayed no hesitation, perplexity and vacillation—expecting only Abu Bakr; who when I told him of Islam tarried not, neither was perplexed." Abu Bakr spent a large part of his fortune purchasing and then freeing slaves who were Muhammad's followers. One of these was Bilal, whom Muhammad called the first fruit of Abyssinia. Bilal's master was furious when he heard that a slave of his had listened to Muhammad and he had Bilal taken into the desert and pinioned to the sand with a heavy stone on his chest. He should lie there, the master said, in the blazing sun, until he renounced Muhammad and worshiped idols of his people, or died. Day after day the tortured slave was carried into the desert, laid on the burning said and the stone placed on his chest. Bilal only cried, "There is but one God. There is but one God." When he was near to dying Abu Bakr chanced to come by. He immediately purchased Bilal and set him free.

For three years Muhammad taught, and made thirty converts among his nearest friends. Then he tried a difficult group, his relatives. He called them together and announced that he was the Apostle of God. "No Arab," he told them, "has offered to his nation more precious advantages than those I bring you. I offer you happiness in this world and in the life to come. Who among you will aid me in this task?"

When no one answered, Ali, thirteen years old, cried, "Prophet of God, I will aid thee."

The others burst out laughing, and the meeting broke up. It was worthy of Muhammad's claims, they thought, that a child should be the only one among them to believe him.

After this, Muhammad taught in public places: in the street, on a hillside, wherever a crowd might be, saying to the people, "There is only one God, he who is Creator and Lord of heaven and earth, who ordains the sun to shine by day and the darkness to give rest at night, who in his love sends water from heaven upon the earth, who makes the palm tree grow and give forth its lucious dates, who made the stately hills and the blue sky, who teaches men to know and understand what they knew not—he is God, and there is no God but him. He and his angel hosts cry, "We will hurl the truth at falsehood, and it shall smite it, and lo! it shall vanish.' "

He called his religion Islam, that is, surrender to the will of God. The glorious doorway through which one entered into God's peace was, "Thy will, not mine be done." Each Prophet was a trumpet blown by the Breath of God, a resurrection morning calling those in the graves of disobedience to God to rise and live again.

As he gave his message Muhammad's eyes shone like burning coals. A child said to his mother, "Describe the lord Muhammad to me." The mother replied, "O my little son, had you seen him you would say that you had seen a rising sun."

While he won a few followers, the large majority of the people considered him just a misguided poet. "Here he comes," they would say, "the son of Abdullah, to talk about his communion with the heavens," he whose words are a "medley of dreams." His revelation?—"He hath forged it. Is he more than a man like us? Unless an angel come down from heaven we will not believe." As to what he said of a resurrection, that when a man is dust and bones he can live again—"Were we dust? Ha, ha, are we the new creation? Are we the resurrected ones?" They laughed him to scorn, refusing to see that we spoke in symbols.

When ridicule proved of no avail they became more violent, placing thorns and refuse in his path when he walked abroad, and throwing dirt at him and his followers.

A practical matter of business was involved in this persecution. Mecca contained the Ka'aba, the small temple which, tradition said, was built by Abraham and Ishmael. In Muhammad's day the Ka'aba housed three hundred and sixty idols, also a Black Stone which the Arabs believed had come from heaven. Muhammad's tribe, the Qureish, the leaders of Mecca, were the custodians of this temple. Once a year Arabs from all parts of the Peninsula came on pilgrimage to Mecca, to worship in the temple and climb Arafat, the sacred mount outside the city. Up and down Mount Arafat the pilgrims tramped. Round and round the temple they marched naked, saying they could not approach so holy a place as the Ka'aba clothed in the garments in which they had sinned. They filled Mecca, and the surrounding hills where they camped; and they brought much business and profit to the Qureish. If Muhammad and his teaching prevailed all this business would be destroyed, for he would take away the idols.

Furthermore, Muhammad forbade gambling, saying it was contrary to the will of God. The Meccans gambled with barbaric abandon. They gambled themselves into slavery, time and again. Muhammad also forbade drinking wine.

"He is a fraud and an impostor," the Qureish cried. What did he know more than they about God and the unseen world! And they fought him with savage fury.

Muhammad continued to teach; and many more of his townsmen believed him. The Qureish decided to deal singly with these believers, each Qureish household agreeing to make away with any Muslims found among them, and there were cruel murders. Some Muslims were thrown into prison, beaten and starved to death. Others were taken into the desert and pinioned to the scorching sand in the terrible heat. When they were about to die of thirst they were offered relief if they would worship the idols of their people. A few recanted, to become Muslims again when the torture was abated; the majority remained firm. Some were violently tortured in other ways and killed.

Muhammad now advised his followers, the Muslims, to seek

refuge in the Christian kingdom of Abyssinia on the other side of the Red Sea; and more than a hundred went there.

The Meccans sent an embassy to the King of Abyssinia requesting the extradition of Muhmmad's disciples, that they might be brought back to Mecca and punished. The king asked the Muslims about their religion. Jafar, Ali's brother, answered for them: "O King, we were plunged in the darkness of ignorance, worshiping idols, and eating carrion; we practiced abominations, severed the ties of kinship and maltreated our neighbors; the strong among us devoured the weak; and so we remained until God sent us an apostle, from among ourselves, whose lineage we knew as well as his truth, his trustworthiness, and the purity of his life. He called upon us to worship the One God and abandon the stones and idols that our fathers had worshiped in His stead. He bade us be truthful in speech, faithful to our promises, compassionate and kind to our parents and neighbors, and to desist from crime and bloodshed. He forbade to do evil, to lie, to rob the orphan or defame women. He enjoined on us the worship of God alone, with prayer, almsgiving, and fasting. And we believed in him and followed the teachings that he brought us from God. But our countrymen rose up against us and persecuted us to make us renounce our faith, and return to the worship of idols and the abominations of our former life. So when they cruelly treated us, reducing us to bitter straits and came between us and the practice of our religion, we took refuge in your country. Putting our trust in your justice, we hope that you will deliver us from the oppression of our enemies."

The king refused to surrender the Muslims to the persecutors.

"You will observe," said Muhammad to his followers, that "he who treats our religion as a lie is the one who thrusts the orphans aside and arouseth not others to feed the poor."

The Qureish tried another tactic. A chieftain approached Muhammad one day as he sat in the Ka'aba and said to him, "O son of my brother, thou art distinguished by thy qualities and thy descent. Now thou hast sown division among our people, and cast dissension in our families; thou denouncest our gods and goddesses; thou dost tax our ancestors with impiety. We have a proposition to make to thee; think well if it will not suit thee to accept it. If thou wishest to acquire riches by this affair, we will collect a fortune larger than is possessed by any of us; if thou desirest honors and dignity, we shall make thee our chief, and shall not do a thing without thee; if thou desirest dominion, we shall make thee our king; and if the spirit [demon] which possesses thee cannot be overpowered, we will bring thee doctors and give them riches till they cure thee."

When Muhammad could not be bribed, the Qureish chieftains told him, "Know this, O Muhammad, we shall never cease to stop thee from preaching till either thou or we perish."

During these stormy years Muhammad composed parts of his Quran. His followers believed that the original book was in heaven and chapter by chapter was given to him. Muhammad could neither read nor write, and dictated to his amanuensis who wrote on whatever might be at hand—a piece of stone, the shoulder blade of an animal dried and whitened in the desert, a palm leaf, a piece of leather. Sometimes the sentences rang in Muhammad's mind like a bell, which thundered and vibrated until it seemed as though he would be rent asunder. Abu Bakr said to him one day, "Ah, thou for whom I would forsake father and mother, white hairs are hastening upon thee." Muhammad answered that it was the intensity of these revelations which turned his hair white.

His book was written in a language suited to the people for whom it was intended, and its effect upon some of them was electric. When Abu Bakr in the coutryard of his home read sentences from the Quran, those passing on the street listened spellbound—until the Qureish ordered him to stop reading aloud in a public place or leave the city.

Umar, a young Qureish chieftain, persecuted the Muslim relentlessly and tried for years to dissuade them from what he considered their crazy idea that Muhammad was a Prophet of God. Unable to compel any Muslim to renounce the new religion, he took his sword one day and, brandishing it, vowed to kill Muhammad at once. Umar was tall and strong, twenty-six years old, and he hated Muhammad and his followers with the vehemence that made him an intrepid fighter. As he rushed through the streets of Mecca, bent on murder, some one called to him, "Where are you going?"

"I am looking for Muhammad," he shouted, "to kill the renegade who has brought discord among the qureish, called them fool, reviled their religion, and defamed their gods."

"Why dost thou not rather punish those of thine own family, and set them right?" asked the other.

"And who are these of my own family?" cried Umar.

"Thy brother-in-law Sa'id and thy sister Fatima, who have become Muslims and followers of Muhammad," replied Umar's informer.

Umar ran to his sister's house. There she was with Sa'id her husband and another Muslim, reading a page of the —Quran.

"What was that sound I heard?" yelled Umar.

"It was nothing," said Fatima.

"Nay, but I heard you, and I have learned that you have become followers of Muhammad," retorted Umar.

He struck at Sa'id with is sword. Fatima, to potect her husband, threw herself in front of him.

"Yes," she cried, "we are Muslims; we believe in God and his Prophet; slay us if you will."

Umar, missing Sa'id slashed Fatima and the blood streamed over her face. Umar's heart softened, and laying down his sword he asked what they were reading. Afraid to tell him, Fatima handed him a manuscript page from the twentieth chapter of the Quran.

Umar commenced to read; and became strangely quiet. On and on he read, his wonder increasing until at last he exclaimed, "Lead me to Muhammad that I may tell him of my conversion."

Umar's change of heart caused a tremendous stir in Mecca and the number of Muslims so increased that the Qureish swore neither to buy from nor to sell to them, nor to have dealings of any sort with them, nor to let any of their people marry a Muslim.

Muhammad had assistance, however, in two ways. His uncle, Abu Talib, who was prominent and influential among the Qureish, protected him from personal injury. And each year came the sacred month of *Ramadhan*, as it was called, when the Arabs made their pilgrimage to the Ka'aba. During this time a truce was declared throughout Arabia and all warfare ceased. Muhammad then went about freely and talked with the incoming pilgrims, although his relative Abu Lahab followed him from place to place shouting to the visitors in derision and hatred, "He is an impostor who wants to draw you away from the faith of your fathers to the false doctrines that he brings; wherefore separate yourselves from him and hear him not"; and the pilgrims answered Muhammad, "Thine own people and kindred should know thee best."

For ten years Muhammad taught under relentless persecution. The next year was the "year of mourning" when Abu Talib and Khadeeja died. For twenty-five years Khadeeja had been Muhammad's best counselor. Through her "was the Lord minded to lighten the burden of His Prophet; for whenever he heard anything that grieved him touching his rejection by the people, he would return to her and God would comfort him through her, for she reassured him and lightened his burden and declared her trust in him and made it easy for him to bear the scorn of men."

Abu Talib gone, the Qureish attacked the Muslims so violently that Muhammad decided to try another city, and went to Ta'if seventy miles from Mecca. With eloquence and spiritual fervor he proclaimed his message to the people of Ta'if and denonced idol worship. At first he was merely ridiculed. On the tenth day of his teaching a mob drove him out of the city and far into the desert, pelting him with stones until evening.

Weary and bleeding, Muhammad sat down under a tree at the foot of a hill. Some kindly people gave him grapes to eat; he was revived, and made anew his prayer that God would dispel the darkness and lead him to victory and peace. He remembered how the prophets before him were laughed to scorn, and what they suffered. Had not Noah prayed, "O my Lord, verily I have cried to my people night and day; and my cry only makes them flee from me the more. And verily, so oft as I cry to them, that Thou mayest forgive them, they thrust their fingers into their ears and wrap themselves in their garments, and persist [in their error], and are disdainfully disdainful." Comforted by this thought, Muhammad returned to Mecca.

It was about this time that he took "the night journey to heaven." when, asleep, he flew on the wings of the spirit to Jerusalem and from there ascended to heaven where he met the prophets of the past.

Howbeit, Muhammad now announced to his followers that they

should pray five times every day, the first prayer to be before sunrise, the second at noon, the third in the middle of the afternoon. Again, in the hush of the approaching eventide when the sun was setting and the stars were making ready to shine from the vault of heaven they should pray. Once more, before the Muslim went to bed, he should remember God. Prayer, said Muhammad, must not be mere words, for "the Lord doth not regard a prayer in which the heart doth not accompany the body. Everyone is divinely furthered in accordance with his character. Adore God as you would if you saw him; for, if you see him not, he seeth you."

In 620, a year after Muhammad's return from Ta'if, among the visitors to Mecca during the annual pilgrimage were seven men from Medina two hundred and fifty miles to the north. Muhammad approached these men and asked them to sit down and talk with him. When they willingly did this, he told them that he had glad tidings for them, for God had sent them a Prophet with a message from high Heaven. And he recited thrilling verses from the Quran.

The men of Medina were not the guardians of any sacred shrine; neither were they the pillars of any old religious order; nor had they other business interests to be interfered with by a new religion. Moreover, they were in dire need of help, for Medina was rent with tribal feuds. Furthermore, they were expecting a Prophet, for in Medina were Jews who continually said, "Soon a Prophet will arise. His time is at hand." When these men saw Muhammad's face bright as though the sun were shining through it, they said to one another, "Surely this is the Prophet of whom the Jews have warned us: come let us now make haste and be the first to join him." Perchance he could persuade the people of Medina to curb their violent passions, and could teach them to live together in peace.

They decided to become Muhammad's followers. "Our countrymen," they told him, "have long been engaged in a most bitter and deadly feud with one another; but now perhaps God will unite them together through thee and thy teaching. Therefore we will preach to them and make known to them this religion, that we have received from thee." They would return to Mecca, they said, at the time of the next pilgrimage.

The following year twelve men came from Medina and met Muhammad at Aqaba, a hill outside Mecca, the place agreed upon by the seven the year before, At this meeting the twelve took "the first pledge of Aqaba." "We will not worship any but the one God; we will not steal, neither will we commit adultery nor kill our children; we will abstain from calumny and slander; we will obey the Prophet in every thing that is right," they solemnly vowed.

On the next pilgrimage to Mecca seventy-three men and two women from Medina met Muhammad in the same place as the previous year, at the foot of the hill Aqaba, outside the city, coming by twos and threes in the dead of night for fear of the Qureish. One by one they swore their allegiance to Muhammad as their Prophet, and told him they were commissioned to invite him to make his home in Medina.

When the Meccans learned of Muhammad's secret understanding with the men of Medina they increased their persecution. To prevent a general massacre of his followers, Muhammad counseled them to leave Mecca by twos and threes, to go to Medina and wait for him. Silently the Muslims slipped away until the Qureish found a part of their city empty.

In their rage they determined to kill Muhammad, and forty men vowed to do the deed. On a dark night Muhammad, at the urgent request of the heroic young Ali, left Ali in his bed to cover his escape and fled from Mecca with Abu Bakr to a nearby mountain where they hid in a cave.

The Meccans at once offered a reward for his capture and started to scour the country for him. In their search they came close to the cave where Muhammad and Abu Bakr were hiding. Said Abu Bakr, trembling, "There are only two of us." Muhammad answered, "Oh no, there are three of us; God is with us." The Meccans thought no one could have been in that lonely place for some time, and they ran on. For three days the refugees hid in the cave and a freed slave of Abu Bakr brought his goat each day and milked her and gave them food.

When the searching parties returned to Mecca, Abu Bakr's slave brought swift camels, and Muhammad and Abu Bakr raced across the desert to Medina.

Each morning during this time of anxiety all the Muslims in

Medina went outside the city and, climbing a ridge of rock from which they could see far over the desert, watched for Muhammad. When he arrived, the news spread like wildfire and a triumphal procession followed him into the city.

Ali was imprisoned by the Qureish and was beaten and abused. After several days he escaped into the desert and, hiding in caves during the day, he tramped on foot by night and made his way over the two hundred and fifty miles to Medina.

# 20

*Arabia Awakes*

FOR MANY YEARS the Arabs of Medina had obeyed no common ruler. Their intertribal language was war; their feuds, it seemed, could never end. They now invited Muhammad to be their ruler and bring peace among them—a task to appall the bravest heart.

Muhammad first cared for the refugees from Mecca, suggesting that each Muslim household in Medina receive one. "You are brothers, fraternize in the name of God," he told his followers. When all the Meccans were housed, no Muslim family was left to care for Ali, and Muhammad took him into his own home.

Muhammad next drew up a constitution for his government, stating the rights and duties of Muslim and non-Muslim. He guaranteed religious freedom to the Jews who lived in and about Medina, promising them protection from their enemies if they in return would defend the new city-state in case of attach. Every one who accepted this constitution agreed to bring his disputes to Muhammad for settlement.

He now set the Muslims to work to build a temple of prayer. Two young people, orphans, gave the land for this first mosque. When Abu Bakr learned that these devoted new believers had given their entire property, he paid them ten dinars for the land. Muhammad laid the first stone for the mosque and smilingly said, "Put one next to mine." Each Muslim brought stones and bricks, and, cementing them with mud, built the temple's walls. Though his followers insisted that he should not do manual labor, Muhammad himself built a considerable part of the walls. The building was also the courthouse and the capital of the new government.

The same month that the mosque was finished another important event occurred: the marriage of Muhammad's lovely daughter, Fatima. Abu Bakr and Umar had sought her hand but
Muhammad refused them, saying Fatima was too young to marry.
One day, as Ali was drawing water from a well, Abu Bakr and
another Muslim asked him why did not *he* marry Fatima. Ali
replied that he was poor and did not have the means to marry. If
that was his reason, they would help him, said the two friends.

Ali, the beloved of Muhammad, went to the Prophet's humble
thatch-roofed dwelling beside the mosque and knocked on the
door.

"Here stands a man more dear to me than any other," said
Muhammad encouragingly when he opened the door. "Speak," he
added, when Ali stood silent.

Ali asked that he might marry Fatima.

"What dowry bringest thou?" inquired Muhammad.

"Thou knowest my poverty. I bring thee all I possess; my sword,
armor and sandals," answered Ali.

His sword, Muhammad told him, belonged to his religion. He
might, if he chose, sell his armor. Ali went off to make the sale.

The friend who was with Abu Bakr bought the armor, setting his
own generous price. Ali returned to Muhammad with the money.

Muhammad divided it into two portions: with one he bought
Fatima's housekeeping equipment—a cup, two water pots, one
leather bag, one sheet, one large pillow and four small ones, two
quilts, a millstone for grinding flour, an a pan for baking bread.
With the other half he purchased some flower and butter, also
dates, for the simple wedding feast. The friend who bought Ali's
armor gave it to him as a wedding present.

Muhammad announced the marriage to an assemblage of the
people. To Ali he said, "Verily, God gave thee my daughter in
heaven before I gave her to thee in this world."

Ali and his bride spent the first three days and nights after their
marriage in solitary prayer. Their first son was Hasan; a year later
the second son, Husain was born. These two brothers were immortal figures in Islam's history.

The Qureish, after Muhammad escaped them, raided the districts around Medina, destroyed the fruit trees, and carried off the people's cattle and other property. When this pillage had gone on for some time, word came to Medina that a caravan belonging to a rich Meccan was journeying from Syria through the desert to Mecca. Some Muslims plotted to attack and plunder this caravan to reimburse themselves for the property stolen from them. The Meccans learned of the plan and sent a thousand men into the desert to protect the caravan, not knowing that the caravan, fore-warned, had taken a route far from Medina. The Meccan soldiers waited in the desert for the Muslims. When for some reason they did not appear, the Meccans, unwilling to go home, marched against Medina.

Muhammad must fight, or let his followers be killed and the new state, the hope of Arabia, be destroyed. If he chose the latter alternative Arabia was doomed. If for God and the truth he fought, a bright future was ahead. He raised an army of three hundred and thirteen men and went to meet the Meccans in the Muslims' first battle.

In the valley of Badr between steep hills both parties camped for the night. Before dawn Muhammad drew up his soldiers, straight-ened their lines with an arrow. He pricked a soldier who was out of line, and the man cried, "Thou art hurting me, O Messenger of God!"

"Take thou retaliation," said Muhammad, baring his chest. The Muslim embraced and kissed him.

"What made thee do this?" asked Muhammad.

"O Messenger of God, thou seest what is before us, and if this is my last time with thee I wished that I might touch thee," said the soldier.

At daybreak the Meccans came running from their hiding places in the hills. Seeing they were so many, and his men were so few, Muhammad prayed, "O Lord, I beseech Thee, forget not Thy promise of assistance and of victory. O Lord, if this little band be vanquished, idolatry will prevail and the pure worship of Thee will cease from off the earth."

In those days single combat was usually the prelude to the battle. The Meccan army, then, halted before the Muslims and sent forward a herald, after whom came three challengers, one on a red camel.

"O Muhammad, sent forth against us our peers of our own tribe," shouted the herald.

"Arise, O Ubaida son of Harith, and arise, O Hamza, and arise, O Ali," called Muhammad.

"Ay, these are noble and our peers," the Qureish shouted back when they saw whom Muhammad sent against them.

Ali and Hamza quickly slew their opponents, and turned to aid Ubaida, who was making an end of the third Meccan. The general battle was now on—three hundred and thirteen Muslims against almost a thousand Meccans. The weather helped the Muslims, for it had rained heavily for two hours on the Meccans' side of the valley, making the ground soft beneath their feet. When the rain storm passed, the sun shone dazzlingly in the Meccans' eyes, and a high wind swept the battlefield. Also, the Meccans thought the Muslims were twice their real number.

The Muslims, believing they were fighting for God whose Prophet was with them, were quickened to almost superhuman heroism. They drove the Qureish back, killing forty-nine and taking almost as many prisoner; and they captured a hundred and fifteen camels and fourteen horses. Only fourteen Muslims were killed. In his Quran, Muhammad explained this amazing victory, saying that the angels helped his followers.

Muhammad commanded the Muslims to protect their prisoners from harm and treat them with lovingkindness. The sword, he said, should be used only in self-defense, as a last recourse. This was unwelcome news to Umar who wanted to put the prisoners to death at once. The chieftain Saad bin Muaz showed his disapproval so plainly that Muhammad said to him, "O Saad, methinks thou mislikest what the folk are doing."

"Yes, O Messenger of Allah. 'Tis the first defeat that Allah hath let fall upon the infidels, and I would liefer see them slaughtered than left alive," grumbled Saad.

Muhammad's strong will prevailed. The victorious soldiers took the prisoners to their homes, gave them the best of their food and treated them as honored guests, excepting two inveterate enemies, who were put to death. Some of the prisoners, arguing that God must be back of people who were so merciful, became Muslims. Said one of them, "Blessings be on the men of Medina, they made us ride, while they themselves walked; they gave us wheaten bread to eat, when there was little of it, contenting themselves with dates."

The Jews in Medina agreed at first to accept Muhammad's charter and obey his government, for he praised the Hebrews' religion and instructed heathen Arabia to believe in Abraham and Moses and the prophets of Israel. The friendly attitude changed when Muhammad added Jesus' name to the Hebrew prophets. Many Jews now broke their compact and became determined enemies, incessantly intriguing against Muhammad. One Jew, Kaab son of Ashraf, went to Mecca after the Battle of Badr and plotted with the Qureish to betray Medina into their hands.

By no means subdued by their defeat in the valley of Badr, the Qureish continued their raids on the Muslims and persuaded other tribes to join them. Reinforced by these marauders and the seditious Jews, the Meccans sent three thousand soldiers, seven hundred of them in armor, across the desert to the hill of Uhud near Medina. Here they camped, and pillaged and ruined the fields and orchards that furnished food for the Muslims.

With an army of seven hundred men and two horses, Muhammad at last went out against them. He camped his men for the night in a mountain defile, and the next morning brought them into the valley under the hill of Uhud. The Meccans came down from the hill to battle, marching to the plain with their idols in their midst, and the wives of their chieftains dancing beside them, singing war songs and beating on timbrels.

In the first hours of fighting the Muslims were victorious and forced the Meccans to retreat. Thinking the battle won, a selection of Muhammad's army disobeyed his command not to dispoil the conquered, and rushed forward to plunder. The Meccans rallied, surrounded them, killed many, and attacking their main army drove the Muslims back, into Medina. The valiant warrior Hamza was killed; Ali, Umar, and Abu Bakr were severely wounded. Muhammad barely escaped death.

In savage glee over their victory, the Qureish went up and down the disolate valley mutilating the bodies of the Muslims. The women tore out Hamza's heart, and made themselves bracelets and necklaces of the ears and noses of their slain enemies. It was at this time that Muhammad gave the stern command that never should his followers mutilate the bodies of the slain.

Across the desert the Meccans came again, ten thousand men this time, and the Banu Qurayzah, a Jewish tribe who had taken the oath of allegiance to Muhammad's government, joined them and tried to open the gates of Medina to them. The army in Medina numbered three thousand soldiers. Muhammad now used the Persians' stratagem, and in six days his men dug a deep trench in front of the unprotected part of the city. Leaving the women and children in Medina, Muhammad stationed his army outside the city behind the trench.

The Meccans had never before seen a trench and could think of no way to get past it. In their perplexity they did nothing. After waiting twenty days for a decisive battle, the tribes who were fighting with the Qureish became discontented and mutinous: their provisions were giving out, their horses were dying, and the heat was intolerable. One night a wind tore in from the desert. It overturned the Meccans' tents, putting out their lights, and away the Meccans ran in panic.

This Battle of the Trench, as it was called, made it clear that the new government could have no security if the Jews of the Medina district plotted against the state they had joined; and Muhammad punished the rebels, tribe by tribe. Some of them now formed a coalition, with Khaibar a hundred miles from Medina for their center and the storage place of their wealth. Khaibar was a group of townships in fertile valleys protected by six fortified castles. Muhammad decided to break up this stronghold of the traitors, and with sixteen hundred soldiers he made a four-day march across the desert and besieged Khaibar.

One fortress was built in an almost impregnable cliff. Abu Bakr led an attack against this castle and failed. Umar tried, without success, to break through the outer walls. The evening of his defeat Muhammad said to the army, "On the next morning I will give the standard to one who will surely reduce the fortress—the man who loves God and his Prophet and is loved by them." That night many a soldier lay awake wondering whether or not he would be Muhammad's choice.

When morning came Muhammad called Ali and told him to go, accomplish the impossible and break the enemy's resistence. Ali went forward, the castle gates opened, and from them came a warrior, the pride of Khaibar, to fight him—a giant whose strength, some records say, was that of a thousand men. The two armies, ready for battle, watched. Single-handed, Ali fought the giant. When Ali won, the Jews fell upon him in fury. The Muslims rushed to his aid, and conquered Khaibar.

For seven years the Qureish harried the new Arabian state. They signed a solemn treaty of peace with Muhammad, and broke it; they intrigued against him; they aided another tribe in an attack on one of his allied tribes. Arabia could have no peace until the Meccans kept their treaties. With an army of ten thousand soldiers Muhammad went across the desert to Mecca.

He camped on the hills outside the city and directed that many fires be lighted on the hilltops. When thousands of fires blazed up, the Meccans thought the army from Medina must number at least a hundred thousand men. Abu Sufyan, a Qureish chieftain and Islam's bitter enemy, went one night to scout the Muslims' camp and learn the army's strength. He was captured by Muhammad's uncle, Abbas, who told him to behold the innumerable fires which bespoke the vast size and strength of the Muslim army; then he took him to Muhammad. Umar was in Muhammad's tent, and when he saw Abu Sufyan he drew his sword to dispatch him. Abbas protested that he had promised the prisoner protection. Muhammad upheld Abbas, and ordered that Abu Sufyan be guarded through the night. The next morning Abu Sufyan declared himself a Muslim, so impressed was he with what he had seen of Muhammad and his soldiers.

Muhammad bade him go to Mecca and tell the people of three ways by which they could save themselves: they could stay in the Ka'aba, in Abu Sufyan's home, or in their own homes, with all doors closed. If they did this no Muslim would harm them. Abu Sufyan returned to Mecca and went through the streets shouting in a powerful voice the three means of safety offered to the Meccans, and practically every one fled to shelter.

Muhammad warned his soldiers many times that they must not harm any property, especially the date orchards, and they must not molest the women or the children. Then he led his army up to Mecca. The city had four gates and the Muslims divided into four groups, one to each gate. Three divisions obeyed Muhammad and entered the city quietly. The fourth group, commanded by a fiery warrior, killed some twenty-eight people before Muhammad could stop them, and one excited officer began a song of triumph but was immediately deposed by Muhammad.

After the conquest of Mecca, deputations from all Arabia hastened to Medina to visit Muhammad and join his state. Soon, by acclamation the Arabs elected him their king. They respected a man of action, who got results, and when Muhammad declared he was victorious because God assisted him, they decided his God must be worthwhile. In the primitive little mosque built by the first Muslims, Muhammad received these envoys; and sent them back to their tribes to destroy their idols and proclaim One God.

Now, Muhammad's word was law, his power was absolute; he could if he chose become rich and worldly. The people of Medina, who watched every incident of his daily life, testified that Muhammad gave away almost everything he received, and lived with rigorous self-denial. They told how his one coat became so threadbare that Ali bought him a new one, for twelve dirhems. A dirhem was then worth about twenty cents. Muhammad thought the coat too expensive for him and went to exchange it for a plain one. On the way to the merchant's shop he met a little girl who was crying bitterly. He inquired her trouble and she told him that she had been sent by her mother to make a purchase, and had lost her money. Muhammad gave her four dirhems and went on. He made the exchange, and wearing his new cheap coat, started for home. He saw a naked man and gave his coat to him. Again he met the little girl. He asked her why she did not go home. She said she had been away for so long she was afraid to go back. The Prophet went home with her and asked her family not to punish her. His townsmen told how "he visited the sick, followed any bier he met, accepted the invitation of a slave to dinner, mended his own clothing, milked his goats, and waited upon himself." The stories of his mercy to prisoners taken in war, to recalcitrant Muslims, and to slaves fill the early records of Islam. His followers were often harsh and overbearing; not so Muhammad. A Muslim cried in wrath, "O Messenger of God, curse the infidels!" Muhammad answered, "I was not sent for this; nor was I sent but as a mercy to mankind." He instructed a Muslim who was about to leave for Yemen on a state commission, "The nearest to me are the abstemious, whoever they be, wherever they be."

His companions described the majesty of his bearing, how he walked quickly and with power like one "who steps from a high to a low place." His followers were so impatient to be with him that they would go every day to the door of his house and stand and shout his name; until Muhammad suggested that they shout not so loud, or better, since he was their Prophet and king, they wait until he came to them. Gibbon quotes a deputy from Mecca who told of his visit to Muhammad in Medina, and how, if a hair fell from Muhammad's head, his followers picked it up and treasured it. "I have seen," said the Meccan, "the Chosroes of Persia and the Caesar of Rome, but never did I behold a king among his subjects like Muhammad among his companions."

His task as Prophet was much of the time difficult and thankless, for the tribes whom he instructed had no desire to change their ways. He had to persuade lawless men to accept God with his exalted ethical requirements, and forgo their idols, who had no inexorable standards. He had to persuade his followers to pray to an unseen Presence five times every day and believe that the Presence heard and would answer them. He must win the Muslims to give a generous percentage of their income to charity. He was dealing with men who had never known obedience to a central authority for the sake of the commonweal; who had never heard of a standard of morality which outlawed fighting and robbery and considered plotting against the government treason and sedition. Some of the Ten Commandments were within their comprehension; others, like the one against covetousness, were much too subtle for them.

Muhammad was a realist who understood just how rapidly he could change human nature; so he hedged his fundamental laws around with many lesser laws of justice and kindness, hygiene and self-control; and little by little educated his followers. To train them out of their drinking, he told them first, there was evil as well as good in drink. Soon he ruled that no Muslim could come to the mosque when intoxicated, for in that state he could not understand the prayers. Finally, he proclaimed that in Islam drinking liquor was forbidden. He decreed that one month of the year should be set apart when all Islam fasted from sunrise to sunset, each day, this to be a time of self-discipline and prayer. He told his followers, "God is gentle and loveth gentleness," and he gave the command that no Muslim should beat his wife. Umar complained at this, saying now that wives had heard this new injunction they had got the better of their husbands. Although the Arab tribesmen had as many wives as they could house and keep their enemies from stealing, Muhammad wrote in his Quran that a man could have four wives—if he could treat them all with perfect justice. This reform was so drastic it must be introduced gradually. In fact Muhammad the ruler was caught in the system which Muhammad the prophet was trying to change. For twenty-five years Muhammad the inconspicuous Arab had one wife, Khadeeja. After her death, when he was king of Arabia and am middle-aged man, he married other women, for the obligations of the king were very different from those of the camel driver. It was the universal custom for rulers to form political alliances by marriage. Also, in lawless and warring times, when women had no career but marriage, polygamy was often a social necessity, for the woman whose husbands and fathers were killed in war would starve unless taken into the homes of the surviving men.

Muhammad's first wife after Khadeeja was a destitute widow whose Muslim husband had died in exile. At the urgent request of Abu Bakr, Muhammad then married Ayesha, Abu Bakr's daughter. Abu Bakr had served Islam so long and devotedly that Muhammad could not refuse his request. Umar also had a daughter, Hafsa. Her husband had died, and she wanted to marry again; but she was so notoriously bad tempered no one would have her. The Muslims avoided her; Abu Bakr and Uthman, one of Muhammad's principal followers, declined when Umar asked one after the other to take his daughter. Umar then went into a terrible rage at

what he regarded as an insult to himself, and an uprising among
the Muslims was imminent. Muhammad married Hafsa and preserved the peace. The beautiful Zainab was married to a freed
slave. She considered her husband beneath her socially, and was
so overbearing toward him that he could not stand her. He di-
vorced her, then went to Muhammad and asked him to marry his
too-well-born wife and give her a home. A tribal chieftain rose
against Muhammad. When Muhammad conquered him, he married the chieftain's daughter, and in this way won the friendship
of the whole tribe, for by this marriage he became their relative.
To conciliate the conquered rebels of Khaibar he married the
widow of one of their chieftains. To prove to the Qureish that he
was their friend he married the daughter of their chieftain, Abu
Sufyan, Muhammad married three middle-aged widows whose
husbands were killed fighting for Islam. Because these women
were Muslims, their relatives, Muhammad's enemies, left them to
starve. He married a poor relative, a woman over fifty who had no
home, and won the allegiance of two influential men, his uncle,
Abbas, and Khalid, one of Islam's foremost warriors. The Christian governor of Egypt who held his office under the Roman emperor sent Muhammad a young slave girl. If Muhammad had
refused to marry her it would have been a deadly insult to Egypt.
In all, after Khadeeja's death, he married eleven women. The
Christian wife from Egypt was the only one of them by whom he
had a child.

It was of utmost importance that the tribes be brought into
friendly relations and Muhammad's followers know each other.
Therefore Muhammad continued the custom of the yearly pilgrimage to Mecca. Mecca, the first home of the King and Prophet,
the scene of his persecutions and his spiritual victories, became the
holy city of the new religion. The idols had been destroyed; climbing Mount Arafat was now but a symbol of the way in which in
sincere prayer man ascended to heights where he attained clearer
spiritual illumination. Nothing remained of the old order but the
Ka'aba and the curious Black Stone, the meteorite.

In February, 632, ten years after the Hegira (Mohammad's flight from Mecca to Medina which marks the year 1 in the Muslim calendar), Muslims from all Arabia made a pilgrimage to Mecca and Mount Arafat. And one evening, as the sun went down behind the desert and indigo shadows crept into the valley, Muhammad climbed to the mountain's summit and talked to the multitude, ninety thousand, it is said, who stood below him. The Prophet paused after each sentence while a man standing near him repeated his words in a resonant voice. The sentence was taken up by man after man, down the mountain's slope, until every one heard it.

"Ye people!" said Muhammad, "listen to my words, for I know not whether another year will be vouchsafed to me after this year to find myself with you. Your lives and property are sacred and inviolable among you, until ye appear before the Lord, as this day and this month are sacred for all; and remember ye shall have to appear before your Lord, who shall demand from you an account of all your actions. Ye people, ye have rights over your wives, and your wives have rights over you. . . . treat your wives with kindness . . . verily ye have taken them on the security of God, and made them lawful unto you by the words of God. And your slaves. See that ye feed them with such food as ye eat yourselves, and clothe them with the stuff ye wear; and if they commit a fault which ye are not inclined to forgive, then part from them for they are the servants of the Lord, and are not to be harshly treated."

"*Talbiyal,*" said Muhammad, his face shining with an inner light. And the pilgrims chanted in chorus, "I stand up for thy service, O God! There is no partner with Thee! Verily Thine is the praise and the blessing and the Kingdom."

The pilgrimage to Mecca grew in later years into an annual visit of from a hundred and fifty to two hundred thousand pilgrims, from many parts of the world:

*Arabs, with eyes of eagles, their complexion of a reddish bronze,*
*Hindus, with faces clear cut and olive tinted,*
*Berbers, fairhaired and rosy cheeked, their eyes blue,*
*Somalis and Soudanese, their black skins shining in the sun,*
*Refined Persians, bold Turcomans, yellow Chinese,*
*All worshipping together on the Mount.*

Muhammad was sixty-three when the great pilgrimage occurred. He celebrated his birthday by freeing sixty-three slaves.
When the time of the pilgrimage was over he returned to Medina.
The next June (A.D. 632) he became very ill, and in a few days his
life in this world ended.

# 21

## The Arabs Acquire an Empire

MUHAMMAD HAD just passed away. His followers were standing around his body. Some thought that a Prophet should live forever. Or, if he left this world he should at least ascend to heaven in his physical body. If Muhammad died, then he was not a Prophet. In the suspense, tense and ominous, Umar drew is sword and shouted fiercely, "The disaffected think that the Apostle of God is dead. By God, he is not dead; but like Christ he has ascended to heaven, and will return soon. If anyone ever say, the Prophet is dead, I will behead him."

Abu Bakr came forward, and asked Umar to sit down. Then Abu Bakr said to the people, "Whoso worshipeth Muhammad let him know Muhammad is dead, but whoso worshipeth God let him know that God liveth and dieth not."

Soon came the question of Muhammad's successor. He had named no one, specifically. He had said, "I am the city of knowledge and Ali is the gate thereof." He also said, shortly before his death, "Verily, I leave two treasures among you, the Book of God, and my family." The head of his family was Ali. Some say he named Abu Bakr as his successor when, during his last illness, he asked Abu Bakr to lead the prayers in the public service. But Muhammad had said previously that anyone could lead the prayers, even a slave or a callow youth.

The men of Medina met to take action. All true Muslims, they argued, obeyed Muhammad, for they believed him to be a Prophet of God. To obey a man from Mecca, one of the Qureish perhaps, would be a different matter. They, the men of Medina, were the ones to choose the Prophet's successor, from among themselves. They had protected the Meccan refugees when their lives were in danger: why should they now let those refugees lord it over them? Dangerous tumult was stirring. Civil war was imminent.

Abu Bakr and Umar were in the mosque preparing Muhammad's body for burial when word was brought them of the threatening uprising. They hurried to the meeting place of the Medina men, and found only a few still there. Umar, much excited, wished to be spokesman, but Abu Bakr checked him. Poised and conciliatory, Abu Bakr said to the men: "We know what you have done to spread our religion and proclaim its laws. The Meccans, however, are the first believers. They are the ones who endured inhuman persecution until Muhammad bade them flee from their homes and city. They are members of Muhammad's own tribe. The succession should go to them."

"Let there be one chief from you and one from us," shouted the men of Medina.

"Away with you," cried Umar. "Two cannot stand together."

The situation was desperate. The tribes might rise; the old feuds break out.

Abu Bakr suggested that the men present choose either Umar or Abu Ubayda, an early Muslim of Mecca, to be khalifa. Both at once declined to serve, and voted for Abu Bakr. The men one by one then stepped forward and, following the ancient Arab custom, grasped Abu Bakr's hand and swore allegiance to him as their khalifa. It was not much of an election; just the old pagan way of choosing the successor to the departed chieftain. But the dispute must not be allowed to spread.

The next day the Muslims gathered to mourn Mohammad's passing. Abu Bakr addressed them: "O my people, now I am chief over you, although I am not the best among you. If I do well, support me, and if I incline to evil, direct me aright. Obey me wherein I obey the Lord and his Prophet; when I disobey, then obedience to me shall not be obligatory upon you."

Many tribes throughout Arabia immediately seceded from the Muslim kingdom. They sent word to Abu Bakr that they did not like the five prayers every day. Their conversion to Islam was evidently a political expedient, which left their characters unchanged; and they reverted to their idolatry and primitive practices. Umar advised Abu Bakr to compromise with them. Abu Bakr replied firmly that he could not change the religion god had revealed. He sent eleven swiftly moving armies against the rebellious tribes, suppressed their uprisings, and compelled them to remain in the Muslim state.

What were the Arabs to do now? Fighting had been their occupation from time immemorial. If they were united they could not fight each other. Abu Bakr sent them off to fight the neighboring countries. And Islam entered upon its era of conquest.

This unfortunate policy was possible because of a widespread misunderstanding of what Muhammad meant when he admonished his followers to fight in the path of God. As Muhammad's service to his countrymen was twofold, since he was their Prophet, and at their request their king, there were for him two kinds of "holy war."

He told his followers they must "fight strenuously in God's cause with your property and your persons" and he promised paradise and its "mighty bliss" to those who so fought. At the same time he told them they must win the same victory Christ and his apostles had won. The spiritually minded understood that he meant the conquest of ignorance, the spread of God's religion, the conquest of self; for this was the warfare of Christ.

Muhammad had declared that his followers must abolish "oppression and civil discord"; for as their king his objective must be to form one law-abiding state. When new tribes voluntarily joined his kingdom, especially those tribes living in the north and the east of Arabia where they were menaced by the Romans and Persians, Muhammad as King must protect them from invasion. He must insist that enemy nations recognize the independence of Arabia.

Muhammad's "holy war" was, first, a campaign of moral and spiritual education; and second, warfare in defense of united Arabia. The large majority of the Muslims, however, wanted to obey him in their own way. When he was no longer among them to restrain them by the strength of his remarkable personality they refused to stay within the bounds he set for them, finding it much easier to conquer their enemies with swords and javelins than to teach them or to discipline themselves.

Summoning the tribes to action under the banner of Islam, and holding before them as best he could Muhammad's central teachings, Abu Bakr pacified the fiery Bedouin. And the united tribes made incomparable warriors. They had absorbed just enough of Muhammad's religion to become energized with high-powered efficiency. To them Islam meant that they were fighting in the path of God; and if they really believed this they would be invincible. If they won their battles they would become rich in spoils. If they were killed they would enter immediately into the joys of paradise. Stirred by the hope of spoils and captive women, and with no thought of failure, the Arab hordes rushed north to conquer the Persians and Romans and take their fields and palaces and lovely gardens. Some of the Christian tribes along the way became Muslims out of sheer amazement at the Arabs' daring. During Abu Bakr's khilafat of little more than two years his armies launched a simultaneous invasion of the Persian empire and Roman Syria. Persia at this time held Mesopotamia, Iraq, and northeastern Arabia; the Romans ruled Palestine, Syria, Asia Minor, and the Eastern Empire west of Constantinople. Any nation but the Arabs would have been satisfied to attack these mighty empires one at a time.

The Roman emperor Heraclius sent an army to Syria to crush the Arabs. The Muslim armies east of the Jordan River drew into a unit and watched as the Romans marched into a wide plain protected by the steep banks of the Yarmuk River and other mountainous borders. This was an ideal place for an army to camp; but it could be entered and left only through a narrow ravine. The Muslim generals saw the trap, quickly brought their army to the mouth of the ravine, and settled down to wait for the Romans to come out.

On August 20, 636, the Roman army came through the pass to battle—one hundred thousand Romans to fight forty thousand Arabs. The morale of the two armies was as different as their numbers. The Arabs believed they were fighting for their faith and for their Prophet, who only four years before was with them. The Christian soldiers cared not at all for the rulers who sent them to the battlefield, nor for the form of Christianity then current at Constantinople, for the Roman-Christian world was now rent with sectarian strife so bitter that the leaders of the differing factions put to death with the most ingenious torture those who disagreed with them on metaphysical or sectarian matters.

When the Roman army was drawn up for battle, hundreds of Christian bishops and monks went up and down the lines pleading with the men to fight, and bravely. The Muslims won, with three thousand of their number slain. In the midst of the battle a Roman general, through fear perhaps, or was it admiration for the Muslims, went to Khalid and accepted Islam.

Soon Antioch fell, and the Arabs entered Palestine with its fields of wheat and barley, its running brooks, its groves of olive, oak and sycamore trees, its hills carpeted with flowers, the beautiful Lake of Galilee, and the snow-capped Lebanon Mountains in the distance. Palestine was populous and flourishing and its fine Roman cities were filled with churches and forums and theaters. Some cities surrendered to the Muslims before even they were attacked. When in 638 Jerusalem surrendered, the Patriarch asked that Khalifa Umar, who had succeeded Abu Bakr, come in person and sign the peace terms.

On receiving this request Umar started across the desert, with one attendant, and arrived in Palestine dressed in his patched robe. When he met Khalid and the other Muslims arrayed in the gorgeous apparel they had taken as loot, Umar got down from his horse and threw stones at them. His followers asked why did not he, the Khalifa, wear better clothes? He replied that his faith in Islam was his dress.

This is the peace treaty Umar made with the Patriarch of Jerusalem, recorded by the Muslim historian, Tabari:

In the name of God, the Merciful, the Compassionate. This is the security which Umar, the servant of God, the commander of the faithful, grants to the people of AElia. He grants to all, whether sick or sound, security for their lives, their possessions, their churches and their crosses, and for all that concerns their religion. Their churches shall not be changed into dwelling places, nor destroyed, neither shall they nor their appurtenances be in any way diminished, nor the crosses of the inhabitants nor aught of their possessions, nor shall any constraint be put upon them in the matter of their faith, nor shall any one of them be harmed.

If a Muslim married a Christian, the husband should not prevent his wife from going to her own church. If the Christians built a church, the Muslims should help them.

The Roman-Christian emperors, Palestine's previous rulers, were arrogant, unjust, cruel, and under them the people were mercilessly oppressed. Most of the Muslim governors appointed by Umar were moderate and just and many worthy Christians held office under them. The Christian inhabitants of the district about Fihl wrote to General Abu Ubayda, there encamped, "O Muslims, we prefer you to the Byzantines, though they are of our own faith, because you keep better faith with us and are more merciful to us and refrain from doing us injustice and your rule over us is better than theirs, for they have robbed us of our goods and our homes."

Comparing the deeds of the Christian emperors with those of the Muslim rulers, many Christians decided that the Muslims were nearer to God than the Christians; and they gave up the complicated creeds and dogmas of Christendom for the simple ethical and spiritual message of Muhammad, brought to them by the Muslim teachers who followed in the wake of the Muslim armies.

Umar's army led by General Amr marched west into Egypt and captured the magnificent city Alexandria, a cultural and religious center of the Greco-Roman world, the home of Origen and Clement and many Greek philosophers and Christian saints.

The Muslim conquerors reported that the city contained four thousand palaces, four thousand baths, four hundred theaters and places of amusement. Umar thanked God for such a conquest, and bade the victorious general, Amr, not to pillage the city.

Alexandria's famous library of more than five hundred thousand volumes had been destroyed by the Romans and by the Christians long before the Muslims entered the city. When Julius Caesar in 48 B.C. set fire to his fleet in the harbor of Alexandria, the great building that held most of the city's library accidently caught fire, and the books burned with the building. More books were gradually accumulated through the years, and another great library arose. Theodosius, the Christian emperor of the West and the East in the latter part of the fourth century, ordered that all pagan monuments in the empire be demolished. The Christians, eagerly obeying him, about A.D. 389 razed the beautiful Greek temple which held Alexandria's second library and destroyed the books.

Six hundred years after the Muslim invasion of Egypt, a Christian living near the border of northwestern Persia wrote that Umar ordered the destruction of this great library and for six months the Muslims used the books as fuel for the furnaces of the city's baths. This story was apparently, told for the first time in the thirteenth century. No contemporary of the Muslim conquest of Alexandria, Christian or Muslim, told it. It is discredited by Gibbon and many other careful historians and scholars, who say the famous library was not in existence when the Muslims entered the city.

While the Muslims were victorious in Syria, they at first were seriously defeated by the Persians. General Muthanna, in command of the compaign against Persia, thought the Muslims should take no further initiative but wait for the Persians to attack. Abu Ubaid, commander of the troops sent by Khalifa Umar to reinforce General Muthanna, became commander-in-chief and insisted on an immediate offensive. Abu Ubaid tried to get his army across the Euphrates River, and came upon the Persian army, near al-Hîra. In a battle fought on November 26, 635, called the Battle of the Bridge, Abu Ubaid was killed, and the Muslims were driven out of the Persian province.

Khalifa Umar faced a serious crisis: Could the Muslims conquer the Persians with their military experience of more than a thousand years? Umar made the chieftain Saad bin Muaz, now forty years old, commander-in-chief of the army in Iraq and sent him to conquer the Persian empire.

Saad's reinforcements swelled the Muslim army to thirty thousand men; the Persian army had a hundred thousand. Rustam, the Persian commander-in-chief also had forty elephants, the tanks of that day and the terror of the Muslims. Thus equipped, Rustam thought it unnecessary to attack and advised Yazdajird, the Persian king, to play safe and let the Arabs take the initiative. King Yazdajird insisted that Rustam attack; and in June 637 a terrible battle was fought in the valley of Kádisíya.

For three days the battle raged. One time the Persian cavalry in front of Rustam turned and fled and Rustam was almost taken prisoner. The Arabs shouted the names of their clans as they fought, or repeated stirring poems or, with strange triumphant faith cried, *"Allah akbar!* God is great!"

Saad, in his camp, lay down to rest. Before he went to sleep he said to a companion, "If they go on shouting, do not wake me, for in that case they are superior to their enemy; and if they cease shouting and the Persians also keep quiet, do not wake me, for then they are equally matched; but wake me if you hear the Persians shouting, for that will be a bad sign."

As the battle drew to a close the armies fought for twenty-four hours without food or sleep. The Muslim poet, Abu Mihjan, before the battle began was put in chains by Saad for writing a poem in praise of wine. Abu Mihjan pled that he be set free to fight, but Saad was stern and unyielding. On the last day of fighting, Abu Mihjan went to the commander's wife and asked her to take off his chains.

"How should I do such a thing?" said she.

Hobbling about in his chains, Abu Mihjan bewailed his fate,

*'Tis sorrow enough for me that here I am left in chains,*
*Fast-bound, while against the foe our horsemen the lancers hurl.*

Saad's wife unlocked his chains. The poet quickly found a horse, and galloping to the part of the battlefield where the fighting was fiercest, with lance and sword he charged the Persian army.

The Muslims knew that Abu Mihjan was in the castle in chains. The stranger on the piebald mare looked like Abu Mihjan, but could not be he. The soldiers thought, at first, he was a general with reinforcements to help them. Then they decided he might be Elijah, or an angel come to encourage them, and they rallied to superhuman effort.

At midnight, when the Persians stopped fighting and the Muslims slowly withdrew from the field, Abu Mihjan returned to the castle, went in by the gate whence he had gone out, laid aside his armor and unsaddled the mare. Then he put back his feet in the irons.

The Muslims won, with eighty-five hundred of their troops killed. The spoils were enormous—jewels and gold and precious stones. The Jewels and gold on General Rustam's body (he was killed) amounted to seventy thousand dirhems. When the spoils were divided, every Muslim soldier received six thousand dirhems.

This victory gave Iraq to the Muslims. When the Arabs entered Ctesiphon, Persia's capital city on the east bank of the Tigris, and beheld for the first time the Persian kings' magnificent palaces, they cried in wonder, "God is great!" In the palaces were gold and silver vessels and marvelous works of art. In one palace was a life-size camel made of silver and on the camel's back was a rider, in gold. The Arabs treated the works of art with respect, and did not harm them.

King Yazdajird raised another army, attacked the Muslims, and was terribly defeated. This time Umar made a treaty of peace with him and set the boundaries for the Muslim and Persian countries, giving the Muslims strict orders to keep on their side of the line. Umar, advised by Ali, set to work to develop and safeguard the land acquired. Irrigation canals were built and the farmers were given financial help from government funds. The taxes the Persian kings had extorted from the wealthy landowners were revised and moderated; and the sale of land was forbidden, lest the native peasants be driven from their homes.

The army clamored for more war spoils. Umar refused them, and sent trustworthy Muslims from Medina to manage and protect the rich lands and hunting forests which had belonged to the conquered king and his princes.

The Muslims strictly observed their treaty with King Yazdajird and kept within their boundaries. Yazdajird, his army, and his overlords, longing for their lost wealth, incessantly raided the districts apportioned to the Muslims who, because of the Khalifa's command, could not retaliate.

When the Arabs could stand this no longer they sent messengers to Umar asking permission to fight the Persian king.

Umar listened to the request and said, "Maybe the Muslims treat the non-Muslims badly, that they break their faith persistently and rebel against us."

"Not so," the men answered, "we do not deal with them otherwise than with honesty and good faith."

"How can that be?" said the Khalifa. "Is there not one honest man among them?"

Yazdajird sent out a call to the Persians to make a violent attack on the enemy. And Umar not only removed the ban from the Muslims but sent them reinforcements. A battle, called by the Muslims the Victory of Victories, was fought in 642. The Persians, outnumbering the Muslims six to one, were defeated. King Yazdajird escaped, and hid in one place after another until, several years later, he was murdered by one of his companions. Persia belonged to the Muslims.

In twenty years the Muslims conquered thirty-six thousand cities, towns, and castles. One may well ask how they maintained their hold on the conquered peoples. The Roman emperors held down their subjects with enormous legions of admirably trained soldiers who suppressed the endless uprisings. Islam had by comparison but a paltry handful of "wretchedly armed Arabs, fighting not in regularly organized military divisions, but by families and clans."

The explanation is first, that the Muslims governed justly and oppression was rare; and second, that the vast majority of the subject people became Muslims and voluntarily obeyed the kalifa as the representative of Muhammad. Before the conquest of Alexandria was completed, large numbers of the Christians of Egypt went over to Islam, for the Muslims were amazingly kind and just to them. Muhammad told his followers to be kind to "the people of the Book," all those whose religion was divinely revealed and written down in a book, and the Muslim rule in the early years was beneficent with few exceptions. The Muslims' subjects who remained Christians were allowed religious freedom, and on the payment of a small tax were protected by the army of their conquerors. In the reign of Khalifa Uthman, 644 to 656, the revenue in Egypt from this tax amounted to twelve million dirhems. From 661 to 679 this revenue fell to less than half that amount because great numbers of Christians became Muslims. The Christian world had by this time entered the dark years of theological strife and ascetic apathy—"sect opposed to sect, clergy wrangling with clergy upon the most abstruse and metaphysical points of doctrine. The Orthodox, the Nestorians, the Eutychians, the Jacobites were persecuting each other with unexhausted animosity," writes Dean Milan in his *Latin Christianity*. The Christian emperor Justinian, it is said, condemned to death as heretics two hundred thousand Copts, the Jacobite Christians of Egypt.

In Islam's first centuries the Christians of western Asia and northern Africa joined the new religion until two-thirds of their fairest provinces were Muslim.

# 22

## The Splendor of Saracen Civilization

IN THE QUREISH tribe were two powerful clans: the Hashim clan, to which Muhammad and his uncle, Abu Talib, belonged; and the Umayyads. The Umayyads were Muhammad's merciless enemies during the years that Islam was being born. When Muhammad was beloved and powerful, and it was clearly expedient, they espoused his religion. One Umayyad, Uthman, became a Muslim before the Hegira. Uthman in his young manhood was very attractive, with fair complexion, high forehead and bright eyes, his face slightly marked with smallpox. He was one of the first men of letters among the Muslims, and at times he was Muhammad's secretary. He was the first Muslim to learn the Quran by heart. He fled to Abyssinia to escape the Umayyads' persecution, and later returned to Medina. He became wealthy but lived simply and wore poor clothes, giving away most of his property, buying and freeing many slaves. The only well in Medina was owned by Jews who would allow no one else to use it freely. Uthman brought this well and gave it to the city. He said, "In the world, I love three things: to feed the hungry, to clothe the naked, to read and teach the holy Quran."

Umar appointed six men to elect his successor. After his death the choice soon lay between Uthman, seventy years old, and Ali who was forty-five. Several people advanced the merits of both. They asked Ali if, were he elected, he would follow the Quran, the Prophet, and the precedents established y Abu Bakr and Umar. Ali replied, "I shall do so as far as I am able, according to my capacity and power." Uthman, asked the same question, agreed without qualification. Uthman had ambitious and unscrupulous relatives, Umayyads who were eager for opportunities to advance themselves. By their intrigues he was elected khalifa.

The Umayyads used to their deadly advantage the precedent of campaigns for conquest established by Abu Bakr and Umar, the first khalifas. Muawiya and his successors conquered all the countries from the Red Sea to Morocco, from Palestine to the borders of India, and appropriated for their own use vast amounts of the wealth belonging to the government. Drunk with riches and power, their oppression of their subjects hung like a black cloud over the empire and their luxuries and debauches were the scandal of Islam. To make themselves, as they thought, secure, they killed many of Muhammad's descendants. For about ninety years they reigned. Then the family of Muhammad descended from his uncle, Abbas, crying the name of Ali, raised an army, drove the Umayyads out and in the year 750 founded the dynasty of khalifas called the Abbasids, after Abbas. This khilafat endured until 1258.

The Abbasids made Baghdad their capital, and instead of the scepter and seal, the ensigns of Umayyad rule, they took for their symbol the Prophet's mantle which, with Ali's sword, Medina had cherished through the years of affliction. The Abbasid standard was black, a sign of their mourning for their chieftains who had fallen in battle or been murdered by the Umayyads, and multitudes of their adherents wore black. The Abbasid soldiers dressed in black and their horses and camels were caparisoned for the battlefield in mourning.

The first nine of the Abbasid khalifas excepting the sixth, were men of ability who concentrated their best energies upon building up their empire. Some of them were incessantly at war suppressing the insurrections of their generals, or tribal chieftains, or incursions of the Romans and Greeks; but they fought only to maintain a united empire and did not continue the Umayyad policy of campaigns for more territory. The Abbasid khalifas founded new cities and equipped them with schools, hospitals, and homes for the poor. They built roads, canals, wayside fountains, and caravanseries. The Umayyads cared little for education or culture and during their reign the scholars and the spiritually minded withdrew from public life. Under the Abbasids the spirit of the Quran and the love of learning, which the Imams of Medina kept alive, spread like a bright light through the empire.

Ali the Younger continued the school in Medina that the first Ali founded. After Ali the Younger, his son, al-Bakir, carried the school forward. Imam al-Bakir appointed his son, Jaafar, to be Imam after him. Imam Jaafar was a profound scholar. He laid the foundation for the philosophic schools of Islam. He trained his students to wrestle with the problem of determinism and free will, to consider the relation between body and spirit, to search for proofs to prophethood. He taught them to ponder God's relation to the universe, to man, to the prophets, and he started many Arabs on the path of experiment and scientific observation. His name is linked with that of Jabir, who became famous in Europe as the chemist Geber. Malik ibn Anas, a founder of Muslin jurisprudence, was his student; and so was Abu Hanifa, who became a foremost teacher of Islam. Imam Jaafar taught that good comes from God and evil from man, that man has freedom to will, at least enough of it to make him responsible for his evil deeds, especially if he has had religious education. Abu Hanifa decided that God was the origin of both the good and evil deeds of man, and he became an exponent of the belief in fatalism.

Muhammad the Prophet declared: "The acquisition of knowledge is a duty incumbent upon every Muslim, male and female," for "it enableth its possessor to distinguish right from wrong; it lighteth the way to Heaven; it is our friend in the desert, our society in solitude, our companion when friendless; it guideth us to happiness; it sustaineth us in misery; it is an ornament amongst friends, and an armor against enemies." Muhammad counseled his followers to study and travel, to learn everything they could from every one, for "he who leaveth home in search of knowledge, walketh in the path of God." Muhammad drew around him a group of devoted followers who became the nucleus for the splendid Muslim civilization of the future. Prince Caetani, the eminent Italian historian writes:

These men were the true moral heirs of the Prophet, the future apostles of Islam, the faithful trustees of all that Muhammad had revealed unto the man of God. Into these men through their constant contact with the Prophet and their devotion to him, there had really entered a new mode of thought and feeling, loftier and more civilized than any they had known before; they had really changed for the better from every point of view, and later on as statesmen and generals, in the most difficult moments of the war of conquest they gave magnificent and undeniable proof that the ideas and the doctrines of Muhammad had been seed cast on fruitful soil, and had produced a body of men of the very highest worth. . . . These men formed the venerable stock of Islam from whom one day was to spring the noble band of the first jurists, theologians and traditionists of Muslim society.

In his Quran, Muhammad often advises the study of nature, its processes, its beauty. In the thirty-sixth chapter he writes, the "sun revolves in a fixed orbit" and the sun, moon, stars, and earth each revolves in its own sphere or heaven—challenging the belief of his day in the Ptolemaic system.

His suggestions roused in his ablest followers an insatiable intellectual curiosity. Guided by the apostolic Imams they studied botany, zoology, geography, the moments of the winds and storms, astronomy, and the laws of hygiene. During the years of the Umayyad rule of terror, these students traveled to Persia, Syria, and Egypt and met many scholars. They returned to Arabia and quietly taught their ever-increasing knowledge, quickening many Muslims to intellectual achievement. When the Abbasid khalifas came into power and openly encouraged scholarship and science, Muslim civilization entered its golden age. The Arab students, imbued by the Imams of Medina with the love of study set to work to learn everything there was to know of science, art, literature, and history; and with characteristic intensity they studied day and night. The Abbasid khalifas and their viziers in addition to their institutions for social service, their hospitals and wayside inns, founded colleges and encouraged learning until immense public and private libraries appeared. A Muslim doctor declined an invitation from his khalifa to come to live in Bokhara, because it would take four hundred camels to transport the scholar's books.

In 786, a hundred and sixty-four years after Muhammad's es-

cape from Mecca, Harun ar-Rashid, grandson of Mansur and immortal hero of the *Arabian Nights* became khalifa of the vast
Muslim empire. He spent much of his life on the battlefield guard-
ing his empire from invasion by the Romans and from internal
uprisings. At the same time he encouraged commerce, science,
and the arts until in his reign and that of his son, Mamun, Saracen
civilization reached its pinnacle of splendor. In times of peace
Khalifa Rashid held his court in Baghdad and received almost
daily reports on the progress of the arts and sciences in his empire.
The Muslims gave Greek learning an ardent reception, some Muslims declaring that through the study of Greek philosophy one
entered into heavenly joy. Khalifa Rashid had Euclid translated
into Arabic and he, and Khalifa Mamun employed a company of
the Christian scholars of the East to translate the masterpieces of
Greek science and philosophy as quickly as the manuscripts could
be secured. In this way the writings of Hippocrates and his school,
of Galen, Plato, Aristotle, Ptolemy, Plotinus, and Porphyry, were
given to the Arabic world. On a single street in Baghdad were
three hundred bookstalls and bookstores. Rashid pronounced music a dignified calling, worthy of degrees and honors like other
scholarly professions. The Khalifa founded in Baghdad free medical clinics and well-appointed hospitals. The colleges held their
classes in the corridors of the mosques; poets, musicians, scholars,
and teachers honored the schools and made them important. Ships
from many nations anchored at Baghdad, and in the city lived
thousands of merchants. The Tigris River was gay with the gon-
dolas that plied its waters, its banks were lined with the marble
palaces of the wealthy, and even the steps that led from the gardens to the river were built of marble.

Khalifa Rashid lived with the magnificence of the Persian court.
The Muslim historian Suyuti tells of Rashid's personal fortune of
more than a hundred million dinars (more than two hundred and
fifty million dollars.) Greek slaves taken in war served in the
Khalifa's splendid palaces. Empress Zubaida, his favorite wife, ate
from gold and silver plates shining with jewels, and her palanquins
of ebony and sandalwood were trimmed with silver. The Empress
made a pilgrimage to Mecca, and when she saw how the people

suffered for water which was so scarce that a bagful was priced at a gold piece, at her own expense she built an aqueduct to bring water though the hills and rocks to Mecca; and she had wells sunk and caravanseries built long the road for the comfort of the multitudes who every year made the pilgrimage to the whole city. Her gifts to the schools in Medina and Mecca amounted to two million dinars, at that time more than five million dollars.

During these centuries of Abbasid rule, while the sovereigns fought to maintain their political power, and the khilafat ascended in splendor, and waned, Muslin civilization climbed to height after height of intellectual achievement. When the too-large empire broke up into many kingdoms, the rulers of the smallest, even the petty Arab chieftains, encouraged education and supported schools and colleges.

"Wisdom is the stray camel of the Faithful, take hold of it wherever you find it," Muhammad told his followers. Learning from all the world, the Arabs became the creators of a new scientific and artistic civilization. Muslim men of science investigated botany and zoology, and studied the flora and animals of different countries. Geographers wrote in detail of the physical construction of lands and continents and of the customs of various peoples. Khalifa Mamun built Islam's first astronomical observatory. Baghdad and other cities acquired observatories, and the finest minds of the Arabic race studied astronomy and trigonometry. The Arab scholars did excellent work on the equinoxes and the orbits of comets and planets. By order of Khalifa Mamun, astronomers and mathematicians measured the circumference of the earth. The fact that the earth is spherical was rediscoered. Later, in Europe, Christian leaders laughed the idea to scorn and punished those who suggested it. Many astronomers, mathematicians, and physicians from India and Syria met in Baghdad. The chemists and alchemists of Islam believed that matter had an underlying unity and elements could be changed one into the other. Knowledge of medicine advanced and the Arab physicians became world famous.

Borrowing from the Chinese, an Arab invented the pendulum and by its oscillations measured time. The Muslim Alhazen was an outstanding influence in Europe during the Middle Ages. He seems to be the first scientific thinker to discover the laws of atmospheric refraction. He showed how refraction is determined by atmospheric density and density by altitude; how through atmospheric refraction bodies are seen before they rise above the horizon and after they set below the horizon. He was the first to discover that rays of light proceed from the object to the eye, not from the eye to the object; that the retina of the eye is the seat of vision, that impressions are carried from the retina to the brain and thus vision becomes possible in man's mind. His original work in optics was a supreme achievement of Muslim science.

Early in the ninth century the Muslim Arabs acquired from India the so-called Arabic numerals, used by Brahmagupta, the renowned mathematician of India, who employed the decimal notation, and determined the quality of numerals by their position. Al-Kwarizmi, a Muslim astronomer, following the lead of his Indian brothers developed arithmetic and algebra and, with other Muslim scholars, gave the West the word "algebra" and the amazing discovery that by the use of ciphers and decimal notation arithmetic could be made a working instrument in science and business. We can appreciate the value of their contribution if we try to multiply say, 10,065 by 851 using the Roman numerals. The Muslims made arithmetic practical and developed algebra into a science. They prepared the way for analytical geometry and founded plane and spherical trigonometry. Their works, when translated into Latin, revolutionized mathematics for the Western world and made possible the exact sciences which have mathematics for their basis.

The Chinese in 751 attacked Samarkand and many of them were taken captive by the victorious Muslims. Some of the prisoners were skilled in the manufacture of a substance called paper, which the Chinese had made since A.D. 105. The alert Muslim governor of Samarkand had the prisoners teach their art to his craftsmen, and soon skilled Persians were making paper from silk and flax. The paper was glossy and firm and remarkably durable. Arab manuscripts written in the time of the Abbasids have been preserved for a thousand years. One of these manuscripts, *Gharíb al-Hadíth* written in 866, is a treatise on the rare and unusual words found in the sayings of Muhammad and his companions. The Muslims evidently also acquired gunpowder and the compass from the Chinese.

Two great Muslim historians, Tabari and Masudi, wrote in the tenth century. Tabari traveled in Syria and Egypt, and then settled in Baghdad. For forty years with indefatigable zeal he studied all the historical records available, and he wrote a remarkable book, the *Annals*, which gives the history of the world from the day of creation to his time A.D. 915. He also wrote from the well-spring of his mmense erudition one of the first important commentaries on the Quran.

Masudi, an Arab of Baghdad, was descended from an early Muslim, a companion of Muhammad. Masudi followed the Prophet's counsel to seek knowledge in far countries. He traveled to India and Persia, and as far as China it is believed, and studied in Ceylon, Madagascar, and Central Asia, acquiring through the years encyclopedic knowledge. He wrote a series of thirty books describing the customs, sciences, and history of Muslim and neighboring countries. he summed up the thirty volumes in a book which he called *Golden Meadows*. In addition, he wrote a book, *The Mirror of the Times*. These valuable works have been lost in most part, except *Golden Meadows*, which is considered one of the most delightful books in Arabic literature.

A fundamental tenet of Islam was brotherhood. All Muslims whatever their race or station were brothers, and in the mosque a prince in his gorgeous robes had no precedence over the ragged beggar. Following this teaching of Muhammad, the Muslims treated their slaves as members of the family rather than as personal property; and some slaves rose to high positions.

Jahiz, the grandson of a Negro slave, became an influential Arabic writer and stylist. When he earned a little money he rented a bookshop for a night, and read the night through. In his writing he was sometimes gay, sometimes sad, and often very witty—the most genial author of his age, and perhaps of Arabic literature. Among the books he wrote were *In Praise of Ministers and Disparagement of Officials* and *The Superiority of Speech to Silence*.

A Turkish slave, Ibn-Tulun, became Sultan of Egypt when in 868 Egypt broke away from the Abbasid rule. He established the Muslim dynasty of the Tulunids who reigned from 868 to 905. He built in Cairo the magnificent mosque, Ibn-Tulun, with its stately arches, arabesques and courts, splendid even in their present broken condition.

In the next native dynasty that governed Egypt, the Abyssinian slave Kafur was prominent. In 946 he became regent for the children of the Sultan, his master, and for twenty-two years he governed admirably. He loved music, he encouraged men of science, poets and other writers, he studied tirelessly, and far into the night he worked on state affairs. When the day was ended he would fall on his knees, and cry, "O God, give no created thing power over me." The people said of him, "The big black eunuch knew how to keep order," and throughout the country he was famous for his generosity, his integrity and justice. When Kafur died Egypt's government collapsed into chaos.

By the eleventh and twelfth centuries Damascus, with its twenty-two colleges, was a brilliant center of learning; Aleppo, Emesa, Baalbek, Mosul, Baghdad, and Cairo had famous schools where scholarly judges and doctors of the law taught their students. The Scholar in politics was now the Muslim ideal, and the doctors of the law were the real administrators of Saracenic society. The great jurists of Islam had built up one of the wisest systems of jurisprudence the world had seen. Muslim law was based on the Quran, the Prophet Muhammad's deeds and legal decisions, and the precedents established by the first khalifas and their companions. Under this guidance the able Muslim jurists made laws to protect and assist the Muslim civilization and the Roman and Christian countries Islam ruled. Muhammad taught that human life is a perpetual struggle between the prophets and friends of God, and the superstitions and rapacity of men. The Muslim lawyers tried to be just to kings and their subjects, to conquerors and the conquered, Muslims and non-Muslims, the weak and the strong, men and women; for Muhammad said the true ruler would protect the rights of both the rich and the poor. Muhammad decreed that the Muslim governmento of Yemen should take care of the poor, the sick, the cripples, the unfortunate; but taxes must be graduated according to the ability of the taxed to pay. The Muslim jurists tried to apply this principle in all Muslim countries. Muhammad said some things contained great evil: like drinking and games of chance. The Muslim jurists must decide how to execute the prohibitions against them: should they use force, or should they trust only to the persuasive power of the Prophet's words. The laws which the jurists framed for every phrase of their social life became with all their niceties the custom, usage, and practical religion of their world; and the law schools and schools of religion were one.

# 23

# The Muslims and Jews Bring
# Glory to Spain

THE BERBERS of northern Africa were rugged, warlike, independent desert tribes full of vigor like the Arabs but more inclined to agriculture. They were conquered by the Umayyads, and many Berbers became Muslims. Always eager for new exploits they looked often, with a more or less possessive eye, across the Straits of Gibralter toward Spain.

Spain was conquered by the Romans in the second century B.C. and was held by them for more than five hundred years, until the Visigoths overran and conquered the land. For three hundred years the Goths and Visigoths ruled the people of Spain: Christians, Romans, and Jews. Under these conquerors from the north, Christianity was nominally the state religion. By the eighth century the Christian clergy continually interfered in politics and forgot their spiritual function. They brutally persecuted the Jews, abused the slaves whom they hardly considered human beings, and neglected the education of the people. The native Spanish chieftains meanwhile had few interests beyond their endless petty feuds.

In 711 some Muslim Berbers decided to live in southern Spain. Under Tarik, their general, twelve thousand Berber and Arab warriors crossed the Straits and landed in fair Andalusia. Roderick, King of the Goths, immediately raised an army to drive them out. He commanded his soldiers himself, riding at their head under an imposing canopy and arrayed in shining armor.

Faced with this army which outnumbered them two to one, Tarik said to the Muslims, "Men, before you is the enemy, the sea is at your backs. By Allah, there is no escape for you save in valor and resolution."

For a week the armies fought. The day after the last battle, King Roderick's horse and sandals were found on a riverbank; the King had disappeared and was never heard of again. The victorious Muslims marched onward and everywhere the Jews and the slaves hailed them as deliverers, the Jews opening the gates of the towns they besieged, and garrisoning the captured cities for them.

In a few months Tarik's army conquered Spain, and the Berber and Arab chieftains became lords of the land. Exulting in warfare and willing to fight all Europe, they led their soldiers through the Pyrenees into France. Their stinging defeat by Charles Martel in the Battle of Tours checked their hopes. They retreated to Spain, and never again invaded France.

Deprived of an all-absorbing war with a foreign enemy, the Muslim chieftains renewed their tribal feuds of the desert and quarreled among themselves as to precedence until Spain was in turmoil. For forty years they fought each other until by a twist of circumstances their master arrived from the east.

When the Umayyads were overthrown in Syria one Umayyad, a young man of twenty, escaped Khalifa Saffár's hungry knife and after five years of wandering and hiding and many thrilling adventures reached northwestern Africa and was given shelter by some Berbers. This young man, Abdur Rahman, decided to cross over to Spain and use the prestige of the Umayyad name to gather together an army from among the Muslims. He landed on the Spanish coast in September, 755, and the Arab settlers, counting him their clansman, received him enthusiastically.

Abdur Rahman was gifted, decisive, daring. This soldier of fortune was a remarkable administrator. He knit together the various sections of Spain and worked indefatigably for their welfare, building bridges, public baths, and mosques in all parts of the land. He built an aqueduct to bring water from the surrounding hills to Cordova; he laid out parks in the city and erected public buildings. An old record says that in Cordova one could now go for ten miles "by the light of lamps along an uninterrupted extent of buildings." For himself he had a garden of rare plants brought from many countries, a garden so beautiful it became world famous. For thirty-two years Abdur Rahman ruled and developed the country; and incessantly fought the rebellious lords, also the Franks and other Christians who raided northern Spain. At times, true to his Umayyad heredity, he was cruel and treacherous. The governor of Africa under the second Abbasid khalifa, Mansur, tried to take spain from him. Abdur Rahman defeated the invading army, killed its commander and sent his head to Mansur secretly by a muslim who was making the pilgrimage to Mecca. The head was thrown before Mansur when he was presiding over his imposing court at Mecca' The startled Khalifa exclaimed, "Thank God there is a sea between that man and me!"

Abdur Rahman founded a dynasty which endured for two hundred and fifty years, and made possible the wonder of the world, the civilization of the Moors in Spain. He was a scholar; and his son and successor, Hisham, who became khalifa in 788 was carefully trained in Muslim administration.

Hisham, like his father, was a firm ruler and held the lawless nobles in check. He gave the people many public buildings; he had the cities patrolled at night and order maintained; he walked the streets of Cordova and mixed with the people to learn their problems and their needs. His charities were boundless; often he visited the poor in their homes and nursed the sick himself. Scholars were welcome at his court and he selected men of science for the important government positions.

Four good kings followed Hisham. They encouraged learning until the sciences and arts developed rapidly. They built schools and mosques, bridges and gardens. And the people prospered.

From 756, and for a hundred and thirty-two years, Spain went forward under good government. During these years much of the nation became Muslim. For with the Arian blight which spread among the Christians in the fourth and fifth centuries; with the anathemas of the sixth century, and the misrule of the seventh; with the return of primitive superstitions which amounted to polytheism; with monasticism and its race suicide at the top of Christian society, the glory of the days of Paul and John and Augustine had departed. Many slaves, and people from the middle class, joined the Muslims, soon to be followed by Christian nobles who found in Islam a vital religion which encouraged science, learning, good government, brotherhood, and social justice. The Muslims allowed the conquered people freedom to follow their religious faith whatever it might be. As late as the year 1602 the Archbishop of Valencia gave Philip III of Spain, as a paramount reason for driving the Muslims out of the country, "that they commended nothing so much as that liberty of conscience, in all matters of religion, which the Turks, and all other Muhammadans, suffer their subjects to enjoy." The Christians celebrated openly and in peace their religious festivals. Their churches, convents, and monasteries were not molested, and often the Muslim government helped them to build new churches. Christians held high offices in the government, they collected from their fellow Christians the Muslin tax, they served voluntarily in the Muslim armies.

Despite the failings of Muhammad's followers, Islam in Spain produced a new civilization. As education and culture spread their beauty and glory over Spain, The Christians forsook the Latin language in which their theologies and their Bible were written for "the exquisite charm and for the eloquence and beauty" of Arabic, until the Bible also was translated into Arabic for the use of the Christians.

In 888 Abdullah, the seventh king of the Spanish Umayyad dynasty, inherited the throne. He was conciliatory and indecisive in his dealings with the overlords, the descendants of the Arab and Berber chieftains, and under his weak rule they became arrogant and insubordinate. Petty chieftains each calling himself the sultan soon made war on the central government hoping to divide up the country. A historian of the time writes, "The State is menaced with total dissolution, disasters follow one another ceaselessly; thieving and pillaging go on; our wives and children are dragged into slavery."

Abdullah died in 912 and his grandson, twenty-two years old, was proclaimed King Abdur Rahman III. Of the many monarchs who ruled Moorish Spain no one was greater than he.

Abdur Rahman III announced at once that he would not tolerate insurrection. He called upon the independent nobles to submit to him, and raised an army to enforce his mandate. With remarkable ability he took command of the army and completely changed its morale. He was handsome, princely in his bearing, with gracious manners. He was a gallant soldier who went with his men as one of them taking no better of anything than they had. His troops in response fought for him so enthusiastically that every city opened its gates to him, until only the Royal City of Toledo remained defiant. Abdur Rahman built a little town near it and settled down to an indefinite siege. After Toledo submitted, he attacked the Christians in their mountain fastnesses within the Spanish border, and fortress after fortress surrendered to this monarch who treated his enemies with mercy and scrupulously kept his covenants with them.

By 930, eighteen years after he became king, Spain was under his control. Abdur Rahman now took the title Khalifa, and his subjects in wonder and awe added "Great."

The measuring rod of a civilization is the prosperity of the masses. The Great Khalifa built a widespread irrigation system and encouraged and developed agriculture until the fields and orchards bore unprecedented harvests. "The country folk returned to the paths of peace and plenty; they were at last free to get rich and to be happy after their own way." The peasants wore clothes of superior quality and the poorest man had his own horse to ride. Public baths were an essential part of every town, for among the Muslims cleanliness was a prerequisite to prayer and worship; many a poor Muslim would go without food in order to buy soap. The Great Khalifa built marvelous gardens along the river at Cordova and piped water from the mountains to supply their lakes and fountains. He opened these gardens to the people.

The artists, architects, and artisans of this golden time, trained in perfect workmanship, made Cordova resplendent. In the city were fifty thousand homes for the well-to-do and the official classes, a hundred thousand homes for the common people, seven hundred buildings for worship and learning, nine hundred public baths. Thirteen thousand looms were used in silk weaving; Cordova's caravans carried her precious fabrics and metal work as far east as India. Some of the most delicate ivory carving in existence belongs to this Muslim period.

Abdur Rahman III made a suburb to Cordova, calling it the City of the Fairest, and there he built a magnificent palace. The Byzantine emperor sent him a wonderful sculptured fountain and a unique pearl; rulers of Rome, Carthage, and other countries gave him lovely columns and adorments for the palace.

The Great Khalifa was celebrated in Europe, Africa, and Egypt. France, Germany, Italy, and the Greek empire sent ambassadors to his court. The schools and public libraries of Spain were famous. Science and learning advanced, medicine developed, women became physicians. The kingdom was so well managed that travelers could go unafraid into the loneliest places. The people prospered, they sang, they enjoyed life as never before.

The Great Khalifa reigned for forty-nine years, and died in 961. Among his papers was found one on which he had recorded the days of his reign that were free from sorrow: fourteen days. He commented, "O man of understanding, wonder and observe how small a portion of unclouded happiness the world can give even to the most fortunate."

Remembering the Great Khalifa's strong hand and how effectually hd had suppressed them, the Arab and Berber lords made no attempt to rebel during the reign of Abdur Rahman's son, Hakim II.

Khalifa Hakim II was a scholar by temperament, and his first interest was books. He fought only when it was absolutely necessary to protect northern Spain from the raids of the Christians. To all parts of the Muslim world he sent his agents to find and buy for him, at any price, rare books. If a desirable book could not be purchased he had it copied. Sometimes when he heard that an author planned to write a book, Khalifa Hakim II sent him a handsome present and requested that he be given the first copy. Printing was unknown and every book was laboriously copied in beautiful handwriting; yet Hakim II acquired, it is said, a library of four hundred thousand volumes. His notes on their margins were greatly valued by later scholars.

Hakim II was a wise, just, beneficent king who truly appreciated the value of education. He protected "even the philosophers, who could now pursue their studies without fear of persecution by the bigots." He finished the palaces his father had commenced; he established in Cordova twenty-seven free schools for the children of the very poor and supported the schools from his own purse, furnishing the textbooks.

After the destruction of Jerusalem by Emperor Hadrian's army in A.D. 135, many Jews fled to countries of Europe, Africa, and the East. There they settled and preserved as best they could their national integrity. In Mesopotamia and Babylonia they fared well and their life gradually assumed a form similar to that in Palestine. Outbursts of persecution came upon them at times, but most of the Persian kings and Muslim conquerors were kind and tolerant to them, and allowed them practically complete freedom.

Encouraged and assisted by the Muslim khalifas, the Jews in Spain entered one of the brightest eras in their history. The great classics of the Greeks which the Muslims had secured they gladly shared with the Jews, who studied them eagerly. The Jews became proficient in Arabic and wrote much of the time in that language. Jewish poets and literary men revised and refined the Hebrew language, which through carelessness in pronounciation and writing had lost much of its elegance during the centuries after the dispersion. The khalifas of Spain made the Jews fellow citizens with the Muslims; every Jew of ability was free to attain wealth and honor.

They could satisfy their love of culture, intellectual and artistic, and could dignify their home life. Their women were honored. Their children were taught mutual respect and service, consideration for others, self-control. The morals of the Jews were high; the records of the Middle Ages show that crime was rare among them. They gave generously to charity and philanthropies and the education of students; they took care of travelers, strangers, and children, and ransomed Jews enslaved by their captors. Jewish children were not allowed to lie or cheat; they were told it was especially wrong to cheat a Christian or a Muslim, for that would bring discredit upon Israel's religion.

The source of their moral training was two books: the Bible (the Old Testament the Christians call it) and the Talmud. The Talmud consists of the Mishna and the Gemara.

The constitution for this Jewish civilization was the laws of Moses in the Torah. The Mishna is the religious and legal decisions of rabbis, over a period of about a thousand years, when applying Moses' laws to problems and conditions.

The Gemara is comments, by rabbis, on the decisions in the Mishna. Interspersed through the discussions of legal and theological matters, in the Gemara are many delightful stories and legends from Hebrew history, also anecdotes that illustrate how a decision came to be, or what happened when it was applied.

The Jews in Palestine finished their Talmud during the fourth Christian century. A compilation of the Talmud made by the Jews of Babylonia was completed about A.D. 500.

The Talmud is of such size that it is a lifelong study. By the ethical, moral, and spiritual training in the Talmud and the Torah, the Jewish nation lived, held together, and survived. The Talmud says:

A sinful desire is at first thin as a spider's thread; [if encouraged] it will at last be strong as a ship's hawser.

Thy friend has a friend, and thy friend's friend has a friend; be discreet.

If thou hast learned much, do not boast of it, for it is for that that thou wast created.

Let thy house be the meeting-place of the wise; sit gladly at their feet, and zealously drink in their words.

More knowledge; more life.

More justice; more peace.

When a Jewish boy attained the age of five his mother and father led him to the school connected with the synagogue. It was a day of rejoicing, celebrated by the whole congregation. The rabbi took the child in his arms and presented him before the Torah which he was going to learn to read. He was then given his first lesson: some Hebrew lines to memorize. They were traced on honey cakes and hard-cooked eggs. When he had learned his lesson he could eat the cakes and eggs. A boy, when ten years old, was given the Talmud and this he studied the rest of his life.

In the Talmud and the Torah is one of the world's noblest systems for character training and cultural development. It carried the Jews forward in times of prosperity, and saved them in periods of disaster. It safeguarded them from the debasing ignorance of the early Middle Ages, and was the flaming sword which halted their deterioration when, after the Renaissance, Jewish education languished.

Under the good Muslim khalifas the Jews owned large estates and were prosperous and influential. They studied astronomy, optics, biology, medicine, mathematics, and were exceptional scholars in these specialities. They were appointed court physicians and ministers in the government. A new note, joy, sounded in their poetry, a contagion caught from this Muslim civilization.

A great Jew in Spain was Hasdai, man of science and student of muslim learning. He commenced his public career as court interpreter and diplomat for Abdur Rahman III, representing the Great Khalifa at the small Christian courts in northern Spain. Due to the Jealousy of the Arabs he ever held any declared office under the Great Khalifa although he was in fact minister of foreign affairs, secretary of commerce, secretary of the treasury. He spoke Hebrew, Arabic, and Latin, and received the ambassadors from the courts of Europe, executing the Great Khalifa's transactions with them. An ambassador from the Byzantine emperor brought a present to the Great Khalifa, a valuable manuscript on medicine. Abdur Rahman was immensely pleased and felt that his library was elevated by it. The only trouble was, the manuscript was written in Greek and no one at the court could read it. Minister Hasdai wrote to the Byzantine emperor requesting that he send a Greek who could translate his present into Latin. The linguist from Constantinople arrived and made the translation as requested. Hasdai, who in addition to his other offices was court physician, was the only physician in Cordova who knew Latin and could retranslate the document into Arabic. The Muslim savants were delighted with this new scholarly treatise on medicine when they could read it in Arabic, and the Great Khalifa proudly added it to the Imperial library.

When Abdur Rahman III died, his son Khalifa Hakim II gave Hasdai an important state office, and he became still more influential. He was a devoted Jew and supported the Talmudic college Rabbi Moses founded. He so encouraged the Jews in Cordova to honor and follow this scholar that Rabbi Moses' college became the most important in the Jewish world.

With gladness the student of history reads that this noble minister of state, Hasdai, lived out his life in peace, confident in the appreciation and protection of two great Muslim khalifas.

The reign of Abdur Rahmen III, and that of Hakim II, his son, was an era when science and poetry reached a pinnacle of attainment. Poets were honored until everyone, nobles and commoners, aspired to write in verse. Centuries later the love of learning which these khalifas fostered was still so strong that a successful Jewish merchant, upbraided by a fellow Jew for preferring his material welfare to the study of science, gave up his flourishing business and went to Barcelona to study. He became a skillful physician and translator of Arabic works on medicine.

Famous in Spain's history is Samuel ibn Nagrela. He was twenty when civil war compelled his family to leave their home in Cordova. Samuel went to Malaga, a town on the coast, and opened a spice shop. Spain was now in the hands of the war lords, who persistently divided and subdivided the country among themselves. In 1020 a Berber prince seized a section in southern Spain and established a kingdom which included the city of Granada, also Malaga where Samuel lived.

Samuel's shop was next door to the palace of the King's Vizier and a slave of the Vizier came to him to write letters for her. She showed his letters to the Vizier who, recognizing the skill and knowledge they displayed, told her to bring the writer to him. Samuel was thirty-two, gifted and well-informed; he spoke seven languages and wrote beautiful Arabic. After his interview, the Vizier took Samuel for his private secretary.

When the Vizier was on his death-bed he advised the king to give Samuel his office, for he has succeeded, he said, only because he consulted Samuel on every state matter and took his advice.

The king made the young Jew the highest official in his kingdom and placed all state affairs in his hands. Samuel was wise and tactful, he treated his enemies with diplomacy and kindness, and under him the kingdom flourished. When the king died, Samuel continued as minister of state for the king's son. He served his Jewish brothers generously, supported their colleges and educated many students, and was in active communication with the Jews of all the Near East.

The great Jewish writer and thinker Ibn Gabirol lived in Spain in this eleventh century. His childhood was sad and lonely, for both his parents died, leaving him penniless. He was still a boy when he turned for relief to the study of philosophy and poetry. At nineteen he wrote in verse a Hebrew grammar, hoping to make the rules of grammar so attractive that young writers would be interested in them. His poems attracted the attention of Samuel Ibn Nagrela and he became Ibn Gabirol's patron, which meant that the young man would have an assured income and could give his time to writing.

Ibn Gabirol when twenty-four wrote a book which he called *The Fountain of Life*. It is in the form of a dialogue between a teacher and his student, and is a remarkable treatise on problems of the human soul: the soul's relation to this world, to the problem of evil, to its origin in God, what it can expect from God, what man should strive for. It was too universal for the pro-Jewish theologians and philosophers, and for a hundred years was little read. A Christian priest and a Jew who had become a Christian finally translated it from Arabic into Latin. It became one of the most widely read books in Europe, and was much discussed by the Christian schoolmen.

In an atmosphere of culture, love of literary excellence and scholarly attainment, thousands of Jews in Muslim Spain became poets. Incomparable among them is Judah Halevi, of the eleventh century. In his youth he wrote love songs, and poems in praise of his friends. When he was older and a successful physician with a large practice, he wrote of his religion. His poems were so beautiful and expressed such depth of feeling that his people likened them to the great psalms of the Bible. Some of his poems were added to the Jewish liturgy and have been sung in Hebrew services for centuries. He was a profound philosopher, and believed that the great prophets saw into the divine world.

For centuries the Jews were a peaceful and favored part of the Muslim civilization in Spain. It would take many volumes to name and do justice to the Jewish scholars, government ministers, poets, and writers of prose who rose into eminence in Spain and other countries. A brilliant Jew of highest integrity became chief minister to an Ilkhan ruler in Persia, descendant of Hulagu. Jewish physicians trained in Muslim medicine served the Christians of western Europe, and taught in Christian universities. When the Inquisitions spread terror through Europe, and Jewish physicians were ordered not to practice on Christians, the Christian nobles secretly and under threat of excommunication had their special Jewish physicians. Even the pope, when he was really ill, called in a Jewish physician.

The greatest genius among the Jews of these centuries was Moses Maimonides. It has been said that in the Hebrew nation the name Moses is supremely great three times: Moses the Prophet, Moses Maimonides, and Moses Mendelssohn of the eighteenth century.

Throughout eight generations Moses Maimonides' grandfathers were rabbis in the Talmudic college in Cordova. His father was the ninth of these scholars. Moses was born on March 30, 1135, and he would probably have lived out his life in Cordova, following in his ancestors' footsteps. But calamity came to his family when he was thirteen. The Almohades from Africa overwhelmed and conquered Andalusia. Fierce and ignorant, they ordered all Christians and Jews to become Muslims. Maimonides' father with his family fled from city to city trying to escape these relentless persecutors and finally went to Fez in northern Africa. Conditinons there were no better and the Holy Land and Egypt seemed their only hope. With his son, Moses, and his daughter, the scholar journeyed to Acre. After six months in Acre they went to Jerusalem and three days later set out for Egypt. In Cairo, Moses' father died.

Moses Maimonides, now thirty-one, with his younger brother, David, opened a jewelry shop in Cairo. David went to India for a supply of Jewels. On the way home his ship was caught in a storm on the Indian Ocean and sank. All the little fortune of the Maimonides family, and the money other people had invested in their business, went down with David. David's wife and daughter were destitute, and to support them Moses commenced to practice medicine.

In their home in Cordova his father had taught him mathematics, astronomy, and the sciences in addition to the Bible and the Talmud. And during their wanderings Moses studied ceaselessly; attending Muslim schools and listening to lectures by Muslim professors who taught him Aristotle's philosophy and the sciences of the Greeks and Muslims. In this way he was trained in medicine also.

Twenty years after he came to Cairo, Maimonides was appointed physician at Saladin's court. When Saladin was at home from the wars with the crusaders, Maimonides, now living in Fostat a few miles away, made daily visits to the palace in his official capacity. A young Jew who asked to study under him received from him a letter giving reasons why Maimonides could not teach him: "As a rule," he wrote, "I go to Cairo very early in the day, and even if nothing unusual happens I do not return before afternoon, when I am almost dying with hunger; but I find the antechambers filled with Jews and Gentiles, with nobles and common people, awaiting my return."

Saladin loaded him with honors, patients came to him from far and near. He was acclaimed the greatest physician of his time. King Richard I of England wanted him for his personal physician but Maimonides declined his offer.

He was also head of the Jewish community in Cairo, and through his writings and letters led the Jewish world. His character and intellect made him a towering figure of his age.

The Talmud, loaded with commentaries by college presidents and other rabbis, had become an almost unmanageable maze of detail. Maimonides undertook to systematize and clarify it, and make it easy to read. He labored at this for ten years, and in his book *Mishne-Torah*, or "Religious Code," accomplished a work of genius.

He also wrote ten treatises on medicine. Following Hippocrates, Galen, and the Muslim physicians, he made many independent contributions. He taught sanitation, good food, simple rational living, and a moderate use of drugs. He emphasized the power of the mind over the body, and believed that some of the superstitions practiced through the ages, though irrational and foolish, had caused healing because of the people's faith in them. He said ignorance was a great source of disease, and to educate people was of utmost importance.

The climax of his work as writer and thinker is his book, *The Guide of the Perplexed* which he wrote in Arabic for a student who asked him to explain the new philosophy of religion the great Muslim thinkers had presented to the world; a system that reached its pinnacle under Avicenna, al-Ghazzali, and Averroës, and attracted and illumined the finest and most progressive minds of Europe, Africa, and western Asia.

To Maimonides, his student was the type of a growing multitude of Jews who joyfully undertook the study of Greek and Muslim science and then discovered their reading had brought them "into collision with religion."

A chief difficulty in uniting science and religion was, in Maimonides' day as it is now, the anthropomorphic passages in the Bible. In *The Guide of the Perplexed* Maimonides considers this problem. Much of the Bible must be interpreted spiritually, he says, for certain passages, taken literally, become superstitions. Well-educated people are bewildered when they read that God came down to earth, ascended to heaven, went to and fro through the earth. They are astonished when told that God has eyes and ears, works with his fingers, covers Moses with his hand; for they think of God as Spirit.

Maimonides explains that the Book of Genesis tries to make God, his power, activities, and perfections, understandable to primitive people who cannot think of him without a body. Form is physical; it is also the mental arrangement and connection of powers and ideas. The Bible, Maimonides says, uses the words "come" and "depart," "stand" and "arrive," "ascend" and "descend" in two ways: sometimes they refer to physical activities; sometimes they mean states of mind: an idea *comes* to a person; God *stands*, that is, is unshakable and eternal.

God *comes*, that is, rises in Moses' mind, in the prophet's mind, in our's. He makes men feel his presence: in the house of prayer, in the Tent of Meeting, on Mount Sinai, and apprehend his glory. His "nearness" is man's consciousness of his presence: men think of him, love him, and lo, they are with him in the secret place of the Most High. A man is active; he moves from place to place. The

Torah says, God moves, God "sees," that is, perceives; he "hears" or listens to and answers prayer. The influence and inspiration which come from him are his movement, his tongue and speech.

Maimonides believes the Torah sometimes dramatizes a vision, making it a physical event. It tells in Genesis that God came to Abraham, and after God had gone three angels visited Abraham; Jacob wrestled with the angel, and afterward saw the angel "face to face." These were really visions, or dreams, says Maimonides. He takes the story of creation, and of Adam and Eve, as symbolic: Adam is man's soul, his spiritual form; Eve is his body; Satan is the body's appetites.

The prophets tell only as much about God as men can understand. They liken him to a rock, meaning that he is steadfast and eternal, "the rock of eternity." When men become firm in their knowledge of God they too become like a rock. As men grow in spiritual capacity the prophets can use more subtle terms.

Says Maimonides, as he observes and follows the facts the laws of nature, he sees within the universe "a certain force which controls the whole," as a man's mind controls his body. This force is God, "the life of the universe," who said to Moses, "I am that I am," meaning he is absolute and eternal. His kindness and mercy are everywhere visible: inanimate things reveal his glory, omnipotence, and wisdom. The world he created is essentially good. Evil comes from turning away from his guidance and truth.

He has given man's soul power to rule his body. Man's condition "varies according to the exercise of this power." "Man sins only by his animal nature," says Maimonides. Therefore it is perilous to think of one's appetites, of sex, of the pleasure of eating and drinking, for thinking of these leads to disaster. Never meet to drink wine, Maimonides admonishes.

Moses Maimonides was one of the world's most influential thinkers. Two great masters of medieval Christianity, Albert the Great and Thomas Aquinas, closely followed his method of uniting reason and revelation. From him they received the idea of God as the supreme Artist, an idea which made a tremendous impression upon the Renaissance.

# 24

## Persia

MUHAMMAD TOLD HIM tribesmen wonderful stories, one in particular about the Persian baths. Those desert dwellers were so curious to see a bath that, as they swept into Persia under Islam's banner, the conquering armies looked everywhere for the phenomenon. Suddenly a soldier saw an eggplant. Knowing not what to make of it he cried, "Oh, this is a Persian bath!"

Swarming through a civilization accustomed to refinement and culture, abounding in palaces and other handsome buildings, with beauty everywhere, the Arabs might have laid waste what they could not appreciate. Instead they made a vital contribution which quickened Persia to undreamed-of achievements.

Persia's beginning is wrapped in the mists of legends. The Avesta, or Zend Avesta, the sacred book of ancient Persia, tells of many prehistoric heroes. One of them is King Yima, who governed his people with wondrous wisdom until in his reign

> Man seemed immortal, sickness was unknown
> And life rolled on in happiness and joy.

This was because "the Glory made by Mazda [God]" descended upon the king. He lived by this Glory and was the good shepherd of his people, and

> The earth became abounding,
> Full of flocks and full of cattle,
> Full of men, of birds, dogs likewise,
> Full of fires all bright and blazing.

After a while King Yima "began to find delight in words of falsehood and untruth," whereupon "the Glory was seen to flee away from him in the shape of a bird." Now he was weak before his foes, and "he laid down on the ground." Through the ages the Glory came upon other kings and as long as they were faithful to it they were wise and successful men.

About 590 B.C., perhaps earlier, a heroic figure, Zoroaster (or Zarathustra), stepped upon the stage. The people of the time were nomadic in their habits, unwilling to settle down to an orderly, agricultural life. It was easier for a man to steal a neighbor's cattle than to raise his own; the cattle were driven hither and thither, the land was untilled, and the people warred upon and plundered each other incessantly. The ancient poems the Gathas, which are much like the Vedas of India in language and meter, give the earliest account of Zoraster's life and teachings. One of the oldest of these Gathas tells in a dramatic dialogue of his call to prophethood:

God created the lowly cattle to help and nourish men. The people on earth "have no knowledge of how right doers act toward the lowly," and do not take care of their cattle. The mistreated animals call to Ahura Mazda, God, that they suffer violence and outrage. "Whom hast thou among men who may care for us twain?" cry the ox and the cow. God replied, "He who alone hath heard our commands, even Zoroaster: he willeth to make known our thoughts." The soul of the ox fears that Zoroaster is only a man. What can he do against the brigands and robbers of the world? God assures the ox that Zoroaster will have power from on high. He will be assisted by Dominion and Righteousness and Good Thought, he will be given "charm of speech," he will found among men "a great society." The ox and the cow cry, "O Ahura, O God, now is help ours: we will be ready to serve those like you."

Zoroaster presented his gospel of monotheism in symbols adapted to the understanding of the childlike people he taught. he declared that Ahura Mazda, "who cloths himself with the massy heavens as a garment" and dwells in endless light is the one God, the First and the Last, Creator through his Holy Spirit of all things. Ahura Mazda's attributes are Good Thought, the Righteous Law, Harmony, Welfare, Immortality, and wonderful Dominion or Sovereignty. Zoroaster pesonified those attributes, that his followers might visualize them and pray to them as mighty archangels embodying the character of God. The highest form of prayer, he taught, was praise to God for his attributes.

The pagan gods of the old Persian polytheism became the daevas, or devils, of Zoroaster's new monotheism. Like the gods of the Greeks, the daevas often sanctioned by their example lying, stealing, and even murder. These forces of evil, especially the Lie, were in age-long conflict with God, his Holy Spirit, and his angelic attributes. Zoroaster summoned his countrymen to enlist on the side of Truth and permanently put to rout the Lie and his daevas who fought to destroy Persia. Addressing the devils, he arraigned them: "Ye Daevas all and he that highly honors you, are seed of Bad Thought—yea, of the Lie and of Arrogance; likewise your deeds. For ye have brought it to pass that men who do the worst things shall be called the beloved of the Daevas, separating themselves from Good Thought, departing from the will of Mazda Ahura and from Right." Therefore "ye defrauded mankind of happy life and of immortality . . . so as to ruin [them]. The teacher of evil destroys the design of life and prevents the possession of Good Thought from being prized."

Zoroaster as one of the first prophets to define heaven as the best state of mind, and hell as the worst. Every good starts with right thinking, he taught; therefore mental purity is the best thing in life. Right thinking rises in a pure mind; right speaking and right doing are its results. "Grant, O Mazda, O God," he prayed, "for this world and the spiritual, that we may attain to fellowship with Thee, and righteousness for all time. Through righteousness, the best, and righteousness, the fairest, may we see Thee and may we come near Thee and may we attain to Thy perfect frendship, O Ahura Mazda." He called this best existence the house of song, the kingdom of righteousness and good thought, the joy of eternal life. Man should understand that this life is for his advantage and should follow it of his own free will:

> *Hear with your ears the best things; look upon them with*
> *clear-seeing thought for decision between the two beliefs;*
> *each man for himself, before the Great Consummation;*
> *Bethinking you that it be accomplished to our [God's] pleasure.*

Zoroaster had a difficult task: winning primitive people to his exalted ethics and to a teaching full of philosophic import. The women calld him a sorcerer and drove him away with curses, and he was abused and persecuted. He declared that while he had he power and strength he would teach men to search for the right, to tell the truth, to resist the oppressor, to settle down and plant their fields with corn, to drain the swamps and irrigate the deserts. He would be a "true foe to the liar," a powerful support to the right- eous. He offered his good thoughts, good deeds, good speech, the strength of his body that, through the assistance of the Eternal Lord, he might win the victory. Continually he prayed, "O Mazda, come near, in thine own person and visibly, O Right and Good Thought, that I may be heard beyond the limits of the people." He prayed for perception, for wisdom, for guidance, for the joys of life "that were, that are, that shall be." He prayed that the poor man might be protected and be granted a sign tha he might worship again "more joyfully."

The Gathas relate that God answered Zoroaster, and told him that his was the prayer of "a mighty one." Though he might wander outcast and poor, and his horses might shiver in the bitter wind at the door of one who would grant them no admittance, yet would Zoraster know that, after all, he had good thoughts, which are the best possession, yea, he had "the glories of the blessed life unto all time." God would assist him. And all who fought on his side, God would prosper. Good Thought would increase their substance and they would attain welfare and immortality. So Zo- roaster set "his heart on watching over the soul" of the people "in unison with Good Thought."

Through the mountainous districts of Persia, with mountain caves for his home, Zoroaster tramped, footsore and weary, pro- claiming Ahura Mazda's message. At the end of ten years he won a disciple, his cousin. With him for companion for two years more he wandered and tried to teach. After twelve years of failure and ridicule he went to the palace and asked to see the king. He was repulsed by the guards; and took his stand at the palace gate. Day after day he stood and waited. Until at last King Vishtasp granted him an audience, and called the court to hear him.

In winged words the Prophet told is royal audience what Good Thought could do for Persia. And King Vishtasp listened. It is said that Zoroaster carried in his hand a fire, but his hand was not burned. He offered the fire to the king, who took it in his hand, and his hand was not burned, for it was "the Glory made by Mazda."

The magicians and pagan priests of the court, jealous of a new favorite tried by false tales and evidence to ruin Zoroaster, and he was thrown into prison. When his cause seemed lost, he was again brought before the king, who finally decided to favor him. The ancient Glory now "clave unto King Vishtasp so that he thought according to the Law, spake according to the Law, did according to the Law." His beautiful queen, and his son, Isfandyar, were converted, also two noble ministers of the court, Frashaoshtra and Jamaspa. With the king's assistance they spread the "good religion" like a fire through the mountains and valleys of Persia.

A powerful king in the north, to whom Vishtasp paid tribute, soon sent word that he would dethrone him if he held to the new religion. Vishtasp's reply was to refuse further tribute. The northern king came with his army, and Isfandyar the mighty warrior went to meet him. Isfandyar was the hero of this and many wars. Whoever his enemies might be, through the assistance of Good Thought he overcame them, until

> *Where'er he went he was received*
> *With welcome, all the world believed,*
> *And all with grateful feelings took*
> *The Holy Zendavesta-book,*
> *Proud their new worship to declare.*

Zoroaster planted, the poet says, a glorious tree before the house of the king. The leaves and fruit of the tree were the civilization which arose from his teachings and around his personality. The sacred Scripture of the Zoroastrian civilization was the Avesta, made up of various books. The first is a compilation of poems and hymns called the Yasna, among which are the Gathas that contain Zoroaster's own words. Another book, he Vendidad, has Zoroaster's teachngs and his detailed social and hygienic laws, written down through the centuries by various teachers. Then come the Yasts, hymns written also at a later time than that in which Zoroaster lived. These books give Zoroaster's teaching of service to man and God. "Action, progress, reform are the watchwords of the Prophet's social teachings," writes M. H. Dhalla in his book *Zoroastrian Civilization*. Ahura Mazda "has instilled in man a burning passion for civilization and progress." Man must redeem and perfect the world, and all his life must work.

To accomplish his great task man must have health; and Zoroaster gave explicit hygienic laws. Purity of body prepares for purity of mind and soul; bodily cleanliness contributes to health. The devout Zoroastrians in obedience to the Prophet's instructions had strict regard for the daily bath in the morning. They must also wash, scrupulously, before prayers, before meals. Their houses and clothes must be kept clean. They must not wash their clothes in the river. They must live in the sunlight, for when the sun is absent the demons of disease prowl about. They must not drink from a dish to which another has touched his lips. Kindness to animals is a requirement, kindness especially to the dog, man's best friend. Detailed instructions are given for the care of dogs and domestic animals. The Prophet taught that it is just as wrong to give bad food to a dog as to the master of the house. The Avesta has thoroughgoing laws concerning chastity and man's relation to woman. It has rules for public health, for physicians and their practice. A law for the surgeon requires him to operate upon three devil worshipers before he practices on the followers of God. If all three devil worshipers die under his treatment he can never operate again on anyone.

The Zoroastrian Scriptures sing their praise "to Ahura Mazda, the Creator, the radiant and glorious, the most beautiful." They describe the soul's beautiful ascent after death to the spiritual world:

> *A Presence sped and hovered over me,*
> *A maiden, roseate as the blush of morn,*
> *Stately and pure as heaven, and on her face*
> *The freshness of a bloom untouched of Time.*
> *Amazed I cried, "Who art thou, Maiden fair,*

*Fairer than aught on earth these eyes have seen?"*
*And she in answer spake, "I am thyself,*
*Thy thoughts, thy words, thy actions glorified*
*By every conquest over base desire,*
*By every offering of a holy prayer*
*To the Wise Lord in Heaven, every deed*
*Of kindly help done to the good and pure,*
*By these I come thus lovely, come to guide*
*Thy steps to the dread Bridge where waits for thee*
*The Prophet, charged with judgment. . . .*
*So with my Angel forth I sped and passed*
*The Bridge of Judgment, passed the heavens Three,*
*Good Thought, Good Word, Good Action, and beyond*
*Soared to the place of Everlasting Light,*
*Ahura Mazda's boundless House of Song.*

The climax of the Avesta is Zoroaster's prophecy that "Future Deliverers," prophets like himself, will come to lead humanity onward until, in the great Day of Judgment, God will win a final victory over the forces of evil, and a glorious age of worldwide righteousness and peace will dawn. The Gathas tell that Zoroaster admonished his son, and King Vishtasp and his prime minister, to "seek the pleasure of Mazda with thought, words, and actions" and make "straight the paths for the Religion of the Future Deliverer which Ahura ordained." It is interesting to Christians that the *Gospel of the Infancy*, one of the early Christian apocryphal gospels, describes how three magi, wise men of the East, because "of a prophecy of Zoroaster" came over the desert to Bethlehem in search of the new Prophet, whose star they had seen in the Eastern sky.

Herodotus, "the father of history" celebrates the Persian religion, which made its followers truthful, moral, noble. In *Alcibiades* Socrates declares the greatness of Zoroaster, and asks Alcibiades how can he think to possess heredity or education comparable with that of the Persian kings and princes. Plato planned to study under the famous Zoroastrian teachers of the East, and was prevented only by the Persian wars. Aeschylus, in his drama *Persia*, praises Cyrus the Great who, it is true, "sorely ravished wide

Ionia," but was "too righteous to provoke the gods to wrath"; and Aeschylus describes the people's devotion to Darius. Xenophon writes of the charm, the beauty, and the courage of the Persians of his time. The biblical books Ezra, Nehemia, Daniel, and Esther have many references to the Persian dominion and splendor. No country had charmed the imagination more than Persia.

The Persians learned the sciences and arts of the people they conquered; and in return taught them the laws of the prophet Zoroaster and spread his good religion. Cyrus the Great and Darius were famous for their kindness to prisoners of war and to conquered communities. King Cyrus' ideal was a federation of the countries of the world into one organization, under one law—each country in this federation to follow its own particular customs, vocations, and religion. True to his ideal he often filled important posts in his government and his army with men chosen from the many countries he conquered. He was humane in his treatment of conquered people; he sent the Jewish captives in Babylon back to Palestine to rebuild their holy city. The Second Isaiah called him "God's Anointed."

Eight years after Cyrus came Darius, great ruler and devout Zoroastrian. He continued Cyrus' plan for a united empire, he developed commerce and industry, and hoped to establish intercommunication among the nations. Darius was tolerant to all religions. He sent many Jews back to Palestine. He freed from taxes and forced labor territory sacred to Apollo. Statesman, organizer, educator, he rose to such heights of power and grandeur that he himself was amazed. On the great staircase of his palace at Persepolis is a long procession of brilliantly carved figures which tells the story of the envoys from twenty-two nations who brought him tribute and gifts.

High upon the precipitous side of Mount Alvand near Hamadan, and on the great cliff at Behistun, he had a record of his deeds carved, in three languages. For his achievements he gave the credit to Ahura Mazda. Some of his inscriptions read:

Thus says Darius the King: Ahuramazda saw this world in confusion and gave it to me. He made me its king, I am king. By the grace of Ahuramazda I established it in its place.

Thus says Darius the King: That which I have done, I have done with the grace of Ahuramazda. ... Ahuramazda brought me help, and the other gods that are there.

Thus says Darius the King: For this reason Ahuramazda brought me help, and the other gods that there are, because I was not wicked, nor a liar, nor a tyrant, neither I nor my family.

North into Armenia, westward to Syria, Zoroaster's Good Message spread, and into Asia Minor where in time kings made it their state religion. The civilization it supported reached its zenith under the Achaemenid emperors Cyrus, Darius, and Xerxes.

Then commenced slow decline. The Persian kings and government officials became enamored of luxury, and enormous wealth demoralized them. The infection spread to the magi, the priests, who grew lax in their ethics and gradually concealed Zoroaster's exalted teachings under excessive ritual and minute purposeless laws. They wrote superstitions and extravagant commentaries into the text of the Avesta, and added to Zoroaster's wholesome teachings those incantations which have associated their name with the word "magic." They encouraged the people to leave the bodies of the dead in desolate places to be devoured by wild beasts. They revived the old nature deities, until Mithras the sun god became so popular he was worshiped in Asia Minor, Palestine, and the western Roman empire.

By 331 B.C. the government and religion were so corrupt that Persia was easily conquered by Alexander the Great. That daring militant hero, sometimes generous and king to the people he conquered, again giving way to paroxysms of anger, entered Persepolis with his army in 331 B.C. and in a mad carousal in Darius' and Xerxes' magnificent palace celebrated his victory over Persia. Then he set fire to the palace, and with it perished the great library where, the Parsee record says, was treasured the Avesta, written in ink of gold on thousands of cow hides.

The Greek rulers looked disdainfully upon the Persians as barbarians fit only to be exploited, and under Greek domination and tyranny the conquered people lost their incentive. In the second century B.C. they were conquered again, by the Parthians from the north, who held them in subjection until A.D. 226. Under the

Parthians they sank into social and spiritual apathy.

After Jesus' crucifixion many Christians traveled to Persia to help the desolate people. Tradition says the apostle Thomas went there with the wondrous story of the Christ. During the first two centuries of the Christian era these messengers of mercy spread their religion and their Greek learning until there were so many friends of Christ in Persia that Emperor Constantine wrote to King Sapur of Persia, "I am delighted to learn that the finest districts of Persia are adorned with the presence of Christians."

In A.D. 226 Ardashir, of the priestly class among Zoroastrians, became King of Persia, and established the Sassanian dynasty, which lasted for four hundred years. He and his successors tried to recover the strength of the Achaemenids, and in their wars with Rome they won back southern Mesopotamia, and at last built their capital, Ctesiphon, near Babylon on the Tigris River.

The Sassanians were handsome, full of energy and enthusiasm, gay, alert of mind, and ready for new ideas. They were devoted Zoroastrians, and in the early years of their rule the religion was purified until much of its original dynamic returned. The Sassanian kings encouraged education, for their Scriptures said, "A poor man who is learned is more beloved of the heavenly beings than a rich man who is ignorant." The schools were usually on the temples' grounds, Zoroastrian priests were the teachers. The teaching profession was held high, and the instructor was admonished that his character, like a mirror, should reflect to his students all good deeds. Students were advised to rise before dawn, and were told that one third of the day and night should be spent in study.

The kings and the noble religious teachers of this dynasty revived in spectacular fashion the architecture, art, and culture of the Achaemenids. To the Sassanian period belong some of the monumental rock carvings of antiquity, and the arts were again developed into marvelous beauty. The Persians now created some of the most beautiful jewelry and textiles of the world. The proud Romans vied with each other to secure Persia's peerless silks and brocades, and paid enormous prices for them. When the Arabs conquered Persia they found in a palace a royal carpet 450 feet long and 90 feet wide on which was woven the picture of a garden.

Gold thread made the ground of the garden, and silver thread its walks; the grass was green with emeralds, the rivulets were pearls, while diamonds, rubies, sapphires, and other precious and brightly colored stones formed the trees, flowers, leaves, and fruits.

The Christians were a potent influence in this recovery. Still aglow with the high-powered radiance of the Christ they influenced the highest ranks of society. Some of the famous Christian saints of this time were Zoroastrian converts. For many years during the Sassanian reign, the Christians were generously treated and allowed to make their own laws and manage their affairs. Given this freedom their religion spread until in the year 302 Armenia, one-time province of Persia, which had been largely Zoroastrian became officially a Christian nation.

Reading the signs of the time some of the Zoroastrian priests became alarmed lest they lose their prestige. They gained the ear of the Persian king, and secured a government order that any Zoroastrian who changed his religion should be punished with death. Under government sanction, they persecuted Christians and other heretics with relentless severity. These self-seeking priests tampered with the teachings of their Prophet, as their decadent predecessors had done five hundred years earlier. Zoroaster's noble and realistic religion, with its book of laws containing beneficent rules for hygienic, moral, social, and spiritual living, with its system of philosophy and teaching of immortality comprehensive, practical, subtle, no longer satisfied the arrogant priests. They added an enormous number of ordinances, also many superstitions, and forced them upon the people. Zoroaster made fire the symbol of purity and light divine which destroys every imperfection. The domineering priests taught the worship of fire itself, and returned the sun god Mithras to his former prestige, until Zoroastrians were classed among the sun and fire worshipers. In the Gathas the devil is Druj, the Lie; the archangels, "the immortal holy ones," are God's attributes, and God is the only ultimate, eternal Power. In this latest form of Zoroastrianism the archangels and the forces of evil were definite persons. Ahriman, the Devil, was so appallingly powerful that he and God divided the universe between them. There is apparently a tendency in human nature to polytheism, that is, the worship of something else than God, which only a vital prophetic personality can even temporarily eradicate.

The collapse of Persia's religion resulted in moral chaos, with kings tyrannical and abusive. In the darkness the noblest of the Sassanian kings, Chosroes the Just, inherited the throne, and during his reign, from 531 to 579, a new hope dawned. Chosroes the Just dismissed the government officials who oppressed the people, and adopted a just form of taxation, which was used later by the Muslim Arabs. In the city of Jundeshapur he founded a university and built a hospital. Under this enlightened and tolerant king, Buddhists, Hindus, Christians, Neo-Platonists, and Zoroastrians made their contributions to Zoroastrian civilization; while Nestorian Christians and Neo-Platonists translated into Persian the works of Galen, Hippocrates, and many eminent Greek philosophers and men of science.

Chosroes the Just wrote his own funeral oration, his legacy, perhaps, to his subjects:

People of the world, conduct yourselves in such a manner that the blessings of all may follow you. Let the conduct of your affairs be accompanied by truthful thoughts. Work strenuously and zealously for mankind. Be just and discreet in your actions. Be of good religion, and you will go to the Abode of Song. Goodness is possible of attainment by anyone, irrespective of his position. Remember that this world is transitory. Prepare yourself by your deeds for the spiritual world. Let this also be said, that everyone should reflect: Whence have I come, why have I come hither, whither have I to go, and what shall they ask of me there? I know that I have come from the creator Ormazd [Ahura Mazda]. I am here to fight evil, and I have to go back to the creator Ormazd.

The kings who succeeded Chosroes the Just were weak and corrupt. They could be approached only through a maze of pomp and cermony, and in their presence everyone must hold his handkerchief before his mouth lest his breath pollute the royal personage. Their sumptuous palaces and their gardens were unparalleled in their world, and the kings were effete with luxury. Under them the social order hardened into caste stratifications which seemed unbreakable, and religious intolerance reappeared. Although outwardly Persia's civilization was imposing, the social and spiritual deterioration was now swift and terrible. The Zoroastrian scholars of the period describe in their writings the darkness of those days, the futile and ruinous wars the kings ceaselessly fought, the hopelessness of the people.

Sixty years after the death of Chosroes the Just, Umar's armies, young, enthusiastic, with no worldly wisdom, entered Persia and in a few years possessed the kingdom.

When the Muslims began to rule Persia they did several unexpected things. They did not harm the civilization they conquered but protected and sustained its colleges and hospitals and the best elements of its government. They did not compel the Zoroastrians to adopt Islam; a Muslim general flogged a Muslim leader who destroyed a Zoroastrian temple to replace it with a mosque. They commenced at once to acquire culture and learning from their surroundings.

The Zoroastrians were greatly in need of the Future Deliverer, whom their Scriptures promised. When the Muslims offered them a Prophet whose influence and teachings were fresh and triumphant, why should they not accept him, they reasoned. Muhammad's teachings were almost identical with those of Zoroaster. Both Prophets taught a dramatic struggle between good and evil. Their laws concerning honesty, just government, social justice, and physical cleanliness were similar. Both taught a brotherhood which meant a noncaste system. Both taught a glorious monotheism. Both Prophets enjoined five prayers daily. Both promised to the righteous immortal joy in paradise.

In a few centuries all the Zoroastrians became Muslims, except a little handful. The wealthiest among this remnant emigrated to India and finally settled in Bombay where, under the name "Parsees," they have cherished their religion until the present day, a beautiful and upright community.

By the time that Islam arrived in Persia the Christians there were also in a deplorable state. Their religion had become dogmabound, priest-ridden, artificial and lifeless to such a degree that most of them joined Islam, and there occurred one of the spectacular conversions in history when a highly cultured people accepted of their own choice the religion of the rough, uneducated Arabs.

True religion kindles an intellectual love of God. Fired with

Muhammad's irresistible spirit of initiative and enterprise, the Muslims sought out Christians, Zoroastrians, and Sanskrit scholars, and transmitted to them a quickening which within two centuries brought to birth in Persia a great intellectual and spiritual renaissance. The Muslims developed the university at Jundeshapur until it became a fountainhead of learning. The Abbasid khalifas from Baghdad, their capital, opened the doors of bounty in the schools and colleges they founded. Under Muslim rule there was no caste discrimination; anyone from any social stratum could become an artist, philosopher, or scientist, if he had the ability. The love of knowledge, of intellectual creativeness returned with new intensity to the Persians. With their learning, accumulated for centuries, and their age-long experience in administration, they were with their new hope the backbone of the Abbasid era.

In these early centuries Arabic, the language in which the Quran was written, became the universal tongue of the Islamic empire, spoken from the Pyrenees to Tibet. Arabic literature came into being, developed in part by brilliant Persians.

Al-Hamadhani, a Persian Muslim from Hamadan, created a most entertaining form of the novel. A contemporary of al-Hamadhani wrote of him that he could "recite a poem of more than fifty lines, which he had never heard but once, remember it all and repeat it from beginning to end without altering a letter."

While the Christians of Europe fiercely suppressed any sign of scientific investigation or intellectual initiative, Muslim rule allowed everyone freedom to acquire knowledge for knowledge's sake. The Muslim Persian scholar al-Biruni, born in 973, observed, studied, thought, and wrote as he chose. After years of study in India he translated Indian books into Arabic, and Arabic translations of the Greek philosophers he rendered into Sanskrit. His monumental, unprejudiced study of the religions, sciences, and social customs of India, finished about 1030, has been translated into English and published in two large volumes. In twelve books, called the *Canon*, he summed up the astronomical science of the Arabs. This work, the result of years of indefatigable labor, he presented to Sultan Mas Súd who, delighted with the achievement, sent al-Biruni an elephant loaded with silver. The scholar returned the present with the message that he did not care for money.

When al-Biruni was on his death-bed, a learned man came to visit him. The dying scholar asked his guest to explain a certain point in the Muslim law of inheritance. The visitor said, "Not now, not in this condition." Al-Biruni replied, "Is it not better that I should bid farewell to the world knowing this question than that I should leave it without this knowledge?" The visitor gave the solution to the problem, al-Biruni committed it to memory, and died.

The greatest genius of the time many think was Avicenna, who lived from 980 to 1037. Man of science, physician, physicist, statesman, musician, poet, philosopher, master of Arabic style, for centuries his was a name to conjure with. From early childhood the love of truth burned in his mind like a consuming fire and, writes the thirteenth-century historian, Ibn Khallikan, "God opened for him the gates of knowledge."

When Avicenna was ten he studied logic and Euclid, and was "a perfect master of the Quran and of general literature." He studied medicine, hoping to improve the existing methods of diagnosis and treatment. Ibn Khallikan tells that "in a very short time he surpassed in that art ancients and moderns, and remained without a rival or an equal." He practiced so successfully when he was sixteen years old that eminent physicians came to him to learn his methods of treatment, and the ignorant people called him a magician.

When he reached manhood he read Aristotle's *Metaphysics* until he knew it by heart; yet after the fortieth reading he did not understand it. Then he found, in a bookstore, a commentary by a Muslim philosopher which cleared away his difficulties. "I was delighted," he wrote, "and the next day distributed alms to the poor in order to show my gratitude to God." Day and night Avicenna studied. He was a devout Muslim, and he wrote, "When I was perplexed by any question I went to the Mosque and prayed to God to solve the difficulty." Often the solution of the problem shone into his mind, sometimes in a dream at night.

Avicenna's book on medicine was for six hundred years, until the seventeenth century, an authority from India to the Atlantic,

from the Sudan to the Baltic and the British Isles. His rules for
health are interesting. The body, he reasoned, reflects the activity
of the mind and is often ill because of fears, worries, and doubts
that harass the soul. Anger, excitement, and fear undermine man's
physical vitality and his ability to resist disease. Whatever could
make the mind more confident and joyous would hasten the healing of the body. Excitement and fear induce fatigue. Prayer and
obedience to the laws of the divine universe bring life. Concerning
diet, he wrote, "Mental excitement or emotion, vigorous exercise
—these hinder digestion. No meal should be bulky enough to
satisfy completely the appetite. One should rise from the table
while some appetite or desire for food is still present. For such
remnants of hunger will disappear in the course of an hour. If one
ate to excess one day, one should fast the next."

Another Muslim physician, one of the greatest in history, was
Rhazes, who lived in the tenth century. He was chief of the hospital of Rayy in Persia, and later of the famous hospital in Baghdad.
Rhazes studied his cases by an empirical method much like that
of the modern man of science. With easy mastery of style he wrote
more than a hundred books.

*The Chahár Maqála,* a delightful book written by a Persian
scholar of the twelfth century, gives the qualifications for the
physician according to the Muslim ideal in this Persian renaissance. "The physician should be of tender disposition, of wise and
gentle nature, and more especially an acute observer, capable of
benefiting everyone by accurate diagnoses." He cannot be of tender disposition unless he recognizes "the nobility of man"; he
cannot be "an acute observer unless he be strengthened by God's
guidance."

A new refinement of perception and an artistic activity seldom
paralleled came to the people of Persia when the breezes of Islam
touched their life. Thousands of artists of highest ability made
designs for textiles and brocades, illuminated books and book
bindings, decorated faience bowls, vases, and polychrome tiles.
Their pottery was plastic and alive, with lines curved to represent
the beauty of life abundant, the pure joy of living. On bowls and
vases they sketched the vigorous human life around them, adding
to their pictures little antelopes and birds, or human beings

mounted on cows or galloping ponies. On bowls ocean blue, they painted golden fishes swimming—a few strokes told the story. Into many charming patterns they so skillfully wove the beautiful Arabic and Persian script that it became an indispensable part of the harmony. Wonderful works from Islamic Persia are to be found in the museums of Iran, Europe, and the United States. One such treasure is a lovely bottle molded evidently by the sensitive hand of a true artist. The blue of the sky is not more beautiful than the turquoise of this little bottle. The grace of its neck and the strange spiritual atmosphere that shines in it gives a glimpse of the beauty of the Persian spirit when Islam was in flower.

In all the arts, the craftsmen and artisans seemed to possess the same love and gift for beauty. Their glassware was exquisite. They manufactured paper from linen and silk, and polished it until it looked like porphyry or agate or marble. They carved wood, making bowls almost as thin as paper and spoons with tiny handles covered with lacework.

One looks at an incomparable Persian rug and thinks of the master weaver who held the intricate, seemingly unwieldy details of the design in his mind and brought them into triumphant oneness. With lines clear, firm, original, he wove all the colors and divergent forms into a perfect unity. As one studies his masterpiece, its construction seems like that of a man's mind where in apparent confusion is stored all that he had heard and felt and learned, the elements of the human and spiritual natures interlaced in orderless tangles like a jungle's lavish growth. The Master Gardener if he is permitted, can assemble this inner life and make it into a harmonious garden.

In the planning and building of their mosques the Persians expressed their thanksgiving to the Prophet who raised them once more into life abounding and poured new beauty into their souls. They developed the pointed arch, they combined the dome and the arch and with astonishing skill placed them on square surfaces. They adorned the walls and floors of their private and public buildings with mosaics and faience tiles brilliant and beautiful. They set the pace for the architecture of western Asia.

Some say this amazing outpouring of artistic genius was due to the dazzling sunlight and the transparent clearness of the air.

Persian sunlight may help clarify the mind, but why did Persian genius develop into resplendent beauty only in periods of especial spiritual awakening? Some say it was contact with the civilizations of India, China, and Greece that stimulated Persia. Buddhist art at its height undoubtedly influenced eastern Asia. By A.D. 600 that dynamic in India had lost its life-giving power and was on the wane. Buddhist China influenced Persia for a while; Persia also contributed to China's renaissance in the days of T'ang. Egyptian, Assyrian, and Grecian art influenced Persia in early centuries. When Greek contact was brought upon her in the days of Greek conquest Persian genius disappeared.

"Men are only creative in poetry and art as long as they are religious; without religion they are merely imitative, lacking in originality," wrote Goethe. When her inspiration was young and vital Persia used the art of other nations as a suggestion for new and original brilliance. When her religion declined and inspiration died, she merely copied the art of the past.

From the ninth to the sixteenth centuries, when Muhammad's influence was at its height and his followers lived by the light of his personality, and his teachings and deeds occupied their thoughts, a host of artists and thousands of poets appeared in Persia. A famous patron of poets and of learning was Sultan Mahmud of Ghazni. He decreed that a great epic celebrating the deeds of the kings and heroes of ancient Iran be written, and from the four hundred poets whom he supported at his court he chose seven for the task.

In the city of Tus lived a student of the ancient sagas of Iran as they were written in old Pahlavi or translated into Arabic. This man, in the prime of middle life, aspired to write the Sultan's epic, although the seven had been appointed. He went to Mahmud's court, sure of the scholar's welcome; and the Sultan was soon so pleased with him that he named him Firdausi, for, said Mahmud, the poet's presence turned the court into paradise, *firdausi.*

The jealous seven decided to humiliate the presumptuous stranger. Three of the seven, to this end, composed a rhyme of three lines. The word that ended each of their lines rhymed with the last word of the other lines. In the Persian language there was no other word that rhymed with any one of these three words. When their trap was set they went into a garden and sat down to wait for Firdausi.

Soon he strolled into the place and they started to converse. They informed him that poets of the first order only were admitted to their presence. Then they suggested that they compose, extempore, a poem, each poet contributing a line ending with a word that rhymed with the last word of the other lines. Firdausi's line would complete the poem. If his last word did not rhyme with the other last words he would be excluded from their society.

Each of the three recited the line he had prepared. And Firdausi was apparently done for. Without a moment's hesitation he completed their verse with a line ending with a proper name from an ancient Persian saga unknown to the others. This name rhymed perfectly with their three last words. The poets inquired who the person with the rhyming name might be? Firdausi described in improvised verse the exploits of a prehistoric hero.

The seven distinguished poets voluntarily relinquished the coveted task to Firdausi, and Sultan Mahmud, delighted with his rare find, offered him a gold dinar for every couplet of the epic.

Firdausi set to work. He searched ancient manuscripts for material for his story and at last discovered, through a dream it is said, an old, forgotten chronicle which gave him most of his data. For more than twenty-five years he worked, and by the light of his learning and his genius he wrote one of the world's magnificent epics. His saga, which he calls the *Shah Namah*, opens with the invocation:

> *Thee I invoke, the Lord of Life and Light!*
> *Beyond imagination pure and bright!*
> *To thee, sufficing praise no tongue can give,*
> *We are thy creatures, and in thee we live.*
> *Thou art the summit, depth, the all in all,*
> *Creator, Guardian of this earthly ball;*
> *Whatever is, thou art—Protector, King,*
> *From thee all goodness, truth, and mercy spring.*
> *Oh, pardon the misdeeds of him who now*
> *Bends in thy presence with a suppliant brow.*

*Teach him to tread the path thy Prophet trod;*
*To wash his heart from sin; to know his God;*
*And gently lead him to that home of rest,*
*Where filled with holiest rapture dwell the blest.*

Firdausi's epic, like the *Iliad*, is a tale of mighty heroes. The greatest of them is Rustam:

*In beauty of form and in vigor of limb,*
*No mortal was ever seen equal to him.*

He fought demons and monsters and vast armies, he served his king faithfully. The secret of his invincible strength was his trust in God. Behold, he said, "what one man can" do "with power derived from God."

Firdausi was a master of romantic song. He was a philosopher, a moral educator whose ethics were high and clear, he was adviser of kings and princes, he was a devoted Muslim, a lover of Muhammad and Ali. In the *Shah Namah* he praises Zoroaster, and one of his heroes declares Moses to be "the best of prophets."

In Firdausi's day lived a druggist, a member of a group of Muslim men who met almost every night to praise God and his Prophet. One evening the druggist took his little son with him to the meeting. The group ate their supper, and when the meal was finished one of the men rose and chanted the verse:

*God gives the dervish love—and love is woe;*
*By dying near and dear to Him they grow.*
*The generous youth will freely yield his life,*
*The man of God cares naught for worldly show.*

The others were so happy in the hope of becoming free from selfishness through loving God that they rose and recited the verse together. To their words they added a quiet, measured dance; and thus they sang to their rhythmic motion until the next day dawned.

Through the night the amazed child watched and listened. He

heard the verse so many times that he learned it by heart. On the way home he asked his father how those lines could cause such joy. "You cannot understand," his father replied. He understood more than his father knew, and in his mind rose the longing for God.

The little boy, Abu Said, listened to the murmur of the waters that flowed through lovely gardens and to the rapturous singing of the nightingales that came to the rose bushes, and he longed to sing with the waters and the birds. So his father sent him to a gifted poet. This teacher asked him one day, "Do you wish to talk with God?" and again, "Do you wish to talk with God?" Then he taught him this poem:

> *Without Thee, O Beloved, I cannot rest;*
> *Thy goodness toward me I cannot reckon.*
> *Tho' every hair of my body becomes a tongue,*
> *A thousandth part of the thanks due to Thee*
> *I cannot tell.*

He said to the boy, "O Abu Said, endeavor to remove self-interest from your dealings with God." With his poet-teacher, Abu Said read the Quran and learned to listen with the ear of the spirit to its melodies. He learned to repeat poems of praise to God so that they sang in his soul. When he became a man he testified that the way to God was thus opened to him in his childhood.

The teacher died, in 990, when Abu Said was in his twenties. For the next ten years he went from one master to another. He met a famous spiritual teacher who told him, "All the prophets were sent to preach one word; they bade the people say, 'Allah, God,' and devote themselves to Him." Said the teacher, if the word but goes into one ear and out at the other it has no effect. It must penetrate heart and soul until one's whole being becomes the word.

How wonderful, thought Abu Said, that all the prophets came to earth to teach men to concentrate their thoughts on God, to repeat his holy name until it possessed their life, to devote themselves entirely to him. Abu Said slept not that night. The next morning he went to the classroom of a celebrated doctor of divinity who, strangely, opened his lecture with the words, "Say, 'Allah, God.' This is the essence of Muhammad's teaching. Concentrate thou on God." As Abu Said listened a door in his heart opened, and he felt God's presence. The teacher seeing what had happened sent him to a noble mystic. When this spiritual leader saw the light in Abu Said's face he exclaimed, "Thou hast been transported, transported, transported." He told Abu Said to go and meditate alone.

Abu Said went to his home and, in the chapel in his father's house, he prayed in ecstasy, "Allah, Allah, Allah." He was like St. Francis of Assisi who in his joy sang all night long, "My God, my God, my God."

To make sure that he had no selfish care for his physical welfare, Abu Said put himself through rigorous ascetic practices. He slept sitting, he stood upright all night. To make sure that he had no pride, he begged for food for the brethren.

One day he met a farmer who told him he was pondering in his heart this matter: If God when he created the world had filled it with millet seed and had created just one little bird, and one man, and the little bird ate one millet seed every thousand years, and the man prayed that he might become conscious of God's presence, and attained it, and lost it, and prayed again, and prayed and longed and purified his heart until, after the little bird had eaten all the millet seed in the world, the vision splendid arose in the man's heart and abode there forever—if the man had to struggle as long as that to attain the consciousness of God, the time was of no moment.

Abu Said was more than forty when he won this consciousness; and for the rest of his life, he testified, he lived in the presence of God. He discovered he could eat what he pleased, he could sit on a soft cushion, he could enjoy the beauty of nature and keep his consciousness of God's presence; he did not have to be an ascetic, he could be joyous and share his joy with others. Sometimes, in these happy years, a rich friend would give him some money. Then Abu Said would spread a feast for the people, high and low, rich and poor. He would have oxen and sheep killed and huge platters of meat served to his guests. And he would do a thing which seemed to the puritans of his day an inexcusable extravagance, he would burn a whole bunch of sweet-smelling aloewood, all at once, and would light a thousand candles in the daytime.

Abu Said is one of the most famous poets and spiritual teachers of Islam. In hundreds of quatrains he sang his love of God and his joy in God. He created the form of verse Omar Khayyám used. he was known as the saint who was not afraid to be happy and jolly.

The Arabs and the Persians were lovers of poetry and some of Islam's finest teachers were poets, who used their verse as the torch by which to light and quicken the spiritual life of their people. A younger contemporary of Abu Said wrote:

> *In the market, in the cloister—only God I saw.*
> *In the valley and on the mountain—only God I saw.*
> *Him I have seen beside me oft in tribulation;*
> *In favor and in fortune—only God I saw.*
> *In prayer and fasting, in praise and contemplation,*
> *In the religion of the Prophet—only God I saw.*

# 25

## The Quran

THE FOUNDATION of this Saracenic–Moorish–Persian civilization
was Muhammad: his laws, his teachings, his dynamic life. Because
Muhammad spoke Arabic it became the language of the Islamic
world, difficult though it was, and Muhammad's style was the
standard. Every chapter but one of the Quran opens with the
ringing words, "In the Name of God." The Muslims therefore
opened their thousands of transactions, written and spoken, with
the phrase, "In the Name of God." A host would welcome his
guest with the words, *"Marhaba, Bismillah.* Welcome, in the
name of God." To the guest this meant, "Be seated." The host
would pass refreshments and say, *"Bismillah;* In the Name of
God," meaning "Have something to eat." Authors dedicated their
books to God and Muhammad. The procedures of the courts of
law, the education of the people from babyhood were built upon
the deeds and words of Muhammad. The Quran was chanted at
banquets, at weddings, at social gatherings; its verses were recited
in unison by the multitudes who filled the mosques every Friday
for their congregational worship, its sentences were intoned from
thousands of minarets and repeated five times every day by millions of Muslims. When the khalifa or another mighty ruler in the
Islamic world sat on his throne in his splendid audience room,
beside him often stood a reader and at intervals during the hours
of conference the solemn words of the Quran were read to the
assemblage.

Even the Umayyads realized how all-important to the Muslim
world were the voice and example of Muhammad. These khalifas'

retainers soon began to invent all manner of sayings and deeds which would be to their advantage and, ascribing them to the Prophet, compelled the faithful Muslims to obey them. Through the years superstitions multiplied, until it was said Muhammad permitted spells for snake bite and the evil eye and many questionable ills. These spurious sayings went under the name of *hadith*, or traditions, and for many years were accepted as authentic.

During Islam's first century thousands of Arab and other pagans lured by the unregenerate desire for conquest and spoils became Muslims. To uphold their lawlessness they dragged the Apostle of God down, until they made him a very ordinary conqueror and self-indulgent king. They tried to prove that their love of war came from the heights of Muhammad's influence, when it was really the drive of their own animal nature. Under their leadership Muhammad's wars were magnified, and his polygamy interpreted as a desirable way of living; whereas they were grievous political and social necessities of his time. Maqidi, a famous Muslim historian of the ninth century who, it was said, had in his library six hundred chests of manuscripts and books, wrote at length of Muhammad's "glorious" wars and declared that the Prophet had lived in luxury, partaking of sensual enjoyments. The words of this historian influenced for centuries the opinions of other historians. The Christian enemies of Islam, comparing this Muhammad with their holy Christ, declared Muhammad was no prophet at all but a rank impostor. Much of the Western prejudice against Muhammad is due to the picture drawn of him by pagan Muslims.

By the time the Abbasid khalifas began to rule Islam the sayings put into Muhammad's mouth had become like the waves of the sea in number, and so fanciful were they that they often contradicted each other. Strange miracles were told concerning him; it was even said a wolf and an ox spoke to him, and a tree moved to meet him.

What was the truth, where was the light of guidance? asked many sincere Muslims. A group of critical scholars—doctors, jurists, and scientific historians—was called to Baghdad by Khalifa Mansur to consider the problem. Among them was Abu Hanifa, student of Imam Jaafar. Noble in character, Abu Hanifa was a tremendous influence for good in Islam. So careful was he to imitate Muhammad exactly that he would never eat watermelon because he could not find in any authentic tradition a description of the way in which Muhammad ate watermelon. Abu Hanifa died in Baghdad, and eight hundred thousand people, it is said, attended his funeral.

The saintly scholar Bukhari, who lived from 810 to 870, before he was eighteen set himself the task of finding among the thousands of false traditions attributed to Muhammad those which were authentic. He had a dream one night in which he saw Muhammad surrounded by flies and he, Bukhari, was driving them away. When he woke he decided this dream was his commission to find the truth in the Muslim records. He traveled through the Muslim dominions, from Balkh to Egypt, and questioned the spiritual teachers of Islam as to purported traditions. He is said to have studied three hundred thousand *hadith*, and finally to have chosen seven thousand he believed to be genuine. If repetitions be eliminated from the seven thousand *hadith* approved by Bukhari, less than three thousand will remain.

His method of procedure was this: no tradition was to be counted genuine unless it could be traced back, through an unbroken chain of guarantors, to a contemporary of the Prophet, an eyewitness who could be proved so trustworthy that his testimony would be accepted in a court of law. When such an eyewitness said, "I saw. I heard," the saying he repeated was accepted by Bukhari.

Muhammad warned, "After my death sayings attributed to me will multiply just as a large number of sayings are attributed to the prophets who were before me. What is told you as a saying of mine you must compare with the Quran. What is in agreement therewith is from me whether I have actually said it or not." Acting on this suggestion other compilers of Muhammad's authentic words used the Quran as their standard. Six books of sayings, some compiled with the aid of the Quran, others by Bukhari's method, were declared trustworthy.

Other eminent scholars compiled four books which a group, the Shias, the Friends of Ali accepted as authentic. The Shias held that the essential authority in Islam after Muhammad was the apostolic Imams; and they required that a tradition be accurately traced to one of these Imams. During the reign of the Umayyads it was very difficult to collect or even quote the teachings of Ali and the Imams, for the House of Muawiya, knowing they had taken the throne from the House of Ali, suspected anyone who was friendly to the apostolic Imams. The Umayyads even employed historians and poets to write sayings favorable to their House and in disparagement of the House of Ali. When the poet, in Mecca, stepped forward from the crowd before the Ka'aba and recited his extemporary poem in praise of Ali the Younger and Husain, that poet was promptly thrown into prison by Khalifa Walid. Ali the Younger sent a purse full of money to the prison for the poet but he returned the purse with the message that he had written so many lying poems in praise of the Umayyad khalifas, poems for which he had received pay, that he would like for once to compose a truthful verse for which he should not receive any money. Not until Harun ar-Rashid's son, Mamun, became khalifa were Muhammad's words in praise of Ali generally quoted, or was the greatness of the apostolic Imams openly declared.

During the Abbasid centuries historians gathered up the incidents in Muhammad's life. They recorded a chain of guarantors for each event they accepted as authentic, and the records read like this: so-and-so told such-an-one (name), and he told (name), on and on through a hundred years or more until the record ends with "and he told (name), a friend, or teacher of his, that Muhammad did or said thus-and-so."

The Muslims built their civilization generation after generation upon the *hadith*, or records, of Muhammad's verbal teachings and his deeds; and upon his book the Quran, that dynamic word picture of a moral, intellectual, and spiritual universe as keenly related to man, as vitally important to him, as is the physical world.

"Time has no indulgence; any veils of illusion which we may have left around an object because we loved it, Time is sure to strip away," writes Matthew Arnold. The Quran grew in influence until centuries after it was written men and women spent the night reciting its verses, and every road of Islamic civilization led to this book. A Jew living in the year 1298 entered a mosque one day, and as he watched the impressive service and felt the sincerity and reverence of the people and their leader as they recited the Quran and bowed and rose in prayer, he decided he was created to be a Muslim. Bosworth Smith, Fellow of Trinity College, Oxford, writes in his book *Mohammed and Mohammedanism,* "By a fortune absolutely unique in history, Mohammed is the threefold founder of a nation, of an empire, and of a religion. Illiterate himself, scarcely able to read or write, he was yet the author of a book which is a poem, a code of laws, a book of common prayer, and a bible in one, and is reverenced to this day by a sixth of the whole human race as a miracle of purity of style, of wisdom, and of truth. It was the one miracle claimed by Mohammed—'his standing miracle,' he called it; and a miracle indeed it is." The Quran has a dignity, solemnity, and dynamic unattainable in translation. Its Arabic verses sing with a tremendous rhythm; and no language but the Arabic in which it was written can do it justice.

During Muhammad's lifetime no effort was made apparently to form the Quran into a book; portions were in writing, but some of it existed only in the memory of Muhammad and the early Muslims. After Muhammad's passing so many of his devoted followers were killed in the battles with the rebel tribes, the very men who knew the Quran by heart, that Umar became afraid Muhammad's book might be lost, and he persuaded Abu Bakr to have a copy made.

The khalifa instructed Zayd, the faithful Muslim who had often taken Muhammad's dictation, to compile a copy of the Quran. Zayd carefully gathered up the ribs of palm leaves, shoulder blades of sheep, flat stones, pieces of leather on which chapters (suras) were written. And he sought out the faithful believers who had learned Muhammad's words by heart, and obtained from them those parts of the Quran they had memorized. Then he made a complete copy and gave it to Abu Bakr. When Umar became khalifa, by right of office the copy belonged to him; and he bequeathed it to his daughter Hafsa, wife of Muhammad.

By the time that Uthman became khalifa copies of Zayd's manuscript had been made and circulated and much controversy had arisen among leading Muslim teachers concerning minute details of transcription. Uthman, at the insistence of one of his generals, commissioned Zayd to make an authoritative copy, and he paid three young men to help Zayd in the task. When Zayd finished his copy all others except Hafsa's, Zayd's original copy, were burned; Hafsa's copy was later destroyed by the governor of Medina. Three copies were made from this last transcription by Zayd and were sent, one to Damascus, one to Basra, one to Kufa. The first copy, from which these others were made, was kept in Medina. From these four copies of the Quran all others have come.

The Quran is the textbook which trained the Muslim nations. Like the other great Scriptures, some parts are eternal, and some, when outgrown, seem strangely unnecessary, since it is difficult to think back sympathetically into primitive conditions.

Muhammad's primary task, and perhaps his most difficult, was to persuade his people to forswear their idols and believe in a God whom they could not see. After many years of training by Muslim teachers, the citizens of Ta'if decided to destroy their idols. They piled them together for a huge bonfire in the public square. As the idols burned, the women of the town stood by and wailed.

As we have already noted, all the chapters of the Quran except one commence, "In the Name of God, the Compassionate, the Merciful," and the book contains ninety-nine names which describe God's glory. God is the Holy One, Lord of Splendid Power, the Judge of Judges, the All-Knower, the Provider, the Forgiver, the Hearer of Prayer, the All-Comprehending, the Help in Peril, the Nearest Friend, the Loving. As time went on and the spiritual understanding of Islam grew, to name these attributes of the All-Glorious God became a prayer; and the Muslims made strings of ninety-nine beads to use with this prayer. Says the Quran:

God, who made you the earth for a resting-place and the heaven for a tent, and formed you and made goodly your forms, and provided you with good things—that is God, your Lord.
Then blessed be God, the Lord of the worlds!
He is the Living One. No God is there but Him. Then call upon Him, purifying your service to Him. Praise be to God, the Lord of the worlds!

God! There is no God but Him, the Living, the Steadfast! Slumber seizeth Him not, nor sleep. Whatsoever is in the heavens, and whatsoever is in the earth, is His. Who is there that shall plead with Him save by His leave? He knoweth what was before them and what shall come after them, and they compass not aught of his knowledge, but what He willeth. His throne overspreadeth the heavens and the earth, and the keeping of both is no burden to Him, and He is the High, the Great!

All that is in the heavens and the earth magnifieth God, and He is the Mighty, the Wise.
His is the kingdom of the heavens and the earth, He giveth life and giveth death, and He is powerful over all things.
He is the first and the last, the seen and the unseen, and all things doth He know.

All that is in the heavens and all that is on the earth glorifieth God, and He is the Mighty, the Wise.
The birds as they spread their wings sing praise of God.
Whoever holdeth fast to God is already guided to a straight path.
God is the light of the heavens and the earth.

Everything they did, Muhammad told his followers, was done in God's presence:

He knoweth what is in the heavens and the earth; and He knoweth what ye hide and what ye manifest; and God knoweth well the secrets of the breast.

O ye who believe, stand fast by justice, bearing witness before God, though it be against yourselves, or your parents, or your kindred, whether it be against rich or poor; for God is worthier than they.

Thou shalt not be in any business, and thou shalt not read from the Quran, and thou shalt not do any deed but we are witness against you when ye are engaged therein; and there escapeth not thy Lord an ant's weight on earth or in heaven.

God is also infinite mercy, and Muhammad said in his Table Talk:

When God created the creation He wrote a book which is near Him upon the sovran Throne; and what is written in it is this: Verily my compassion overcometh my wrath.

God saith: Whoso doeth one good act, for him are ten rewards, and I also give more to whomsoever I will; and whoso doeth ill, its retaliation is equal to it, or else I forgive him; and he who seeketh to approach me one cubit, I will seek to approach him two fathoms; and he who walketh toward me, I will run toward him.

Muhammad told his followers that in order to prosper they must form into a brotherhood in which all were socially equal. His many laws for the administration of the brotherhood were adapted to his particular time, for it would have been useless to give his country-men regulations far beyond them. They were people who, when they came together to make a town or city, built it in sections, one for each tribe, with a wall around each division; and when there was trouble of any sort each tribe withdrew within its own walls and locked the one gate to its section. This was as much as they knew of cooperation. Muhammad had to win them to take the first step in real community life. He told them:

Say not, if people do good to us, we will do good to them, and if people oppress us, we will oppress them: but resolve that if people do good to you, you will do good to them, and if they oppress you, oppress them not again.

Merchants shall be raised up liars on the Day of Resurrection, except he who abstaineth from that which is unlawful and doth not swear falsely but speaketh truely as to the price of his goods.

The bringers of grain to the city to sell at a cheap rate, gain immense advantage by it, and he who keepeth back grain in order to sell at a high rate is cursed.

He wrote in his Quran,

It is not righteousness that ye turn your face towards the east or the west, but righteousness is [in] him who believeth in God and the Last Day, and the Angels, and the Scripture, and the Prophets, and who giveth wealth for the love of God to his kinsfolk and to orphans and the needy and the wayfarer and them that ask and for the freeing of slaves; and who is instant in prayer, and giveth the alms; and those who fulfil their covenant when they covenant, and the patient in adversity and affliction and in time of violence, these are they who are true, and these are they who fear God.

If ye give alms openly, it is well; but if ye conceal it, and give it to the

poor, it is better for you, and will take away from you some of your
sins; and God knoweth what ye do.

In his Table Talk, Muhammad said:

Doing justice between two people is alms; and assisting a man upon his
beast, and his baggage, is alms; and pure words, for which are rewards; and answering a questioner with mildness is alms, and every
step which is made toward prayer is alms, and removing that which
is an inconvenience to man, such as stones and thorns, is alms.

Muhammed forbade gambling and drinking alcoholic liquor. He
gave hygienic laws for bathing and moderate eating, and warned
against harmful foods; he made brushing the teeth almost a religious duty.

His strict penal laws were much like those in the Torah. To give
alms and to free slaves were noble deeds, he taught. If his followers
were not willing to free their slaves, they must treat them as
members of their family. The man who struck his slave must free
the wronged one immediately. Muhammad's teaching concerning
marriage was similar to the Mosaic law. Of war, Muhammad wrote
in the Quran, "Fight in the way of God against those who fight
against you, but begin not hostilities. Lo, God loveth not aggres-
sors."

Muhammad taught that prayer should be more than a request
for favors of presents from God; it should also be meditation upon
God's mighty characteristics. He required his followers to pray
five times every day, and as much during the night as they were
able. Those who prayed in the night would have bright faces
during the day, he said. The month of Ramadhan, the month of
fasting, was a special time of prayer. "Whoso loveth to meet God,
God loveth to meet him," he told the Muslims, and advised them
to pray at dawn while the sun was slowly flooding the world with
light. In later years, when their Prophet was no longer with them,
his devoted followers remembered that, after praying half the
night, Muhammad would be in the court of the little mosque in
Medina for the dawn prayer. For love of him all Islam, centuries
after he lived, rose at every dawn prayer. For love of him all Islam,
centuries after he lived, rose at every dawn and prayed as he had
taught them to pray; and to the earnest ones it seemed that they

could understand Muhammad better and come closer to him during this prayer.

According to the Quran, all true prophets are mouthpieces of the One God; they teach the same law and supplement each other. Many prophets have come, for "to every people was sent an apostle." Muhammad taught his followers to believe in Noah, Abraham, Isaac, Jacob, and Joseph, and told them stories about Aaron, David, and Solomon. These heroes he saw as nobler, more significant for all time than the Old Testament historians made them. He selected tales about them which were current among the Jews although they had never been incorporated in the Bible, and used them not so much to tell a story as to illustrate moral laws and show the spiritual strength by which the prophet triumphed over his vicissitudes. When Muhammad told of Noah, it was not the ark and the flood he made important but the fact that Noah came, a prophet to an unbelieving people. The Book of Genesis tells that after the flood, Jehovah seemed pleased with the sweet odor of the (animal) sacrifice Noah offered, and Jehovah repented him of floods and resolved never again to send one like that through which poor Noah had just lived. Muhammad told his people that Noah had a message from God, but those to whom he delivered it tauntingly replied, "We see not in thee but a man like ourselves," and they added that only the meanest and most common people would follow him, those of "hasty judgment." So is it in every age, cried Muhammad. "O the misery of men! No apostle cometh unto them but they laugh him to scorn," and call him a liar. Muhammad's Abraham is a more illustrious figure than the patriarch of the Old Testament. The Quran tells that in his boyhood Abraham comprehended God's Oneness and went and destroyed the idols around him. Muhammad saw Isaac, Jacob, and Joseph as a succession of prophets; and Moses was to him glorious. Of David he wrote: God said, "We established his kingdom; and wisdom and skill to pronounce clear decisions did we bestow upon him." Solomon knew the language of the birds even, and was assisted by unseen angels. Of Christ, Muhammad wrote with almost breathless adoration, calling him the Spirit, the Word.

Muhammad gave two realistic sanctions for righteous living: fear of the punishments of hell; hope of the rewards of heaven. The only way to make heaven and hell real was to liken them to the best things in this world, and the worst. The greatest blessing in a desert is water: Muhammad said heaven was a place where water was abundant. In his time sex relations were indescribably lax. Muhammad portrayed heaven as a place where women were chaste. A modern translator of the Quran shows plainly that, when Muhammad wrote of the "houris" of heaven he did not mean physical maidens but ideal companions, angels as the Christian Bible knows them. Like every prophet he spoke in highly symbolic language; and in three chapters of the Quran, written in Mecca, are verses which could be interpreted as referring to physical pleasures in heaven. It is significant that in one of the chapters in which he uses physical symbols is the sentence, "Is the reward of goodness aught but goodness?" and as soon as he had educated his companions somewhat he no longer used this kind of symbols. In Medina, he wrote:

Fair in the sight of men are the pleasures of women and children; fair are the treasured treasures of gold and silver; and fine horses; and flocks; and corn-fields! Such is the enjoyment of this world's life.

Shall I tell you of better things than these, prepared for those who fear God, in his presence? Theirs shall be gardens beneath which the rivers flow, and in which they shall abide for aye, and wives of stainless purity, and acceptance with God, for God regardeth his servants.

They who say, O our Lord, we have indeed believed, pardon our sins, and keep us from the torment of the fire; the patient are they and the truthful, the lowly and the charitable, and they who ask for pardon as each days breaks.

Muhammad's Resurrection Day is twofold: the appearance of the soul before its Lord when it enters the spiritual world after death; and the time when the call of the new Prophet is raised in the land. Both times are also the Day of Judgment. He taught that life in this world passes quickly; the life to come is eternal.

Through the Quran is the cry: Prepare to meet thy God, O Islam! for "God taketh souls unto Himself at death," and "man is a telling witness against himself." Those obsessed with "the desire of increasing riches, surely ye shall see hell fire." If a man worships "other gods than God," on the judgment "day will we [God and his prophets] say to Hell, 'Art thou full?': and it shall say, 'Is there more?' "

Souls may be resurrected by recognizing the new Prophet. These souls shall drink, here and now, of knowledge which draws them nigh unto God and they shall enter into paradise. Using the word "resurrection" as Paul, and the Gospel of John use it, Muhammad said of his uncle, Hamza, that he was dead while on earth, but God gave him light by which to walk among men; and Muhammad declared that some of his followers had already been raised from the dead and had become a new creation. Khalifa Ali wrote that a dead man sold a piece of land to a dead man, meaning that neither of them was spiritually alive.

The Muslim historian Ameer Ali writes: "During the ten years Muhammad presided over the commonwealth of Islam, a great change had come over the character of the Arab people. The reckless freedom of heathenism was abandoned, and manners became decorous, almost austere; gambling and drunkenness were forbidden. Before this there had been no privacy in houses; from this time, it became customary to have special apartments for women." By the eighth century A.D., the second century of the Islamic era, the Arabs had so advanced intellectually that in their treaties with some of the conquered nations they made the term that they should have access to any ancient Greek documents owned by the subject people.

Plato tried to frame in his *Republic* a pattern for the best possible government, maintained by the authority of philosophic guardians. As his observation of facts grew clearer and his experience deepened he brought to the aid of government, in his *Laws*, the almighty authority of religion and the sanctions of reward and punishment not only on earth but after death.

The laws of he Islamic civilization were enforced by the executive arm of kings and princes; but the foundation of the civilization was love of its Prophet. Islam believed it was Muhammad's purpose to bring the maximum of welfare to all people, that he spoke truly when he said God wished for them his wealth of good things. For eight hundred years Islam held together under one law, one language, one brotherhood. The people and their monarchs were instructed by their men of science, their doctors of law and philosophy, their religious leaders, who in turn looked to Muhammad and his Quran for guidance as to what laws and what paths of investigation they should follow. And the whole civilization moved forward by the light and by the power of its religion.

# 26

## Sufis and Dervishes

THE TEACHERS and notable of Nishapur, a great city of Persia, asked the eminent Muslim lawyer and theologian, al-Qassár to "mount the pulpit and preach to the people." Al-Qassár declined, saying, "My heart is still attached to the world, and therefore my words will make no impression on the hearts of others. Speech is permissible to him alone whose silence is injurious to religion, and whose speaking would remove the injury."

Al-Qassár was asked why the words of his contemporaries. He replied, "Because they discoursed for the glory of Islam and the salvation of souls and the satisfaction of the Merciful God, whereas we discourse for the glory of ourselves and the quest of worldly gain and the favor of mankind."

Al-Qassár lived at a time when the Muslims were so prosperous and powerful that they were enmeshed in luxurious living, that ill-starred harbinger of social decline. On the crest of this torrent of wordly power were the Muslim jurists and theologians, who now interpreted the Quran as straitjacket thou-shalt and thou-shalt not, which was easier than explaining what Muhammad meant when he said so-and-so. In time these leaders fitted Islamic theology into the channel of fatalism, determinism, literalism, and anthropomorphism which they dug for it. This impoverished version this they served to the masses.

Companion to these latter-day theologians were the kings and officials who ignored Muhammad's emphatic instruction that slaves should be freed, and Muhammad's wish that Muslims should have no slaves. The kings made slaves of the captives of their wars; and the sensual rich bought the beautiful captive girls who were sold on the open market and made them their wives or concubines, forgetting that Muhammad, aiming at the ultimate elimination of polygamy had limited the number of wives a man should have and had virtually abolished the concubine.

Whether it was frozen into theologies, or was soiled with self-indulgence, Islam was in perpetual peril. But reforming movements arose; among them the Brothers of Purity and the Sufis.

The first Brothers of Purity were a group of scholars who lived in Basra in the tenth century. The requirements for membership in the Brotherhood were exacting. A candidate was a scholar of exceptional ability, fearless and unselfish, ready to teach scientific truth although threatened with persecution by the Muslim clergy; he must live so nobly that his example would be an inspiration to his companions and his students. From the initial meetings in Basra in the home of a Brother, similar groups were formed in every city of the Muslim world where were scientists and scholars able to carry on the work. These broadminded, learned men discussed in their meetings science, literature, philosophy, history. They wrote treatises on mathematics, astronomy, music, geography, mechanics, physics, chemistry, botany, physiology, geology, meteorology, biology, logic, ethics, immortality, and the like, and sent them throughout their world. Their books were the encyclopedia of the time. They preserved freedom in scientific investigation, and educated the people in every branch of learning then known. The movement was a powerful force for progress in Muslim civilization.

A second renewal group was the Sufis. They fully appreciated the value of education, but differed from the Brothers of Purity in their emphasis upon a direct consciousness of God. They were deeply interested in spiritual perfection, and they glorified poverty and simple living; accepting troubles as blessings, they imposed privations upon themselves for their spiritual training. They prayed: O God, break with thy blows this shell of self, until thy light is reflected in glory from the hidden mirror at the foundation of my soul. The Quran told them, "God is the light of the heavens and the earth." Thousands of earnest and gifted Muslims went to spiritual teachers, *shaykhs,* to learn how to attain to this light. Under their teachers' direction they practiced self-discipline, unselfish living, and prayer.

The Sufis had societies, and their Brotherhoods and Sisterhoods owned buildings where men and women of any age or calling who wished to study and pray might find a home, for as long a time as they wished (no life vows were required). Women who were widows or had been deserted by their husbands could find protection in a Sufi retreat, where a Mother Superior kept strict discipline. Of the Superior of a famous convent in Cairo the historian al-Maqrizi wrote, "She was acquainted with jurisprudence, of great learning, an ascetic, content with little, God-fearing, exhorting others, zealous in what was profitable and in religious exercises." Some homes were in Mecca snd Medina; some were in the high mountains, for the Sufis loved nature. One of the first Sufi retreats was built and endowed by a Christian prince in Syria. The Orders were recognized by insignias—a patched robe, or a coarse woolen robe, or a blue robe. Muhammad discouraged monasticism; therefore most of the Sufis married and lived in their own homes. They believed that "knowledge should not be separated from action."

A descendant of Muhammad, the Lady Nafisa was a famous Sufi teacher. She lived in Egypt and to her home came many scholars, and students of the spiritual life. Two of Islam's most famous Sufi teachers were named Rabia. One Rabia lived in Syria and for centuries thousands of pilgrims visited her shrine on Mount Tor. The other Rabia was a slave girl of Basra. Her master saw, in a vision, her spiritual radiance and set her free. Her students treasured her prayer, "O my Lord, if I worship Thee from fear of Hell, burn me in Hell, and if I worship Thee from hope of Paradise, exclude me thence. But if I worship Thee for Thine own sake then withhold not from me Thine Eternal Beauty."

Hasan of Basra, a foremost Sufi scholar and teacher of his day, believed that, as the high-spirited Arab horse was put on short rations for forty days before he ran from the prize in the hippodrome, so must the Sufi train himself for his journey to the City of God. And Hasan prayed and fasted, day and night. One evening this cultivated gentleman passed by the hut of Habíb; and Habíb called to him to come in and pray with him. Habíb was a usurer, and in Islam usury was forbidden. Unable to endure Habíb's company, Hasan pretended not to hear him and hurried on, explaining to himself that Habíb's mispronounciation of Arabic offended his ear. The next night, in a dream, Hasan asked, "How can I praise thee, O Lord?" The answer came, "If yesternight you had said your prayers after Habíb, and if the righteousness of his intention had restrained you from taking offense at his pronounciation, I should have been well pleased with you."

The Sufi Fudayl had been before his conversion, a notorious highwayman. He plied his trade on the road between Merv and Vayard, and few dared travel that way. Fudayl was, however, gentlemanly and discriminating. He seldom robbed women; he let his victims keep part of their property according to their means; he did not take from those whose funds were meager.

One day a merchant found he must travel through Fudayl's district. He was advised to take a military escort, but declared it unnecessary, for, said he, "I have heard that Fudayl is a God-fearing man." He took the only precaution a devout merchant about to meet a God-fearing brigand required. He hired a man, mounted him on a camel, placed him at the head of the caravan, gave him a copy of the Quran, and told him to read loudly and clearly, day and night.

The caravan approached Fudayl's ambush. And the reader recited, in a very loud voice, "Is not the time yet come unto those who believe, that their hearts should humbly submit to the admonitions of God?"

Something happened in Fudayl's mind when he heard these words and suddenly he repented. He retreated to his lair, and soon afterward set off for Mecca to study under the saints of God. He became a Sufi ascetic and practiced the spiritual laws with the energy he had expended on his secular affairs. Much of the time he was very sad; thinking perhaps of his evil past and fearing the punishment that might come to him if he did not attain the spiritual station required of him. Deeply in earnest, he was as rigorous with others as with himself. The khalifa visited Mecca, and one day knocked at Fudayl's door. Fudayl was intolerant of the rich khalifa and his many luxuries, and wished it understood that he wanted nothing from a khalifa. He called out, "What have

I to do with the Commander of the Faithful?" and for a while would not open the door.

Of the Quran's ninety-nine names for God, the Sufis liked "Truth" the best. By the end of the tenth century, under the guidance of gifted teachers, the Sufis had developed a clearly defined spiritual philosophy and were able to meet the questions of al-Ghazzali when, in his quest for ultimate truth, he came to them.

This scholar was brilliant among the many who flowered under the instruction of the Prophet, Muhammad. Al-Ghazzali was born in 1058, in Tus in Persia. His father died when he was a little boy, and the Sufi who adopted him sent him to a Muslim school where board, room, and tuition were furnished by the government. When al-Ghazzali was thirty-one he was appointed a professor in the great university of Baghdad.

In his youth al-Ghazzali observed "how easily the children of Christians become Christians and the children of Muslims embrace Islam." He was not satisfied to accept in this way the conclusions of others, whoever they might be. He must investigate for himself every assertion. "The thirst for knowledge was innate in me from an early age; it was like a second nature implanted by God, without any will on my part," he wrote in his autobiography.

His fundamental problem was to find a basis which would enable him to be as sure of his own conclusions as he was of his existence.

The senses, he decided were not sufficient as a basis, for they often led one astray. "Our sight, for instance, perhaps the best practiced of all our senses, observes a shadow, and finding it apparently stationary pronounces it devoid of movement. Observation and experience, however, show subsequently that a shadow moves not suddenly, it is true, but gradually and imperceptibly, so that it is never really motionless.

Miracles had for him no significance as proof of truth. "Suppose, for instance," he wrote, "a man should come and say to me, who am firmly convinced that ten is more than three, 'No; on the contrary, three is more than ten, and, to prove it, I change this rod into a serpent,' and supposing that he actually did so, I should remain none the less convinced of the falsity of his assertion, and although his miracle might arouse my astonishment, it would not instil any doubt in my belief."

He accepted the proved conclusions of the exact sciences, of physics, astronomy, mathematics; but how far could reason go? Reason interpreted and clarified the testimony of the senses, and undoubtedly "it is a great injury to religion to suppose that the defense of Islam involves the condemnation of the exact sciences." But might there not be a higher authority which corrected the assertions of reason?

Al-Ghazzali decided to study the beliefs of those people who claimed to have attained certitude.

First among them were the Scholastic theologians. They proved useless for him. They might heal some people, he said kindly, but they could not help him.

Next he turned to the philosophers and scientists. Of them he wrote, "There are past masters in every science who are entirely ignorant of other branches of knowledge. The arguments of the ancient philosophers are rigidly demonstrative in mathematics and only conjectural in religious questions." The men of science were gifted; and certain of their knowledge in their own field only.

Finding no abiding certitude in Scholastic theology, or Greek philosophy or science, he turned to the Sufis, who had written many treatises "which clearly proved that their minds were filled with divine thoughts."

Islam's theologians believed that only a great intellect could have knowledge of one so vast as God. The Sufis said that often the child who loved God knew him better than the eminent philosopher. Those who really knew God, the Sufis taught, were those "whose hearts He hath vivified with Himself." Al-Ghazzali read exhaustively the writings of the scholarly Sufis, studying their systems of thought and their conclusions. He found himself then in the position of the learned man who, having completed his study of the Sufis, went to his teacher and said, "What shall I do now?" The teacher replied, "Practice what you have learned, for theory without practice is like a body without a spirit."

Was al-Ghazzali willing to follow the Sufis when they said God was at the far end of the path called Renunciation? What had al-Ghazzali to renounce? He was at the top of his world, widely acclaimed as the greatest philosopher of his age. He was a dynamic personality, and from far and near students poured into his classroom. His genius was the pride of the people of Iraq. He liked this applause. Did he like it more than he desired the presence of God, he asked himself. He decided that he could go no further in his search for truth until he resigned his professorship, for, he wrote, "worldly interests encompassed me on every side. ... When I considered the intention of my teaching, I perceived that instead of doing it for God's sake alone I had no motive but the desire for glory and reputation."

For six months he struggled with himself. He wrote in his autobiography, "In the morning I was sincerely resolved only to occupy myself with the future life; in the evening a crowd of carnal thoughts assailed and dispersed my resolutions. On the one side the world kept me bound to my post in the chains of covetousness, on the other side the voice of religion cried to me, 'Up! Up! thy life is nearing its end, and thou hast a long journey to make. All thy pretended knowledge is nought but falsehood and fantasy.' ... Then my resolve was strengthened, I wished to give up all and flee; but the tempter returning to the attack, said, 'You are suffering from a transitory feeling; don't give way to it, for it will soon pass. If you obey it, if you give up this fine position, this honorable post exempt from trouble and rivalry, this seat of authority safe from attack, you will regret it later on without being able to recover it.' "

When he decided to take the drastic step he dared not let it be known, but only said he intended to make a pilgrimage to Mecca. He made provision for his family, and took a small endowment for himself, for, he said, "there is surely nothing more lawful in the world than that a learned man should provide sufficient to support his family."

He started off for Damascus, Jerusalem, and Mecca; and for ten years he traveled and studied. He wrote, "During my successive periods of meditation there were revealed to me things impossible to recount. All that I shall say for the edification of the reader is this: I learned from a sure source that the Sufis are the true pioneers on the path of God; that there is nothing more beautiful than their life, nor more praiseworthy than their rule of conduct, nor purer than their morality."

Some Sufis believed that to spend their life in solitary mental contemplation of God was the highest activity. Al-Ghazzali did not think this allowable. When he had attained to the spiritual rebirth he went back among the waiting people with the good news he could tell them; and the rest of his life he taught.

In his writings he brought together all that was best in the philosophy, theology, and science of the Muslim centuries. He wrote a masterpiece, *The Renovation of the Sciences of Religion,* and tried to stabilize religion on a proved scientific basis.

The essence of his philosophy he explained in one small volume, *The Alchemy of Happiness.* Man's body is weak, but his spirit is lofty, he writes in this book. The process of spiritual emancipation he calls "the alchemy of happiness." In this alchemy there are four constituents: knowledge of self, knowledge of God, knowledge of the world as it really is, knowledge of the next world as it really is. It is quite clear that man did not create himself, "nor can he now make a single hair," he reasoned. Yet, "there are some who, failing to find God by observation, conclude that there is no God and that this world of wonders made itself, or existed from everlasting. They are like a man who, seeing a beautifully written letter, should suppose that it had written itself without a writer, or had always existed." "Those whose eyes never see beyond the world of phenomena are like those who mistake servants of the lowest rank for the king. The laws of phenomena must be constant, or there could be no such thing as science; but it is a great error to mistake the slaves for the master."

Man is the microcosm, God is the macrocosm, reasoned al-Ghazzali. As a "close study of the niceties and shades of language in a great poem reveals to us more, and more of the genius of its author," so a study of the microcosm, man reveals a "more intimate knowledge of God." Man, in fact, is a "little world in himself." By "knowing himself," al-Ghazzali did not mean knowledge of man's body, for "if thy knowledge as to that which is within only extends so far, that when thou art hungry thou eatest, and when thou art angry thou attackest some one, wilt thou progress any farther on this path, for the beasts are thy partners in this. But real self-knowledge consists in knowing the following things: What art thou in thyself, and from whence hast thou come? Whither art thou going, and for what purpose hast thou come to tarry here awhile, and in what does thy real happiness and misery consist? Some of thy attributes are those of animals, some of devils, and some of angels. . . . The occupation of animals is eating, sleeping, and fighting; therefore, if thou art an animal, busy thyself in these things. Devils are busy in stirring up mischief, and in guile and deceit; if thou belongest to them, do their work. Angels contemplate the beauty of God, and are entirely free from animal qualities; if thou art of angelic nature, then strive towards thine origin, that thou mayest know and contemplate the Most High, and be delivered from the thraldon of lust and anger."

"The rational soul of man," he writes, "abounds in marvels, both of knowledge and power. By means of it he masters arts and sciences, can pass in a flash from earth to heaven and back again, can map out the skies and measure the distances between the stars." Man's "five senses are like five doors opening on the external world."

"More wonderful than this, his heart has a window which opens on the unseen world" Prayer opens this window of the heart. Al-Ghazzali describes prayer as having three stages. In the first stage one repeats words. In the second, with much effort one succeeds in concentrating his thoughts on divine things. In the third stage one thinks spontaneously of God, and it is difficult not to relate every thought to God; this attainment the Sufis called "annihilation of the self in God."

"The love of God," writes al-Ghazzali, "is the highest stage of our soul's progress." Love of God is the goal and dynamic of existence. "how can he who understands only the love of sensible things believe in the joy of looking upon the face of God Most High?" Al-Ghazzali answers, "Stones, plants, animals, the earth, the sky, the stars, the elements, in fact everything in the universe reveals to us the knowledge, power and the will of its Originator." "The world is a masterpiece; he who studies it loves its invisible Author in a manner which cannot be described."

Many Sufis were gifted poets and some were truly inspired. They worked out a set of symbols by which to express their spiritual life. They called God "the Friend" or "the Beloved." His teachings were a cup of wine; the joy which came from living according to God's will was intoxication. He who longed to become conscious of the presence of God, he who sought the Beloved, they called the lover. The place where the wine of God's teachings was given to the Sufi, the place where some one told him of God's love and God's purposes for mankind was the tavern; the spiritual teacher was the tavernkeeper. There are many variations to their terminology. Those who take their words without poetic or spiritual meaning are much confused. Nizami, a Sufi poet of the twelfth century, wrote a spiritual masterpiece, *Laila and Majnun*, in which he describes the soul's search for God. Nizami commences his poem with this prayer for inspiration:

> *Cup-bearer, thou know'st I worship wine;*
> *Let that delicious cup be mine.*
> *Wine! pure and limpid as my tears,*
> *Dispeller of a lover's fears;*
> *With thee inspired, with thee made bold,*
> *'Midst combat fierce my post I hold; . . .*
> *Bring, bring the liquid gem, and see*
> *Its power, its wondrous power, in me.*

Shabistari, a Persian poet of the thirteenth century, lets one see the Sufi's soul, in his beautiful poem:

> *Descending to the earth,*
> *That strange intoxicating beauty of the unseen world*
> *Lurks in the elements of Nature.*
>
> *And the soul of man,*
> *Who has attained the rightful balance,*
> *Becoming aware of this hidden joy,*
> *Straightway is enamoured and bewitched.*
>
> *And from this mystic marriage are born*
> *The poets' songs, inner knowledge,*
> *The language of the heart, virtuous living,*
> *And the fair child, Beauty.*
> *And the Great Soul gives to man as dowry*
> *The hidden glory of the world.*

A citizen of Nishapur had a thriving drug and perfume business. It is said that five hundred patients a day came to him that he might feel their pulse. One day, as he directed the many servants who were busily carrying out his orders, he noticed a wandering dervish standing at his door and quietly looking in. Faríd ud-dín'Attár, the druggist, bade him, be gone. Replied the dervish, "That is easily done, I have only a light bundle to carry, nothing in fact but my clothes. But you, with your sacks full of valuable drugs, when the time comes to go, what will you do? Had you not better consider a little?"

Faríd ud-dín'Attár pondered these words, and decided to acquire something he could take with him when he left this world. He disposed of his drug business and traveled to Egypt, Mecca, Damascus, and India. For thirty-nine years he collected the verses and sayings of Sufi saints. He wrote memoirs of the greatest saints, and became a poet and mystic himself, one of the renowned teachers of Islam. His widely read allegorical poem, the *Conference of the Birds* describes the soul's journey to God through seven valleys: how the soul, longing to know and meet God takes the necessary steps.

When 'Attár was an old man he met a college president and his little son. Holding the child tenderly in his arms, 'Attár said to the father, "Take care! This son of yours will light a great flame in the world."

The father thus cautioned was a distinguished Persian scholar, head of a college in Balkh. He married a princess, and their son Jalálu'ddin was the little boy whom 'Attár loved. Jalálu'ddin's grandfather, also a famous scholar, had married the daughter of his king. Jalálu'ddin had every advantage of birth, environment and education. When Jalálu'ddin, or Jalál as he was called, was still a small child his father was banished from Balkh, for he took issue with the skeptical and decadent theologians, then in favor with the king. The exiled family wandered from city to city, and finally settled in Iconium in Asia Minor, where Jalál's father accepted the presidency of a college. Since Iconium was a Roman city, Jalál was called Jalálu'ddin Rumi.

When he was five years old, it was said he talked with the angels. "They come to present themselves before you to offer you gifts and presents from the invisible world," his father told him.

Jalál studied under his father and other Muslim professors, he traveled to Damascus and Aleppo to visit celebrated teachers in those cities, he read Plato and the Greek philosophers, and studied the Quran. He became a professor himself, and taught in four colleges simultaneously. His students so loved him that they would crowd around him when his lectures were over and follow him through the streets to his home.

One day as he was making his way along the street, riding a donkey and surrounded by his students, he met a barefoot dervish dressed in a coarse black robe. Shams of Tabriz, illiterate and inspired, had come on foot from Tabriz, for Shams' teacher had told him, "In the land of Rum is a Sufi who glows with divine love; you must go thither and fan this glow into a clear flame."

Accosting Jalál, the dervish asked, "What is the aim of all the teaching you give and the religious exercises you practice?"

"The regulation of conduct as prescribed by the traditions and the moral and religious law," answered Jalál.

"All this is mere skimming the surface?" said Shams.

"But what is under the surface?" asked Jalál.

"Only when knowledge frees thee from thyself is such knowledge better than ignorance," replied Shams, quoting the Sufi poet Hakim Sanai.

Jalál was evidently electrified by these words, for immediately he put himself under the tutelage of the far-seeing Shams. Jalál neglected his classes and spent hours discussing profound problems of life with the new acquaintance. His pupils and friends became angry and declared that Shams of Tabriz had come "to lead the pattern of believers astray"; Jalál called him the peerless teacher, "perfect in word and deed."

What could a profound scholar like Jalál learn from a poor illiterate dervish? Jalál tells in his poems. Every one, he writes, who travels the spiritual road is like a man riding a donkey. The donkey is his body, and the man must be careful and watch the donkey's every step, for "he is madly in love with fodder" and is always straying off the spiritual path in search of places where green herbs are plentiful. The man must have a spiritual guide who knows the way the donkey should go; for without this help the "journey is exceedingly full of woe and affright." If a man finds a guide who lives what he teaches, he discovers that "men inspired by God are the foundation of life." "Other people are like the night, and the spiritual guide is the moon." Others are like the autumn, but he "is the summer." "If you lack perfect wisdom, make yourself as dead under the shadow of the wise, whose words give life." When the austere and ardent Shams had taught Jalál all he knew, he declared himself the disciple, for Jalál's wisdom now exceeded his own.

Jalál's book the *Masnavi* is a treasure-house of anecdotes of Islam, Persia, and the Near East, and is full of stories of Christ, Moses, Solomon, and the many immortals who make up the history of Judaism, Christianity, and Islam.

He uses these anecdotes to illustrate spiritual laws. Commencing a story, he works out a fundamental principle, holding the conclusion of the story in abeyance until the analysis is completed. Sometimes he runs two stories parallel, one from the Christians, one from the Muslims, becaue both illustrate the same principle.

In the *Masnavi* he tells of Ayas, the Persian youth who was raised to a high place at the court of Sultan Mahmud of Ghazni. It being "a characteristic of evil doers to think evil of the saints," the courtiers became jealous. Observing that Ayas went every night to a room in the palace and shut himself in they told the Sultan that Ayas had stolen gold and was hoarding it in a secret chamber, or he had alcoholic drink in that room. The Sultan ordered the courtiers to search the room. They broke the lock and opened the door—and found only the old shoes and ragged garment Ayas had worn in the days before the Sultan favored him. Every night Ayas went to his room and put on these old clothes that he might remain humble and obedient to the admonition in the Quran: "Let man reflect how and from what he was created."

Jalál was interested in the things that are eternally profitable. "A mule said to a camel, 'How is it that I am always stumbling and falling down, while you never make a false step?' The camel replied, 'My eyes are always directed upwards, and I see a long way before me, while your eyes look down, and you see only what is immediately under your feet.' Just so, said Jalál, partial reason cannot see beyond the grave, but real reason looks onward to the day of judgment and, therefore, is enabled to steer a better course in this world."

Differences of opinion he illustrates by the story of the elephant that was brought into a dark room where many people were assembled. No one could see the elephant; so each person felt it, to discover that the beast was like. One felt its trunk and declared an elephant resembled a waterpipe. Another touched its ear and said the creature must be a large fan. One person put his hand on the elephant's leg and thought it a pillar. Another felt its back and was sure an elephant was like a throne room.

Jalál protested against the vagaries of asceticism and appealed to his students to see the futility of mere physical austerities. A peacock, he said, was found tearing off his beautiful plumage because it was a temptation to his vanity. Respect the beauty God has given you, said Jalál, and "tear not off thy plumage, it cannot be replaced; but avert thy heart from it."

The personality of the great Prophet, Jalál explains in this way: When a man is training a parrot to speak he holds a mirror before the parrot and from behind the mirror the man speaks. The parrot, looking in the mirror, thinks it is a parrot that is speaking and imitates this one like himself, this fellow bird, of his own species. Just so is the Prophet the mirror behind which God conceals himself. Looking at the mirror, men think it is a man who is speaking; but lo, it is the Eternal Lord. All the great Prophets and their religions are essentially one, and One speaks behind them. Jalál writes:

> In the adorations and benedictions of righteous men
> The praises of all the prophets are kneaded together. . . .
> Because He that is praised is, in fact, only One.
> In this respect all religions are only one religion.

Jalál taught that the miracles in the scriptures are parables. He asked his little son, Valad, how it could be that Moses' rod when it swallowed up the rods of Pharoah's magicians became no thicker than before. The child at once replied, "In a very dark night, if a lighted taper be brought into a large room or hall, it instantly devours all the darkness, and yet remains a little taper." Jalál took the boy in his arms, "kissed him and said, 'May God bless thee, my child! Verily thou hast strung a pearl of the very first water on the string of illustration.' "

To Jalál heaven and hell are states of consciousness. "Toothache and a serpent's bite are hell.'. And "What is ascension to heaven? It is annihilation of self." Some think annihilation, or extinction, is blotting out the individual's identity. To the saints it has meant the permanent conquest of the lower, the selfish characteristics until, in concentration upon God, the soul forgets even its attainments, and thinks only of God. In other words, he that loseth his life shall find it. "Give up your life and live anew," says Jalál.

Of God, the Life of the universe, he writes:

> *Thou art the Source that causes our rivers to flow.*
> *Thou art hidden in thine essence, but seen by thy bounties.*
> *Thou art like the water, and we like the millstone.*
> *Thou art like the wind, and we like the dust;*
> *The wind is unseen, but the dust is seen by all.*
> *Thou art the Spring, and we the sweet green garden;*
> *Spring is not seen, though its gifts are seen.*
> *Thou art as the Soul, we as hand and foot;*
> *Soul instructs hand and foot to hold and take.*
> *Thou art as Reason, we like the tongue;*
> *'Tis reason that teaches the tongue to speak.*
> *Thou art as Joy, and we are laughter;*
> *The laughter is the consequence of the joy.*
> *Our every motion every moment testifies,*
> *For it proves the presence of the Everlasting God.*

God offers men the best possible life, but is not dependent upon their decisions. It affects not the all-glorious God "whether ye accept or reject" him, writes Jalál. "The moon sheds her light, and the dogs howl," but the moon does not stop shining in the heavens "because of the howling of the dogs on earth."

The reigning prince of the country requested Jalál to instruct him. Jalál asked the prince whether or not it was true, as he had heard, that the prince had committed the Quran to memory. The prince replied that he had done this. He had been told, said Jalál, that the prince had studied, with a learned teacher, *The Elements*

*of Jurisprudence;* was this so? The prince answered that, he had
studied this book. Said Jalíl, "If you know the word of God and
do not practice it, how can you expect that words of mine will
profit you?" The prince wept, changed his policy, and became a
just ruler.

A group of college students came to Jalál to decide if he was as
learned as another professor, a famous linguist. Perceiving their
purpose Jalál told them a story: A worthy jurist and a celebrated
linguist were traveling together. They came to a ruined well and
the jurist recited a verse from the Quran about a well. In Arabic,
*bir* is the word for well. When the jurist finished the verse the
linguist told him that he had mispronounced *bir*. The vowel was
not long, as he made it, but short with a hiatus after it. The two
learned men fell to arguing and disputing and became very angry.
The linguist said his pronounciation was pure and according to
classical usage. The jurist replied that the linguist was wrong. The
scholars disputed all day. Night came and it was very dark. The
scholars were by this time so excited that the linguist fell into the
well. From its depths he called to the jurist, "O my most courteous
fellow-traveler, lend thy help to extricate me from this most dark-
some pit." The jurist answered back that he would reach down his
hand if the linguist would admit he was mistaken about the pronounciation of *bir*. "Never," cried the linguist. And he stayed in
the well.

Some poets write of frustrated hopes, of vain regrets, of lives
misspent, telling the world their inner life is a failure. Jalál sang,
with the triumphant note of one who is master of his destiny, his
love for God and men. "My existence is the life of my friends,"
he wrote. Someone repeated to him the king's remark that Jalál
was a matchless sovereign but his disciples were a disreputable lot.
Jalál wrote the king, "Had my disciples been good men I had been
their disciple."

As Jalál walked along the street one day he came upon two men
who were quarreling. "Whatever you say to me," one man shouted
at the other, "I will answer back with a thousand words." "Ah,"
said Jalál to the fluent one, "if you say a thousand words to me I
will answer back just one." The men, abashed, stopped quarreling.

A miracle told of Jalál is symbolic of his influence upon the people. One day, it was said, he entered a large assembly room in which were many tall, unlighted candles. When he came in, with just a tiny candle in his hand, all the tall candles began to burn although they had not been touched by fire.

When Jalál passed into the unseen world, many Jews and Christians were among the multitude who came to his funeral. Asked by the Muslims, why they had come to the funeral of a Muslim sage and there repeated in his honor passages from the Torah, the Psalms, and the Gospels, the Jews and Christians replied that Jalál had explained for them the mysteries of their Scriptures and they were his adherents and disciples. The beloved teacher was buried by the Seljuk Sultan in the royal mausoleum.

Al-Ghazzali was the teacher of scholars. Jalál went a step further and was the teacher of everyone.

# Book IV

# Encounter and Renewal

# 27

# The Crusades

WHEN THE ROMAN empire collapsed under the onslaught of the barbarians, systematic education, refinement of living, and efficient government disappeared from western Europe. The Christians, by this time having set their faces against Rome's "pagan" learning, had no science, no plan for stable government, no widespread school system, no art and culture to teach the conquerors. Only their religion remained, and this they reduced to two extremes: an otherworldliness which would have nothing to do with normal social life; and a materialism which used the sanction of religion to acquire all the good things of this world which were obtainable.

Under these conditions, with few voices to cry in protest and rouse some lingering conscience, Europe abandoned itself to darkness. Kings, lords, and minor vassals fought each other ceaselessly, relentlessly, and if they lived to do it, fought again. From the year 500 the advantages of the Roman civilization slowly disappeared. Cities, trade, and the excellent Roman roads which had made travel possible, the hospitals and hospices the Christians had contributed—all fell into ruin. Uncleanliness became the mark of godliness, until a nun to prove her spirituality boasted that she had not bathed in sixty years except to wash the tips of her fingers before taking the Eucharist.

The feudal lords, unrefined and unlettered, wrung their maintenance from the serfs who lived in wretched hovels on their lands. Only the Christian clergy could read and write, and after a while they forgot so much of their Latin they could not read the Bible intelligibly to their illiterate hearers. However, they often performed valuable clerical and other services for a king or great lord, who paid them with the commodity which he had, land. As the Church acquired immense tracts of land and the monasteries became rich, the clergy assumed the political power their wealth made possible. State and Church then struggled for priority. The feudal lords, seeing a way to increase their authority and income appointed as bishops and abbots those men who would be subservient to them, and exacted payment for their patronage. The church appointees passed this personal expense along to the peasants, and collected from the people. During Europe's Dark Ages the monasteries owned a large part of the land and wealth of western Europe, and bishops and abbots became feudal barons in their own right. They did not beat the serfs on their lands quite so hard as did the barbarians around them, nor extort taxes from the people quite so heartlessly, but few of these churchmen heeded Christ's mercy, as the early Christians practiced it. They left the peasants to their terrifying superstitions born from the depths of ignorance; to their belief in demons invisible and malevolent that infested the forests along with the robbers and wild beasts. At times these church officials fought in wars of aggression as boldly and savagely as any secular lord.

In the seventh century, while Buddhism gave an impetus to Chinese learning and culture which caused them to flower into the splendor of T'ang, and Japan joyously responded to Prince Shotoku and the Buddhist teachers, while Arabia gazed in wonder and growing appreciation at the light held high by Muhammad, Ali, and the apostolic Imams, and India safeguarded her treasure, the brilliant Gupta Age, a few sporadic lights flared up in barbarous Europe, and quickly died away.

In the eighth century, Charlemagne, King of the Franks and formidable Christian, swore to wipe out paganism. He declared his conquest of the vast lands east of Gaul was a part of his missionary campaign. For thirty-three years he fought the Saxons, and annexed alien territory until he became a great emperor. His first requirement of the Saxons whom he conquered was immediate baptism and acceptance of Christianity. The alternative was death. As quickly as possible he built churches and monasteries in Saxony and filled the monasteries with monks and nuns. When he turned his attention to his wars in other parts, the Saxons massacred the Christians and burned their buildings. Their conversion was a matter of the sword and their retaliation was the sword.

Charlemagne laid the foundation for the clergy's political power through the centuries. He made the bishops and other high officials of the Church equal in rank with dukes and counts, and in his Council meetings received the churchmen on this footing. The clergy, however, were subject to conscription if needed in the emperor's wars. He allowed the monasteries in Gaul enormous grants of land; and for the support of the clergy levied the tithe, a special tax on laymen of one tenth of their income, including farm produce and animals.

The emperor wished to educate his subjects, and he ordered the priests of Gaul to teach the people to read; their education to consist of enough Latin to enable them to read the Bible. Charlemagne had a school in his palace, and induced Alcuin of England, the foremost scholar of the time, to live at his court.

Charlemagne died in 814 and his son Louis the Pious became his unwilling successor. Louis preferred religious austerities to court life and was always on the verge of retiring to a monastery. Time proved him unable to carry on his father's enormous activities, and Louis' sons, seeing his weakness, rebelled against him and divided up the empire; the avaricious nobles took what plunder they could get during the general anarchy. Charlemagne's efforts to rouse Europe to intellectual interests were smothered under chaos, warfare, and brutality as kings, prelates, and nobles seized each other's property and power, each man trying to advance himself.

While Charlemagne's grandsons were fighting their father, Louis the Pious, for an immediate division of the empire, they let the defenses against the barbarians which Charlemagne had built up—the armies and forts at the mouths of the rivers, and the strong fleet—go to ruin; and when the Norsemen from Scandinavia and the Baltic's shores fell upon Europe, Gaul was defenseless. The barbarians appeared in almost every city and fertile district; they made their way into Italy; they pillaged Flanders and Germany. In Spain only did they meet armies sufficiently organized to drive them off. Because they found most of Europe's wealth in the monasteries and churches they attacked those first, taking what they wanted and burning the buildings.

They overran Britain, burned the monasteries and convents, ruined the cities and farmlands, and got possession of all but a fragment of the country. Alfred the Great fought them under the king, his brother. When Alfred became king in 871 he fought them for many years longer, and finally won.

Alfred the Great was a statesman with a gift for organization, a lover of learning whose interests included many countries and peoples. In the intervals between the desperate years of fighting he tried to rebuild the ruined country. Any desire for education, any inclination to learn to read had died in the desolation brought upon Britain by the Vikings.

King Alfred started a palace school like Charlemagne's, and schools in the cities which he rebuilt. He brought from the Continent scholars of high character to live in Britain. He taught the people handicrafts, and built two monasteries where only monks of exemplary character should live. He translated books which the clergy and the people might use, and urged them to learn to read. He was one of the noblest kings in history. Like a strong searchlight he stood against the abysmal darkness. The hope he offered through education flickered in the hands of his successors for seventy-five years, then vanished.

From 1095, for two hundred years, the Crusades were an absorbing interest, and successive hordes formed in Europe and started off for the Near East to conquer and plunder the Muslims. It has been said that the first Crusade was proposed by Pope Urban II in the hope that the feudal lords, the soldiers, and the robbers of Europe would go to fight in Palestine, and Europe might, at least for the time they were away, have peace. The declared purpose was to save the Holy Sepulcher from the Muslims.

Early Christian leaders, wise men like Augustine and Jerome, opposed pilgrimages to Palestine, saying each Christian's daily life should be a holy pilgrimage. The followers of every religion, however, have loved the places where their Prophet lived and taught, and there have always been many people who wanted to see these places.

After Umar's peaceful conquest of Jerusalem in 638, Palestine was in Muslim hands for centuries. The Quran taught reverence for the Christ; and the Muslims under their good khalifas were sympathetic to the Christians' desire to pay homage to the places where Christian history arose. Jerusalem and Galilee were wide open to Christian visitors, who would come and go as much as they wished. Harun ar-Rashid allowed Charlemagne to hold the keys of Jerusalem, and declared Charlemagne owner of the Church of the Holy Sepulcher. Charlemagne encouraged pilgrimages to the Holy Land. He ordered that this subjects give a night's lodging to the passing pilgrims; he built hospitals along the main highways and arranged that the pilgrims be provided with certain small comforts. He also sent money to build a hospital in Jerusalem.

It was believed that he who made the pilgrimage to the Holy Land and bathed in the Jordan River was purified from sin. When he returned home he was as one set apart, ready for heaven's rewards. There were also immediate and practical results from the pilgrimage. The Holy Land contained an apparently inexhaustible supply of relics related in some way to the life of a saint or an apostle, also innumerable pieces of the True Cross. The pilgrims brought these back and sold them at fancy prices. After a while the pilgrims became merchants and returned with the products of the East, rare to Europe: silks, spices, and other things.

Under the good khalifas all went well. But Hakim, the insane khalifa who ruled Egypt and Palestine from 996 to 1020, took at times a maniac's delight in malice. Not content with the many and terrible murders he perpetrated among his palace associates and high officials, he had the Christian churches in Egypt razed, and destroyed the Church of the Holy Sepulcher in Jerusalem, the most beloved church in the Holy Land. He harrassed the Christians with capricious orders that they must ride on mules or asses, never horses, must wear a heavy cross, although his mother and many of his best government officials were Christians.

Added to this persecution were political troubles: the Fatimid and Abbasid khalifas were struggling for supremacy. The heads of Christianity, the pope at Rome and the patriarch in Constantinople, were tirelessly jealous each of the other's power. And in 1071 the Seljuk Turks conquered Jerusalem; their ruling dynasty was in decline and anarchy prevailed. Any one of these conditions would have reacted against the comfort of visiting pilgrims; the sum total was disastrous. Pilgrims came back to Europe with tales of mistreatment by the Muslims in Jerusalem, and of persecution along the way.

In November, 1095, Pope Urban II, at his Council meeting in Clermont in southern France made a speech which resounded for almost two centuries. His description of the sufferings of the Christian pilgrims and his impassioned appeal that Jerusalem be saved from the polluting presence of the infidels struck home among the nobility, kings, and organized soldiers. Peter the Hermit took care of the common people. Bareheaded and barefooted, carrying a crucifix, and riding an ass, Peter traveled through the highways and byways of France and nearby Germany proclaiming a Crusade.

He roused the common people to a frenzy of excitement to go to Palestine and save the Sepulcher. A terrible famine had wasted the country the year before and the poor of eastern France were almost desperate. They heard tales of the wealth and plenty in the Holy Land. What might they not find to better their earthly as well as immortal existence! Pope Urban II declared, "The wealth of your enemies shall be yours; ye shall plunder their treasures." He told the people that Christ was a God of battle and would direct the war. He promised to each crusader immediate release from every worldly obligation, and God's forgiveness for all his sins. For about a century the Church had cried that the Day of Judgment was at hand; the wickedness of the world was proof. Many a guilty soul knew he would feel more comfortable if he could slough off his sins in a crusade to Palestine. If he should die in the Holy Land, all the better for his reception into the next world.

In the spring of 1096 the first Crusaders started for Palestine, in five divisions, each under a leader. One division, in addition to their leader, had a goose and a goat, which they placed in front of them, believing that these two were inspired by the Holy Spirit and would lead them to the Holy Land. Frantic multitudes of the poor of France swelled the throngs, who were unorganized and were provided with makeshift arms.

The only way to get what they needed was to take it as they journeyed on. Two divisions arrived in Hungary and like locusts commenced to feed upon what they could find. They broke into the cities and appropriated gold and silver and quantities of food. The Hungarians rose to save their property and killed them by the thousands.

Another horde made their way along the Rhine and, after brutally robbing and destroying some ten thousand Jews in the German cities, appeared in Hungary when they were slain or dispersed.

A division led by a soldier, Walter the Pennyless, passed through Hungary without mishap, to the border city Malevilla near Belgrade and crossed the river into Bulgaria. Sixteen of this party stayed in Malevilla to purchase arms. They approached some citizens, and were immediately set upon and stripped of their money and clothes. They fled to Walter and told him of their misfortune. Walter considered returning for revenge but decided it would take too long. He went on to the next city and his men seized the sheep and cattle they found grazing in the fields nearby. The Bulgarians came from the city to save their herds, and slew many crusaders. His party much depleted, Walter finally reached the outskirts of Constantinople and waited for Peter the Hermit.

With a multitude which, according to one record, was as "innumerable as the sands of the sea" Peter got through Hungary to Malevilla. He heard now what had happened to the sixteen crusaders of Walter's party; and ordered his followers to take revenge on the Hungarians. The crusaders ran up to Malevilla in overpowering numbers and poured in such a storm of arrows that the Hungarians fled. The attackers pursued them and murdered or drowned in the Danube River so many of the citizens that almost none were left. The crusaders took possession of the city, which they found richly stocked with what they wanted—food, wine, horses.

The King of Hungary came with a large army to save Malevilla. Peter's horde then tried to get away into Bulgaria. To do this they had to cross the river. They found a hundred and fifty boats on the bank, and with these and rafts of poles which they made, they endeavored to get their vast numbers over the river. They evidently took care of the food and livestock first, for although many crusaders drowned, those who survived marched into a mighty forest in Bulgaria with plentiful supplies taken from Malevilla. The King of Bulgaria received them kindly and counseled them to make haste through Bulgaria, for the Emperor of Constantinople could hardly wait to see them.

Peter the Hermit and Walter the Pennyless joined forces outside Constantinople. The hordes they had led, starting out ostensibly for Palestine to save their religion from contamination by the infidels, for a summer pillaged, murdered, and destroyed their fellow Christians and the peaceable and hapless Jews they came upon along the way. Most of these crusaders were killed in Europe. The remnant who finally reached Asia Minor were quickly disposed of by the Seljuk Turks.

The second portion of the first Crusade was made up of knights. They were well equipped with arms and were commanded by a bishop and princes of France. In three divisions, and in little bands, they made their way southward, and by June of 1097 assembled in Constantinople, some one hundred and fifty thousand men.

The next autumn they were in Syria. For two years they conquered cities and country districts, and in June, 1099, reached Jerusalem, the goal of their efforts. On July 15, after a month's siege, they entered the city. The distinguished English historian Henry H. Milman, dean of St. Paul's Cathedral, describes what then took place in Jerusalem:

No barbarian, no infidel, no Saracen, ever perpetrated such wanton and cold-blooded atrocities of cruelty as the wearers of the Cross of Christ (who, it is said, had fallen on their knees and burst into a pious hymn at the first view of the Holy City), on the capture of that city. Murder was mercy, rape tenderness, simple plunder the mere assertion of the conqueror's right. Children were seized by their legs, some of them plucked from their mothers' breasts and dashed against the walls, or whirled from the battlements. Others were obliged to leap from the walls; some tortured, roasted by slow fires. They ripped up prisoners to see if they had swallowed gold. Of 70,000 Saracens there were not left enough to bury the dead; poor Christians were hired to perform the office. Every one surprised in the Temple was slaughtered, till the reek from the dead bodies drove away the slayers. The Jews were burned alive in their synagogue. Even the day after, all who had taken refuge on the roofs, notwithstanding Tancred's resistance, were hewn to pieces. Still later the few Saracens who had escaped (not excepting babes of a year old) were put to death.

The French princes divided up the land they had conquered and settled down upon their territory, which for a time stretched from Edessa and Antioch almost to Egypt. The new owners called the southern part of this region the Kingdom of Jerusalem, and they maintained at Jerusalem a king and his court, which gave them at least a semblance of unity.

The Muslims, who had held this country for nearly five centuries, so persistently endeavored to drive the invading Christians out that for two hundred years popes and priests roused Europe to fresh Crusades to save the Sepulcher. Many Crusaders settled in Palestine, married Muslim women, and became a part of the Muslim civilization. These contented ex-Europeans were among the most resentful in the land when new hordes arrived from Europe. The first Crusaders did not know the Muslims, had never seen any of them, and hated them: the Muslims had a religion other than Christianity; they must be slaughtered until not one remained to gasp the name "Allah." As the Christians became acquainted with the Muslims they liked them, began to copy their gentle manners, even to appreciate their superior learning.

The Crusaders saw many things: better methods in medical treatment, well-organized armies; soldiers equipped with fine armor and swords of tempered steel. In their attacks the Muslims used a weapon that had never occurred to the Franks—firebrands, which they threw over the walls into the enemy's city.

Latin Europe before the Crusades knew little of community life, of cooperation through mutual interests. Almost the only cooperation from the sixth to the eleventh centuries was fighting a common enemy. Travel to Rome, Constantinople, Palestine, and Egypt enlarged the world for the Crusaders beyond all their dreams, and gave them something to think about besides fighting.

Slowly they began to admire the courtly bearing and manners of the cultivated Muslim gentlemen; and they wanted for themselves beautiful houses, silks, ornaments, delicious foods, sanitation. They carried back to Europe many recollections, and gladly greeted the merchants who brought them comforts and luxuries of the Muslim world.

When Italian merchants established regular trade with the Near East all kinds of rare and lovely things made by Muslim craftsmen were brought to Europe. *The Legacy of Islam*, written by eminent Western scholars, tells that of these Muslim treasures "not a few have rested secure for ages in churches, where a casket that had served as a Caliph's jewel-case became the repository of sacred relics, perhaps brought in it from the Holy Land wrapped in a scrap of splendid silk cut from a Muslim robe of honor." The two-headed eagle which was the royal insignia of the Seljuk sultans of the twelfth century was used in the fourteenth century by the emperors of the Holy Roman Empire as their coat of arms. Arabic script was copied by European artists as an adornment for their paintings. Giotto's painting "The Resurrection of Lazarus" shows Arabic script on the right shoulder of Christ. Fra Angelico and Fra Lippo Lippi ornamented the sleeves and the robe of the Virgin with Arabic script. In his painting "Coronation of the Virgin," Fra Lippo Lippi covered with Arabic script the long scarf the angels hold. Perhaps the great artists did not know where those highly decorative marks came from. In the British Museum is an Irish cross of bronze-gilt, made in about the ninth century. In the middle of the cross is a small glass piece on which is inscribed in Arabic the phrase, *Bismi llah*, the phrase which opens every chapter but one of the Quran. At Oxford University is a Muslim astrolabe dated A.D. 984. This instrument for measuring the altitudes of heavenly bodies was invented by the ancient Greeks, and improved and used by Ptolemy. The Muslims perfected and used it to guide them at sea and to tell the time. It was brought to Europe by traveling Christian scholars who found it in Muslim countries, and it became invaluable to mariners. The Muslims had for centuries exchanged their treasures with China. They imported and copied T'ang pottery and porcelain, and gave to China the beautiful blue color which the Chinese called "Muhammadan blue" and used with striking effect. In the eighth century Chinese prisoners taken at Samarkand taught the Muslims to make paper and the invention spread quickly through Muslim countries. Paper was brought to Europe in the twelfth century, but for a hundred years or more its value was not understood.

The mosques of Islam contained lovely glass lamps that looked like jewels when they were lighted. Beautiful silk textiles were to be found in the homes of the wealthy Muslims. The marvelous Muslim glassware and pottery and textiles were highly treasured in Europe. Venice owns a superb rock-crystal ewer on which is engraved, "al-Aziz," the name of the second Fatimid khalifa of Egypt; the ewer evidently was made for him. It was on Persian pottery that the people of Europe first saw pictures of some of the flowers of the Orient; bulbs of one of these flowers, the tulip, were later brought to Europe. In a famous Muslim weaving-house in Sicily the Italians learned the art of silk weaving; also Greek weavers captured in war taught the Italians, until by the thirteenth century Italian weavers were successfully copying the Muslim textiles and designs.

The fruits, the flowers, the entrancing gardens, the singing and games, the music on instruments like the guitar and the lute, the joy of life in the well-ordered cities, the interest in medicine and chemistry and astronomy, the reading of romances and stories, the palaces that beautified the large cities—all these things which made up Muslim culture in Tunisia, Morocco, Sicily, Egypt, Palestine, Syria, and Spain amazed the somber Europeans. When Ferdinand and Isabella conquered Muslim Spain they did not know what to do with the astronomical observatories they found there, and made them into belfreys. Neither did they know what to do with the public baths and discontinued them.

Knighthood, chivalry, was the idealistic side of life during Europe's dark centuries. Devotion to one's religion, romantic love of adventure, giving one's self with abandon to a noble cause, the joy of risking one's life with reckless ardor in an honorable deed, rescue of the oppressed and the helpless and giving them hope and at least temporary security, were ideals for the Christian knight.

There was, however, an exception to these living rules: when the knight became a Soldier of Christ he could set them aside in dealing with the Saracens. With the infidels, the Christian knight could be bloodthirsty, remorseless, freed from every moral obligation or vow of humane behavior.

The Soldiers of Christ who went to Palestine on the third Crusade met the true knight, Saladin, now Sultan of Egypt and a large part of western Asia. During the whole of his life Saladin never broke a treaty. No circumstances released him from honor and self-respect.

One day in Palestine a terrified Frankish prisoner was brought before him. The man said, "Before I saw his face I was greatly afraid, but now that I am in the presence and can see him, I am certain that he will do me no harm." Saladin set the man free.

Another day a woman frantic with grief was brought to Saladin by a scout, who said the woman had come from the Franks' camp and asked to be taken to the Sultan. She told Saladin some Muslim thieves had stolen her little girl the night before and had carried her off. All night long the mother had begged the Frankish princes to help her recover the child. They advised her to go to the King of the Muslims, saying, "He is very merciful. We will allow you to go out to seek him and ask for your daughter." Saldin's eyes filled with tears as the woman told her story. He sent a messenger to the marketplace of the camp, with money to buy the child if she was there. The messenger returned within an hour, carrying the little girl on his shoulder. The woman when she saw her child threw herself on the ground at Saladin's feet in an agony of gratitude. Saladin gave her a horse to carry her and her daughter back to the Franks' camp.

In the interim after the second Crusade, Saladin made peace treaties with the Franks who held Palestine, these treaties guaranteeing the Muslims' merchant caravans safe traveling between Syria, Arabia, and Egypt. The brother of the King of Jerusalem, a lawless Christian warrior living on his holdings beside the Dead Sea, three times broke the treaties, descended upon peaceable caravans, and stole their rich goods. This warrior, Reginald of Châtillon swore to destroy the Ka'aba and Muhammad's tomb, and he sailed a fleet to a port on the Red Sea, whence he planned to march upon Medina and Mecca. Arab warriors slew his troops as fast as they landed, and Prince Reginald fled back to Palestine.

Fully aware that peace treaties with the Franks were not to be relied upon, Saladin had long foreseen the time when he must fight the invaders. Reginald of Châtillon brought matters to a crisis in the summer of 1187 Saladin massed a large army in Palestine.

In a battle with the Franks near Hattin, a small town west of the Sea of Galilee, the Saracens won a tremendous victory and captured a great number of Franks, among them the King of Jerusalem, Reginald of Châtillon, and many important nobles and knights. Saladin executed Reginald of Châtillon and two hundred incorrigible treaty breakers. With honor, he sent the King of Jerusalem and other chief nobles to imprisonment in Damascus.

Two months later all Palestine, except Jerusalem, Tyre, Ascalon, and a few scattered castles, was in Saladin's hands.

Ninety years before, the Crusaders had taken Jerusalem from the Muslims, to whom, also, it was a holy city. The Muslims were now strong enoughto recapture it. Saladin's army advanced upon Jerusalem, and on October 2, 1187, the Christians surrendered.

A Frankish prince and warrior, Balian of Ibelin, was captured at Hattin. He came to Saladin and asked permission to take his wife and children who were in Jerusalem, to Tyre in southern Lebanon. Saladin agreed, after Prince Balian promised never again to fight against him and to stay only a night in Jerusalem. When Balian arrived in Jerusalem the Christian citizens greeted him as their commander and deliverer, for no knight of rank was left in the city. The patriarch absolved him from his promise to Saladin; and Balian took command of the city's resistence to the Muslim army. When Jerusalem fell, Prince Balian now in Ascalon just west on the sea coast had the effrontery to ask Saladin for safe conduct for his wife and children whom he wished to send to Tripoli in northern Lebanon. Saladin furnished him fifty horsemen for the journey.

When Jerusalem surrendered, Saladin's most trusted soldiers kept order in every part of the city and protected the citizens from marauders. The Christian chronicler Ernoul, squire of Prince Balian, writes that not a single story was told of a Christian's mistreatment by a Muslim. Saladin's only requirement of the conquered Christians was a ransom payment; allowed by the laws of war. Everyone who paid it would be freed; and the Muslims bought the goods of those who desired to leave the city, helping them to raise the ransom money. Saladin decreed that every man who paid ten gold pieces could go free; and two women or ten children might, for the same sum, take the place of a man. He ordered that seven thousand destitute Christians should be ransomed, the thirty thousand besants which was their ransom price to be taken from money the King of England had sent to Jerusalem.

The Patriarch of Jerusalem, a man without integrity or conscience, paid his ten gold pieces and left the city carrying an immense amount of gold plate and other treasures from the Church of the Holy Sepulcher, also a vast hoard of his own. Saladin let him go with these riches. Some Christian women, who had fled to Jerusalem after their husbands or fathers were taken prisoner in the battle of Hattin, came to Saladin and begged release for these relatives. Saladin gave the women money from his own fund, and told them that as soon as he was able he would go to the prisons and find and free the men; this promise he carried out. He ordered that a handsome sum from his fund be given to all the Christian women, married or unmarried, who were in want because the men who supported them had been killed in battle. Ernoul writes, "And he gave them so much that they gave praise to God and published abroad the kindness and honor which Saladin had done to them."

Al-Adil, Saladin's brother, after the conquest of Jerusalem said to him, " 'Sire, I have helped you by God's grace to conquer the land and this city. I therefore pray you give me a thousand slaves from the poor people within.' To Saladin's question, what he would do with them, he answered he would do as pleased himself. Then the Sultan gave him the thousand slaves, and al-Adil set them all free as an offering to God."

Ernoul tells that Saladin allowed all the old people in Jerusalem who were too poor to pay the ransom to leave the city if they wished. The number of those who left was so great that from sunrise to sunset they were passing through the city's gates, unmolested. Ernoul adds to his chronicle that these poor ones whom

Saladin freed, when they came to Tripoli, held by their Christian brothers, found the city's gates closed against them and no admission granted.

The loss of Jerusalem was a severe blow to the promoters of the Crusades. Straightway a "Saladin tax" was levied in Europe on every able-bodied man who would not go on another Crusade; and many men joined the marching crowd rather than pay the tax.

King Richard I of England was a leader of this third Crusade. He raised money for the campaign by selling to the highest bidders the most important offices and honors of England. When he returned to England he took these away from the buyers; but did not give back the purchase money.

Richard reached Acre, Palestine, with a large army, and quickly conquered that city, which had held out against the Christians for two years. Saladin's generals, evidently intimidated by King Richard's extraordinary bravery and leadership, made timorous surrender terms without consulting Saladin. By their agreement the Saracens would pay the Christians, in three monthly installments, two hundred thousand pieces of gold, and would release a thousand or more prisoners whom they held, some of them great nobles. In return, the Christians would set free twenty-seven hundred Muslim soldiers in Acre.

Saladin was greatly chagrined when he was told of this agreement. He accepted his generals' decision and made the first money payment. Remembering how often the crusaders had broken their promises to him, he announced that the would not release all his prisoners at one time but would keep certain ones as guarantee that the Muslims would be freed.

When King Richard heard this, he had the twenty-seven hundred Muslim prisoners taken outside Acre on the Friday after a Christian holy day and beheaded. The Saracens who were near enough to see this threw themselves upon the butchers, but could not save their countrymen. A Christian contemporary wrote admiringly of Richard's deed, commenting that the King was always eager to destroy the Muslims and uphold the law of Christ.

After sixteen months of fighting in Palestine, with little accomplished and much bad news from England, King Richard was about to sail from Acre when word was brought him that the Saracens were taking the coastal city Jaffa, about sixty miles away. Richard hastened in his ship to Jaffa, jumped into the waist-deep water, and dashed for the shore, calling to his men to follow. Only a few hundred knights were with him, but the king fought so furiously that his party drove off the thousands of Muslims who had made their way into the city.

For several days after this victory for the crusaders, Richard and Saladin negotiated, unsuccessfully. Then the Saracens attacked, early one morning, in seven formations of a thousand horsemen each. King Richard, with only fifty-four knights on horseback and two thousand infantry, held back the Muslims until three o'clock in the afternoon. When the Saracens began to withdraw, Richard, with fifteen knights made a reckless attack, and himself slew so many Saracens that the others fled. In the thick of the combat the king lost his horse. As he continued to fight, a Turk suddenly rode up with two beautiful Arab horses, a present from Saladin who was watching the conflict and thought it unworthy Richard's courage that he should fight on foot.

After this victory, due to King Richard's initiative and valor, Richard and Saladin made a three-year peace treaty, and Richard left Palestine. He was ill with fever, his brother John was intriguing for his throne, and the third Crusade was a failure.

# 28

## Heresy and the Inquisition

LATE IN the twelfth century Pope Innocent III proclaimed a fourth Crusade, and he labored to rouse the nations of Latin Europe to what he called their duty to Christ. Finally, four great lords of France responded, raised an army, and sent envoys to Venice to ask assistance in transporting their army by water to the enemy's land. The Doge of Venice conferred with the city's other rulers and agreed, for a heavy price, to carry the soldiers overseas. When the Crusaders could raise only three fifths of the cash payment the Venetians demanded, the Doge consented to accept, as the equivalent of the money deficit, the capture of Zara, a prosperous Christian city across the Adriatic. The crusading army accepted the Doge's terms and set out for Venice.

Some years before this Crusade the Byzantine emperor, Isaac, an extravagant and pleasure loving ruler, was driven out by his brother who usurped the throne. Isaac's son, Crown Prince Alexius, after several years' imprisonment in Constantiniple, escaped and fled to northern Italy.

There Alexius heard of the crusading army of thousands of soldiers assembling in Venice. He sent messengers to Venice beseeching help to regain his throne, and hastened to Germany to ask the support of Philip of Swabia, his brother-in-law and one of the powerful princes of Europe.

The crusading lords answered Prince Alexius that they would aid him if he would assist them in their campaign against the Saracens.

The crusaders in Venice keeping their terms with the Doge, in the autumn of 1202 crossed the Adriatic with an army of Venetians who had joined the Crusade, and attacked Zara. They captured the city and stayed there through the winter to pillage its wealth and food.

While they were so engaged, messengers came from Philip of Swabia with a proposal:

If the Crusaders would make a detour and attack and recover for Prince Alexius the city of Constantinople, if they would drive Alexius' uncle from the throne of Byzantium and reinstate him and his father, Alexius would pay the Crusaders two hundred thousand silver marks, would furnish ten thousand soldiers to accompany the Crusaders to Egypt or Syria and fight with them for a year, would provide food for the entire army for a year, and during his life would maintain in the Holy Land a standing army of five hundred knights. Also, he and his subjects would be submissive to the pope at Rome.

In view of the state of affairs between the Western and Eastern Christians, this was a very attractive offer.

The Christians of Byzantium never discarded the learning and culture of Greece as entirely as the Christians of the West repudiated them, and through the centuries the East respected law and just government.

The Eastern Church also disagreed with the West on many details of the religion they held in common, the Greeks declaring they had the true version, for they were the first to hear and accept Christianity:

The Greeks said the Holy Spirit emanated from the Father. The Latin Christians were sure the Holy Spirit came from the Father and the Son. Rome commanded celibacy of the clergy, and tried to enforce it. The Greek Church required celibacy only of its bishops.

A great rift between the Western and Eastern Churches was about images and pictures in the churches.

During their first centuries the Christians resolutely fought the worship of statues of gods and goddesses. By the seventh century, however, their own churches were filled with statues and pictures of Christ, the Virgin, and the saints. These images and pictures, the Christians now said, actually were the persons represented. The people worshiped them, as though they were alive, and told all manner of stories about them. Images spoke, it was said, or gave away a ring from a finger, stretched out a hand to a supplicant, or performed some other astonishing miracle.

In 717 an energetic man, Leo III, became emperor of the Eastern, the Byzantine, empire. He vehemently believed that the people of his empire had made idols of the images and pictures in the churches. In 726 he sent out an edict to put a stop to this form of worship. In his edict he ordered that images in the churches should be placed so high above the people they could not kiss them. Also, no one should prostrate himself before an image. When this was not effective, Leo commanded that all images be destroyed, and the pictures on the walls of the churches be plastered over.

Italy was now a province of the Byzantine empire and came over this edict. The people of Italy especially loved the images and pictures in their churches; and the Italian women wept publicly at the possibility of losing them. Pope Gregory II rose in his authority to uphold this worship his subjects adored. He rebuked Emperor Leo III for interfering in matters of worship, defied his rule over Italy, and urged the cities to continue in the current adoration of images.

The next pope, Gregory III, added to Rome's already large collection, magnificent images in marble and silver of the Christians' holy ones. By his order a statue of the Virgin was bedecked with a gold diadem set with jewels, a golden collar with jewel pendants, and earrings set with six precious stones. On a statue of the Virgin and the Christ Child he placed large handsome pearls. Gregory III called a Council in Rome and they denounced Emperor Leo and upheld image worship .

Emperor Leo III sent a fleet and an army against Italy. His ships encountered a storm in the Adriatic Sea, and many were lost. The soldiers who survived bravely landed and attacked Ravenna. In a battle, which lasted all day, the Greek army was driven back to the Po River and destroyed.

Soon after this, central Italy seceded from the Byzantine empire and sent to the pope the revenues which had gone to Constantinople.

For more than a hundred years the Greek emperors who succeeded Leo III fought image worship. The women who ruled the Byzantine empire favored it. Empress Irene, regent for her son, called in 787 a great Council at Nicaea. Under her guidance, the Council anathematized everyone who did not revere images and ordered that this adoration be restored. Then came emperors who repudiated these decrees. So it went, back and forth, one ruler undoing the work of another, During these years, the popes were always in favor of image worship.

A Council called in 794 at Frankfurt, composed of high ecclesiastics and members of Charlemagne's Diet, opposed it. Charlemagne presided at the Council and followed up their decision with a statement which he hoped would end the warfare: an image, he said, should not be worshiped or adored as though it was actually Christ, or the Virgin, or an apostle. Nor should images be reverenced, nor should lights or incense be burned before them, nor should they be kissed. Neither should images of the saints be considered living men or women. Charlemagne was willing that images and pictures be allowed in the churches if they were looked upon as reminders and ornaments only.

The Western Church, in the main, adopted Charlemagne's decision. The Greek Church ceased to worship statues, but held, to an extent, to the adoration of pictures.

Through the centuries that followed, many conflicts of varying degrees of violence, on diverse matters, between the Christians of the East and the West tore at the heart of Christianity. The West tried persistently to re-establish the pope as the center of Christendom; and was so successful that the patriarchs of Constantinople sometimes appealed to the popes to settle altercations. In the eleventh century, after heated disputes and defiance from the Greeks, the pope excommunicated the Christians of the East. In retaliation, the Greek Christians separated from Western Christendom and repudiated the pope's authority.

It seemed to many of the Latin Christians, when they received Philip of Swabia's message, that the time had come to end the controversies—by conquering Byzantium. Western Europe, temporal and spiritual, would right the wrongs of the Byzantine prince and place him on his throne, he having promised unqualified allegiance to the pope of the West.

To this was added Venice's ambition to dethrone Byzantium, her commercial rival, and become supreme as the merchant city of her world with wealth uncountable pouring into her hands, from the Far and the Near East.

With politics at its heart from the beginning, the fourth Crusade utterly miscarried, and became a bitter war among the Christians.

Prince Alexius appeared in Zara, reiterated his promises made in the message from Philip of Swabia, and the war lords and Crusaders decided to make an immediate attack on Constantinople, the capital of Eastern Christendom and one of the beautiful cities of the world.

In the spring of 1203 they sailed, and soon arrived before the great city. The Venetians, skilled in attack by sea, undertook that phase of the siege. The other Westerners attacked by land. The usurping emperor quickly fled the city. And the old blind emperor, Isaac, was brought by the Greeks from his dungeon and seated on the empty throne.

He at once proclaimed a truce and sent a message to the besiegers requesting that they return to him the prince, his son. In reply, four envoys appeared at the city's gates. When the gates were opened they marched to the palace and told Isaac he could have his son when he had met the promises made by him: cash, and soldiers, and submission to the pope. Greatly astonished, Isaac gave his trembling assent to the terms, and the prince was allowed to enter the city. He was enthusiastically received by the Greeks, and in a grand ceremony in the Church of Hagia Sophia was crowned co-emperor with Isaac.

During the days that followed, the Crusaders visited Constantinople and were amazed to see wealth and beauty of which their own barren homes knew nothing.

Meanwhile the Greeks became aware of the price at which their prince had sold them to the Christians of the West, and they were bitterly discontented. They were to be submissive to the pope; they were to pay an enormous sum to the Crusaders; they were to invade Palestine although they were trading with that country on friendly terms.

While a portion of the French army was away with Alexius, the new emperor, trying to make secure his throne in the provinces, a band of Crusaders, roaming about Constantinople, came upon a mosque. This meant the presence of infidels, their original quarry, and the Crusaders attacked those round about who were not of their party. Many Greeks quickly came to the aid of their Muslim friends, and in the fighting the Crusaders set fire to the mosque. A high wind was blowing and the fire spread fiercely through the most thickly populated sections of the city. It burned for eight days and nights, and destroyed palaces and beloved churches and an almost incalculable amount of property in the business section, also the homes and possessions of thousands of people.

Alexius returned to Constantinople, to share the throne with his father—who was blind, and too old to rule. The young emperor's success was of short duration, for the Greeks refused to be taxed to make payments to the Latin Christians, and besought their Senate to give them another emperor. Repudiated by the Crusaders and the Venetians because he did not keep his promises to them, and reviled by the Greeks who felt he had betrayed them, Alexius through the treachery of a high palace official was thrown into a prison, and after several days in chains was murdered. His father also was killed; and the Greeks proclaimed a usurper emperor.

The Crusaders and the Venetians now locked with the Greeks in a deadly struggle for Constantinople. When the besiegers after some three months' fighting entered the city, they were lighted by the third great conflagration they had started. The usurper's personal guard, and those who had held the city's gates, fled in terror. Constantinople lay open for the taking.

The barbaric horde from the West went into an unrestrained orgy of plunder and sensuality, worse than the sack of Jerusalem by the first Crusaders. Their victims this time were their fellow Christians. They looted the beautiful churches and brought their horses and mules into the buildings that they might the more easily be loaded with the treasures. They used for gambling, tables on which were painted the holiest reminders of their religion. They brought a prostitute into the Church of Hagia Sophia, had her sit on the patriarch's throne and lead them in ridiculing the church services. Nothing was sacred. No persons were safe from their wildness, neither monks, nor nuns, nor the saints, nor the Christ of their religion.

The city contained many works of art belonging to the pre-Christian Roman and Greek civilization, treasures the Christians of Constantinople appreciated and honored with conspicuous places in the city. The Crusaders broke them to pieces for the bronze or other valuable materials they contained. Some of the foreign mob found another prize, and collected an enormous number of crosses, also bones and images of the saints, which they carried back to Europe and sold at greater profit than any other loot, not excepting the treasures they rifled from the tombs of the Christian emperors in the Church of the Apostles.

The form of religion then commonly practiced in western Europe resembled Christianity only in name. Most of the manasteries and convents were worldly institutions, and kept their hold on the people through intimidation; until fear of God dominated their religion. God, the priests taught, was wrathful, interested chiefly in punishment. His Son the Christ being his representative was, like him, watching absorbedly for sin.

In the twelfth century, in many places someone tried to teach a form of Christianity better than that practiced by the clergy. In one way or another these reformers attacked the rituals of the Church: some would discard them, some would keep baptism and the Eucharist. The reformers were unanimous in their disapproval of the ungodly lives of the clergy. For the wealth and worldly power of the prelates, and the priests' extortion of money and obedience from the people were not in accordance with the deeds of Christ and the apostles.

The promoters of the Crusades told the Christians to hate the Muslims, who differed from them in religion. In Europe this hatred was turned against a foe considered equal to, perhaps worse than, the infidel—the unorthodox Christian.

The clergy rose against the spiritual insurgents. Two groups of offenders were prominent: the Waldenses and the Albigenses.

The Waldenses were peasants of the Alpine valleys and nearby regions. Their leader, Peter Waldo, a rich merchant of Lyons, used his wealth to take care of the poor, and gave up his business that he might teach the Christianity of the Gospels. He paid a scholar to translate the Gospels and some other parts of the Bible into the vernacular, and gave these books to the people. The Waldenses had no wish to leave the Church; they only insisted that the Christian clergy return to the teachings and life of Christ and the apostles. The clergy ordered them to stop their revolt, and when they refused to do this labeled them with the deadly nama "heretic."

The Albigenses in southern France were in open rebellion. They practiced their own form of Christianity in defiance of pope and clergy, and were the first to be attacked by the Church. The people of this beautiful land had the most advanced civilization in Latin Europe. They were on friendly and courteous terms with the Muslims of Spain. They did not persecute the Jews but associated with them as equals. They chose for their religious leaders not the mercenary officers of the Church, but those among themselves whose lives were blameless.

In April, 1198, Pope Innocent III sent a command to the archbishops, nobility, and people of southern France to get rid of the heretics among them. The count who ruled this section of France, also the princes and barons who were his vassals, paid no attention to the mandate. They were not willing to make war upon their devoted subjects and personal friends.

Time went on, and Pope Innocent III placed in the most important church offices in that part of France archbishops who were cruel and relentless. Again he ordered the nobility of southern France to destroy the heretics in their midst.

In 1207 Innocent III sent out a letter calling on the faithful Christians in France to rise against the heretics in the south. He promised all who entered on this Crusade absolution from their sins as though they were going against the Muslims in the Holy Land; also the same privileges of pillage and seizure of property. The Christian heretic was no better than a wild beast, and should be treated as such.

Southern France had long been independent of the northern section, almost independent of the king. The opportunity had come not only for the soldier of fortune but for the King of France to plunder the lovely and prosperous country. From all over France Crusaders poured by the thousands into Lyons, an assembling place, while in western France another huge army formed. Monks, abbots, bishops, archbishops, knights in armor, the vultures made ready to destroy their fellow Christians, in the name of God and his Son the Christ.

Led by the highest dignitaries of the Church, the Pope's special ambassadors, the horde attacked the walled cities and sacked the countrysides. In Béziers during a massacre which spared no one, seven thousand Christians were killed in one church. One account tells that fifty thousand Christians in the city were killed, and then the city was set on fire.

After conquering five hundred castles and towns, the Crusaders went home for the winter. In the spring they renewed the attack and pillaged, murdered, and burned their human prey. At one place the conquerors made a huge pyre and burned four hundred heretics at one time. The king's son, with a cardinal, a bishop, and Count Simon de Montefort held a secret conference to decide whether to pillage or burn Toulouse, the largest city of all. Count Simon decided to keep the splendid city for his personal fortune; later he and a bishop sacked Toulouse and stripped it of enormous wealth. In September, 1213, the last battle was fought and it only remained to divide southern France among the secular and ecclesiastical nobles, with Count Simon de Montefort as first lord of the land.

Time after time the people of southern France tried to regain their freedom. In 1226, a vast army almost openly for political conquest was sent against them by Louis VIII. Louis IX made a treaty in 1229 which gave at least the appearance of peace. The persecutors continued, however, through special inquisitors a secret and cruel torture. Their victims' public life was ruined. The plan now was to wreck their private life, to pry into the most intimate home life, into the very thoughts of the people and uncover insubordination.

The Inquisition in southern France had an inhuman program. Adopted in 1229 by the Council of Toulouse, and amplified through the years, it was made the law of the land. Four inquisitors must be appointed in every parish: a priest and three laymen, who were to search, house by house, for heretics and bring them to the high officers of the Church. The lord of the district must be responsible for an equally drastic search on his part. Anyone found hiding a heretic would forfeit all his property and become a slave for life; the building in which the heretic had hid must be razed. Anyone could search at any time the lands of anyone. If a heretic recanted he must be taken from his home, to live in a city among loyal followers of the Church, the recanter wearing always two crosses on the front of his dress, one on each side and made conspicuous by a color that contrasted with the dress. Anyone suspected of recanting through fear would be imprisoned for life. Everyone, commencing with boys of fourteen and girls of twelve, must, under oath, declare faith in the established Church and its tenets. Everyone must confess and take the sacrament three times a year, or be under suspicion. No one suspected of heresy could hold a public office, or practice medicine, or come near a sick or dying person. Any priest who did not publicly denounce those who failed to come to the services in his church would be deprived of his office. No layman could have a copy of the Old or New Testament. Wills could be made only in a priest's presence. Heretics who had outlived the armed war against them must be hiding somewhere, probably in the forests or in caves or behind rocks; anyone who captured a heretic would be paid a mark by his town or village. The lord suspected of allowing a heretic to hide on his land must pay a fine of twenty-five livres. Cabins were torn down, caves and other possible hiding places were closed up in the search for victims.

The Crusades, which began as a battle against Muslims across the sea, became in this way, crusades against Greek and nonconformist Christian groups. They shifted from persecuting the unbeliever outside to accenting the heretic within.

# 29

## The Struggle for Intellectual Freedom

WHILE SELF SEEKING rulers dominated Europe, out of the jungle they made rose men with the originality of genius and the courage of the martyr to blaze the way to Europe's recovery.

St. Dominic told the Pope and his princely prelates that a campaign of education would rid Christendom of the Albigenses' beliefs, but this education could not be effected by cardinals and bishops in gorgeous robes and with expensive retinues who marched in pagaents through city streets; for a first tenet of the Albigenses was simple living. Devoted and self-sacrificing, Dominic undertook the task, and for ten years traveled barefoot up and down the country to the cities, to the castles, to the country highways, reasoning with his listeners as to the true meaning of Christ's teachings.

During these years a little band of disciples joined him and the idea of an order of traveling monks grew in Dominic's mind. When he despaired of influencing the Albigenses, he went to Rome for the pope's permission to found his Order. Pope Innocent III, and after him Pope Honorius III, gave him every encouragement; and Dominic sent his sixteen followers through Europe to teach the common people true Christianity. Many monks were ready for his message of service in action, and in six years' time five hundred had joined his heroic movement and were teaching western Europe. Dedicated to his work, Dominic traveled incessantly, teaching by his noble life of austerity and sincerity as well as by eloquent arguments.

Simultaneously and under the protection of the same popes, St.

Francis of Assisi taught that Christianity was not merely theological beliefs about the nature of Christ and God; it was an inner experience of God through Christ who made him reality. This inner experience could be attained only by living as the Christ has lived: Christ had pure love for everyone, he had no property and lived in poverty, he came to earth not to rule but to serve, he traveled from place to place and taught many people. Francis renounced his home and its luxuries, accepted his father's threats and curses, and commenced to teach his simple message: a return to the life of Christ and the apostles. His townspeople ridiculed him and drove him away; a robber took his last garment.

From his love for his fellow men and his life of exquisite beauty rose the Order of the Franciscan monks, who did not shut themselves up in self-centered monasteries but spent their lives in service to the common people.

As these two movements educated the masses, great men taught in the universities and made them important and independent. In time the universities became so strong they had their own charters for self-government, given them by the popes. Popes and kings sometimes submitted their disputes to the University of Paris for settlement.

Robert Grosseteste, a revered bishop of England, from the prestige of his high office tried to reform the clergy and did not hesitate to oppose pope and king when he considered their demands unreasonable. He was more interested in the natural sciences than in philosophy or theology and served as a teacher in the new University of Oxford. Later he was its chancellor. His students honored him as the first authority of the time on mathematics and physics.

His brilliant student, Roger Bacon, hampered by the prejudice and jealousy of his less able contemporaries gave his life that his age might have light. Trained at Oxford in clearn thinking, Bacon when about twenty went to the University of Paris. He found the teachers there using faulty translations of Aristotle and supplementing their ignorance of the physical sciences with outworn dogmas. Bacon advised the French professors to learn Arabic, Hebrew, and Greek that they might read their scholarly documents in the originals.

He returned to Oxford; and when he was about thirty-six joined the Franciscan Order. His fame as a scientist grew; but his knowledge was called black magic and heresy. About seven years after he joined the Franciscans he was commanded by the general of the Order to go to Paris and to cease his scientific writing. He submitted to this punishment and for ten years lived in Paris in poverty, closely watched lest he publish something.

Pope Clement IV was interested in his work and, setting aside the dictum of the Franciscan general, requested Bacon to write out his findings in the sciences and send them to Rome. With much difficulty, for he lacked paper, instruments, and assistants, Bacon wrote three lengthy manuscripts and sent them to Pope Clement IV. In 1268, evidently under the pope's protection, Bacon was allowed to return to Oxford, and there he worked for ten years more. Another general of the Franciscans then condemned all his works and ordered him to prison; and for the next fourteen years he was a prisoner.

Roger Bacon was a pioneer in the study of optics, mathematics, chemistry, and the sciences that led to biology. Like other scientific thinkers of the Middle Ages he built his study of optics on the Muslim scholars, al-Kindi and Alhazen. Bacon saw the magnifying possibilities of convex lenses, and the force latent in gunpowder. He realized that flying machines were possible, that boats could be propelled by machinery. He believed that by means of the experimental method, all kinds of industrial and useful implements could be invented. He studied and used the philosophy and sciences of the Arabs; and counseled the pope that the Christians, if they encouraged the study of science, could educate and win the world. His chief work, an encyclopedia of science, philosophy, and theology he addressed to Pope Clement IV.

Albert of Cologne, called because of his vast learning Albert the Great, joined the Dominicans in 1223 when he was seventeen. He was allowed an amount of freedom which Roger Bacon seldom knew and spent most of his life in scientific study, teaching among the Dominicans and writing. Distinguished in birth, for he belonged to the nobility, he was Count of Bollstädt; distinguished in mind and character, he was considered by many the most learned Christian scholar of the Middle Ages.

In the thirteenth century many ordinary phenomena were explained by superstitions: some birds were said to be born out of trees and to live upon the sap of the trees. Other birds, it was believed, sprang from wood that was decaying in the sea. Bad weather was made by magicians and witches. Chemistry, which the Christians obtained from the Muslims, was counted black magic. Albert the Great tried to find the facts, to discover the laws of nature and destroy such fantastic ideas. He studied Muslim mathematics, medicine, and chemistry. He was a founder of modern botany and biology. Drawing upon Aristotle's full works as translated by Michael Scot and others, as well as upon the original contributions of the Muslims, he wrote an exhaustive encyclopedia of the sciences and philosophy of his day. In 1890 his works were republished in Paris in thirty-six volumes. He and his ablest student, Thomas Aquinas, taught that the earth is round. He might have become one of the great scientists of the Western world. A barrier of literal interpretation of the Scriptures, however, placed across his path by the reactionary church hierarchy effectually blocked his advance.

Thomas Aquinas, son of the Count of Aquino in the Kingdom of Naples, was closely related to several of the royal families of Europe. When he was five he was sent to the school in the monastery of Monte Cassino. Arabic learning was then at the height of its influence and was taught by the monks of Monte Cassino and also in the University of Naples, where Thomas Aquinas studied for about five years after he left Monte Cassino.

He decided, when he was nineteen, to join the Dominican Order. His mother was determined he should not become a friar and had him kidnapped and taken to her ancestral castle. After more than a year's imprisonment here he escaped in a basket lowered from the castle wall and fled to his Dominican brothers, who received him gladly.

He went to Paris and studied philosophy, theology, and the sciences under Albert the Great. This great scholar was made head of the new Dominican college in Cologne, and Thomas worked with him there. In 1256 Thomas became a professor in the University of Paris. He was now an authority on philosophy and theology, and was consulted by popes and kings on state matters. He was a devoted Dominican, and traveled and taught tirelessly in the service of the Order. On his way to a Council in Lyons called by Pope Gregory X in the hope that the disputes between the Latin and Greek Churches might be settled, he was taken ill. He died a few weeks later, on March 7, 1274.

When a little boy he pondered, What is God like? and tried through much praying to find a satisfactory answer. During his imprisonment, he studied the Bible, Aristotle's *Metaphysics*, and the *Sentences*, a book by Peter of Lombard who summed up in systematic fashion the teachings of the Church Fathers.

Thomas Aquinas decided that the most essential knowledge is knowledge of God and the nature of the soul. Being a profound thinker, he knew that the physical sciences can never solve the problem of life, its origin, its continuance, its goal.

Adolf Harnack writes in *The History of Dogma*, "Augustine taught that it was only possible to obtain a firm grasp of the highest questions by earnest and unwearied independent labor." Rejecting conservative thinking, acceptance of less than the best, unwillingness to work to his utmost capacity, Thomas Aquinas set himself the task of giving his age in logical simple reasoning, satisfactory and enduring arguments for the Christian religion; hoping that all Christendom would see the truth when it was made clear and differences of opinion, quarrels, and enmities would then vanish as clouds before the sun.

Like his teacher, Albert the Great, he was unconscious of prejudice and unaware of any essential antagonism between science and religion. Truth for him had no label: it was not Muslim or Greek, Jewish or Christian; it was truth. He did not hesitate to search for it in the Greek, Muslim, and Jewish writings as well as in the Christian Fathers and the Bible.

Thomas Aquinas delighted in the study and researches offered by the Muslim scholars. He read Aristotle, Averroës, al-Ghazzali, Maimonides, and Avicenna; guided in his reasoning by Aristotle he often used the ideas of the profound Muslim thinkers, and their method of presentation, to prove his faith in God and his Christian theology. He was considered the foremost Christian thinker and teacher after Augustine and was quoted by all the universities of Europe as their authority. The four great Fathers of the Latin

Church were Ambrose, Jerome, Augustine, and Gregory the Great. Thomas Aquinas became the fifth. Unlike the first form, however, he was a university teacher.

In Latin Europe the earliest universities were founded in Bologna and Paris. The University of Bologna specialized in Roman and church law. In Paris, theology, logic, and church law were studied, with training in argument as a primary interest. When a student could hold his own in public argument with an authorized teacher he won his degree, a permit to teach. The University of Naples commenced in Salerno as a medical school. It was founded, tradition says, by four teachers, a Greek, a Latin, a Saracen, and a Jew. In this school were Muslim, Christian, and Jewish teachers and students. In 1224 Frederick II moved the now famous school to Naples, broadened its curriculum, and gave it a charter under the title University of Naples.

By the twelfth century many young men were looking hopefully to the training offered by theological study, and to positions in the Church, from which no one was debarred by birth or poverty. It was the custom for a man to decide under what teacher he wished to study and go to him, and students traveled over Europe in search of some teacher. It is said that Abelard had thirty thousand students from many parts of Europe, and from among them came fifty bishops and twenty cardinals.

The Muslims had for centuries lived upon Greek science and philosophy. Khalifa Mamun in the ninth century employed Christian scholars of the East to translate into Arabic the Greek classics and scientific writings, that all Muslim students might have access to the works of the great Greek physicians, Hippocrates and Galen, and the writings of Plato, Aristotle, and other masters. Guided by these superior minds the Muslim scholars commenced their own independent work, which continued well into the twelfth century. Obedient to Muhammad, they searched the world for knowledge and availed themselves of the sciences of Persia, China, India, and central Asia. Towering intellects appeared in Islam and carried forward the scientific achievements of other nations. The Muslim physician Rhazes, skilled in the treatment of the eye, was one of the first to show the difference between smallpox and measles. He was a master of the history and practice of medicine, and was profoundly learned in philosophy, mathematics, physics, and astronomy. Avicenna, the great physician and philosopher, wrote also on physics. Averroës was a philosopher, whose many commentaries interpreted Aristotle, and in time shook intellectual Europe to its foundations.

Timidly and secretly at first, for Muslim learning was considered not only black magic but untheological, young men of inquiring minds made their hazardous way to the Muslim countries most accessible to the Christians, Spain and Sicily, where strange new sciences might be studied; and to some the intellectual quickening was as exciting as was the life of adventure to the knight in armor. The scientific and philosophic works of Islam were written in Arabic; Latin Europe could read neither Arabic nor Greek. The problem was to get Latin translations.

The eager students of Christendom found in Spain many brilliant Jewish scholars who were proficient in Latin and Arabic. Here also were scholarly Christians who, with the Jews, lived at peace with the Muslims. These scholars helped the Christian students translate Arabic manuscripts into Latin—all in utmost secrecy for fear of the Christian clergy. The Christians went back to northern Europe to show their treasures to other daring minds. Arabic philosophy and science were also smuggled into Europe by merchants who traveled in many lands.

After the sack of Cordova in 1010, Muslim learning in Spain was centered in Toledo. When Alfonso VI conquered Toledo in 1085, its libraries became easily accessible to Christians. Even before Toledo fell, Christian kings encouraged Greek and Muslim learning; and Jewish scholars translated, into Hebrew and Latin, Arabic translations from the Greek, as well as the works of the Islamic philosophers.

Petrus, one of the greatest of the Jewish scholars, was baptized a Christian in 1106 when he was forty-three. He went to England and became the physician of King Henry I. The Christian physicians of Europe were lamentably in need of scientific medicine. They used relics of the martyrs, bones of the saints, and charms to drive away the demons that caused illnesses. In some cases they used special prayers. If the first joint of the right thumb was in trouble they prayed to God the Father. The second joint of this thumb was under the care of the Blessed Virgin. St. Clare could heal sore eyes. St. Pernel watched over and cured ague. The priests helped with the prayers and were paid for their services. Hippocrates, Galen, and later the Muslim physicians worked out more scientific formulae. For consumption they prescribed sunshine, fresh air, good food, and rest. Petrus introduced into England the rational medicine and methods of the Greeks and Muslims.

He also brought a book called *Training School for the Clergy.* It was full of folk stories of India that the Muslims had translated into Arabic. Petrus read these stories while he was in Spain, and retranslated them into Latin. Some of the tales in Petrus' book were in time published in England in a volume called *Gesta Romanorum* and became very popular. *Gesta Romanorum,* writes Professor Charles Singer, "is the source of many of the stories in Chaucer and Shakespeare. It was first printed about 1510, by Wynkyn de Worde. The edition survives in but a single copy, but was reprinted in 1577. Shakespeare probably read this later issue."

Petrus' contemporary, Adelard of Bath, after many years of study in Muslim countries returned to England and taught the sciences he had learned from the Muslims; to whom he gave full credit for his scholarship. The Arabs told him the ancients became authorities by the free use of their reason, and gave him the great idea which he proclaimed to western Europe: Use your reason. Do not accept a statement just because an authority has declared it. Reason it out: Is it right, or is it perhaps wrong?

Gerard of Cremona, Italy, a scholar of the twelfth century, heard that the Greek astronomer Ptolemy wrote a book, *Almagest.* Gerard tried to find it but no one in Italy had a copy, nor could he get one in all Latin Christendom. Hoping the book might be in Spain, he went there, and in the great Muslim libraries found not only Ptolemy's *Almagest* but hundreds of other books of which he had never heard, written by great philosophers and scientists, Greek and Muslim. Gerard resolved to stay in Spain among these riches. Here he lived for many years, learning Arabic, then translating the Muslims' books, that Europe might have them.

A large part of the medical works used by the universities of the later Middle Ages were Gerard's translations. He rendered into Latin all of Avicenna's vast *Canon of Medicine,* an encyclopedia of general medicine giving information on diseases that might attack any part of the body and prescribing simple treatment. In the latter part of the fifteenth century, three hundred years after Gerard lived, his translation of the *Canon of Medicine* was printed sixteen times, and in the sixteenth century twenty more editions came out. Innumerable handwritten copies made of other translations by him were fervently studied. That future scholars might not forget their debt to Gerard, his students attached to one of his translations (of which there were almost eighty on various subjects) a short biography telling their master's labors and achievements.

A remarkable school of translators founded in Spain in the twelfth century by Raymond, Archbishop of Toledo, has been likened to Khalifa Mamun's support of such work, three centuries earlier in Baghdad. The services of these many translators to those in Europe who were thirsting for knowledge can hardly be overestimated. By the thirteenth century translations from the Arabic were so popular that translating was made almost a profession, and Christian kings appointed scholars to render the books of the Muslims into Latin.

Alfonso the Wise, King of Castile, highly appreciated and admired the Muslim learning and culture around him. He founded a university in Toledo, his capital, and appointed Christian, Jewish, and Muslim scholars to be the teachers. He ordered the translation of the Quran and other Muslim books, and had the Jewish Talmud translated.

The scholars who worked under the king's direction drew upon the Muslims for much of their information. With the assistance of the Arabs, King Alfonso wrote a world history. And guided by the high achievements of the Muslim astronomers he directed the work of two Jews who compiled the Alfonsine Tables. These astronomical Tables were consulted by Kepler and Galileo and for centuries were a basis for scientific study in Europe.

To a world that had only fragments of Aristotle and Plato, and practically no Plotinus; to whom Hippocrates and Galen were almost unknown, except perhaps in the southern tip of Italy; to a world that had almost no Greek science or medicine, a wonderful door was opened to the biology and philosophy of Aristotle, to

Plato's great mind, to mathematics, astronomy, medicine, and other Greek sciences. With these came the Arabs' living philosophy and science and the interpretations and knowledge the Muslims had added to Greek science and medical practice. A few manuscripts containing a very small part of the writings of Aristotle had lain around in Christian monasteries for centuries, and a few copies of them had been made; but no one read them, for pagan learning except in brief censored digests like those of Boëthius and Isidore was taboo.

Translations from the Arabic were at first violently rejected by the clergy. By the fourteenth century, all the large medical schools in Europe used Avicenna and Rhazes as supreme authorities and, writes Professor Rashdall, Arabic medicine was "everywhere in full possession of the medical faculties." At the University of Montpellier in southern France, by 1340 all the medical books used for lectures, except perhaps two, were Latin translation from the Arabic.

For two hundred years Europe leaned upon the works of the Greeks and the great Muslim scholars and scientists, translated from Arabic into Latin. But gradually Christian scholarship awoke and began to lay the foundations of its own characteristic science. Even when the terrifying designation "heretic" was used to silence the scholar, courageous thinkers like Roger Bacon, Albert the Great, and Thomas Aquinas were opening avenues of thought that would never again be closed.

# 30

## Mysticism and Renaissance

IN THE THIRTEENTH century, Dante saw his world bristling with war: the little city-states of Italy fighting each other, fighting the pope, fighting the German invaders—and Dante decided that the only hope for the world was peace. He wrote: "O human race! what tempests must need toss thee, what treasure be thrown into the sea, what shipwrecks must be endured, so long as thou, like a beast of many heads, strivest after diverse ends!"

In the opening sentences of his *De Monarchia* Dante reveals the inner urge which he felt compelled to obey: "All men on whom the Higher Nature has stamped the love of truth should especially concern themselves in laboring for posterity, in order that future generations may be enriched by their efforts, as they themselves were made rich by the efforts of generations past." The sublimity of his vision, his soaring genius, the eternal truth and beauty in his writings are evidence that Dante was assisted by divine Reality. The "footprints of eternal power" are apparent in his sentences; for no man of himself could think so sublimely and call to his contemporaries so eloquently to rise above the beasts and live nobly.

Dante believed it is man's destiny to attain perfection in thought and action, for God made men little lower than the angels. As God is one, Dante declares, the human race, made in his likeness, must be one and live under a universal law which all people obey in their hearts, saying, "Behold how good and how pleasant it is for brethren to dwell together in unity."

A first step toward this universal unity must be Europe at peace under one ruler to whom the princes are loyal. This ruler must realize that the government is not for his personal benefit, to make him greater than others; but he exists for the governed, to bring them the best possible prosperity. Only by absolute and binding moral and spiritual practices can good government be maintained; therefore this ruler must obey God.

In his *Divine Comedy* Dante warns the Christians that the moral and ethical issues taught by Christ are unescapable, and there is no abatement of the law that as a man sows so shall he reap. In an allegory he describes what he witnesses around him: he visited Paradise, he writes, and "rapacious wolves in garb of shepherds are seen from here on high all over the pastures"; fables are taught in place of the Gospels, everyone strives for display.

Dante was a profound student who investigated every avenue of thought open in his day. Among the authors whom he read were Averroës, Avicenna, and al-Ghazzali.

The poet and philosopher Ibn Arabi, who lived from 1165 to 1240, was particularly interested in the story of Muhammad's visit to heaven. This vision, described by Muhammad in the Quran, was much elaborated by Muslims of imaginative minds. They multiplied Muhammad's heaven into nine, and tried to harmonize these with Ptolemaic science and astronomy. First, they decided, came the heaven of the moon, second the heaven of Mercury, and so on.

Modern scholars have discovered in their researches that Dante's heaven and hell closely resemble the writings of the Muslims. Professor R. A. Nicholson of the University of Cambridge writes that Ibn Arabi "certainly influenced some of the Christian medieval schoolmen, and, as Professor Asín Palacios has recently pointed out, many peculiar features in his descriptions of Hell, Paradise, and the Beaitific Vision are reproduced by Dante with a closeness that can scarcely be fortuitous. 'The infernal regions, the astronomical heavens, the circles of the mystic rose, the choirs of angels around the focus of divine light, the three circles symbolizing the Trinity—all are described by Dante exactly as Ibnu'l-Arabí described them.' Dante tells us how, as he mounted higher and higher in Paradise, his love was made stronger and his spiritual vision more intense by seeing Beatrice grow more and more beautiful. The same idea occurs in a poem of Ibnu'l-Arabí written

about a century earlier. . . . It may be added that Ibnu'l-Arabí too
had a Beatrice—Nizám, the beautiful and accomplished daughter
of Makínu'ddín." Each poet personified his revelation from on
high as a lovely maiden.

One of the heavens the Muslims had Muhammad visit was
Mars, where lived the souls of good soldiers. In the heaven of
Mars, Dante put the great Crusaders, the Soldiers of the Cross. To
combine these Muslim and Christian poetic ideas would cause the
good Crusaders and the good Muslims who died in Palestine
fighting each other to live together in the same heaven.

Contact with the intellectual, industrial, and artistic life of Islam
was a momentous step toward Europe's Renaissance. Another
impetus was the mystics. Some mystics were philosophers, political reformers, believers in emancipation through knowledge of
God, like Dante and St. Thomas Aquinas. One day, toward the
end of his life, as Thomas Aquinas was celebrating the Mass, and
thinking of Christ as the bread from heaven, he suddenly saw the
Christ as the Spirit of God. This wonderful moment brought him
such mental freedom and knowledge that he testified it meant
more to him than all the proofs he had reasoned out in his books.
Other mystics were men like St. Francis and St. Dominic who by
their sheer spiritual strength became the educators of their age.
Some mystics were great artists.

Mysticism is often interpreted to mean anything that is irrational and mysterious. It also means a direct consciousness of the
divine, the unseen world; when the veil is lifted from men's eyes,
they look at a higher reality and are reborn. To the empiricist's
claim that his findings are based upon an immediate experience of
the surrounding physical universe, upon his direct awareness of
fresh air and sunshine and the life in his body, the mystic replies
that he trusts an equally vivid experience of the sunshine and
breezes and life of an invisible universe which sustains and sur-
rounds the physical. The characteristics of this invisible universe
are, he says, love, a sense of freedom, peace, quickening of the
intellect, and joy. These phenomena are so real that the physical
world grows pale and unstable beside them.

As thoroughgoing in their researches as the most conscientious scientists, the mystics discover that God is not an hypothesis but a reality; that he may be known in the same direct way in which one recognizes true love when it shines as a feeling in the mind; that he may be found if one follows the path to him blazed by his Messengers; that no man can make his own terms with God but must accept God's terms. Those who experience God's presence enter a life so glorious that no calamity is comparable to losing this inner reality. The way, the mystics testify, is concentration of mind and deeds upon God.

What a marvel they were, the mystics of the fourteenth century, rising in a brutal and ignorant environment gloomy with a religion largely defined as punishment for sin. The mystics made the dignity of man the center of their teaching. They declared the common people were sons of God and as valuable as any high-born prelate. They proclaimed Christianity to be a religion of joy, good cheer, and love.

Twenty-six years after Dante died, one of these mystics, a girl, was born in a well-to-do home in Siena, a city-state of northern Italy. She was the twenty-fifth child of the dyer Jacopo Benincasa and his wife, Lapa. Catherine grew up sweet and attractive, and her family easily arranged an advantageous marriage for her.

Catherine would have none of it, for when she was six years old she saw in vision the Christ; and when she was seven, in the sanctuary of her heart she took the vow of celibacy. To punish her disobedience her father and brothers put her in the kitchen to do a servant's work. Catherine was so happy at her tasks that they were no hardship. Her father, a sincere and generous man, soon befriended her and let her do as she pleased. The young girl shut herself in her room, vowed to speak to no one but her confessor, and for three years lived in this room in her father's home as the ascetic lives in the desert, praying day and night with the intensity of an unusually strong character.

In three years' time her mind and will were trained to find, in God and the Christ, the way through every blank wall on the bleak paths where human beings are lost. Catherine was sure God's love for humanity was fathomless; that he created men and women to give them perfection and that his plan was checked only by their obstinate refusal to receive his wonderful bounty.

Remarkably original and independent, she decided she could do nothing for God himself, for he needed nothing. She could, however, show him her love by serving his children, not for themselves but because she so loved their Maker. She went to the hospitals and nursed repulsive cases everyone shunned; she became a peacemaker between individuals and, later, between groups. She was as much at home with the nobility as with her family, for she lived in a realm where there were no class distinctions. The people felt she had insight and knowledge beyond ordinary experience, and she became famous as a saint.

The sorrow and responsibility of her life were the demoralized clergy. She was sure the pope could correct this social condition. Gregory XI, then pope, was living in Avignon in southern France, his court the center of the luxury and wordliness of the time. Catherine saw the first step in reforming the Church must be that the pope return to Rome. The next step must be that he appoint to church offices holy and honorable men who sincerely wished to live according to Christ's teachings. She wrote many letters to Pope Gregory explaining her ideas, urging him to live in Rome, to cease quarreling with Florence, with the King of France, with this one and that one. Pope Gregory allowed her to write him as plainly as she wished. He gave her an audience at his court in Avignon, and with a suite of attendants came to interview her in Florence. By her spiritual radiance and unswerving conviction she at last persuaded him to move his court to Rome. He was not strong enough to dominate the political and private corruption there and disasters multiplied. When Gregory XI died the situation became worse, for with the election of Urban VI as Gregory's successor an opposition party formed and set up a pope at Avignon.

Catherine grieved so acutely over the political chaos, and the unworthy prelates, that she died of her grief when she was thirty-three. To her the church organization, with the pope at its head, was established on the Word of God. It only remained to bring the organization back to Christ.

By her own attainment she showed what the spiritual life could give to the individual. Apart from her distress for the Church, she was radiant and joyous. To her came an endless stream of visitors seeking healing of mind and body. Priests, professors, poets, monks, nuns, patricians, the rich and the poor—all came to her as to a physician for inspiration and counsel. Even intolerant and domineering Pope Urban VI sent for her to help him bring peace among Rome's factions.

Of plebeian birth and environment, St. Catherine carried herself like a queen. When she stood before Pope Gregory XI in the interview he arranged in Avignon—an awesome occasion, for the room was filled with cardinals, bishops and other grandees listening to her every word—she was as poised and sure as though it were a time of private prayer. In her letters to her students, to cardinals, laymen to near-holy monks, she offered each, with her spiritual insight, the cure for his self-indulgence or laziness.

The Dominican monk Eckhart raised the cry for freedom of thought in Germany. He was a founder of German prose and is often called the Father of German philosophy. A profound scholar, he studied the Greek, Muslim, and Christian classics. He taught that God created because he loved; that "one should not have a theoretical God and be satisfied therewith, for when the thought vanishes, God vanishes also." His ideal was God at the foundation of man's thinking. He was tried by the Church for heresy and accused of believing the world was eternal, for he had written that as soon as God was, the world was created. In his defense he quoted Avicenna, Aristotle, Bernard of Clairvaux, Thomas Aquinas, and Augustine.

Eckhart's great theme, that God is in the human soul, a spark of light, was taken up by his disciple, the famous preacher Tauler. Tauler taught spiritual democracy—that the humblest workingman, married and supporting his family, could attain perfection, as well as the eminent priest. It was becoming apparent that by right use of the intellect the real Christ could be rediscovered.

Another scholar and mystic of the fourteenth century, Ruysbroeck, became a monk when he was twenty-four and worked quietly among the people of Brussels until he was fifty. With his uncle and another monk he then went to a hermitage in the forest given them by the Duke of Brabant. The three hoped, in the quiet and seclusion of the forest to pray and meditate as they could not in the city. However, Rysbroeck's fame as spiritual teacher was too widespread, and through the years many disciples came to him; from Germany and Holland, France and Belgium. He could not turn them away; and his sacrifice bore much fruit, for among his students rose the Brethren of the Common Life.

Some priests asked Ruysbroeck if he thought them holy men. He answered that they were as holy as they wished to be. His student Gerhard Groot, hoping to cherish and encourage the wish for holiness, founded the society known as the Brethren of the Common Life: groups of men who lived the ascetic life in their community houses but took no religious vows. They supported themselves by manual labor and by copying manuscripts, and their earnings went into a common fund. They lived unselfishly, at peace with each other and the world, and made it their supreme aim to serve and educate all who came to them. By the middle of the fifteenth century they had a hundred and fifty schools in northern and central Germany, in the Low Countries, and in England. For more than two centuries they worked to educate Europe. The book *Imitation of Christ*, compiled by Thomas à Kempis, gives the teachings of their founder, who received his instruction in the spiritual life from Ruysbroeck.

To know the Christ again, even dimly, gave impulse to the building of churches and cathedrals, and by the thirteenth century this great movement was educating the people. The first cathedrals were massive, somber, unadorned strength and endurance. As the people became more conscious of the gentleness and sweetness of the Christ, refinement of feeling and reverence grew in the artists' souls and to the churches they added soaring towers, arches and spires, lovely statues, and stained-glass windows. The artists' names were not recorded but their tribute to the greatest thing in their life remained to remind the coming generations of the Artificer of civilizations. The cathedrals soared above city and congregation, a symbol of Christ's teaching of unity. They became the community homes and were used by high and low, the great lord and the beggar. Everyone could find a refuge and at least a temporary home in the cathedral dedicated to Christ.

In the fourteenth century came Giotto, the emancipator of art and friend of Dante, the liberator of literature. Giotto loved human beings and with the eye of genius entered into their joys and tragedies, and painted them as they were. His teacher, St. Francis, showed him the sweetness and ardor, the vitality and love of Christ and the early Christians, until Giotto saw heaven's loveliness shining in the stories of Joseph and Mary and the apostles and painted by this inner sight. In his picture "The Flight into Egypt," little Jesus is more than a child, he is divinity, waiting; and the boy who leads the donkey looks up into Joseph's face as though he beheld divine beauty and looked forward to a sublime hope. After Giotto came other artists who could pass through the door he opened—and the Renaissance began.

As though in answer to the skeptics who might say that mystics like St. Francis and St. Catherine and the early Christians could prove in no tangible way their assertion that in their minds they met God, an artist came who was able to paint this experience. When the great Michelangelo studied the faces Fra Angelico had painted, he said the good monk must have gone to heaven and seen angels to paint such faces.

Fra Angelico painted his lovely spiritual life on the walls of the monastery of San Marco in the monks' cells and in the hallways, to help the brothers to find and feel in their prayers the divine Presence. He painted the Christ Child, a sweet, strong, adorable boy, through whose eyes the eternal world was looking, for he was the Christ. Fra Angelico painted the mature Jesus, and in his picture shone the mighty spirit which made Jesus the Messiah. After five hundred years, and now through faded colors, the glory of Fra Angelico's visions may be seen in his Holy Virgin, his paintings of angels and apostles. His spiritual life set him free from the limitations of this world and made him a saint. He cared not at all for the pomp of Florence then rising into the material magnificence of the Renaissance. He sought no rewards from the rich and officially great. His blameless life, his confidence in himself and his powers have ennobled the centuries.

In the fourteenth century in which Catherine lived, a vital liberating movement commenced when Petrarch through his unique originality broke with the conventional attitude and opened an era in education.

Petrarch loved beauty as the church prelates loved power. He saw the beauty in Rome's ancient temples and works of art and tried to overcome his countrymen's indifference to these treasures. He found charm in the Latin language as it was written by Cicero and Virgil. His soul drank in the loveliness of the French and Italian scenery. In verse and prose he described what he saw and felt: human life and its emotions quite apart from theology and philosophy. His theme was culture, and he presented his ideas with such consummate art that he became the leader of education for culture and the appreciation of beauty.

Petrarch's father hoped to make him a lawyer like himself, and to please his father the young man studied law for seven years, first at the University of Montpellier and then at Bologna. His passion for literature could not be quieted and he surreptitiously secured and studied the classics. The father surprised the unwilling law student with his manuscripts and threw them into the fire, but relented in time to save half-burned copies of Virgil and of Cicero's *Rhetoric.* When Petrarch was twenty-two his father died, and what estate he left was stolen from the heirs, Petrarch and his brother, in the settlement. Petrarch then followed the only course open to a well-born and well-educated young man who was destitute: he became a monk. Things went well for him and before long he acquired a patron, a rich nobleman who soon became a powerful bishop; and another prelate, Cardinal Giovanni, befriended him.

When Petrarch was thirty-three he began in earnest his profession as a writer. In April, 1341, when he was thirty-seven, a celebration by commoners and patricians was held in his honor on the Capitoline at Rome and he was given the poet's crown. He was now an international celebrity and was welcome at the courts of Europe. Although he could have a prominent position in the Church he refused the offers made him and jealously guarded his independence and his leisure to write. He finally became an ambassador for his patron, the Archbishop of Milan, and was sent by him and his successors on many important commissions to the courts of Europe.

With scholarly care Petrarch studied Cicero and Virgil, also the monuments, statues, and temples of ancient Greece and Rome. In literature he gave first place to the Bible and the Church Fathers; next to these he put the ancient classics. He carefully selected the passages in Greek philosophy and the Bible that harmonized, and compared them to show their similarity. His appreciation of Greek and Roman culture spread through Italy and France as a fire flies from tree to tree in a forest. Even the illiterate farmer who managed Petrarch's estate handled his few priceless books with awe.

Boccaccio was Petrarch's devoted friend and worked with him to spread classic learning. Boccaccio was a finished scholar and he lectured in Florence on Dante and Greek literature. From his writings and those of Petrarch and Dante emerged a new Italian literature, to which the letters of St. Catherine of Siena made an important contribution. But the greatest impetus to the new education did not come for almost a century after Petrarch died.

On Marcy 6, 1447, Nicholas V became pope. To preserve his authority he put his trust in the spirit of primitive Christianity, not in armies of paid soldiers. Until his death in 1455, he lived and worked for peace, for the advancement of learning and art, and for every worthy cause.

It was his great desire that Rome become a city of spiritual grandeur. To accomplish this he was as practical as he was idealistic. The Jubilee which celebrated his triumph over the spurious pope of Avignon brought to Rome wealthy visitors from all Europe. These princes, temporal and ecclesiastical, poured their gifts into Rome's empty money box until the total sum was immense.

With this wealth Nicholas V commenced to rebuild Rome and fortify it against invasion and civil war. He restored outer walls and bridges, and repaired churches and other public buildings in the city ruined by war. He spent lavish sums repairing churches, fortifications, and waterways in all parts of Italy. He employed the best engineers, architects, and artists of Italy. He brought Fra Angelico to Rome to paint for him. It was the hope of this great Pope to make Rome spiritually, intellectually, and physically grand. Then might return the respect and reverence for the holy Christian religion, which was almost lost when Rome became the center from which radiated gaudy display, scheming politics, and a sensual clergy.

As the Turks pressed upon Constantinople in the middle of the fifteenth century, and the fall of the Eastern Christian empire was a matter of time only, many Greek scholars fled to safer Italy, carrying with them their Greek manuscripts. Pope Nicholas V greeted these scholars with enthusiasm and set them to work translating their documents into Latin. He sent messengers to England, Germany, and France to search the monasteries for their rare old manuscripts, which for centuries had been unwanted and forgotten. He had Constantinople and Greece ransacked for manuscripts the scholars had overlooked. Nicholas' collection of five thousand volumes was the astonishment and pride of Europe. With these books he founded the Vatican Library.

The translation of the Arabic manuscripts taught the scholars of Europe to think and reach out for knowledge. The Muslim commentaries explained Aristotle and Plato and lifted Europe to mental levels lost for centuries. The Latin and Hebrew translations from the Arabic, however, were full of mistakes, for the translators did not understand the Arabic language. To the scholars of Italy, the original Greek manuscripts now in their hands seemed treasures from heaven. Their accurate Latin translation created intense eagerness for Greek learning. With better knowledge of Greek philosophy, science, and literature came an understanding of Greek art, soon to be followed by a love of beauty equally that of Periclean Athens.

The Greek scholars from the Byzantine empire translated for Nicholas V the histories of Herodotus, Thucydides and Polybius, as well as Xenophon's *Cyropaedia.* They translated works of the great Jewish philosopher Philo, Aesop's *Fables,* Epictetus, Plato, and many other masters.

The Pope gave Manotti, a learned scholar of Florence, the task of translating the Bible from the Hebrew and Greek. Manotti made a translation of most of the New Testament, and from the Syriac he translated the Psalms. Boccaccio had supervised a prose translation of Homer, but Pope Nicholas wanted to read Homer in verse. He offered the translator, Philelpho, "a fine palace in Rome, and farms in the Roman territory, which would maintain his whole family in ease and honor, and to deposit ten thousand pieces of gold, to be paid when he should have finished the Iliad and the Odyssey."

Pope Nicholas V, by his innate love of books and study, set in motion a tremendous movement toward the Renaissance in Italy.

The popes who came after Nicholas V, though they carried on or allowed the Inquisitions, gave freedom to scholars and artists. They called to their service the greatest artists of their time and encouraged and supported them while they accomplished works which honored and dignified the world. The artists, sculptors, architects, the scientists and men of letters who lifted Europe into splendor were so many and so gifted it would seem they came not by chance but by a heaven-formulated plan to ennoble the life of men after centuries of brutality.

# 31

## Reform and Renewal

IN ITALY the Renaissance reached its zenith in Michelangelo and Raphael. Then came reaction. The educated people of Italy read with boundless appreciation the literary classics upon which the ancient Greeks and Romans had lived—and had died morally. Calling it culture, Italy delighted in the tales of the Greek gods and goddesses and their depravities, and in the dramas which in elegant style told of illicit loves, of revenge and murder. Under this influence Italians lost their moral balance, as had the ancient world. The artists retained their creative skill and superb technique, their mastery of perspective, composition, light, shadow, and characterization, their almost faultless standards of beauty. But they now chose subjects from Greek mythology, and were ready to invoke at any time the very deities whom the early Christians had fought and had given their lives to drive forever from the world. Again men imitated the immoralities of these gods and goddesses. Again men thought their horrible banquets and excesses, their bestial sensuality were the last word in culture. The Christian religion in Italy made no organized protest, for the morals of the monks and priests were also in full and tragic decline. The monasteries of the fourteenth and fifteenth centuries owned enormous property; the clergy were the scandal of Christendom.

The monk Savonarola tried singlehanded to reform Florence. He used gentle persuasion, and made no headway. Then he discovered he could be a highly emotional speaker. He mounted the cathedral pulpit and, working himself into frenzied feeling, denounced the clergy and the humanists. As he pictured the moral depravity around him and prophesied the calamities about to envelop the world, his audiences swayed and shuddered with him. His violence opened no gate to heaven, and save for a conversion here and there the clergy and the humanists went their way. Savonarola made other blunders: he mixed religion with party politics; he did not pay due respect to Pope Alexander VI, probably because he considered this pope a first cause of the Church's wickedness. The pope was stronger than Savonarola, and he had the troublesome reformer burned at the stake.

Since the time of Anselm and Bernard of Clairvaux, efforts were made to reform the clergy: sometimes by groups like the Waldenses, sometimes by a university teacher. A century before Savonarola, John Wycliffe courageously attacked the abuses which spread from Rome. Wycliffe was the most eminent and influential professor or Oxford University, for some years Master of Balliol College. He was appointed by the King of England to a rectory and held this post until he died. He preached often in London and became famous for his eloquence and for his many books and pamphlets in which he analyzed the falacious practices of the Church. For centuries the kings of western Europe had struggled with the popes and prelates for supremacy. Sometimes the kings held the balance of power; more often it was the popes. Taking the established feudal system as the basis for society, Wycliffe argued that a feudal lord held his fief in return for the services he rendered to the lord above him. So also was it with the popes and the prelates. The lord above the ecclesiastical nobility was God. The service God required was righteousness, justice, and holy living. The prelate who did not give this service ought to forfeit his office, his wealth, and his authority. Wycliffe told his audiences that the clergy should not own great estates, should not live in luxury, and should have nothing to do with politics.

He called the Bible the charter of Christendom and said all Christians should own and read this book. With the assistance of two friends he translated the Vulgate into the English vernacular. He sent out itinerant laymen to teach the people of England the truth about their religion. He did not choose as his teachers any monks, for, he said, they were too easily deflected. His messengers were gladly received, and as they preached against the evil ways of the clergy, they roused much discontent with the Church.

Wycliffe was called before the Bishop of London for trial. Pope Gregory XI also condemned him. He was protected for a time by the king and some of the nobles of England who wished to undermine the Church's power; and though he was much persecuted he lived until he was sixty, when he died of a paralytic stroke.

The prelates who could not wreak their indignation upon him during his life had some satisfaction after his death. The Council of Constance pronounced him a heretic, and decreed on May 4, 1415, that his body be disinterred and burned. At the command of Pope Martin V this was done in 1428, forty-four years after Wycliffe died.

His followers, called Lollards, did not organize into a sect or distinct group; but they were to be found everywhere in England, among nobles and peasants, in the royal family. An enemy declared that half the men one met were Wycliffites. In after years, being of the material of which martyrs are made, many were burned at the stake.

Princess Anne of Bohemia became Queen Anne of England, wife of Richard II. In England she, and her countrymen, in her train, accepted Wycliffe's version of Christianity. The Bohemian scholars carried many copies of Wycliffe's writings back to Bohemia, where they were widely and sympathetically read.

His writings also reached Bohemia by way of Paris, and came into the handsof John Huss, the accomplished and remarkably popular Rector of the University of Prague. Huss read Wycliffe's books carefully, and announced in many public addresses that he agreed with Wycliffe that the clergy should give up their vast wealth, should renounce their worldly power, and should live irreproachably as Christ and the apostles had lived.

If the clergy relinquished their property and secular authority they would deprive themselves of what they counted valuable, for righteous living was to them a poor thing beside the riches and dictatorial powers which were theirs. Wycliffe's ideas must not be allowed to spread; Huss was too persuasive. The hierarchy at Rome began a relentless persecution and summoned Huss to the city of Constance to appear before the grand assemblage of European prelates there in counsel. Betrayed by the Emperor of Germany who had promised him protection, Huss was finally publicly burned at the stake.

Bohemia continued to believe as he had taught, and fought desperately for his principles. Only when they quarreled among themselves were Huss' followers conquered.

Wycliffe's writings found their way into the universities and were read by many leaders of thought. Discontent with the arrogant cardinals and bishops and with worldly popes who levied heavy taxes increased among the educated and the common people.

Groups arose within the monastic orders and tried to reform them. One such party, the Spiritual Franciscans decried the worldliness of the Franciscans of Italy and reminded the monks who bore St. Francis' name that the first leader of their Order abhorred wealth. These reformers, also, were cruelly persecuted and murdered.

"Beware when the great God lets loose a thinker on this planet," wrote Ralph Waldo Emerson. When Martin Luther in 1517, nailed his ninety-five theses to the door of Elector Frederick's castle church, his challenge resounded through Germany. Large numbers of the German people had ceased going to the church services. There was almost no preaching. The people heard that the taxes the pope extorted were spent in Rome in incredible extravagance. When the monk Tetzel appeared and offered for sale the new indulgences Pope Leo X had prepared, Martin Luther's theses gave good reasons for not buying them.

The declaration Luther nailed to the church door was printed in Latin and German and quickly spread through Europe. Luther had no idea of leaving the Church, or creating another organization. But he sincerely believed the Church should be reformed and that clear thinking could accomplish it. To him one of the boldest of the false beliefs was the indulgences, papers promising the pope would secure forgiveness for persons suffering in purgatory for their sins. Popes or bishops signed these papers, and monks went off to sell them to people who were uneasy about their relatives in the other world. The money from the sales swelled the pope's treasury.

Pope Leo X, son of Lorenzo the Magnificent, wanted money and more money to build St. Peter's Cathedral. He prepared a new issue of indulgences and sent Tetzel to Germany to sell them. Luther argued in one of his theses that if the Pope was really Christ's representative he would have Christ's mercy, and if he had power to forgive sins he would forgive them without requiring a money payment.

Just one person saved Luther from Huss' fate. Elector Frederick of Saxony was a powerful prince, his university at Wittenberg was the apple of his eye, and Martin Luther was a professor in that university. Elector Frederick determined to protect him. As Elector Frederick had friends who also were powerful princes, with their help he saved Luther from the combined intrigues of Pope Leo X and Emperor Charles V.

Unable to reform the Church from within, Luther turned to the next great interest of his life, the education of the people of Germany, for only through widespread education could they become free.

The current method of education was the whip: when the children did not learn, whip them. When they did learn, whip them on to more knowledge. Luther testified that the schools in which he spent his childhood were "hell and purgatory," and the punishments he received in his boyhood produced in his mind a fear that never entirely left him. He said, "Where such fear enters a man in childhood, it can hardly be rooted out again as long as he lives. As he once trembled at every word of his father and mother, to the end of his life he is afraid of a rustling leaf." He told of a time when he took without permission one nut, and for the offense his mother whipped him until the blood came.

He was an advocate of education through joy, and he believed music was a great joy-bringer. During his convalescence from an accident he learned to play the lute and made it his lifelong companion. He composed songs which became the popular melodies of Germany, and later the rousing hymns of the Reformation, especially his clarion call, "A Mighty Fortress Is Our God." The effect of music on the life of mankind has been so momentous, one

ENCOUNTER AND RENEWAL

is constrained to believe great music is an echo of God's way of
thinking.

Luther read the Bible, and slowly realized that many of the
Church's customs and laws, which he had accepted from boyhood,
laws like celibacy for monks and nuns and priests, were not to be
found in this book. He decided the Bible contained true Christianity and the people of Germany should have it to study. He made
a translation, and the simple homely idiom he used became the
standard in the development of German prose. He translated with
such feeling and simplicity that many of his devoted followers
believed he was inspired to write in German, as the apostles were
inspired to write in Greek and the prophets in Hebrew. His translation was printed and read until the people were better acquainted
with the Bible than were the priests. The common people went to
school that they might learn to read the Bible; and as they read
they reasoned: the priest says so-and-so, the Bible says the opposite; and they compared the priests' deeds with what the Bible
taught.

Luther was very human. When he saw his popularity, how the
people loved him and read his pamphlets, he was at times not sure
he was right. The mind which is always sure is very great, a divine
prophet; or it is very small, a mind pitifully conceited. Luther was
neither. Intensely conscientious, he agonized over the questions:
what should be his attitude to the pope, to the dogmas of the
Church, to the sacraments. He read his Bible for guidance, and
prayed into the small hours of the night. His friends, men like the
artist Dürer, were sure he was divinely inspired.

Luther was at times irritable, too prone to cut off his opponent's
head with the sword of his keen logic and fluent speech. Some of
his best friends thought he plunged into argument too quickly. But
it was an age of controversy and worse. Everyone was fighting—
nation with nation, class against class, reformer with reformer. The
Inquisition with its torture chamber was in full action. No one
seemed able to escape the prevalent violence and the belief that
it was right to carry a dispute even to the battlefield and there put
antagonists to death.

Luther was accused by his enemies of all the sins a self-centered
monk might commit. It was said he broke with the Church because

he wanted to marry. If he could commit the sins of which he was accused why did he bother to marry? The monks around him had concubines. Even the much admired and fastidious Petrarch never married, yet his two children born out of wedlock were pronounced by the reigning pope to be legitimate.

The Muslims say, If you be sincere seek death; be willing to be martyred for your beliefs. From the moment Luther nailed his theses to the church door he faced death. And he was, he said, naturally timid and full of fears.

He found the balance wheel of his life in his friend Philip Melanchthon, who was to him as was Jonathan to David.

Philip Melanchthon was cultivated and refined, his father was famous for his integrity and his spirituality, his mother was the niece of the celebrated scholar John Reuchlin. There was no finer family in their world. They were people of robust intellect, independent thinking, nobility of soul.

Guided by his great-uncle, Reuchlin, young Philip studied, in the universities of Tübingen and Heidelberg, the Greek and Latin classics, art, physics, history, mathematics, philosophy and theology, and read Galen until he knew much of him by heart. When he was twenty-four he was called to be a professor in the University of Wittenberg.

Luther greeted the brilliant young scholar with unfeigned joy. He said, "I am rough, boisterous, stormy, and altogether warlike. I am born to fight against innumerable monsters and devils. I must remove stumps and stones, cut away thistles, and thorns, and clear the wild forests; but Master Philip comes along softly and gently, sowing and watering with joy, according to the gifts which God has abundantly bestowed upon him. . . . Whoever does not recognize Philip as his instructor, is a stolid, stupid donkey, carried away by his own vanity and self-conceit. Whatever we know in the arts and in true philosophy, Philip has taught us. He has only the humble title of Master, but he excels all the Doctors. There is no one living adorned with such gifts." To Philip Melanchthon, Luther seemed the successor of the apostles and the Church Fathers.

Luther gave his students a fine blending of vocational, intellectual, and spiritual education. Melanchthon trained a generation of university teachers, and wrote textbooks which were studied in

Germany for a hundred years. With the assistance of many gallant teachers, these two reformers laid the foundation for schools supported by the state, the modern public school system. Melanchthon wrote, "By our example we must excite youth to the admiration of learning, and induce them to love it for its own sake, and not for the advantage that may be derived from it. The destruction of learning brings with it the ruin of everything that is good—religion, morals, and all things human and divine. The better a man is, the greater his ardor in the preservation of learning; for he knows that of all plagues ignorance is the most pernicious. . . . And a terrible darkness will fall upon society, if the study of the sciences should be neglected."

While Luther and Melanchthon were working in Germany, a daring and able reformer, two months younger than Luther, led Zurich, Switzerland, to revolt against the Church. Ulrich Zwingli's father commenced his son's education when he was eight years old and kept him in school until he was ready for university work; and then sent him to Vienna. He studied for two years in Vienna, and graduated at the University of Basel. When he was twenty-two he was ordained a parish priest. In 1518 he was given an important post in the central church of Zurich, with permission to preach the truth as he saw it.

Zwingli's teachers in school and university were men who severely questioned the prevailing church doctrines. They told the young man to study the New Testament for himself. Zwingli learned Greek that he might read this book in the original; and he studied Erasmus' Latin translation of the New Testament. From his studies he concluded that the New Testament contained the right version of the Christian religion, that the additions imposed by the Church were unnecessary, and that even the early Church Fathers made mistakes.

For years, Zwingli quietly worked for religious and political reforms, and in Zurich and southern Germany he was a trusted leader. When he was thirty-five he publicly defined his unorthodoxy—he had already persuaded the rulers of Zurich to shut the city's gates against a seller of indulgences who was trying to glean an extra money harvest for the pope. Zwingli proclaimed that celibacy, the worship of saints, the Lord's Supper as conducted by the Church were requirements not found in the Bible. He declared in a sermon that the pope and his Councils were not needed to explain the Christian religion. Zurich stood solidly with him; five cantons of Switzerland opposed him. Zwingli persuaded his townspeople to carry the dispute to the battlefield. In October, 1531, the army from Zurich was defeated and Zwingli, forty-seven years old, was killed.

He could never agree with Luther concerning the interpretation of the Lord's Supper, and in this dispute the Protestant Reformation at its very beginning broke into two parties.

Revolt against the Church was growing in France where many people read Luther's writings, also a French translation of the Bible, made for them by Jacques Lefèvre, a priest and scholar, who taught about as did Luther. The University of Paris and the French Parlement denounced the Protestants, and the Parlement appointed inquisitors to hunt out and destroy these heretics. As the Reformation gained momentum, King Francis I favored or persecuted the religious rebels in accordance with his political interests; for he followed the pagan form of the Renaissance, and cared nothing for religion. The King's sister, Marguerite d'Angoulême, who married King Henry of Navarre, was devoted to the new cause and while she lived Lefèvre and the reformers had her strong protection.

The young Frehchman John Calvin spent his youth in arduous study and became an accomplished scholar in the Greek and Roman classics and in law. He was twenty-four when he was branded an enemy of the Church and fled for his life from Paris.

The hostility against him soon ceased for the time being; and he continued to study, narrowing his interests to religion. He decided not to try to graft his heretical ideas upon the established theology but definitely to break with the Church, which meant that he must resign the Church benefices by which he lived.

He became the leader of the Reformation in France, for it was evident that intellectually, morally, and in his daily life he was almost a superman. Things moved swiftly for him in the momentous years of 1533 and 1534, and he was so conspicuous that he was obliged to leave France. He fled to Basel, Switzerland, and there, when twenty-six years old he wrote his brilliant and powerful book, *Institutes*, a comprehensive statement of the Protestant faith.

After two years in Basel he was persuaded by his friend Guillaume Farel to come to Geneva. Here Calvin quickly started many schools, and he wrote a catechism which the children in the schools were taught. The reforms he suggested were opposed by influential citizens. When he tried to simplify the ritual of the church services the disputes became so bitter he and Farel were banished from the city. The opposition gradually disappeared, and three years after he left the city, Calvin consented to return to Geneva.

His leadership and authority were now unquestioned, and Geneva became the laboratory in which his plan for a spiritual and secular democracy was tested. Church members governed the city, and by their civic authority maintained their form of religion. The elaborate church service was discarded and the sermon was made the central feature, with an impromptu prayer and congregational singing of psalms and hymns. The organization was democratic, the churches chose their officers, all church members were socially equal; yet the little city of twelve thousand people was severely ruled. Under Calvin's direction the Consistoire was formed of the Protestant ministers and twelve laymen; a committee with power to enforce obedience to the city's laws concerning compulsory education for the children, attendance at the church services, no dancing, no extravagant dress, no breaking of the first or the seventh Commandments. The Consistoire could enter any home and question persons suspected of undue levity, and could try heretics and those who broke the moral law. The punishment for sedition and heresy was death.

Calvin worked indefatigably for the welfare of Geneva; under his leadership the city developed a model sanitary system, and its weavers and tradesmen prospered. He founded the Academy, which later became a university; he taught in this Academy, and his students from all western Europe carried his liberal ideas to their own countries. The Huguenots of France looked to him for guidance; Flanders, where freedom of thought flamed into singular strength, read his books; in Scotland, John Knox thought Calvin's life and Geneva his city were as near to Christian perfection as was attainable on this earth.

The blot on Calvin's memory is Michael Servetus, the heretic. Condemned to death by the city of Vienne, Servetus appeared in Geneva the same year that he published a book in which he questioned the authority of the Scriptures, and seemed to favor pantheism. The rulers of Geneva tried him and condemned him to burn at the stake. Calvin told him if he would repent he would try to secure his forgiveness, and Calvin endeavored to have Servetus' penalty changed to death by the sword, for Calvin thought the stake a terrible sentence. Geneva's rulers would not change their verdict; and Servetus was slowly burned to death. The reformed churches, generally, approved Servetus' sentence; even the gentle Melanchthon declared it just.

Sick unto death with asthma and fever, never considering his own welfare, Calvin labored for Europe's emancipation. Teaching, counseling, preaching, deciding many civic problems of the little city, writing far into the night, or all night, he worked until he died on the twenty-seventh of May, 1564. As a thinker he ranks with Augustine and Thomas Aquinas.

Another prince of scholars, Desiderius Erasmus, traveled quietly through Europe teaching by his writing and his example. He believed that moral, political, and social education could change the characters of the monks and nuns and purge Europe of the gross ignorance which smothered the nations; therefore to stay in the Church and reform it from within was better than to break with it.

Refined, quiet, poised, Erasmus appealed, in hundreds of letters and in his books, to all intelligent people to realize the incongruities in their religion and social customs and to unite to reform their society. He wrote: "A commission of pious and learned men should bring together into a compendium from the purest sources of the gospels and the apostles and from their most approved commentators, the whole philosophy of Christ, with as much simplicity as learning, as much brevity as clearness. What pertains to the faith should be treated in as few articles as possible; what belongs to life, also in few words, and so put that men may know that the yoke of Christ is easy and pleasant, not cruel; that they have been given fathers, not tyrants; pastors not robbers; called to salvation, not betrayed into slavery."

Sincerity of motive was Erasmus' ideal, and with biting and kindly sarcasm he exposed the inconsistencies practiced in the name of religion. He visited Thomas à Becket's shrine and saw the many costly presents hoarded there by the custodians. He asked these keepers if Thomas à Becket had not given all he had to the poor. Was he ever known to hoard anything for himself? Why then did those who paid him honor not use in good works this wealth which really belonged to him, since it was given in his name? Erasmus attacked the worship of saints to the exclusion of the remembrance of Christ; and the practice of celibacy which forbade the monks and nuns the normal life of their society. And he prayed for the little children of the Christian world that they might be educated with kindness, not by beating.

His contemporaries in England, John Colet and Sir Thomas More, gave invaluable service to the end for which Erasmus worked: the reformation of the Church from within. Colet, dearly loved by Erasmus, was a popular teacher of Oxford University when he was thirty. His lectures were attended by the scholars of England, young and old, who listened to him deferentially. When he was appointed by King Henry VII dean of St. Paul's Cathedral he at once commenced many reforms; and he lived with the frugality and self-discipline he required of others. He revived and endowed the public school at St. Paul's, one of the first of its kind in England; under his guidance Greek, pure Latin, and the Christ-life were taught there. London's leaders filled the great cathedral to hear his remarkable sermons.

In 1491, in his father's castle in western Spain near the Pyrenees, a boy was born, the youngest of a large family. He was not named Ignatius at first, but chose this name himself, because he loved the story of Ignatius of the second Christian century, who died for his faith in Christ. Ignatius of the sixteenth century became Ignatius of Loyola, since his father was lord of the Castle of Loyola.

The young man was a soldier by profession and no one in Spain fought with more zest. He fought so hard to save the citadel in Pampeluna after the French had captured the town that in the struggle both his legs were severely wounded. The French took care of him for two weeks, then sent him to his home. The surgeons did their best for him; their bungling operations, however, made him worse, and he lay in bed for weeks. One day he asked for something to read. He wanted tales of knights, but the only books in the castle were a Life of Christ by a Saxon monk, and *Lives of the Saints.* At first Ignatius read these books because he had no better. Then he became interested in the stories; and as he read he pondered: if the story of the Christ made saints of other people why should it not have this effect upon him? He determined that it should, that as soon as he was able to walk he would go in search of Jesus' pearl of great price. His brother, now head of the family, was much distressed, for Ignatius was handsome, charming, well-born, and his reception and success at the Spanish court were assured.

The brother was no persecutor, and when his arguments for court life did not change Ignatius' resolve, he let him go, with two attendants to take care of him, for he was weak from his illness. Ignatius soon dismissed the servants, and riding a mule made his way alone toward the east.

Ill and exhausted he finally reached Manresa, about thirty miles from the Mediterranean, and was taken in and cared for by the kind monks of the little town's Dominican monastery. He now determined to commence his search for the spiritual life, and since asceticism was believed to be the way, he put on a hair-shirt next to his skin, and over it a sackcloth robe with a girdle of a thorny plant, which he bought. For a year, like St. Anthony in the desert, in his monastery cell he fought to hold his wandering thoughts on spiritual subjects. He tried by starving to control his mind and twice was found in a dying swoon by the monks, who nursed him back to life.

He won triumphantly, and became so pure of motive and thought that the secret place of the Most High was revealed to him, and he was given wisdom not to be found in any worldly way. When he was at the head of his far-reaching Order with many followers he advised against austerities, saying that a weak body could not serve the spirit.

He decided on a pilgrimage to the Holy Land and set out on foot for Barcelona, whence he would go to Rome as he must have the pope's permission to make the journey. It was a perilous undertaking for a penniless ascetic, and often it seemed he could go no farther; yet always he was helped by some kind person. In Barcelona as he sat on the steps of a church, surrounded by curious children, a well-to-do woman passing by thought she saw a halo encircling his head. With her husband's permission she took him to her home and gave him the food he desperately needed. And in the night, in Venice, a rich senator dreamed a voice told him a holy man was lying on the hard stones nearby. The senator called for his servants and torches, found Ignatius lying under an arcade, and brought him to his house. Revived and cheered by a few hours in the senator's luxurious home, Ignatius continued his journey the next morning, for he must not pamper himself with comforts. The senator later became the Doge of Venice.

When his pilgrimage was over and he was again in Barcelona, Ignatius decided to study theology and philosophy, for he might have to argue with educated priests. He did not know the rudiments of Latin grammar and joined a children's class. Two years he studied, and he found it as difficult to keep his mind upon Latin conjugations as in his monastery cell it had been hard to think of spiritual subjects. For now he could communicate with the spiritual world and even in the classroom its unseen wires brought him the most beautiful messages.

He began to preach in the streets, an unheard-of thing for a layman, and was arrested and sent to prison. The Inquisitors questioned him repeatedly but could find nothing in particular against him. Wishing to be rid of him, they forced him to leave Spain.

He went to Paris and entered the Collège de Montaigu of the University. The students of the University of Paris were at this time a lawless lot, famous for their street brawls. The public debates held under university auspices on Sunday afternoons were the only meetings the professors could be sure they would attend. Even these were forgotten when Ignatius commenced to preach in the streets on Sunday. The professors determined to arrest Ignatius as a disorderly person and flog him in the way customary at the university: the student to be punished walked down a long college hall and the professors, lined along both walls, whipped him as he passed them.

Against the advice of his friends, Ignatius went to the Rector's office on the day he was to be arrested and punished. While the angry professors waited for him with their whips, he explained to their Rector his purpose in talking to the students. When he finished, the Rector accompanied him to the hall. Before the convocation of students and professors he knelt at Ignatius' feet and, tears streaming from his eyes, asked forgiveness for his intentions against him.

For two winters Ignatius studied in the University of Paris, begging funds during the summer for his next year's work. After the third summer, some generous merchants in Flanders arranged to send him regular amounts of money. When he was forty-four he won the Master of Arts degree.

The next year he went to Spain, and denounced the depravity of the clergy and laymen. He was promptly arrested and brought before the Inquisitors. They tried him repeatedly, threatened him each time with torture and death, and sent him back to prison. It seemed impossible for him to teach in Spain and he left that country for Rome, to lay before the pope his wish to start an Order for those who truly wanted to follow and serve the Christ. Pope Paul III granted him an interview and promised him approval and protection.

Ignatius believed the hope of Europe was the young men and he labored especially for them. A book he wrote, *The Spiritual Exercises*, became the textbook by which he trained his students in holy living and thinking. As the years passed, and his Order became the hope of the failing Church, he made strict rules to protect his followers from the lure of wealth and political power which had demoralized the Christian clergy. A novitiate under Ignatius must study for ten years, and then spend a year in prayer and in teaching the peasants and children of his community. When this time was fulfilled, the best students were taken into the ranks of the most faithful, the Professed, and of them every disinterested service was required. The Professed took the vow of poverty, and were bound by vow to seek no position of authority in the Order or the Church, nor any worldly honor. Their monasteries must not accept endowments, nor should contributions be expected during the church services; and the monks must go in quest of alms when needed. They were sent to far countries to teach and must go penniless; in this spirit St. Francis Xavier went to India, Japan, and China. Those who stayed at home must educate the under-privileged.

For a hundred and fifty years the Jesuits preserved the ideals and the remarkable personality of their founder. When they were true to St. Ignatius they were saviors of their society.

Others reformers within the Church, among them St. Francis de Sales and St. Teresa, taught widely in Italy, France, and Spain. St. Teresa in Spain was almost as active in her practical social service as was St. Ignatius. She achieved the spiritual life and taught others the way. Her books, especially her autobiography, are immortal in Spanish literature. Her uncompromising integrity was as important contribution toward a saner religion.

Many reformers, Protestant and Jesuit, founded schools and universities, where teachers devoted to the welfare of their communities worked for more liberal education.

# 32

## Recovering the Bible

MEN OF THIS caliber in England saw that the greatest spiritual need of their nation was a translation of the Bible into the vernacular the people could read. For years the clergy had threatened all translators of the Bible with excommunication and had tortured and burned at the stake anyone found with the Wycliffe Bible. The people were so eager for the Wycliffe translation that they persistently read it secretly, and paid exhorbitant sums for a few manuscript pages.

As Zwingli taught in Switzerland, and Luther's work approached cataclysmic proportions, a gifted young man studied at Oxford University and became distinguished as a scholar. William Tyndale, this student, soon went to Cambridge. There he read Erasmus' Greek edition of the New Testament. As he read the wonderful account of God's love, a story seldom told by a Christian priest, he determined that the people of England should have this book and began at once to translate Erasmus' Greek text.

He must have a quiet place to work and, hearing that the Bishop of London was a scholarly man, he asked for a room in his palace. The Bishop was interested in classical learning, not in a heresy like giving the Bible to the common people, and he made his displeasure clear. An alderman of London, Sir Humphrey Monmouth, took Tyndale to his home. There he worked secretly for six months, translating the Greek and Hebrew documents he had secured.

By this time Luther's writings had reached England, and Tyndale heard that those who had copies were sent to prison and executed. He knew a translation of the Bible would be a worse offense than Luther's books and decided he must leave England. He went to Germany, and, in dire poverty and peril of discovery, finished his translation of the New Testament. While he was printing his work in Cologne, some of the printers gave away the secret to John Cochlaeus, dean of an important church in Frankfurt. Cochlaeus persuaded the rulers of Cologne to forbid the printing of Tyndale's manuscripts, and sent word to King Henry VIII and Cardinal Wolsey to watch lest Tyndale's translation appear in England.

Tyndale gathered up some of his printed pages and fled to Worms. There, under the shadow of the Reformation, he finished his work—printed copies of an English translation of the New Testament. Warned by Cochlaeus, the bishops of England watched for Tyndale's translation; he must therefore be cautious. He printed smaller volumes that might elude the enemies, and in every possible manner they were smuggled into England. They were very cheap and very numerous, they were joyfully and secretly received and in a few years were scattered far and wide through the country. Every package that came to the English ports was searched by the bishops' agents and thousands of copies were found and burned. But many thousands escaped.

The Bishop of London thought of a plan to put an end to the smuggling: he would buy up all the copies that had not been shipped to England. He chose a certain merchant for his agent, not knowing that the merchant was Tyndale's friend. The bishop gave his money to the merchant. He sent it to Tyndale, who collected all the copies at hand and shipped them to the bishop. The bishop received his books and had them burned. Tyndale by the transaction paid off his debts and printed another edition.

A man who was known to be one of Tyndale's assistants was brought before Sir Thomas More, in a London court, and the judge promised him favor if he would tell who supplied Tyndale with money. The prisoner said he was quite willing to tell: it was the Bishop of London who had bought the copies of the New Testament to burn them. He was their comfort and helper.

For years William Tyndale struggled on against poverty, persecution, and delay, and accomplished his purpose, for the people of

England now owned parts of the Bible and would never give them up. Unable to stop the circulation of Tyndale's translation, the English clergy attacked it from their pulpits. Many people in England sympathized with Luther's Reformation, and they ably defended Tyndale's version.

His enemies in England determined to have at least the satisfaction of torturing Tyndale and tried to entice him home. Failing in this a clergyman, Henry Phillips, by wiles and protestations of friendship, won Tyndale's confidence, although Tyndale's landlord warned him the man was treacherous. One day Phillips lured Tyndale to a place where men were waiting to seize him. They carried him to Vilvorde Castle near Brussels and locked him in a dungeon. There he was kept for nearly four months, cold and sick and in rags. On October 6, 1536, he was taken to a stake, strangled, and his body burned to ashes. His crime? He gave the New Testament to his nation.

He translated directly from the Greek and Hebrew, not from the Vulgate, for due to many transcriptions it contained mistakes. His translation is a marvel of dignity, grandeur of feeling, spiritual insight and musical expression, the rendering of a spiritual and intellectual prince who could write for the common people.

The merchants of London continued to smuggle Tyndale's books into England, also Luther's pamphlets, and many of Wycliffe's. The scholars of Oxford and Cambridge universities secretly obtained and discussed these heretical works, and the educated people throughout the country read them insatiably.

Henry VIII and Cardinal Wolsey, who were ruling England, classed Tyndale's books, since they came from Worms, with Luther's writings. Luther was to them anathema, a destroyer of unity, a promoter of revolution. Cardinal Wolsey burned quantities of the books, seized the libraries of many Oxford University scholars and sent the scholars to prison. But Cardinal Wolsey had also, on his hands, the king's determination to get rid of Catherine of Aragon and marry Anne Boleyn, and Henry's ambition to increase his power.

What Wolsey could not accomplish through diplomacy, Thomas Cromwell, his successor as King Henry's trusted adviser, effected by a reign of terror. On and on Cromwell led willing

Henry: past submission to the pope into open defiance and independence of the pope; past consultation with an outspoken Parliament to pseudo-consultation with a deferential Parliament; until there was no law in England but the king's will, largely guided by Thomas Cromwell. The churches of England, the universities, the monasteries, religion and learning lay at Henry's feet. Henry's despotism sent some of England's noblest men to be hanged or beheaded.

After a while King Henry and Cromwell set about to reform England's religion. Purgatory and pardons, masses for the dead, pilgrimages, images and relics supposed to have magical powers were dismissed. The result was almost Erasmus' dream come true.

The despoliation of the monasteries of England, when Henry VIII broke with the pope, resulted in a wild demonstration from the Protestant youth. They not only joyfully abandoned the old orthodoxy but made it the victim of all manner of practical jokes as they stripped the churches of their wonder-working shrines and images, and insulted and humiliated the monks.

To this lawlessness King Henry reacted with energy. He ordered that every person in his realm should believe in transubstantiation, should confess, should attend Mass. Those who refused to accept transubstantiation should burn at the stake. And a struggle to the death began with the Protestants.

The king decided to have an English translation of the Bible, but not Tyndale's. The bishops were invited to render the service. No translation appeared; so Cromwell employed Miles Coverdale, a churchman of London. Coverdale had already made a translation, using the Vulgate, Luther's German translation, Tyndale's translation, and others. His version was published in 1535, the first complete Bible printed in English.

A friend of William Tyndale's was living in Antwerp during this time. This man, John Rogers, put together a Bible in English, using all the parts Tyndale translated and taking Coverdale's translation for the rest. Tyndale had translated the New Testament, and the Old Testament to Second Chronicles; he printed the New Testament, and the Old Testament to Second Chronicles; he printed the New Testament, the Pentateuch, and Jonah. John Rogers had Tyndale's manuscript copy of the unprinted section of his translation, and used it in the version he made.

John Rogers took the pseudonym "Thomas Matthew" as translator of his compilation, sent the manuscript to England, and there it was printed. A copy came to the hands of Thomas Cranmer, Archbishop of Canterbury. He was delighted with it and said the bishops could not have done better.

When Coverdale was asked by Cromwell to make an official translation, he merely used John Rogers' compilation, with the assistance of some scholars improving the parts he, Coverdale, had translated and leaving Tyndale's work almost untouched. Coverdale's final manuscript was approved by Archbishop Cranmer and King Henry. It was published in 1539 with a frontispiece which pictured Henry VIII sitting on his throne and handing the Bible to Cromwell and Cranmer, who were to pass it on to the multitude of clergymen waiting at the bottom of the picture. The book was called the Great Bible. The King commanded it be placed in every church and the people be allowed access to it. It was published three years after Tyndale was murdered.

For centuries the Church had used a Latin book of services for the offices performed by the priests: marriage, baptism, the church rituals, and others. Under the boy king Edward VI, son of Henry VIII, Archbishop Cranmer undertook a translation of this book into simple English, and the convocation of English bishops attempted to remove the superstitions that filled its pages. The work was completed; but Edward VI, then fourteen, sympathized with the Reformation and wished the book to be more Protestant in form. The bishops hesitated to make more changes; Edward threatened to take the matter to Parliament. The result was a second Prayer Book. Edward died two years later, in 1553. Mary, the daughter of Catherine of Aragon, became Queen of England.

Embittered by her mother's humiliation and the implication of illegitimacy against herself, for which she blamed the Reformation, Queen Mary determined to reduce England to unconditional subservience to the pope. By her order prominent bishops of the Church, as well as many lesser people, were chained to the pyre, a sack of gunpowder tied around their necks for additional fuel, and crowds assembled to watch their death agony. John Rogers, who compiled the Matthew Bible, was the first victim, and he died heroically.

Queen Mary thought to intimidate her subjects into submission. The effect upon the English people was just the opposite, for with every martyrdom the nation became more antagonistic to Rome. Although she was determined to reduce her people to obedience, when Mary herself was ordered by the pope to do things contrary to her wishes she did not trouble even to break the seals of the papal communications.

A great day of hope dawned for distressed England when in 1558 Mary died and Elizabeth became queen. England now gradually achieved a mean between the radicals of the Reformation and the reactionaries at Rome. Wise reformers endeavored to preserve all that was good in the established Church, in the interpretations of the first Church Fathers, in the rituals, and all that was true and purifying in the Renaissance reformers. This pursuit of the mean between the extremists is one of the triumphs of English attainment.

Queen Elizabeth's reign was an era of enthusiasm, energy, and initiative when remarkable men opened a new world in science and literature, and explored new countries. The service book of Edward VI was retranslated and purged of many medieval theologies and superstitions. The stately rhythmic English of the new rendering gave a thrilling quality to the services of the English churches, different from the church at Rome which held to the Latin book, understood by few.

More translations of the Bible appeared. A group of Protestant scholars living in Geneva printed in 1560 a translation which became immensely popular in Great Britain and later in New England. In 1568 the bishops of England published their rendering, an authorized version which was read in the churches.

James I, Queen Elizabeth's sucessor, was already considering a translation when the Protestants petitioned him for one that would be satisfactory to them. James I chose a group of England's foremost scholars from the Church and from Oxford and Cambridge universities for the task. They used the best Hebrew and Greek manuscripts available and after careful study and consultation revised the previous translations. They worked for seven years, and in 1611 brought forward the Authorized Version, or King James Bible. In this Version, 90 per cent of the New Testament is Tyndale's translation. Of the parts of the Old Testament that Tyndale translated, 80 per cent are as he rendered them.

Suppose the only religion people know is built upon fear. They expect terror to haunt their daily life, for the tyrants who surround them may descend upon them at any moment. Suppose they have the same fear of God and believe he waits to pounce upon them the moment they leave this world; and suppose they are told that the only way to save themselves and those they love is by continual payments to priests who have access to God and can influence this awful Judge in their favor. One day the Bible in their own language is placed in their hands. They open it, and what do they read that God says to them: "They that wait upon the Lord shall renew their strength; they shall mount up with wings as eagles; they shall run, and not be weary; and they shall walk, and not faint. Fear thou not; for I am with thee: be not dismayed; for I am thy God: I will strengthen thee; yea, I will help thee; yea, I will uphold thee with the right hand of my righteousness. For I the Lord thy God will hold thy right hand, saying unto thee, Fear not; I will help thee. Ho, every one that thirsteth, come ye to the waters, and he that hath no money; come ye, buy, and eat; yea, buy wine and milk without money and without price."

Another book came to England, written by John Bunyan, the son of an itinerant tinker. Bunyan's *Pilgrim's Progress* was so beautiful and easily understood that it was almost a continuation of the Bible. These two books became the most popular in the English-speaking world.

The Reformation brought hope to millions of people, and to a smaller number intellectual freedom; its path was drenched with the blood of countless martyrs. The Inquisitions raged in Spain, in France, the Thirty Years' War paralyzed Germany, in the Netherlands the number of people of the new faith who were slaughtered was appalling. The issues were not altogether creedal; for politics often used religion to cover its presence. The Inquisitors confiscated the properties of wealthy heretics and divided the spoils with the crown or the pope. When the Protestants won, king and nobility took over the vast property belonging to the monasteries and to many of the churches.

The reformers won release from thraldom to the past. They cried out for freedom—unhampered freedom to study facts, to observe existing thought and test its finality leads to more knowledge. Without this freedom progress is not possible. Such study of facts is today called the scientific method.

By this method great men in the universities were sure of scientific law and progressive knowledge, and staked their life's work upon their certainty. Scholars of genius came, in a brilliant succession, each making a priceless contribution which carried their civilization forward. Copernicus had discovered, or rediscovered, that the earth and the planets move around the sun. Galileo rediscovered this truth and dared write explaining it. Harvey made an epochal contribution to medical science. Kepler and Newton were intellectual giants.

And the spiritual life of the nations was led by men and women who dared commune directly with God. Jacob Boehme, an illiterate shoemaker of Germany, became wise from an unseen fountain. In Paris, Fenelon, Brother Lawrence, and Madame Guyon simply and quietly attained knowledge of the spiritual world that brought hope to many. George Fox and William Penn practiced and spread their belief that God does not speak in the tempest but with a still, small voice which will guide those who hear it into green pastures where they may live by love.

Pascal combined the two schools of thought and was both scientist and philosophic mystic. With his powerful scientific intellect and his spiritual intuition he endeavored to bring science and religion, the physical and the spiritual worlds, into harmony. He wrote, "The infinite distance between body and mind typifies the infinitely more infinite distance between the mind and love, for love is above nature." He saw that the spirit must be guided by knowledge and that knowledge must be illumined by the Spirit. This is the principle of life. It was the principle out of which Christianity was reborn and renewed.

Book V

The Perfection
of Days

# 33

## *World Horizons*

FOR THOUSANDS of years one nation after another has taken a first place on the world's great stage. From elemental beginnings a nation developed dexterity in thought and action, and progress seemed assured. Men built themselves comfortable houses, good highways, systems of irrigation. Community life advanced and public buildings appeared. Wealth piled up, jewels and lovely apparel were purchased for personal pleasure, physical comforts were invented. Soon the very rich, and those in power wanted to surpass their companions; also, they must have diversions. They began to exploit the poor and take their earnings, forcing them back into primitive living while the masters acquired more luxuries. The rulers of the people quarreled; or a leader, a king, tried to gratify his insatiable desire for more wealth and power. The result was war, revolutions, vineyards and harvests ruined, frantic emotions, the misery of the conquered. Some civilizations went down to complete ruin; where was once the splendor of Babylon or Ninevah or Ur wild beasts made their lair in silent desolation. After many centuries archaeologists explored the ruins for traces of what had been the envy of the world.

We are living today in the most advanced age of history. Must we also collapse; must we reach a certain intellectual, artistic, scientific height, and then sink into oblivion. Is there not a science of remaining, as well as a science of becoming?

Since the dawn of history people have experimented with living. In the laboratory within us we try out behavior until we know what is helpful and what is disastrous for ourself. In the laboratory composed of groups, some small, some large enough to be called nations, people have experimented with almost every form of behavior. People have tried justice and injustice; running their civilization with morals, and without morals; living only for material goals; living for social and spiritual goals. They have tried polygamy, monogamy, promiscuity, chastity, easy divorce, strict divorce; selfishness, domination in family relations; loving consultation and mutual yielding in family relations. They have exacted blind obedience from their children, and have given them freedom. People have built their national life upon force; they have built it upon education, knowledge, and character. They have made the intellectual life first. They have made the spiritual, moral life first. They have lived by economic exploitation; and by cooperation and socialization. They have lived individually and nationally as wolves and tigers live. There have been cooperation, coersion, business for profit, business for service. People have tried different forms of religion from the lowest to the most divine. They have tried living with God; and excluding God.

People have experimented with economic determinism, the belief that human beings are shaped and determined by economic forces. Place men in a favorable environment, say the advocates of this theory, give them good remuneration that they and their families may live in comfort, and they will become rich in body and mind. This idea has been tried out in various ways in different parts of the world. Its advocates believe that man is the passive product of his environment and, like wax, will take the impress of his surroundings; or like a small machine he will respond mechanically to the great machine, the economic order. Reform, socialize the environment, says this theory, and men will automatically become public spirited and socially minded; and society will endure. Such socialized communities, however, have deteriorated into self-seeking, loafing on the job, and other quite unsocial attitudes due to man's animal nature, which urges self-preservation and self-promotion at any cost to society, for this nature, unless it is educated in social motives and absolute moral values causes ruin.

Only when men rise above determinism, and live by another nature, which is higher than physical urges and social pressure, can civilizations be saved from ruin. The men of science, the teachers, the soldiers who sacrifice income, career, and life that they may work for humanity; the many physicians, nurses, social workers, and others who in this spirit serve their state or another great cause upon which the world's welfare depends; the statesmen, the men of wealth who serve humanity often at the risk of every economic self-interest; such people cause their society to progress. When self-interest had almost ruined China, India, Palestine, and Persia, great Prophets called into action an army of people who were willing to live by their higher nature and save their nations. In Egypt, Greece, and Rome the flame of Christian civilization rose from the wreckage of materialism.

Through the centuries many peoples have discovered the quickening touch of one culture upon another to vitalize civilizations. When travel was difficult and hazardous journeys must be undertaken in fragile ships, on horse- or camel-back, or by foot for months, people saw the value of intercommunication. Persia, Palestine, and Greece acquired the art of Assyria and Babylonia. Science and the alphabet came to Greece from Egypt and Syria. Greece then quickened Phoenicia, Palestine, Egypt, Assyria. Alexander the Great marched his army into India and in his wake came Greek art to Persia and India, to be taken on to China and Japan. India carried her life to Ceylon, China, Tibet, Cambodia, Siam, Java, and all central Asia. Japanese civilization was born from contact with China and for centuries Japan's schools and government, art and culture followed the pattern of T'ang. Persia responded to Greece and taught the West her beautiful techniques. Assyrian, Grecian, and Persian arts were taken up by the Byzantine, and the Byzantine by western Europe. Islamic civilization gave new life to Spain. Islam and the Christian scholars brought Greek learning and culture, with Muslim arts and sciences, to Europe and the result was the Renaissance, to which China contributed paper, wallpaper, china, porcelain, gunpowder, and probably the compass, and India gave her sciences, her storybooks, and many other treasures and wonders. Confucius' political science lent a hand to social science in France and helped that science to a higher level of service. Voltaire, Goethe, and Lessing were in debt to Islam and the East. In the nineteenth century

Whistler and other pioneers discovered Japanese art and copied it. The art of India, China, and Persia is still quickening artists and idealists in the West.

Many people say that science will save our civilization, for scientific experimentation in medicine, industry, engineering, agriculture, education, and the social sciences has transformed present-day life. Modern science has also made it possible for us to have knowledge of every nation and people, of almost every spot on the earth. It has destroyed national exclusiveness and caused each nation to interpenetrate the life of other nations. It has made the world an open book, for everyone to read, has outlawed provincialism as ignorance. It has caused the nations today to depend upon each other as never before, has bound them together by ties which cannot be severed, until no nation can say, "We live for ourself alone."

Science has brought humanity to the gates of a great world community. But science does not open these gates. Instead, science's miracle-working skills are commandeered by one nation after another in a vast effort at domination. Physical science creates, and also destroys. More truth than science possesses is needed to preserve a civilization. What truth does modern science lack?

When learning was revived in the Renaissance organized religion in Europe controlled education. The theologians continued to fight scientific research and refused the modern scientists any part in the reconstruction of the Church. The scientists, embittered by the theologians' insistence upon the acceptance of many superstitions which could not bear scientific scrutiny, decided to rule religion out, and to create a strictly materialistic science. This was really a help to them for it expedited and simplified their thinking and enabled them more easily to put their science into quantitative and mathematical terms.

Having excluded God and any spiritual data from the postulates of their science, the scholars did not find God anywhere in their science. Not finding him, after they had excluded him, they came to think he was superfluous to their universe. With no trace of God in their system, many scientists became agnostics or materialists. With their course dogmatically chartered in advance, these scientists, when they studied physics, biology, medicine, and psychology, also economics and political science found only material causes. Historians, soon catching up with them, omitted from their accounts of the doings of mankind any spiritual causes, and triumphantly announced there was no God in history. The literary critics who wished to be ultra-modern searched their data with a new point of view, and wrote to proclaim that modern times really began when the Victorian period ended, for then men reverted to the absence of morals.

It takes all the genius on earth and more to civilize and keep civilized that mixture of mind and body, beast and angel, and other men's opinions which we call human beings. Both science and religion are needed for the task. Today there is a ringing call for accuracy. Let science and religion be accurate and bases for disagreement will disappear. Religion should face the facts of modern science and discard those doctrines science has proved to be superstitions. Men of science should accept the fact that true religion proves history contains more than the play of physical forces.

Details which concerned the economic and social conditions of the Prophet's day are outmoded. The essentials in every religion are still as fresh as when they came from the Teacher's lips. If an economic world order was built upon the Golden Rule taught by every great religion neither science nor religion would suffer in any way.

Right relations are essential to all stability and progress. The right relation of thought to invention, humility to research, mind to mind, idea to truth, past to present, teacher to pupil, labor and management. Right relations between mind and mind, between mind and reality, between friend and friend, parent and child, husband and wife, a Christ and his followers for two thousand years—these are the warp and woof of civilization and the unities by which alone men can really live and endure.

Right relations between science and religion are absolutely essential, for unless science and religion can work together our civilization will fall.

# 34

## The Education of Character

RIGHT RELATIONS in living are attained through right education; they are not possible in unguided thinking and undisciplined emotions. How do we secure the right education? Almost everyone will answer: by the acquisition of knowledge. It used to be knowledge of the classics and the great books of the past; of history, languages, music, and mathematics; understanding of our native tongue and how to use it easily and clearly. In recent years we have added instruction in hygiene that we may have a strong and well body, knowledge of the sciences which are revolutionizing our civilization. On every side today, boys and girls say they want training that will fit them to get a good job and make a living. Others say the goal of their endeavor is culture, the cultivation of good taste in books, music, art. Some want training in self-expression, self-realization. Others stress education for citizenship, that they may make a contribution to good government. Some think knowledge of economics, of the social and psychological sciences most important. Some emphasize training for home-making. There is education of the consumers, that they may buy efficiently. As the sciences move forward, education becomes a lifelong process and no matter how diligently we work we can never cover the entire field of knowledge, for it is like an ocean and we can attain but a few cupfuls though we study all our life.

To make study and work attractive is now the goal; the day of education in sorrow is ending. Educators emphasize not only instruction which stores knowledge in the mind, but training in useful skills, techniques. They show that the student learns more readily through doing, acting, serving. The apprentice system in past centuries was founded on this principle, and was supplemented in the homes, where mothers trained their sons and daughters. Today farmers, mechanics, engineers, lawyers, internes, businessmen, and teachers learn by doing.

It is believed that by experimentation our goals may be achieved; and educational experiments are bringing important results. We want also to profit from the returns already rendered by the worldwide laboratory of history, and train ourselves as quickly as possible to live according to those systems of behavior which have proved beneficial. Experimentation with every generation of human beings is too costly.

Great medical scientists like Pasteur were not satisfied with trying to cure the patient after he was stricken, but determined to find the cause of the disease and root it out.

The world's greatest social scientists, the Prophets, announce that the fundamental cause of human happiness and stability is right motives; that wrong motives eventually destroy the nations. To Confucius, the man of good motives was the superior man. Confucius told his students, "The man of perfect goodness is sure to possess courage, but the courageous man is not necessarily good. The nobler sort of man is proficient in the knowledge of his duty; the inferior man is proficient only in money-making. The princely man never for a single instant quits the path of virtue; in times of storm and stress he remains in it as fast as ever. The nobler sort of man is dignified but not proud; the inferior man is proud but not dignified. The higher type of man is calm and serene; the inferior man is constantly agitated and worried. The nobler sort of man emphasizes the good qualities in others, and does not accentuate the bad. The inferior sort does the reverse." The superior man is universal "in his sympathy and free from party bias." His supreme virtue is love.

Truth is a fire. Expediency is water. They cannot both live in the same mind for one always extinguishes the other. A man's prevailing motives are his character. Good character is the appreciation and practice of ethical and spiritual values. These values are pushed into the background when men concentrate upon material ends. Materialism uncontrolled by the government will ruin the natural resources of a country and will exploit a nation's children, as though there were no future, even ten years distant. Alexis de Tocqueville writes, "Materialism is among all nations a dangerous disease of the mind." He comments that those who prove for themselves they are only beasts, instead of feeling humble become, surprisingly, as proud as though they had proved they were gods.

The man without good motives who makes politics his career is a menace, for nothing is so dangerous to society as the profit motive in politics, except self-seeking in religion. Lacking, integrity, the public employee will loaf and steal his country's time, the politician will multiply jobs for "the faithful" and play for his particular interests heedless of the cost to his country, will make laws for those who press the hardest upon him. Men in politics from personal motives do good deeds for love of fame and power. To superficial minds a deed is a deed, whether motivated by fear, or hope of favors soon to come. To profound minds the motive is all in all. A good deed becomes truth when it shines from an unsullied conscience.

Certain health relations, when preserved, mean life abounding. They are relations between city and country, promise and performance, nation and nation. They are essential connections between the laborer and his conscience, between performance and perfection, hidden motive and overt action, the rights of the individual and the common good, education and efficiency, the public servant and real public service. They are relations between energies and ideals, the boy and his wishes, the girl and her hero, the person and his definition of pleasure. Like the relations between hand and brain, foot and eye, digestion and the blood stream, they determine our life. Only by education on good character are they rightly achieved.

A supreme objective today is the efficient mind trained to use the scientific method in arriving at truth. Can the student relate this method to his character, which regulates his daily life? Has he acquired in school and college a scale of values by which to put his knowledge together, giving each phase its proper place and setting, forming all into a unified system of values which will be adequate to guide him at all times? When he leaves the classroom with his diploma in his hand can he summon an array of facts and reach his own conclusions as do those who blaze the way ahead? Or will he merely get the results which orthodoxy expects? Can he judge a worthwhile book for himself? Can he assess the character of the people he meets, seeing more than well-trained manners, or a rough exterior? If disaster comes upon him, if he loses his position, if he becomes ill, if the world talks back, does he know how to keep serene and confident and patient? Or will he waste his energies when he needs them most, and worry, and resist conditions, piling up more trouble for himself? Suppose he is financially successful, will he lose his humane qualities, allowing his conscience to become blunted and his heart rigid like steel, cold and calculating? Has he learned while he studied in school or college that art of replenishing his soul with love, and calling back to life the mind that is dying to everything but worldly success? Has he learned to turn his will to high ideals by reading the potent words of someone who lived and thought nobly? Has he so established certain qualities of character that he is almost automatically honest, faithful to his task, loyal, loving truth, knowledge, beauty, perfection? The love of perfection enabled Milton to transcend the tragedy of blindness, and Beethoven to forget his deafness—until these great artists could penetrate through the physical and transmit the melodies of heaven. No one can calculate what the love of perfection did for Dante, Shakespeare, Michelangelo.

Good character pays in business, engineering, medicine, the law, and above all in teaching; it pays dividends to the social order and to the individual. William Penn, a gentleman of old England, wise and far-seeing, came with a little party of his Quaker friends to "uncivilized" America. The fashion of the day was the conquest and exploitation of the new world. William Penn did not follow this reigning practice. He made a straight, honest, and generous bargain with the Indian owners of the country. He bought land from them and paid for it, and he made with the Indians a solemn peace pact, which was almost never broken. As a result, while the Indians with tomahawks ravaged and scalped the colonies to the north and south, William Penn and the Quakers built in the wilderness a city of brotherly love. A successful salesman sat at his desk one morning planning his day's work. His employer arrived after a night of drinking and became brutally angry at the first sentences exchanged. The salesman, excited at the injustice done him, retaliated with harsh words. He was dismissed on the spot. He had a good position. But he could never get another, for he was sixty years old. It would have paid him handsome returns if he had thought ahead and said to himself, "Why should I lose my self-control, because someone else has none?"

Some persons see only themselves: what, how much can they get for themselves. Some have a broader horizon; their sympathies reach out to other lives and classes, sometimes to other races and nations; they desire material welfare, knowledge, art, literature for all earth's multitudes. Some see the inner life of the universe. They see it expressed when Christ or Buddha is spurring a whole civilization to disinterested social service and self-sacrifice. They see it in the patriot who voluntarily leaves the security of his good position to serve his country. They see it in every man and woman who prefers integrity to self-interest.

The conscientious public servant today seeks education in jurisprudence and commercial law, economics, the social sciences, the way to universal peace. He wants to know the psychology of human nature, and men and their destiny. When we appreciate the value of others no one will attempt to exploit anyone. To understand others we must be informed concerning their life, occupations, aspirations, and needs. Therefore we will study sympathetically, on a worldwide scale, past history, and history in the making. We will inform ourselves not only of the tragic mistakes of the many rulers of the past who lost their way and forced their nations into wars which destroyed them. We will learn about the people who under such rulers lived their lives courageously and served their civilization nobly when social conditions were almost unbearable. We will investigate the wonders of the East and the West; what the nations have accomplished through their courage, faithfulness to their tasks, the love of perfection. We will become acquainted with and understand the literature, music, dancing, art, and wisdom of every country. We will study constitutional government as it has been developed by the freedom-loving countries of the world, for it will be our desire to perfect and protect free and stable forms of government.

It is indubitable that the first essential is character education; in the family, in the school, in business, in government. For the multiple interests and activities of men will fall into their proper places when good character is established. Milton wrote of the time when, through education, men will "hate the cowardice of doing wrong."

Some declare good character to be a gift of nature; one passively receives or does not receive it. Even if this postulate were true, it is a fact that good character is preserved only by constant attention and care. Parents without virtue destroy it for their children. Priests and theologians without God, scholars without conscience destroy it for civilizations. Wherever we may turn, civilization is shaped by personal character.

Religion is the only force which has ever appeared which is able to control for any length of time hate, malice, selfishness, self-advancement at the expense of others, cruelty, falsifying, disregard of promises given, coveteousness, theft on small or large scale, unbridled appetites. If human life held nothing but these attitudes and actions and their results, humanity would be more brutish than the beasts. When people cease to live for virtue, intellectual and artistic activity, reverence, sympathy, and self-control; when they harbor and encourage the hangover of the animal instincts, civilizations go down in terrible wars.

A president of the United States once said: "I do not know of any adequate support for our form of government except that which comes from religion.

"I can conceive of no adequate remedy for the evils which beset society except through the influences of religion.

"There is no form of education that will not fail, there is no form of government that will not fail, there is no form of reward which will not fail.

"Redemption must come through sacrifice, and sacrifice is the essence of religion.

"Without that faith [religion] all that we have of an enlightened civilization cannot endure."

Nothing has happened to disprove the essentials of religion. Science has refuted only the superstitions.

Good character is the flower and fruit of the human tree. Love of the great Prophet is the sun which makes it grow. The endeavor to educate humanity without knowledge of God is like trying to establish the science and practice of agriculture without the sun and rain. When the Prophet's influence is potent, to please him becomes to his followers the highest prize. For love of him they become and do as he directs. During such a time civilizations take a short cut in attaining right relations in living.

The purpose of life is the attainment of perfection, in character, in workmanship, in the thoughts we alone hear, in the deeds we alone know of.

Those individuals in whose minds enthusiasm for truth and goodness is glowing furnish the motive power for true civilization. Without this assistance scholars languish, artists blindly imitate the models of the past and the tendencies of the present, statesmen are sterile, businessmen become self-centered, men of science miss the highest goal.

Put men and women of high character and ability in positions of prestige and they will reanimate the life of the nations. Peace on earth will be possible only when the nations are guided by many people who can control their lower emotions, and rise above prejudice and self-interest.

In the Buddhist religion the highest ideal is the bodhisattva, who, having attained perfection of character until goodness, strength, and beauty are innate for him, lives that he may train and serve others. So perfect is he that he may if he chooses ascend into heaven where sin and suffering are excluded. Instead, the Mahayanna Scriptures say, "as on from strength to strength he runs," he cries,

> *How shall I seek the goal to gain*
> *While others live in fear and pain?*
> *Should I this self of mine preserve*
> *And fail those other selves to serve?*

High character is reality in action, it is the great purifier in any realm. It revitalized Persia at the beginning of the Achaemenid and Sassanian periods. In the early centuries of the Christian era it created two universal brotherhoods: the Buddhists of the East, the Christians of the West. In the summer season of Confucian,

Buddhist, Hindu, Hebrew, Zoroastrian, Islamic, and Christian civilizations it ennobled millions of lives. Taught by heroes of the Renaissance and later centuries, it quickened the moral, intellectual and social life of Europe and the Americas. It created modern science and the splendid institutions for social service that beautify our civilization. Good character enables one to think clearly, to decide wisely. When it is achieved on a worldwide scale it will synthesize and unite the nations, for by its light everyone will look at what is best in every nation. The structural steel for a world civilization is the moral law. The moral law is the creator of good character.

# 35

## The Joy of Religion

CIVILIZATIONS HAVE KNOWN periods of creative splendor and periods of docile imitation.

As an era comes to its close the river of inspiration sinks to low tide. Then the swamp grass, the bogs and unpleasant flats of the time lie bare and repellent in home life, art, and literature.

A new era opens. The ocean tide again enters the estuary of a people's life. Currents of glory flow with a swift, joyous inrush. The higher levels gleam with sunshine. Civilization is once more a river of light and people gladly bathe in its fresh, shining waters.

In the new light women take their rightful place among the leaders of the world. And art becomes an ennobling influence.

In early Buddhism the women were as free to progress as were the men; and women had much to do with the spread of the new life. Seventy-three of the early Buddhist women described so vividly their conversion to the Buddhist faith that their poems were placed in the Buddhist Scriptures, and brought joy to millions of people. Beautiful Queen Khema by her wisdom and radiant virtues inspired the women of many centuries. Queen Maya, the Buddha's mother, was almost deified. One famous Buddhist woman before her conversion was a militant debater. From village to village she tramped, to plant her walking stick in the ground and wait for someone to present to her a difficult question. She never lost in argument until Sariputta came by, and asked: What is truth? From that day, this debater taught Buddhism vigorously. Paticara, whose many students considered her second only to the Master, came into Buddhism through pitiful calamity. In one swift twenty-four hours she lost her husband, her two babies, her father, mother, and brother. She went insane with grief and wandered around in circles weeping for her dead. The townspeople threw stones and mud at her and shouted to her to go away from them. One day the Buddha spoke to her words which entered into her soul and cleared her mind. Lady Kuan, a devout Buddhist of the thirteenth century, was called with her husband to Kublai Khan's court. The mighty monarch gave her the title of a feudal lord, that all might know the degree of culture and learning Kublai Khan admired. Lady Kuan was as famous for her philanthropies as for her writings.

When old-time China was influenced by the Sages, women associated with men on an equal footing, and often surpassed them. Among China's Immortals is Chiang-Hou, the wife of King Hsüan Wang of the Chou dynasty. Hsüan Wang followed the wise advice of experienced statesmen, and brought his country better days. He then relaxed his vigilance, rose late in the morning, and could find no time for state matters. Queen Chiang-Hou saved him by a clever stratagem. One morning she refused to dress in any royal apparel, and sent word to the king she could no longer be Queen for she was unable to prevent her husband from indolence in high office. Her antidote had an immediate effect; and never again was Hsüan Wang self-indulgent. Lady Pan Ch'ao, the illustrious scholar of the later Han era was one of more than three hundred women who became famous under Confucian guidance; and the men of China gladly honored them.

Mary Magdalene was the first to see the risen Christ. Through Christian history women have worked and served as heroically as men. The Christian religion shines with the names of saintly women.

For the first hundred years of Islam's life the best Muslims had no thought of interfering with the freedom of women. Muhammad's daughter Fatima was a famous speaker and writer among the Muslims. Because of her beauty and many gifts Islam called her "Our Lady of Light." Her son, Husain had a talented daughter whose home was a center for the intellectual life of her community. Until the eleventh century Muslim women were at the head of their households, at liberty to receive their guests. The

Umayyad, Walid II, who became khalifa in 743, was the cause of the first seclusion of Muslim women. This depraved khalifa took the girl who attracted his attention. Damascus, his capital, became under him so lawless that a woman of rank was safe only in her own home. Walid II was the first khalifa who made eunuchs the keepers of the royal women of Islam.

For a hundred years after Walid II, Muslim women still had freedom, and they were celebrated as scholars and writers. The Muslim scholar Ameer Ali writes, "The system of absolute seclusion and segregation of the sexes does not seem to have become general until the time of Kadir b'Illah, who did more to stop the progress of the Muslim world than any other sovereign." The khalifa reigned from 991 to 1031. Until his time women even went to war as commanders of troops. They were hostesses in their homes; they were educated and intellectual, and much respected by the men; some of the queens assisted their husbands in state matters. Two Muslim women of the twelfth century were famous scholars. One, Shaikha Shudha, taught history and literature in Baghdad; the other received from the men scholars of her day her diploma as a doctor of law and a license to teach law. The best Muslims looked upon marriage as a solemn rite. Mothers were acknowledged to have the most important service of their world: the training of the future generations. In Muslim Spain women went about freely and attended the public festivals and games. Some of the gifted Muslim writers, and many of Islam's saints, were women.

In Japan, Empress Suiko, with Prince Shotoku, was responsible for a new civilization, through Buddhism. Women opened the renaissance in Japanese literature. Lady Murasaki may be counted a founder of the modern novel.

Humanity is meant to have a happy childhood, an adventurous and idealistic youth, a creative and socially useful maturity. Women can start the human race on this splendid highway. Muhammad said, "Heaven lies at the feet of mothers." When Buddhism was effective, women were the balance wheel of their families, active in the education of their children, in service to the poor, exerting a beneficent authority which shaped the character of millions of people.

When the life-imparting light of true religion in the floodtide of its youth illumines different parts of the world, art becomes a creative energy. All great art in literature, poetry, painting, sculpture, architecture, and music is inspired. Homer told that Odysseus said to Demodocus, "If you will now relate the tale in its due order, forthwith I will declare to all mankind how bounteously God gave to you a wondrous power of song." Plato took it for granted that to write good poetry one must be inspired. Milton opens his immortal epic, *Paradise Lost*, with the prayer:

> *What in me is dark*
> *Illumine, what is low raise and support;*
> *That, to the height of this great argument,*
> *I may assert Eternal Providence,*
> *And justify the ways of God to men.*

To the thoughtful people of China art was more than aesthetic and poetic expression; it was a divine thing. They saw it in nature, which they looked upon as God's glorious apparel, and in this spirit they painted rolling ocean waves, or plant life bending to the breeze, or the misty light on a mountaintop.

Today, the love of beauty is the only religion many people know. And beauty is wonderful. If its followers would be true to it they would find themselves in pleasant fields. But it must be true beauty, not a sham. Literary style is sometimes like a beautiful dress on a figure in a store window; it is harmonious in design, sometimes quite dazzling; but when one looks for the person who wears it, nothing is there. Some works of art, by their faultless communication of experience do a shameless thing, for they publish to the world how impoverished and unwholesome, how blind to real beauty, how deaf to refinement, how dead in character, how dust-swept and beclouded are the men and women who create them. This kind of writing, or painting, or music, going under the name of art, is but an awful exposure of the soul's secrets. Some artists abound in ideas. Others, having nothing to say, continue to compose, forgetting that art consists of both form and content. The child tells everything that he does and sees, on and on with no feeling for the significance of what he does or observes. So the uninspired artist may make a man simply a bundle of mineral salts entombed in a mass of flesh, with face distorted, weary of life, a living ugliness and a walking death.

We say, in art be true to nature. But many a naturalist in literature, sculpture, or painting portrays only the sordid aspects of a really beautiful world, never seeming to see the sweetness of little children and their charm, the loveliness and laughter of happy homes. To delight in the idealism of youth, in kindness and self-sacrifice, in a will firm as adamant, a mind luminous with the wisdom of the Spirit is beyond this artist. If art holds no eternal beauty, it has technique only.

Art for art's sake is only an alluring phrase. People wish for a work of art because it amuses or thrills, instructs or tranquilizes them, liberates or uplifts them. Which nature in us does it please, this book or play, this picture or song? Does it evoke the animal and nourish him, or does it quicken our intellect, our unselfish love? Does it stimulate the beast or the angel; confusion, or order and harmony; death or life? Our taste depends upon what is living and growing within us: is it dislike or love, prejudice or knowledge, apathy or intelligence, the eye of the mind or the eye of the flesh? To associate with degraded thoughts and deeds, in books or pictures, by the law of contagion may make one degraded. Bad company corrupts good taste and morals; it also drags one into the dark caverns of gloom and despair.

Knowing that corrupt literature can never produce incorruptible character, Confucius chose for his nation's reading a collection of maxims, stories, and poems which could upbuild China's civilization. He admonished his students, "Have no depraved thoughts." Dr. Herbert A. Giles, eminent Professor of Chinese at Cambridge University, writes in his book, *The Civilization of China:*

Throughout the Confucian Canon, a collection of ancient works on which the moral code of the Chinese is based, there is not a single word which could give offense, even to the most sensitive, on questions of delicacy and decency. That is surely saying a good deal, but it is not all; precisely the same may be affirmed of what is mentioned above as high-class Chinese literature, which is pure enough to satisfy the most strait-laced. Chinese poetry, of which there is in existence a huge mass, will be searched in vain for suggestions of impropriety, for sly innuendo, and for the other tricks of the unclean. This extraordinary purity of language is all the more remarkable from the fact that, until recent years, the education of women has not been at all general, though many particular instances are recorded of women who have themselves achieved successes in literary pursuits. It is only when we come to the novel, to the short story, or to the anecdote, which are not usually written in high-class style, and are therefore not recognized as literature, proper, that this exalted standard is no longer always maintained.

The vulture flies over valleys and hills ever in search of the dead. The nightingale flies through the night ever in quest of the rose. The vulture gloats over the bodies of the unsuccessful and the slain. The nightingale even in the darkness goes straight to the rose and when he inhales its fragrance bursts into the most thrilling song known to the kingdom of birds. The nightingale like the vulture senses the dead body, but he does not pause in his search until he finds the rose. He perceives true values.

The real artist, in writing, and painting, building, and living, acknowledges the existence of the ugly side of life, but he prefers the rose; for those who are victorious look up and not down. The early Buddhists wrote psalms of freedom and attainment. They knew all about devils. But they could also describe heaven, for love opens the artist's eyes to the beauty in the universe. Love also opens his heart to the Godlike forces which may inspire his brush and pen. What appears in his painting or his poem must first rise in his soul. He becomes a true artist when the vision and harmony of the Over Soul enter his mind. The Chinese said a god or an angel guided the brush of the great Wu-Tao-tzu. Sir Laurence Binyon writes, of the Chinese artist, "The universe in its wholeness and its freedom" is "his home. The winds of the air have become his desires. . . . mountain peaks are his lovely aspirations, and torrents his liberating energies."

A government official and his wife lived in China in the days of Sung. From his salary they saved enough to buy every two weeks a lovely masterpiece of Chinese painting or writing. For two weeks they delighted in the beauty of their treasure. Then the official brought home another piece of food for their souls. A delightful Chinese picture of the Ming dynasty shows the joyous expectancy of a party of scholars and artists who have assembled in an exquisite garden to see a Chinese painting. Every face looks happy. The artist who painted the wondrous scroll was that day king of their hearts.

We want beauty of style. We also want beauty of soul. When a true artist appears he reveals the value of the combination of technique and inspiration. A supreme artist comes upon an auditorium stage with his violin, to play to thousands of attentive people. He is relaxed, unself-conscious, his whole being lifted in listening concentration upon, receptive adoration of, an invisible harmony, already composed, and now to be manifest. As he silently worships the unembodied melody it rises from his violin, and tones sweet, powerful, ethereal go singings, shining, radiating through the hall. The audience is lost in wonder and admiration approaching that of the artist himself. He becomes a mediator of invisible beauty.

The great Prophet adores, and then transmits the melodies of Reality. Easy master of his will, he listens only to the quiet, radiant note Reality gives him. He is endowed with power, his love is creative, his every deed is sublimated, glorified. He thinks God's thoughts, until the beauty which fills his soul possesses him so completely that he becomes the beauty. He makes known to the listening, watching millions of people, God the Composer, from whom he receives the music of life eternal.

# 36

## Our Certainty of God

MATERIALISTS SAY that nature is a vast machine which, having started like any other machine in good condition, goes on and on. And human beings are small machines. Connected up with the cosmic mechanism they are as completely determined by their heredity and environment as are their watches and automobiles, the product of the factories in which they were made.

The fact that we try to express scientific truth proves we are not machines. What does a machine know of truth? What machine is conscious of its motions, its speed? Can a machine contemplate its own degradation; when did we hear of a machine being conscience-stricken if it broke down. What machine ever prayed that it might be a better machine? Can a machine conceive ideals, or plan its destiny?

The objective of scientific investigation is facts, the truth. If we are machines, determined by physical or even social forces only, truth does not exist. According to the deterministic hypothesis, each person believes what he is compelled to believe, what he must believe. Two men believe what happens to be put into their minds by inexorable causation. Their beliefs may be quite different yet both are equally right for both are absolutely determined. Ten plus two is tewelve, in one brain. If the dull child says it is eleven, he is as right as though he were Sir Isaac Newton. The dunce and the man of science are equal. There is then no right or wrong. Criminal and angel are what nature makes them. Christ and Judas are alike; goodness and evil are illusions; beauty and ugliness have no more reality than the mists of the morning.

If we say one machine is good, and another is defective, we immediately pass out of the mechanistic order into that of truth and error, and accept the reality of values. These are not at all mechanistic.

Human determinism means that certain minds in authority say to others, You shall not think. There are always men and women however who at any cost make choices through reason; who discover their mind is strangely creative, that it selects what it will believe, what form of activity it will follow. The child may seem to be determined, physically and mentally, by his environment. When he grows to maturity he sloughs off his childhood's dependence, and selects, arranges, and creates his environment. The scientific investigator exults in freedom of thought, for he is awake, resourceful, creative. He sorts, rearranges, and considers the existing knowledge, using it as a steppingstone to new and daring discoveries.

Man becomes more than a machine when he chooses his attitudes and deeds. The world exalts the hero because he could be a coward, and the saint because he has chosen to advance far beyond the sinner. The Buddha could have passed his life in his palace. The Christ himself chose the cross. Freedom makes virtue valuable. Under determinism praise and blame have no meaning.

According to mechanistic materialism man's mind is physical only, and he thinks because his brain cells somehow get connected with each other. These cells associate ideas and hook up with memories and sensations, with the result that consciousness emerges. When very many cells are thus connected Newton's laws are discovered.

Some say that chance is creator, lord, and king; that all the worlds and stars, the evolution of men and women, even the greatest among them, came to be through the fortuitous sticking together of atoms. Could the great truths Newton, and Faraday, and Clerk Maxwell discovered be chanced upon by the fumblings of immovable brain cells? How many times, one wonders, would it be necessary to throw down a font of type that by the law of chance a play of Goethe, or the *Divine Comedy* might appear? To say a thing happens by chance means we do not know its cause. To say the whole universe happened by chance means we do not know how it came into being. To exalt our ignorance into a theory of causation is the essence of superstition.

We decry the old theology because it made us worms of the dust. Modern mechanistic materialism makes us machines of the dust, which is no more desirable. All spiritually minded people live by the hope that through the help of God, the Mind whom they believe to be back of and within the physical universe, they may escape from determinism and bondage. Such darkness is well enough for the animal. It is impossible to awakened men and women who live in the light of the freedom, unselfish love, and beauty of holiness by which good people ascend to the mountain-top of human society.

The practical materialist says: "I am what I eat and own and wear. I must get money and exchange it for these things, lest I perish. My body rules my mind, is my mind. I am only an animal. Therefore I must live and end like an animal. While life lasts let me enjoy myself, for tomorrow I go out of existence." A medical student once dissected a human body, and announced triumphantly to his fellow students that not a niche or cranny could be found where the soul might take up its abode.

Thus does the skeptic deride the idea of the soul and God. But he can no more put God out of existence than can a cup annihilate the ocean by saying the ocean is a futile idea because it, the cup, cannot contain anything larger than itself. Nor can the skeptic find the living soul in a dead body, in the crumbling house from which it has departed.

Suppose some of us are constrained to believe there is, within and beyond the physical world, a mighty Being, a Mind wise beyond all our hopes, who works through universal laws. He is just, as no man or woman can ever be, for he knows every subtle motive and cause of the deeds and thoughts of each human soul. He tempers justice with perfect love for he is responsible for the existence of every human being; yet he is always just. He brings failure to ultimate victory. He wants our love and is ready to make himself known to us the moment we take the right initiative. Suppose we are willing to believe in the existence of such a Being; can we find proofs which the rationally minded may accept?

Modern science with its world-shaking discoveries is founded on faith in a rational order of cause and effect permeating and sustaining the universe. Although once in a while scientists tap the wire of exceptions to the law of causation, the uniformity of nature is the foundation, the prerequisite of all science.

Scientific search for natural laws implies a universal order or truth in nature which our minds can comprehend. Order and unity and truth are mental realities. The physical world is composition and decomposition in endless flux. A natural law by its nature does not pass away. Therefore the laws of change, because they are changeless, must be a mental and not a physical reality. Science then rests upon a mental order.

Finding geometrical patterns in this order, we must infer that in it is an Intelligence, for only mind geometrizes. Also, when we learn that light traveling a hundred and eighty-six thousand miles a second takes untold millions of years to reach some provinces of the universe, we confront an immensity of space before which we fall back confused. Even the best machine needs a mind that fully understands it to keep it in order. Could such an unthinkably large machine as this universe move in absolute rhythm forever unless a mind was directing it? Every machine has a maker, the mind that planned and brought it into being. There must then be a mind which directs the physical universe. According to Xenophon, Socrates reasoned, "When you know that you have in your body but a small portion of the earth, which is vast, and a small portion of the water, which is vast, and that your frame is constituted for you to receive only a small portion of each of other things, that are vast, do you think that you have seized for yourself, by some extraordinary good fortune, intelligence alone which exists nowhere else, and that this assemblage of vast bodies, countless in number, is maintained in order by something void of reason?"

When we say, "This is an error," we affirm there is a truth by which we decide that such and such is error. Even the most unscrupulous man demands that other people deal honestly with him. The author who ridicules morals and makes the life of the profligate seem attractive can make his book interesting or temptation exciting to his reader only by contrast with decent living. He is like the monkey up a tree, breaking off the branch which alone protects him from the lion on the ground below him. The virtuous society the author laughs at makes it possible for him to live in safety and write his virtue-destroying books.

Every valid criticism, every demand for social justice that a man voices implies that a better pattern is possible. Every error presupposes truth, else how do we know it to be error? To say a thing is evil acknowledges the existence of goodness. Ugliness declares the existence of beauty. Each value judgment requires for its authority that values exist in reality. The idea of evolution implies ever-higher values. Every step toward perfection opens a higher vista of perfection, on and on beyond the immediate reach of man's mind. Each perfection when attained becomes an existing reality. Therefore absolute perfection, wherever it may abide, is the Ultimate Reality, which is God. Ralph Waldo Emerson writes, at the beginning of his essay on *The Over Soul*, "We grant that human life is mean; but how did we find out that it was mean? What is the ground of this uneasiness of ours; of this old discontent? What is the universal sense of want and ignorance, but the fine innuendo by which the great Soul makes its enormous claim?"

Ideals are therefore a partial reflection of the real. We see them as in a mirror, broken lights from the real world. Progress in science, education, art, business, government, and good character is possible only by obeying certain standards that soar above us. The standard of perfection for scientific research is truth; for art it is beauty and truth and the gift of expression; for government it is the welfare and happiness of those people who are within the sphere of its sovereignty or influence. We call these standards: laws, ideals, the will of God, for they are charged with the life of Reality.

The Director of the universe is then a mind which is Reality. Since he is not to be seen as a physical phenomenon on this planet we must infer that he lives without a physical body; and as mind cannot be seen with the physical eye, we cannot thus see God. How then can we have knowledge of his character and attitudes?

The branch reveals the nature of the tree. The Rational Order in the universe is the tree; a Buddha is the branch. The stream cannot rise higher than its source. The stream is the Holy Spirit which is in the Christ; the source is God. The macrocosm is reflected in the microcosm which is the Christ: the mind of Christ is controlled by perfect love. The product reflects the standards, the nature of the producer. The highest human products are the greatest prophets. Since God created them he must be beyond them in perfection and genius, for to him they ever aspired.

God then is a Mind which is the beginning and the end of ultimate truth and of every quality of good character and of genius that has appeared among men. He lives without a physical body. We live in bodies. Why should we believe we have any relation to him?

We live in physical bodies for a time only. Then we leave our body, as we discard an old garment, and live like God as disembodied spirit.

How do we know we can live without our body? The animal has certain bodily needs, such as hunger and thirst, and finds in his world the elements which he must have to appease them. So far man is like the animal. The animal has no intellectual hunger, for the animal has not a human intellect. Nor can he think of God's Spirit, for he has no like spirit in him. Man's intellect forges forward century by century. The animal makes no such progress.

Man's brain is a composite of separate cells; but every activity of human consciousness is the activity of a unit. Human consciousness unites feeling, reason and purpose into one activity, and directs this activity to its goal.

The fact that the human mind can surmount the limitations of the animal; that it can think as a unit and transcend time and space; that it can organize, unite, and utilize the sensations of the physical world proves it is quite distinct from a body made up of separate cells. The martyrs who submitted to torture for their faith lived in thought far from the condition of their bodies, entering a mental environment. A magnificent succession of scientific thinkers, rising mentally above and beyond their bodies dwell in thought in the remotest spaces and discover the universe we know today. Congnizant of the laws that govern the physical world they become the masters of that world, breaking with their thought its supposed limitations. They make it possible to bridge, and tunnel under, great rivers, to fly through the skies in a heavier-than-air carrier, to drive a vessel through the waters of the under sea, and send the human voice around the world on the wireless. The man of science has explored nature and used its forces, has traveled in thought to the farthest star, has rebuilt the history of past ages.

Man's hunger for intellectual and spiritual progress does not come from his body. His body wants to play, rest, be comfortable; its nature is self-preservation. The mind and spirit often compel the body to work far beyond its instinctive desires, and sometimes press it on to martyrdom. Man at his best proves at every moment that he is spirit, living in a timeless, immortal world.

What does man's spirit mean to him, more than his body means? The fearful, or the glorious thought of immortality, that whether we like it or not we are undying spirits who cannot escape our immortality, becomes one of the mightiest incentives to face life, and to triumph, that ever confronted man.

When religion is in decline and belief in materialism is current, many say the idea of immortality is only wishful thinking. Wishful thinking works both ways. The materialist may wish to go out of existence; to lie down in eternal sleep and forgetfulness may seem to him desirable. In all lands and ages some have feared to face the awesome fact that what kind of immortal life came to them was determined by the deeds they had done and the habits they had acquired on this earth. Therefore they preferred to believe they were extinguished by the death of the body. The Wisdom of Solomon, written in the first century B.C., expressed this skepticism:

> ... *By mere chance were we born,*
> *And hereafter we shall be as though we had never been:*
> *For the breath in our nostrils is smoke,*
> *And our reason is a spark kindled by the beating of our heart,*
> *Which being extinguished, the body shall be turned into aches,*
> *And the spirit shall be dispersed as thin air;*
> *And our life shall pass away, as the traces of a cloud.*

The poem continues:

> *Thus reasoned they, and they were led astray;*
> *For their own ignorance hath blinded them.*
> *For God created man to be immortal,*
> *And made him an image of his own eternity.*

*In the eyes of the foolish they seem to die;*
*And their departure is accounted to be misery,*
*And their journeying away from us to be their ruin:*
*For the souls of the righteous are in the hand of God*
*And there shall no evil touch them.*
*Their reward is in the Lord.*
*And the care for them with the Most High.*

Plato wrote in his *Phaedo* that Crito asked Socrates, on the eve of his martyrdom, where he wanted to be buried; and Socrates smilingly answered that they must catch him first. They could do anything they pleased with his body: he himself was immortal. The same triumphant faith was held by Plato, Plotinus, and other positive thinkers of Greece and Rome. It has been proclaimed by the best thinkers of Israel and Christendom, of Buddhism, Islam, Zoroastrianism, and Hinduism. The Chinese services in memory of ancestors have no meaning unless the ancestors are living and immortal.

Professor William James explains immortality by the simile of the organ and the organist: Man is the musician who plays for a time on an organ, his body. The organ pipes are the brain cells. If the organist breaks a pipe, he cannot play certain notes, for there is a localization of function in the pipes. If the whole organ is injured or deteriorates beyond repair, the organist cannot play at all on that instrument. But the musician is never limited to one instrument; he can play his music elsewhere.

The love of perfection, which means progress, is man's highest life. Yet no one who aspires ever lives long enough to achieve his ideals. As soon as he reaches a goal, another and higher opens to him. If we as a race strive and climb and discover science and God, yet are still only brain cells tied to a fleeting composition called the body which will pass away, then are we of all creatures the most pitiable, for we live to be defeated.

God is the meaning and the hope of our superphysical life. The voice of conscience is a cry for God, from whom it came. The content of conscience may come from our environment; its imperative is from God. Unless the soul be immortal how can we believe in God's justice? How can we believe in God? For justice to everyone, not only for those who fail but for those who achieve, requires immortality. If God could let the most valuable people who have ever lived struggle the whole of their lives, partially achieve perfection, and then go out of existence, God's work and purpose for humanity would continually come to naught. If God gives us every gift, and withholds immortality, he is like a father who brings a son into existence, trains him with devoted love and every promise of assistance until he reaches maturity, and then annihilates him. Can we condemn such a deed in human beings, and then attribute it to God, on an everlasting scale?

For those who experience the activity of mind and spirit, the center of gravity in the universe shifts from the transitory to the eternal. When we survey the thousands of years of human evolution, all that gives real meaning to existence is the spirit's capacity to vault the barrier of death.

The early followers of the Buddha, Christ, and Muhammad lived by the certainty that every individual is immortal, and their Teacher was even more vitally active in the unseen world than he was on earth. The sun's shadow causes nothing to grow. Paul had no vague, shadowy experience on the road to Damascus; he saw with his spiritual eyes the immortal Christ and heard his voice. Nor was his experience limited to the one instance. His consciousness of the living Christ sustained Paul through the rest of his life, a period of perhaps thirty years. This consciousness was repeated in different degrees of vividness and glory by millions of Christians. It was because the Buddhists, Christians, and Muslims knew their Prophet to be living after he left this world that they worked to spread his teachings.

Jesus told his disciples that the kingdom of heaven has many mansions; that is, different levels of perfection. Muhammad made reward and punishment in the next world a sanction whereby to persuade his first wild followers to become temperate in their behavior, and socially minded. The Buddha taught the soul's progress through immortal worlds.

The Prophets give mankind the laws which govern the approach to the Real Life of the universe and promise that everyone who lives and prays aright can, in his own experience, have knowledge of God. The secret of prayer, that is, companionship with the

THE PERFECTION OF DAYS

Unseen Being, is concentration upon the thought of God, his glorious attributes, his love, his guidance when the individual truly turns to him. The dedicated ones, the saints, in all religions, who desired the presence of God as earnestly as other men and women desire their worldly successes were rewarded beyond all their hopes. They testified that to them came a mind-transforming, will-renewing, heart-expanding experience: direct consciousness of God's divine and eternal life within them.

The Buddhists call this consciousness nirvana, or paradise. The Christians call it the birth from on high. To the Jews it is "the secret place of the Most High." To the Muslims it is awareness of the Living Light. Paul says that eye hath not seen nor ear heard, nor hath it entered into the mind of man to imagine the immortal wonders prepared for those who love God.

# 37

## The Unity of Nations

MANY PERSONS REASON: I could believe in God if all the world was good. But when I see maimed children, broken lives, premature deaths, the insane, slums, pestilence, earthquakes, poverty, the madness of war, I lose faith in a well-wishing Creator.

Before man, was nature, with its mighty upheavals, its violent hurtling hurricanes, its crashing earthquakes, its floods. Of themselves these were not evil. They became an evil when they affected man. The savagery of wild animals, the way they kill and devour each other, is not for them unlawful, but according to their nature.

Right and wrong, good and evil appeared with man. The laws that govern the animals permit them to prey upon each other, to fight for what they want, and get it at any cost. In the human world this is evil, for man is more than an animal and must not be ruthlessly destroyed.

How does man know that the behavior of wild animals is evil in him? Because man can see that he causes suffering, a faculty the animal does not possess. A despot when entertaining a number of guests at dinner let loose in the room a boxful of scorpions, and commanded, on pain of death, that no one move. It was his pleasure to watch the agony of his guests when stung. The scorpions in themselves were not evil. The human being who released them was the degraded one. Napoleon Bonaparte was brilliantly endowed; his intellect, his indomitable will, his gift for planning great undertakings were remarkable. But he made his genius serve his insatiable thirst for power, his cruel desire to be master of the world.

Century after century people do the things that create misery, that all but wreck humanity, and then say there is no God. Of a truth, God has no part in the tragedies human beings bring upon themselves and others through the misuse of their God-given freedom.

Men of ability use their talents to take from others the barest necessities, piling up for themselves more than they can ever use. Others, seeing what they think to be the prominent position of the rich, would like to be prominent also. When by the manipulation of labor, perhaps, or by political power they attain such a position they often become stealers of the common good themselves.

So arise the problems of poverty, unemployment, corruption and graft, strikes, and strife between capital and labor, lack of profits, lack of consumers, war.

Modern scientific and technical knowledge has built up a system of warfare terrible beyond the most murderous hopes of any conqueror of the past. By this means the barbarous policy of conquest is carried on: stealing territory and forcing the conquered people to submit to the distasteful government of the oppressor or be killed. A man or woman who deliberately kills another human being is sent by society to the electric chair. The ruler who destroys a million or more "foreigners" and annexes their country is called, by his nation, a valiant patriot. "Hands off" has been the cry of the conqueror since historic times began: leave me alone while I take from other nations their lands, their possessions and taxes.

Being today socially one humanity, we suffer vicariously for the lawlessness of others. Being one body, all the members are affected when any nation is out of order. Our present-day unity visits upon us the iniquity of any of us. Some groups cry for splendid isolation and a self-sufficient nation. The problem cannot be solved in this way, for the recent discoveries of science and technology and our unescapable economic and scientific interdependence have eliminated national self-sufficiency.

We are free to live by the laws of the animal world, or by those of the intellectual and spiritual world. We know by long experience that to live by our lower nature brings upon us ignorance, poverty, sorrow, frustration, war, crime. When the people who form the nations follow the laws of mutual consideration, and hold

in check those who do not value these laws, the whole world will move forward simultaneously. Suppose Canada and the United States had to fortify the three thousand miles of borderland between them. Suppose each of the states that make up the United States had to equip itself with armies and fleets of airplanes, with border forts and tariff barriers against the other states. Instead, these states are the United States. Their interstate differences are settled by their Supreme Court. A universal Congress legislates for the good of all. This is possible because all the states can trust each state to keep the faith.

A universal society of the nations with an International Court of Justice, universal limitation of armaments, lowering of tariff and trade barriers through reciprocal or general consent, just access for all to natural resources, raw materials, and world markets are essential to world peace. Certain national defenses are necessary for internal peace; collective security under international law is the only permanent safety. If a large majority of the nations formed into such a society they could control the unruly ones, open a new era of international cooperation, and keep universal peace.

The establishment of a beneficent world society can be brought about only through a fundamental change in international attitudes, acceptance of the essential unity of mankind, and a sincere agreement to settle international differences by arbitration under universal law. It is imperative that all the nations be willing that every nation is treated with the same justice each nation wants for itself; that each nation consents to subordinate its own interests for the good of all, and makes real economic and national sacrifices to maintain world peace.

A stable world society is possible only when the nations can trust each other. We can be sure of a ntion's behavior when we know it is based upon belief in a universally righteous order of which all nations are a part, and to which they are under perpetual obligation to be trustworthy, when we know the nations are working under the direction of God's Prophet, who guarantees their good character. When a nation's belief in God and the moral law breaks down, with the result that the people discard religion as useless, they have no standard of values but their own desires.

If the world was secure in a universal peace, sums of money vast beyond all dreams would be released for economic advancement, education, and the betterment of every nation. Social security is essential to stable civilization: international, national, economic, personal security. Security for libraries, schools, universities, for childhood, for middle life, old age, for investments and savings. Security for the employer and the employed. Ordered security. Through the centuries some kings have considered their subjects merely as objects for taxation. A society where a few own everything, and the poor have nothing but their poverty is in peril.

Every civilization that does not encourage individual enterprise, initiative, and freedom of thought declines. But social freedom must be controlled; for social security requires economic justice. The extravagant wages demanded by workmen in times of prosperity, the equally extravagant prices demanded of the consumer, the extortionate claims of landlords, the unrestricted freedom of the capitalist or the labor leader soon paralyze society. Justice is the strength of the international, the industrial, the social order. The most enlightened self-interest is justice, for only justice can see far enough to be truly enlightened. Only justice can decide how large a profit a man should collect, and the wage he should pay or receive.

All who live in free countries are part owners in the most important business of the world: government. The objectives of good government are protection and security for the governed. Governments have protected the well-to-do from thieves, landlords from tenants, creditors from debtors, the family from dissolution, the poor from destitution. Governments have made citizens secure against foreign invasion and civil sedition. Good governments have interfered in business with tariffs and taxes, with laws for the preservation of contracts, the collection of debts, the prohibition of usury, with laws forbidding the employment of women and children in factories at starvation wages and body- and soul-killing hours of work, with laws protecting the farmer, the inventor, the worker, the investor, the consumer.

Business for business' sake, even science for science's sake, will have to give way to science and business for the sake of all men. Charles Dickens presents an ideal from the heavenly world, in his *Christmas Carol:* " 'Business!' cried the Ghost, wringing its hands again. 'Mankind was my business. The common welfare was my business; charity, mercy, forbearance and benevolence, were all my business. The dealings of my trade were but a drop of water in the comprehensive ocean of my business!' " The men of pre-eminent ability who have used their genius and vast fortunes in this way are a glory of the world. Attaining character and intellectual education themselves, they devote their gifts to others less privileged.

When the social problems that bring calamity to all the world are solved and the nations make concessions for the sake of the general welfare—and this must come about if humanity is to progress or even survive—the personal problems of daily life still remain: why my illness, accidents, loses, failures, frustrations? How can my problem be solved so my soul will be satisfied?

We are born to live by our mind and spirit and the Godlike power hidden in our will, not by our animal desires. We are free to choose either world; and herein lie our hope and our misery. If we advance because we have no alternative, achievement loses its meaning. When, of our own free will, we climb toward perfection and God, we appreciate the prizes we win. If God forced us to be his friends, our love, our friendship would have no value. A personality made perfect by free choices is humanity's glory.

Life is a school in which we are meant to prepare ourselves to become companions of God. Difficulties are a stimulus to activity and achievement. What would we think of the student who registered in a university with the request to his teachers, "Now be careful to make my work easy. I am really interested only in walking a pathway of roses." This is what many of us demand of life: it must hold no troubles. If we do have trouble, we will not believe in God. If we do not have trouble, God is quite unnecessary to our universe.

If we understand them, our troubles become steppingstones to ever higher attainment. Moral perfection, writes Emerson in his *Journal*, "is always the glory that shall be revealed; it is the 'open secret' of the universe." We wrestle with poverty and sickness and unemployment, with an adverse environment; and like Jacob, we do not let our adversary go until he blesses us. Mencius wrote,

"When Heaven is about to confer a great office on any one, it first exercises his mind with suffering and his sinews and bones with toil; it exposes his body to hunger and subjects him to extreme poverty; it confounds his undertakings. In these ways it stimulates his mind, hardens his nature and supplies his incompetencies. Life springs from sorrow, and calamity and death from ease and pleasure. When men are possessed of intelligent virtue and prudence in the management of affairs it generally arises from their having been in distress." Yet, in the school which graduates heroic perfection, most of us are, at least part of the time, unwilling students.

The soul's highest aspiration is communion with God. When this communion is attained the answer to every personal problem is immortality. The life beyond death was the great thought which sustained Paul through his years of persecution. It was the hope of Jesus' disciples; it is the final sanction for righteous living. It is a vital challenge, belief in an eternal world, where everyone receives justice, according to his ability and his striving. In this immortal world no one can injure another. Everyone is governed by perfect wisdom and love, for his own highest good. Such a life, coming some time, makes this life well worth living. God did not make this physical world perfect lest we become too attached to it and fail to learn the lessons that will help us in the eternal world. To justify the travail of childbirth and the weakness of childhood one must see the grown man. Only the life beyond the death of the body can reveal the spiritual strength and ineffable glory achieved through overcoming the personal problems and frustrations of this world. Through the centuries, many noble people were sustained by the certainty that if they did their part, a Golden Age would come upon the earth, and for them individually there was an immortal life in which the injustice of this world would be rectified.

The problem of evil is in the main the problem of social and mental mismanagement of the resources God has given us. When we subtract all the harm man has done to man and we have done to ourselves through lack of knowledge, spiritual education, self-control; and add all the equipment science has furnished us today for the control of pestilence, dire poverty, famine, for the healing of physical and mental ailments, we find we could go a long way toward eliminating evil. God did not give us a ready-made world and ready-made instinctive habits, as he gave them to ants and birds and bees. He made us his free partners in building a just and righteous world, revealing to us the plan and assisting us with the power to carry it into action, while waiting for us actually to create it. We know what the skilled gardener accomplishes by planting and cultivating trees and flowers, how he remakes and beautifies the land. So can human activity, rightly directed, remake this world.

The great evils and the causes of evil are ignorance, prejudice, exclusive nationalisms, greed, hatred, cruelty, selfishness, lust, and fear; and these are preventable. Religion and science working together can destroy them. The method of prevention is education: science and religion working hand in hand to eradicate them. When education in true democracy, brotherhood, knowledge of God as the Father of all races and nations wins in the war with education for racial fanaticism, class struggle, and the lust for domination and conquest, then a large part of the problem of evil will vanish as the darkness of night disappears at the rising of the sun.

There is only one way to permanent safety. God has shown us this way through the great Prophets, who have carried humanity through periods of dire calamity into the light. When we spread their teachings with the thoroughness and untiring devotion that the nations committed to world conquest use in their life-destroying purposes, we shall finally so firmly establish the Prophets' great moral, social and spiritual laws that the majority of the world's people will recognize and immediately root out every death-breeding doctrine.

Science and evolution have brought us to the crossroads. The only way now possible is to follow the laws which lead from the jungle to the security of a permanent peace.

## 38

### Science and Inspiration

RELIGION MAY BE divided into three parts: superstitions, transient laws, eternal truth. Superstitions are the invention of the ignorant. They are passed on from century to century by imitative minds and by the connivance of those for whom superstition is profitable. Sometimes a truth gets caught among the superstitions and there it remains until the scientifically minded investigate and find it belongs with eternal truth.

Belief in inspiration is today often pronounced a superstition. Yet it is by means of inspiration that God in historic crises has come to humanity's assistance. Long ago, Isaiah testified that God said to him, "I am God ... declaring the end from the beginning, and from ancient times things that are not yet done." The Hebrew prophets were brought forth into a larger place than their contemporaries knew, and were clearly aware of God. Then did they cry that God was everywhere, like the light, inhabiting eternity, infinitely merciful, so glorious that only his signs might be seen by mortal man. One of his signs was inspiration, from which came true prophecy. By means of their inspiration and their knowledge of the future, these prophets transcended the childish ideas of their age, declared the solution of many social problems, and anticipated the character of the true Messiah. They soared above and ahead of their time because they lived, at least for the moment of their inspiration, close to the timeless world. In the face of a hostile society they kept burning the fire which would otherwise have died out.

Can this sign of God, inspiration, be accepted by men of science?

Ahab, King of Israel, says the Old Testament, wanted to take the city of Ramoth-gilead from the King of Syria. Ahab asked Jehoshaphat, King of Judah, who was making him a visit, to help him.

Jehoshaphat said to Ahab, "Inquire now, I pray thee, for the word of the Lord."

Ahab called together about four hundred prophets and asked them, "Shall I go against Ramoth-gilead to battle, or shall I forbear?"

"Go up: for the Lord shall deliver it into the hand of the King," answered the four hundred as with one voice.

Said Jehoshaphat, "Is there not yet another prophet of the Lord? If so, what will he say?"

Ahab replied, "There is yet one man by whom we may inquire of the Lord, Micaiah, the son of Imlah; but I hate him; for he doth not prophesy good concerning me, but evil."

"Let not the King say so," counseled Jehoshaphat.

Ahab called an officer and ordered him, "Fetch quickly Micaiah the son of Imlah."

The kings in royal robes sat on their thrones surrounded by the crowd of prophets. Micaiah was brought before them, and Ahab put to him the matter in hand: should he make war on the King of Syria, or should he not?

Micaiah answered that he had seen in vision the Lord of Hosts, and with him all the hosts of heaven. Micaiah heard the Lord say that a lying spirit was in the mouth of the king's prophets. If Ahab made war on Syria he would lose and would be killed.

One of the men standing by the king stepped forward and struck Micaiah in the face. And Ahab gave the command, "Put this fellow in the prison and feed him with bread of affliction and with water of affliction until I come in peace."

Ahab went to take Ramoth-gilead. On the first day of battle he was killed. His army returned home, defeated. How did Micaiah get his advance information?

Jeremiah made prophecies which every intelligent person of his nation counted impossible: that the Jews would be taken captive and carried off to Babylonia, and after seventy years would return to Palestine. For his heresy Jeremiah was grievously punished. Yet his prophecies were fulfilled.

The Second Isaiah prophesied that the Jewish Messiah would in no way resemble a worldly king. He would be meek and lowly, and would be martyred by his enemies.

When the prophet Zechariah witnessed in vision Israel rising against the Greeks, he also saw the Messianic King entering Jerusalem, riding on an ass. Zechariah wrote, "Rejoice greatly, O daughter of Zion; shout, O daughter of Jerusalem: behold, thy King cometh unto thee; he is just, and having salvation; lowly, and riding upon an ass . . . and he shall speak peace unto the nations: and his dominion shall be from sea to sea, and from the River to the ends of the earth."

What strange prophecies were hidden away in the 22nd Psalm, which begins with the cry, "My God, my God, why hast thou forsaken me?" And there flash out the words, "They look and stare upon me: they part my garments among them, and upon my vesture do they cast lots. But be not thou far off, O Lord: O thou my succor, haste thee to help me. Deliver my soul from the sword."

Zechariach foretold, in a dramatic prophecy, how the Christ, God's beautiful Staff who was to shepherd and unite the nations, would be betrayed for thirty pieces of silver:

"I said unto them, 'If ye think good, give me my hire; and if not forbear.' So they weighed for my hire thirty pieces of silver.

"And the Lord said unto me, 'Cast it unto the potter, the goodly price that I was praised of by them.'

"And I took the thirty pieces of silver, and cast them unto the potter, in the house of the Lord."

Centuries after this prophecy was written the man who, Zechariah foretold, would make this confession was proved to be Judas. Repenting his terrible deed, Judas threw down in the temple the thirty pieces of silver the chief priests gave him in payment for his betrayal of Jesus. The priests, counting it blood money and unclean, repudiated it, saying, use it to buy a potter's field; that is, a cemetery for strangers.

In A.D. 100 probably not a philosopher or man of science in the Greco-Roman world would have conceded it possible that Jesus' poor uneducated followers could spread his gospel. Yet the prophecies were fulfilled that his teachings would be known throughout the world.

These prophets, recorded in the Bible, announced, far ahead of their time, events and truths which, they declared, were given them by God.

The man of science believes there is an ocean of hidden knowledge which can be tapped and from which new facts can be ascertained. He deliberately probes this unseen reality for its secrets. The prophets declared their information was revealed to them to their surprise. How does the man of science gain new truth?

In their search for truth, scientific men are guided by observation, inference, experiment, deduction, verification. With these and mathematics they explore the universe.

The senses must at once be checked by reason, or experience, or authority, lest they lead to a mirage. Said a little girl as she gazed at the horizon, across a great lake, "What an awful noise that water must make when it falls out there." The scientific investigator uses the senses plus reason and experiment; and, by exact measurements with instruments which he guides by the senses and by reason, verifies, modifies or disproves the conclusions of the authorities who have gone before him.

How does he advance to the next conclusion, an idea perhaps so far in advance of reason that it may take years of experiment to verify?

Many scientists and philosophers have declared that new knowledge comes through disciplined intuition or inspiration. John Tyndall, the eminent English physicist, questioned concerning Pasteur: was his wonderful gift his "intuitive vision which discerns in advance the new issues to which existing data point," or was it his skill in proving his intuition true in "the ordeal of test and experiment"? Of Michael Faraday the great physicist, John Tyndall wrote, "We have [in him] flashes of wondrous insight and utterances which seem less the product of reasoning than of revelation." Jules Henri Poincaré, the famous mathematician, tells how he would think over and struggle with a problem; and as a complete surprise the momentous solution would come into his mind, when he was entering an omnibus perhaps, or walking in the country. The idea would always have "the characteristic of brevity, suddenness and immediate certainty." A questionnaire sent to leading inventors and scientific investigators of America asked how often their remarkable discoveries were intuitive. Half of those who replied testified that after months of patient research, from out the blue as it were came the "bright idea" which solved their problem. To some it seemed a voice spoke. Others visualized the new idea. To some it came in a dream or just after waking in the morning. To all it came in moments of relaxation. Worry, anger, "periods of worldly success, if accompanied by a general softening of attitude," inhibited these "scientific revelations." The results of this study were analyzed and presented in the *Journal of Chemical Education.* Professor Bancroft, the chemist, in his *Methods of Research* records the immense import of the "flash of genius" to scientific discovery.

Many times, statesmen have anticipated the trend of politics and the rise of mass movements of mankind. By insight, they have chosen the right men for high positions, and presented right issues at strategic moments. Disraeli, a biographer noted, had this intuition; it was a chief source of his genius.

From "the subliminal self," which is nobler and wiser than the conscious mind, these intuitions come, say many psychologists. Others frankly declare this more-than-normal knowledge to be from a higher world. William James writes in one of his essays, "We have a right to believe the physical order to be only a partial order . . . the external staging of a many storied universe in which spiritual forces have the last word and are eternal." Take away this assurance, he says, from those who have it, and "all the light and radiance of existence are gone." William James was convinced that what the naturalist calls "normal" is "a small part of actual experience. . . . Other kinds of consciousness bear witness to a much wider universe of experience." He studied this wider experience in saints, writers, and many others and found it gave them knowledge, also an indomintable spirit which broke down barriers, opened a path of action, and enabled them to follow that path.

An authoritative witness to inspiration is Ralph Waldo Emerson, one of America's greatest thinkers. His original ideas came to him, he testified, from the vaster region of his mind, which he believed communed with the Over Soul. As these ideas came he wrote them down in his Journal, and later wove them into his essays and poems. He writes, "Man is a stream whose source is hidden. Always our being is descended into us from we know not whence.... When I watch that flowing river, which, out of regions I see not, pours for a season its stream into me—I see that I am a pensioner—not a cause, but a surprised spectator of this ethereal water; that I desire and look up, and put myself in the attitude of reception, but from some alien energy the visions come." Genius he was convinced "is a larger inbibing of the common heart," and has access to inspiration. He writes, "This energy does not descend into individual life on any other condition than entire possession. It comes to the lowly and simple; it comes to whosoever will put off what is foreign and proud; it comes as insight; it comes as serenity and grandeur."

Professor Oliver Elton in his *Memoir* of C. E. Montague gives a manuscript which Montague never finished. In this beautiful document Montague, distinguished thinker and writer of England, describes how there came to him moments when the bondage of self was broken and "you were for an instant ennobled and saw like a god" into a glorious world, vaster, higher, more luminous than our ordinary consciousness. With this world we are connected. It is in us as water is in the flower and the tree. "It seems to me," writes Montague, "that if I could sustain my own mind and heart at the pitch of clarity and tenderness to which they rose and stood poised for some of those odd seconds ... then I should be in Heaven. ... A kindred form of rapture is achieved, in greater or less measure, by every artist of high gifts." The "artist's own mind, or some part of it, seems to look on at the happy miracle from without, enchanted or awed by the strange uncalculated rightness of each effortless touch that he gives to the thing that takes shape in his hands. ... And, yet again, a kindred rapture may visit a man suddenly faced with peril and opportunity in a battle or an accident. He is released—that is all you can say. Fear and desire, his two keepers through life, to preserve and enchain him, are suddenly gone, and he goes to self-sacrifice as lightly as a child draws its breath, with so perfect a freedom from all sense of effort, danger, or pain that presently he is surprised and abashed ... when people credit him with heroism."

The Prophet says, "I was in the presence of God. I heard God speak within my soul." Thousands of men and women believe him, and apply his teachings to their daily life, testing them out in the laboratory of experience.

There are acid tests which may show the prophet's inspiration to be true or false. Does his message vary according to expediency. The real Prophet is never influenced by expediency. Poor Micaiah spoke the truth, and for it he got imprisonment and starving; while the four hundred false prophets enjoyed the favor of the king. A false prophecy may be termed "revelation" for the time being when everyone shouts applause. Authentic revelation is abiding reality.

Said Socrates of the Sophist, "If you only give him money enough he will make you wise." No true prophet of God ever betrays his revelation by turning it to worldly advantage.

Revelation is very particular. It does not come to those who are weak in character, who capitulate to their own safe-keeping. A true communication from God often instructs the prophet to expose injustice, which may be a dangerous thing to do, for injustice, if powerful and pressed to the wall, will persecute. Revelation sometimes requires that the recipient stands alone, for an unpopular truth. Then indeed does he need divine reinforcement, when the crowd hisses its anathemas, and his friends and social stratum ridicule, despise, and disown him.

True inspiration contains exaltation of thought, and authority. It does not follow worn-out convention but announces new truth. The first recipient of true revelation is often the most amazed of all who hear it; wherefore Moses argued solemnly with the Lord, beside the burning bush.

The Hebrew prophets give us rare glimpses of God's method of communicating with them. Jeremiah tells how the prophet is taken by surprise; how God called him, who had small opinion of his ability, to be a prophet to the nations and when he hesitated, said to him, "Be not afraid of them, for I am with thee to deliver thee. Behold, I have put my words in thy mouth." God told Jeremiah that he must know the difference between true messages from the Eternal and fictitious imaginings, as a man separates wheat from the chaff. The Word of God is sudden, tremendous, awesome, "a consuming fire." It strikes at human superstitions like "a hammer that breaketh the rock in pieces." Cried Amos despairingly, "When the lion roars who can but fear; when God speaks who can but prophesy." To John on Patmos, and to Ezekiel by the river Chebar, came glorious visions, like motion pictures from the eternal world flashed upon the screens of their minds, showing the present, the future, and their part in them. In the silence of the desert Moses' spiritual eyes saw what has never happened on earth —a bush burning and undiminished by the fire—and with the vision came the consciousness of a holy Presence, the Angel of the Lord. Isaiah was made to see a glory which, he said, was like a robe of light covering the Lord of Hosts.

As there are different degrees of light all the way from the solitary candle to the sun which illumines and gives life to the world, so are there different levels of inspiration. To some God comes as an impulse to self-control, to speak a kind word, to forbear with others. To those whom he has singled out to do his particular work he comes in grandeur.

Gotama's experience when he sat under the Bodi-tree and looked upon Eternal Law is one of the most epochal cases of inspiration recorded. In the *Iti-vuttaka,* a collection of sayings in the Pali Scriptures, the Buddha says, "He who sees me sees the Truth." In the *Digha Nikaya,* one of the earliest of the Pali documents, he says that he is "one with Brahma," God. That is, he reflected the very light or life of God, Brahma. As these passages about Brahma are contrary to the later Buddhist theology in the Pali Scriptures, one concludes they remained in the later recensions of the Buddhist Bible because they were so genuine and well known they could not be omitted. They represent the earliest tradition, the pillar sentences of Buddhism.

Buddhism began as a mighty movement for self-control and divine love. The early Buddhists testified that the Buddha's inspiration poured upon them like precious rain, and his love spread from mind to mind like a holy fire. Custom is the mightiest force in society save one, the God-sent mind who changes for the better the custom that a social order counts inviolable. The Buddha is glorious against the custom-enslaved, caste-ridden, superstitious, and often cruel religious order of his day. For more than two thousand years he was a tremendous force for good and just behavior, for honest civil service, brilliant art, the inspirer of heroic individuals, patient, conscientious, creative craftsmen. Buddhism produced millions of trustworthy, incorruptible men and women, and vast communities which, bound together by brotherly love, carried forward the civilization of Asia.

Confucius' influence and the spread of his teachings were due to the lure of truth that was in him. He was an effective and perpetual foe to superstition. He never offered any easy road to high moral and intellectual attainments nor condoned the frailties of the flesh or the mind. He sternly cautioned his students, "The scholar who is bent on studying the principles of virtue, yet is ashamed of bad clothes and coarse food, is not yet fit to receive instruction." Again, he said, "With coarse food to eat, water to drink, and the bended arm as a pillow, happiness may still exist. Wealth and rank unrighteously obtained seem to me as unsubstantial as floating clouds."

Should we try to account for Chinese character at its best and the endurance of China's civilization by saying that the Chinese were a superior race, it becomes apparent that the Chinese were superior only when they followed the teachings of their Sages. Mencius said, "Wherever the superior man passes he civilizes; and he leaves behind him an atmosphere of spirituality."

Although the spiritually deaf invented the dogma that God does not speak, and the Confucian scholars mechanically endorsed it, through the centuries emperors and scholars preserved in the Confucian Classics the sentences which disproved their dogma. In the *Chung Yung* we read, "Confucius remarked, 'The power of spiritual forces in the Universe—how active it is everywhere! Invisible to the eyes, and impalpable to the senses, it is inherent in all things, and nothing can escape its operation.' . . . Like the rush of mighty waters, the presence of unseen Powers is felt; sometimes above us, sometimes around us. The intelligence which comes from the direct apprehension of truth is intuition. It is only he, in the world who possesses absolute truth who can get to the bottom of the law of his being." The Confucian *Book of Odes* relates:

> *God said to King Wên,*
> *"This is no time to be idle,*
> *No time to indulge in your desires."*
>
> *God said to King Wên,*
> *"I am moved by your bright power,*
> *Your high renown has not made you put on proud airs,*
> *Your greatness has not made you change former ways,*
> *You ... follow God's precepts."*

Confucius made known his inspiration from God when he said to his students, "Since King Wên the Cause of Truth has been lodged in me."

When Muhammad invalidated the idols and gods of Mecca and destroyed his townsmen's business, it required more than ordinary power to save him from the Meccans' fury. The fact also that Muhammad's teachings and influence so revived the fading civilizations of Egypt, Palestine, Mesopotamia, and Persia that once more they made remarkable advance is proof that Muhammad was much more than a camel driver. Real effects presuppose real causes. For a thousand years and more the best Muslims found a vital spiritual strength in Muhammad and the Quran. By this energy they learned to pray until they became heroic, humble, and united, their minds filled with love for God and humanity. By this power, brilliant and influential minds acquired fresh originality and the gift of expression until the Muslim architects built glorious temples of worship, Muslim scientists discovered new and life-transforming sciences, artists, writers, and craftsmen perfected their unique gifts, and there arose one of the world's most splendid civilizations.

Jesus, deserted by every one in his world, stood before Pilate to receive the death sentence. Jesus' family thought him slightly insane. Few among his contemporary teachers of religion deigned to notice him save to curse his preposterous pretensons. After his crucifixion, when his eleven chosen disciples recovered their belief in him and rallied to teach what they had learned from him, they were laughed to scorn, and when that was not sufficient to discourage them, they and those who joined with them were beaten and burned and crucified, until it seemed that not one among them would be left to tell their story.

Without family or official influence, with no promises, to anyone, of worldly prosperity, for this might be taken away at any moment, Jesus prevailed. And why? Because in the world are always people who can hear the call from God which the great Prophet gives to their inmost souls, who will answer this call and rise to serve under the Prophet's direction. In Jesus' name thousands of people gave up the prizes of this world, believing that the kind of life Jesus taught was more desirable. In his name they told others what they had learned and proved to be true. In his name they found a spiritual quickening in the Old Testament, and in the new book written for them by Jesus' first apostles. In his name bitter enemies became friends. In his name the martyrs made superhuman sacrifices and were reinforced by a superhuman energy and power of patient endurance. Their heroic spirit shone through the records of their deeds and quickened multitudes of others to similar heroism. In his name Jesus' followers healed the sick, and raised the spiritually dead, dreamed true dreams, and saw true visions not of this earth.

That is truly inspired which make for the good of all classes and races. By this test the vital words of Jesus, and the Hebrew prophets who have lived in the Bible, are proved to be divine. The spiritual power which prevailed in spite of later corruptions of Jesus' teachings; which was transmitted even through the bewildering dogmas that sought to encase and preserve but really obscured Jesus' words; the power of Christ's spirit to transform, sustain, and upbuild civilizations through the centuries despite his misguided and sectarian followers is proof that he came from God.

Why do the church bells ring every Sunday morning in thousands of cities and villages all over the world; why are innumerable services held to repeat the words and glorify the names of a workingman and his humble friends who lived nineteen centuries ago?

Why even in the modern world with its science and mechanical skill do we still honor the names and revere the words of Jesus and his apostles? Whence came the devotion which caused the French people to build in the heart of Paris a church to Mary, the simple village girl of Magdala? Why do we name our children in honor of Jesus' apostles, and date every letter that we write, every newspaper that hastens from the press, every business contract we sign, from the day Jesus was born? Some ideas, although true, are inert. Others, because they are alive with the drive, the authority, and the creative potency of life eternal are quoted, loved, and obeyed by many nations for centuries. Such ideas shine upon human society with a fruitfulness like the sun. The divine dynamic they transmit strengthens men to practice a code of life quite contrary to the pull of the lower nature. Such ideas prevail against all the opposition, all the mistakes of those who amplify and misapply them. They are so potent that at last kings and people declare them the will of heaven and the voice of truth.

The great Prophet reveals, and then creates, a new world. The power in him which makes for righteousness we call "God." After the Prophet leaves the world he continues to be a living presence, drawing humanity to him. He calls into action men's latent capabilities. When the Prophet's influence is potent, barriers of caste and race are broken down; governments here and there become just and beneficent; more and more kings and ministers live and reign for the happiness and welfare of all people and become a glory and a blessing to their countries; religious tolerance and freedom of thought are maintained; and nations rise into social unity, international friendship, and peace.

# 39

## The Inner Light of Civilization

THESE GREAT RELIGIONS which accomplished so much in the past are now outgrown, many say. Their Scriptures are written in a language of long ago, for a social order which is out of date. They are not adequate for this machine age and its economics. They cannot solve the overwhelming problems of the new industrial and international order. The cycle of social change surges past them. We must have another authority.

Eager for something new, we greeted modern science as the latest authority. The masters of science, we said, have the facts, perform the experiments, sift the evidence, interpret experience and arrive at truth, as far as it can be known on any subject.

In this century, we have seen how science, expanding unrestrained by the balance wheel of true religion, can wreck the world. Equipped with science, leaders of nations have said: The civilization of the future shall be built upon the law of the survival of the fittest; that is, the cleverest, the strongest, the most ruthless. Harden your heart. Kill and be killed. Blessed are the war makers for they shall inherit the earth. Be exclusive, self-centered. Use the sciences to get money and power. Trust to your physical strength and mental cunning. Hate those who, you think, hate you. If anyone thwarts you, say to yourself, he is my enemy, I will get even with him, I will have revenge.

Wars of aggression are today intolerable; and the pitifulness of nations forced to receive the blows of the mechanical and human war machines wrings our hearts as never before. For such oppression is now outlawed by reason, and by all the best human beings who cry that they will not be dragged back into the jungle from which they have struggled but insist that they shall enjoy the advantages of their life as sons of God. For they have climbed high enough on the mountain of evolution to see and appreciate this destiny.

We look about for someone to answer the vital question: How are we to manage our lives? We go to science, we go to the technological schools and the universities, we question everyone. Authorities on social management undertake with their trained intellects to solve our problem. We find that their capacities are limited to one, or a very few, specialties. Strong in criticism, the specialists will be weak in appreciation. Brilliant in analysis, they do not synthesize. Intellectually developed far beyond the average, their sympathies may be atrophied.

We find that doubt fills every mind, that no one knows where he came from, where he is going, how he thinks. No one knows how he inherited characteristics from his ancestors, or how much he has derived from his environment. Not even a genius knows how his ideas are original: some visions of beauty and truth came into his consciousness with a rush of inspiration; whence they came he does not know. No one can comprehend the nature of life and living. The essence of our mind or soul or nerve currents, how consciousness arises, what happens in the cortex of the brain even in the simplest sensations, no one can tell. Nor can those whom we question tell us our possibilities, our future, our immortal destiny, what makes for our ultimate degradation or exaltation, for inner peace or turmoil, for life or death. Knowledge of ourselves, even with the assistance of the most advanced psychology, is but a drop; our ignorance is the ocean. The masters of the sciences are at a loss to find our connection with the unseen source of our life which is as hidden from most of us as is the sun unknowable to the tree. The tree lives by sun and showers, air, and the chemical food elements taken in at its roots. But it has no consciousness of its life. We are told a little about our physical environment. Know thyself, said the Greek philosopher. How shall we know the most unknowable thing on earth, which is man. Even Plato could not answer the question, What is man? Who can explain little Mozart, composing when four years old, astonishing the Austrian Court by his virtuosity at six years of age? Yet we insist that unless we fully understand God, his abilities, his mind, his activities, his plans, we will not believe in him. The Prophets tell us the way to become conscious of God's presence; few of us bother to try it out. Our interest in the physical universe causes us to go to incredible lengths to discover any one of its forces and secrets. Our interest in God is casual.

National defense is imperative. Therefore we maintain navies, air fleets, and armies. What we owe to them and to the police we can hardly estimate. By them we live in comparative security. But civilization depends for its vitality and continuance upon a moral, mental, and spiritual education, which in turn depends upon that inmost life force, God's guidance to his fathomless knowledge. Who shall keep out the sly enemies of ignorance, self-seeking, hatred, prejudice, indifference, and the blasé, unbeliever who takes away our faith; those forces that undermine the foundations of society. Who shall defend our higher vision?

Civilizations are saved from disintegration when the people who form them prefer virtue. This is accomplished when educators make good thoughts, good words, good deeds more attractive than their opposites.

The Muslims tell of a man with a rasping voice who read the services and led the prayers in a splendid mosque, in the golden days of Saracen civilization. After a while the ruler of the city sent for the man and offered him a hundred dinars if he would go to live in some other place, and not spoil the beautiful services of that particular mosque.

In India the people were brought up on their great epics, the Ramayana and the Mahabharata, and their sacred Scriptures. They learned by heart inspiring poems and prayers, and passages of the Upanishads.

In the Buddhist civilization the Jataka tales with their teaching of self-sacrificing service, love, and mercy were the spiritual food of millions. Gentle Buddhist teachers told these stories to the people in the moonlit evenings. Such stories and the Buddhist services and festivals were the motion pictures of the Buddhist world and became a far-reaching influence. Sir Laurence Binyon writes in his *Flight of the Dragon*, "The substitution of the conception of a divine pity at the core of things for the conception of ruthless power shows us the change wrought by Buddhism."

China read the Confucian Classics, which students committed to memory until they became part of their soul's rhythm and existence.

Christ's language of love, in the Gospels, called forth a slumbering spirit which neither Stoic nor mystery cult nor Neo-Platonist could awaken. Keats wrote:

> *All lovely tales that we have heard or read;*
> *An endless fountain of immortal drink,*
> *Pouring unto us from the heaven's brink.*
> *Nor do we merely feel these essences*
> *For one short hour; ... they become a cheering light*
> *Unto our souls, and bound to us so fast,*
> *That, whether there be shine, or gloom o'ercast,*
> *They always must be with us, or we die.*

The parents in the homes, the teachers in the schools and universities who can direct the youth of the nations to the books, the pictures, the people in whom virtue is shining—teachers who not only recognize truth but have themselves the power to live it—can transform the world. The certainty of the love of God which the great Prophets brought to many souls quickened them into a life far beyond any they had thought possible.

Faith is the pathway to light. Faith is built upon evidence. Faith is also a decision of the will. We assemble proofs of God's existence, and the evidences of his love. We assemble from many sources evidences for God and immortality. We weigh this evidence rationally. Then we make a decision of the will. Faith in God's love for humanity releases the deepest powers of the soul, and those priceless elements of personality—confidence and kindness. It quickens men and women of genius; it cleanses and unites the social order. It gives the science of education an objective, all men a sense of human values, art a new and divine inspiration. It makes clear that unity of mankind which will result in universal peace. Belief in God is the immediate sanction for belief in an immortal life in the soul of man. God is absolutely impartial;

therefore all humanity is endowed with immortality.

Said Muhammad, "Unbelievers try to put out the light of God with their mouths." What is the light of God?

Moses says it is the holy laws, which God gave him.

The Buddha says it is fully enlightened reason, the cosmic law sublime which shone into his mind the night of his illumination.

Confucius calls it the moral law, by which nations prosper.

Zoroaster announces it to be the good thoughts, good words, good deeds revealed by the Wise Lord.

The Upanishads say it is the divine Spirit made known in the Vedas and present potentially in the human soul.'

The Gita says it is God manifest in human form.

Muhammad proclaims it is God's will, announced by all true Prophets and Scriptures.

Jesus declares it is the truth, the life which sets men free from wrongdoing and its consequences.

The greatest attainment of the mind is to recognize truth and act upon it. The highest truth is God's presence. No one can know God's presence without loving God. No one can love God and not enlist on his side. He is working for a divine social order among all nations and classes, impartially. As God will win in the end, those who enlist with him are bound to be victorious.

We turn away from our Bibles, which contain rarest jewels, because, we say, in these books are so many mistakes. Science also makes mistakes, is constantly discarding its theories and trying out new ones. The central facts and laws in science do not change; on them the scientific structure is founded. So is it with the Bibles of the world. They proclaim laws for human relations which long experience has proved are forever valid.

The world today awaits a universal synthesis. The human law divides. The divine law unites. The human law says, my Prophet has sealed up revelation forever; God can never speak again as he spoke through Moses, Muhammad, Jesus; no one will ever have the innate knowledge of Confucius, the perfect illumination of the Buddha. The divine law says, you cannot limit God. The law of evolution requires that he send his children on earth a succession of prophets. This is the glorious theme of the Gita, the Quran, the Bible.

The solution of our present confusion must of necessity be universal. Nothing but our untoward effort to limit divine truth to *my* sacred Scripture, *my* creed can account for our missing the fact that God's revelation is universal and progressive. No true Prophet ever denounces the teachings of the other true Prophets; that is the undertaking of his overzealous followers. Each Prophet of God builds upon the mission of his predecessors and, renewing eternal truths, applies them to the needs of the age in which he is living. In the international day that is coming the names of the great world Prophets as revealers of one moral law will permeate the universe.

Zoroaster promised the time when all men will speak one language and have one law. The Hindus have long foreseen an era of universal righteousness. The Hebrew Bible says the time will come when men will run to and fro, knowledge will increase, and all from the least to the greatest will know the Lord. Then they that are wise will shine as the brightness of the firmament; and they that lead many to righteousness as the stars forever and ever. In that glorious day God's law will arbitrate for many peoples. Nation will not lift up sword against nation. Neither will they learn war any more. And God's living law will establish a universal peace.

This age, this day of universal resurrection is promised by Zoroastrian, Jewish, Muslim, Christian, and Hindu Scriptures. The Buddhist Scriptures call it the cycle of renovation, or the Western Paradise. The Confucian Bible describes this era as the day of the great unity and brotherhood, the day of perfect justice.

The Buddhist Scriptures describe life cycles of humanity's civilization and religion. They tell of such numbers of years before Gotama was born that they seem to stretch back into infinity. In the Jataka Scriptures we read:

> *A hundred thousand cycles vast*
> *And four immensities ago*

a Buddha taught the people. His work was taken up where he left it and carried forward by a long succession of Buddhas, until the Buddha who was Gotama appeared. These accounts of course are not historically correct; they are valuable in that they reveal the

Buddhist belief that Gotama was but the last of a magnificent succession of prophets, and he would be followed by another Buddha, and other Buddhas. If the Buddhist time-span be projected into the future we have the inspiring hope of thousands of years to come when God's plan and laws will be accepted by humanity as the best way of life. It was such a hope which caused the early Christians to hold so tenaciously to their belief in the Christ that they eventually saved their world from the savagery of Roman decadence and the northern tribes. What the Christ Spirit accomplished once can be accomplished again. In the perspective of thousands of years of time perhaps this present period of disintegration may not be so long as it now seems.

The strongest force for beneficent social control is a world religion at the zenith of its influence, when it guides, unites, purifies, animates, and glorifies the moral, intellectual, artistic, and social life of many nations.

The King of the universe sent a message, full of love and practical suggestions, to his subjects in India. Buddhist India repeated this message far and wide, until all central and eastern Asia responded to their King with the lovely society, art, and holy lives of the Buddhist civilization.

The King of the universe sent another message, to Palestine, and the early Christian society replied, for more than three hundred years, with one of the most united, self-sacrificing, dynamic brotherhoods humanity knows. After the Dark Ages the Christians again responded, with science, universities, Renaissance art and literature, saints, and workers for social righteousness.

The King sent his message through Muhammad's compelling voice, almost the same message that the Hebrew prophets transmitted. Muslim civilization, as ardent in achievement as some of its first members were tempestuous in self-seeking, answered with a far-flung brotherhood, sustained by millions of saintly lives, and from which appeared remarkable art and architecture, science and philosophy.

Religion is the science of spiritual dynamics which realizes that the first and last thing in knowledge is the knowledge of God; that everything gets out of date but God; when everything crashes, God remains.

Oh that we might learn in our youth how to know God, ere those who grind wheat for the bread of life shall cease, and the silver cord that connects us with God be severed, and the golden bowl of our receptivity be broken, and we lose our longing for God, and the windows of our mosques and churches and temples be darkened, and our pitchers that receive the water of life be broken at the fountain. God is beauty. Every beautiful landscape, every lovely mountain scene is his thought. God is wisdom; every act, every idea that makes for progress, for social betterment was first thought by him. God is truth, reality, love. Whenever beauty or wisdom or true love enters our mind, God comes to us.

We stand in the dawning light of a world springtime of science and invention and brotherhood. The old world is ending. The new is beginning. Spring is promise and destruction, fruition and frustration, storms and the coming of flowers and perfect days. The sun seems in the evening to be fading out. In reality it is preparing for a new sunrise.